AF845118

Comparative Capitalism

Comparative Capitalism

A Global Perspective

Magnus Feldmann

BLOOMSBURY ACADEMIC
LONDON • NEW YORK • OXFORD • NEW DELHI • SYDNEY

BLOOMSBURY ACADEMIC
Bloomsbury Publishing Plc
50 Bedford Square, London, WC1B 3DP, UK
1385 Broadway, New York, NY 10018, USA
29 Earlsfort Terrace, Dublin 2, Ireland

BLOOMSBURY, BLOOMSBURY ACADEMIC and the Diana logo are trademarks of Bloomsbury Publishing Plc

First published in Great Britain 2025

Copyright © Magnus Feldmann, 2025

Magnus Feldmann has asserted his right under the Copyright, Designs and Patents Act, 1988, to be identified as Author of this work.

For legal purposes the Acknowledgements on p. vii constitute an extension of this copyright page.

Cover design: www.simonlevyassociates.co.uk
Cover images: Welder © Danie Wiadro / unsplash.com; Graph and magnifying glass © Shutterstock; Women working on SodaSteam devices © Remy Gieling / unsplash.com

All rights reserved. No part of this publication may be reproduced or transmitted in any form or by any means, electronic or mechanical, including photocopying, recording, or any information storage or retrieval system, without prior permission in writing from the publishers.

Bloomsbury Publishing Plc does not have any control over, or responsibility for, any third-party websites referred to or in this book. All internet addresses given in this book were correct at the time of going to press. The author and publisher regret any inconvenience caused if addresses have changed or sites have ceased to exist, but can accept no responsibility for any such changes.

A catalogue record for this book is available from the British Library.

Library of Congress Cataloging-in-Publication Data
Names: Feldmann, Magnus, author.
Title: Comparative capitalism: a global perspective / Magnus Feldmann.
Description: New York: Bloomsbury Academic, 2025. | Includes bibliographical references and index. |
Summary: "The debate surrounding Varieties of Capitalism has been limited by its excessive focus on Western Europe and North America. Comparative Capitalism takes a global perspective to understand capitalist diversity, considering not only liberal and coordinated market economies but also networked, hierarchical and new market models. The book accounts for the significance of state structures, global integration and natural resources, and includes a range of case studies from across East Asia, Latin America, and the Middle East. Offering tables, figures, and overviews of key features of each economy, this book is essential reading for students of political economy and international development"– Provided by publisher.
Identifiers: LCCN 2024026763 (print) | LCCN 2024026764 (ebook) | ISBN 9781350423091 (hardback) | ISBN 9781350423107 (paperback) | ISBN 9781350423084 (epub) | ISBN 9781350423077 (ebook)
Subjects: LCSH: Capitalism.
Classification: LCC HB501 .F3855 2025 (print) | LCC HB501 (ebook) | DDC 330.12/2–dc23/eng/20240816
LC record available at https://lccn.loc.gov/2024026763
LC ebook record available at https://lccn.loc.gov/2024026764

ISBN: HB: 978-1-3504-2309-1
PB: 978-1-3504-2310-7
ePDF: 978-1-3504-2307-7
eBook: 978-1-3504-2308-4

Typeset by Deanta Global Publishing Services, Chennai, India

To find out more about our authors and books visit www.bloomsbury.com and sign up for our newsletters.

CONTENTS

PREFACE

How do capitalist systems work? How and why do market economies vary? How does the institutional context affect the operation of capitalism? The field of comparative capitalism has provided distinctive answers to such questions and been one of the most active and influential fields of research in the first quarter of the twenty first century. It grapples with fundamental questions that are of great importance to scholarship and policy. These questions are also highly relevant to students across a wide range of social science disciplines. Given that the literature on comparative capitalism is already very large, one might ask why we need a new book on this topic. This book was written with two goals in mind.

First, given the centrality of comparative capitalism to the teaching of political economy both in political science programmes and in other social science disciplines (including modules on the global business environment in management departments and business schools, and in some modules in cognate fields, such as international development, economic sociology and economic geography), there is a great need for an overview of the field that is accessible to students. The rapid growth of research on comparative capitalism over the past few decades and the expansion of the debate to cover new countries and topics have made it increasingly difficult for students to get a good understanding of the field. The literature is vast and wide-ranging, and much of it is not very accessible to students without prior training in political economy. My hope is that this book can serve as a map of the field, thereby giving students a good starting point to navigate the terrain and encouraging them to explore it further.

Second, the book is designed as contribution to the wider debate about comparative capitalism. The study of comparative capitalism has evolved over a long period of time and always been characterized by debate and contestation. Yet there are many open and controversial questions about the field, and this book makes the case for a global and pluralist approach.

On the one hand, many open questions relate to the implications of an increasingly global economy for comparative capitalism, a field that initially focused primarily on Western Europe and North America. Whilst the literature on other parts of the world has grown very rapidly, this book is one of the first attempts to look at comparative capitalism from a global perspective. By integrating a wider range of economies into one study, this book seeks to contribute to a broadening and 'globalization' of the debate.

On the other hand, comparative capitalism is also characterized by active debate and contestation. Such debates are useful as they help advance the field, but competing perspectives can also be viewed as complementary. The book discusses both the Varieties of Capitalism (VoC) framework, which has been the most influential model of comparative capitalism for over 25 years, and some of the most influential alternatives to VoC. The book can be regarded as a plea for pluralism – it suggests that we need more, not fewer, theoretical tools in our toolboxes when we study comparative capitalism.

ACKNOWLEDGEMENTS

This book has been a long time in the making. It builds on many years of research, reading and thinking about capitalism, initially as a student, and later as an academic at the University of Bristol. I have accumulated many debts of gratitude, and I would like to acknowledge some of the help and advice I have received, whilst stressing that the usual disclaimer applies: I am solely responsible for all the weaknesses of this book.

First and foremost, I would like to thank the School of Sociology, Politics and International Studies at the University of Bristol for providing a congenial academic home. I am very grateful to my colleagues, and I would particularly like to thank Glenn Morgan and Mark Wickham-Jones, who have been exceptionally important interlocutors, collaborators and sources of advice and support. I am also grateful to Jeff Henderson and Mircea Popa for our research collaborations on related topics. I have been teaching a final year undergraduate seminar on states and markets for many years, and multiple cohorts of brilliant students have engaged with my ideas about most of the topics covered in this book. Working with these wonderful students has helped me to sharpen and clarify my own thinking, and I am very grateful to them. Two former Bristol PhD students – Nada Ghandour-Demiri and Samuel Rogers – were very able research assistants and supported me with data collection in the very early stages of this project.

I would like to thank the six anonymous reviewers, Aleksandra Stelmach and Daniel Kinderman for exceptionally useful suggestions on a draft of this book manuscript. I would also like to thank my successive editors, especially Stephen Wenham (who helped me launch this project), Andrew Malvern and Tallulah Griffith (who helped me bring the project to completion), for their support and patience.

The years spent in the PhD programme at Harvard predated this project, but they were decisive in shaping my interest in comparative capitalism. Torben Iversen was an outstanding and inspirational PhD adviser. I am very grateful for his support and advice and for our many conversations about political economy that have had an enduring impact on my academic work. Peter Hall's influence as one of the founding fathers of the Varieties of Capitalism debate is obvious and profound, and I am very grateful for all the guidance and inspiration that he has provided over the years. Dwight Perkins played a crucial role in helping me bridge my interests in different regions and various approaches to political economy. Our conversations and the opportunity to serve as Dwight's teaching fellow shaped my approach to political economy from a global perspective. My friend Robert Fannion also deserves a special acknowledgement given the importance of our many discussions for my understanding of capitalism and many other topics.

The wider Harvard community, including both professors and fellow PhD students, influenced my thinking on political economy, and I would like to acknowledge my gratitude to Ben Ansell, Fiona Barker, Tim Colton, Pepper Culpepper, Alexis Diamond, Gergana Dimova, Grzegorz Ekiert, Margarita Estévez-Abe, Jeff Frieden, Daniel Gingerich, Vessela Hristova, János Kornai, Jason Lakin, Steve Levitsky, Shannon O'Neil, Sonal Pandya, Susan Pharr, Alison Post,

Robert Putnam, Tom Remington, Gilles Serra, Jiyeoun Song, Elina Treyger, Robert Urbatsch and Jong-sung You.

I would also like to thank Ngaire Woods, Razeen Sally and Andrew Walter for their excellent teaching, mentoring and encouragement during my earlier studies, which played a crucial role in my academic development and helped awaken my interest in political economy.

Many colleagues around the world have generously offered advice on related topics over the years, and I would particularly like to thank Sarah Ashwin, Will Bartlett, Dorothee Bohle, Clemens Buchen, Helen Callaghan, Vladimir Gimpel'son, Jane Gingrich, Béla Greskovits, Steffen Hertog, Krzysztof Jasiecki, Vytautas Kuokštis, Martin Myant, Andreas Nölke, Jonas Pontusson, Janez Prašnikar, Ben Ross Schneider, David Soskice, Miroslav Stanojević, Wolfgang Streeck, Kathleen Thelen and Linda Weiss for their suggestions and help.

Finally, I would like to thank my family for their support. This book is dedicated to Harald and Eleonora who enrich my life every day and provide much-needed distraction from comparative capitalism.

PART I

Introduction

1

Why comparative capitalism in global perspective?

Markets feature prominently in people's lives. In the twenty-first century this statement applies across most parts of the world. It is sometimes said that we now live in market societies, where markets increasingly penetrate into new spheres of life (Sandel 2012). Beyond the markets for goods, services and labour, there are now markets in a variety of new and often unexpected areas. Many traditional market places can still be found in town squares, but in many countries they are marginal or specialize in niche products or local produce. They are often overshadowed by large retail outlets or increasingly sophisticated electronic markets that are underpinned by companies organized around digital platforms like eBay or Amazon. Whilst people increasingly view markets as an inevitable part of their lives and a certain market culture has taken hold, markets still inspire political conflict and public controversy. For example, questions surrounding privatization and the proper degree of regulation are often controversial and at the core of political disputes.

Much of the twentieth century was shaped by the clash between two superpowers – the capitalist United States and the anti-capitalist Soviet Union – but it is not much of an exaggeration to say that capitalism now seems to have conquered the world, much as Karl Marx and others predicted in the nineteenth century. Virtually all economies in the world, including the erstwhile communist world, had embraced markets and private property by the end of the twentieth century, if they hadn't already done so in the past (there are only a few exceptions that have largely resisted market reform, such as North Korea). Whilst the word 'capitalism' can be used in a variety of ways, sometimes polemically or with strong ideological undertones, this book uses the term to denote a market economy with mostly private property (Kocka 2016). Hodgson (2015: 259) identifies six defining features of capitalism, which relate to the role of the legal system, market relations, ownership, the organization of production, wage labour and the financial system in underpinning market-based economic systems.

This book has three aims. First, it seeks to introduce readers to the study of comparative capitalism and make what are often highly technical debates accessible in a way that promotes greater understanding of capitalism. Second, unlike much of the literature on comparative capitalism, this book adopts a global approach. It synthesizes and integrates a vast literature on the OECD with a significant literature on the Global South. A key premise of the book is that a global perspective contributes to a fuller and more nuanced understanding of capitalism and capitalist diversity. Third, comparative capitalism has long been a field characterized by intellectual contestation between competing paradigms. This book is also intended as a plea for pluralism. Whilst much of the book focuses on the Varieties of Capitalism (VoC) literature that has had a central position in the comparative capitalism literature, it highlights some weaknesses associated with this approach and how they can be addressed. In doing so, the book discusses refinements to the VoC debate, but it also introduces a range of alternative theoretical perspectives that can enrich our understanding of comparative capitalism. Rather than aiming for an intellectual mono-culture or one dominant paradigm, comparative capitalism benefits from pluralism. A theory can be a straightjacket if it is deployed uncritically. Having multiple theories in our toolbox means that we can answer a wider range of questions and approach problems in a nuanced way. By drawing on different approaches for different purposes we can harness their strengths and even combine them in novel and eclectic ways (Sil and Katzenstein 2010). The book is an invitation to readers to approach these theories critically and with an open mind and to reflect on the tools that are most compelling and relevant to their interests.

Why comparative capitalism?

Capitalism and markets are central to contemporary societies, but these concepts almost invariably generate controversy and competing interpretations. Some accounts of capitalism border on the triumphalist. In one influential incarnation of it, Andrei Shleifer (2009) speaks of the 'age of Milton Friedman', a period of increasingly free markets, which largely coincides with what is often described as the 'neoliberal era' (see Chapter 8). For Shleifer, this is a period of economic success as measured not only in rates of economic growth and progress but also following the title of Friedman's bestseller *Capitalism and Freedom* in terms of expanding freedom and liberty. Even in more measured accounts, such as Iversen and Soskice (2019), who consider the role of democracy and institutions more systematically, the core message is almost as upbeat. Capitalism generates growth and progress, and it has been surprisingly resilient over long periods of time, even during the turbulent twentieth century. The emergence of capitalism in the late eighteenth century was associated with rapid increases in economic growth rates, which have gradually spread beyond the corner of Northwestern Europe where it originated. After millennia of very limited growth, the Industrial Revolution and emergence of capitalism led to dramatic accelerations of growth. Often associated with the image of the 'invisible hand' from Adam Smith's *Wealth of Nations*, the appeal of capitalism lies in its decentralized decision-making. If everyone pursues their own self-interest, market advocates argue that the aggregate outcomes will be beneficial to society at large and maximize the country's welfare.

If this account of capitalism was enthusiastic, another influential perspective is virtually its polar opposite. In this alternative view, capitalism is a profoundly unjust and unstable system, which may not even be sustainable in the longer term. The history of global capitalism is bound up with empire and colonialism (Anievas and Nisancioglu 2013; Bhambra and Holmwood 2018). Capitalism is associated with chronic challenges, such as high inequality and persistent unemployment, which are related to its exploitative nature. It is also prone to periodic economic crises that wreak havoc on people's livelihoods and bankrupt firms and entire economies (Harvey 2015). It is rooted in an appeal to base instincts – greed and selfishness – which undermine community spirit and may even ruin the planet as everyone pursues growth without limits whilst disregarding its effects on the planet and the communities around them (Marglin 2008). For Karl Marx and many critics of capitalism after him, such problems with capitalism would eventually lead to its downfall and collapse.

Which of these two stories is correct or most important is a question to which every reader may need to find their own answer. In some sense both are valid. Capitalism as an economic system has generated unprecedented economic growth since the Industrial Revolution, but it has always been a controversial and contradictory system. Even for critics like Karl Marx, capitalism was both progressive (compared to the preceding feudal era) and exploitative.

The distinctive perspective on these matters that comparative capitalism offers can be captured by one of the puzzles animating Andrew Shonfield's *Modern Capitalism* (1969). Shonfield wanted to understand why capitalism had been so remarkably stable and successful in the post–Second World War decades, when it had seemed so dysfunctional in the interwar period. At that time the world economy was hard hit by the Great Depression, and international economic exchange was undermined by national rivalries and war. And most international institutions, including the monetary system based on the Gold Standard, were perceived as straitjackets that worsened economic crises.

The study of comparative capitalism can help elucidate why capitalism sometimes seems remarkably successful at generating growth, and sometimes even growth with low levels of inequality. Whilst capitalism has led to dramatic increases in global GDP over long periods of time, economic growth has been highly uneven, with economic convergence at best conditional and mostly limited to regions within countries (Barro 2015). Success stories of economic growth, like the East Asian miracle, were described as 'miracles' precisely because such outcomes are rare and unexpected.

Whilst capitalism is not always successful, there is more than one path to economic prosperity. This is why the claim that the whole world is capitalist in some shape or form tends to obscure as much as it reveals. Markets work very differently across countries. All the richest countries in the world can be defined as capitalist, but many low-income economies in the Global South can also be defined as capitalist, at least if a general definition is adopted. If differences in living standards across capitalist economies are striking, so are differences in inequality. If we consider the Gini coefficient as the most common measure of inequality (which can range from 0 to 1, where 0 indicates perfect equality and 1 the situation where one household earns all the income and everyone else nothing), the most recent World Bank scores for each country indicate that the country with the highest level of inequality, South Africa (see Chapter 5), has a Gini coefficient of disposable income of about 0.63, whereas the corresponding figure for Slovakia (see Chapter 6) and Slovenia (see Chapter 3) was 0.24. This is a very significant difference in inequality. Markets are also regulated in very different ways. In some countries, employment is predominantly informal – some kind of agreements are made, perhaps underpinned by a handshake, but without written contracts, and workers do not have any easy recourse to the legal system if they are unfairly dismissed or maltreated by their employers. In other countries, the employment relationship is regulated by a variety of laws and regulations. In yet another group of countries, including some Western European countries, organized interests – trade unions and employers' associations – negotiate binding agreements on behalf of their members, which determine pay and various other benefits and regulations. In a further group of countries, the employment relationship is underpinned by a variety of norms – such as the principle of lifetime employment that was once sacrosanct in many Japanese companies (Dore 2003).

In other words, whilst all of these examples might fit the label 'capitalist', they differ from each other in many ways. Given the importance of capitalism and markets, it is important to make sense of these differences and to explore where they come from and how they matter. Why have some capitalist economies been very successful in generating economic growth? Why do levels of inequality differ across capitalist economies? Are all capitalist economies inherently vulnerable to periodic economic crises? Is globalization likely to wipe out differences between national economic systems and institutions? Are new technologies transforming the ways in which capitalism works? Finding good answers to such questions is a key challenge for all social scientists and anyone else interested in the functioning of markets and contemporary societies.

This book tries to make sense of these issues by discussing the most influential contemporary approaches to these topics.

Understanding capitalist diversity: Approaches to comparative capitalism

How should we understand differences between capitalist systems? The analysis of markets and capitalism has a long pedigree. There is a large literature on this topic, and the term 'comparative capitalism' refers to a variety of theories and perspectives that are designed to explain capitalist diversity. It is worth highlighting four families of traditional approaches to comparative capitalism, which the contemporary literature builds on.

First, one of the most common approaches, which is implicit in much economic analysis and also very influential in public debates, is to focus on the *size of the state*, which is measured by public spending and sometimes analysed in relation to the size of the economy or the industrial sector. On this view, 'more state' generally means 'less market'. In other words, there is a sharp state/market dichotomy. This maps on to a simple view of politics, where the centre-right seeks to roll back the state and the centre-left wants to rein in markets and extend the reach of the state. People using this lens do not necessarily agree on the desirability of markets. For many free-market economists, in particular, state intervention prevents markets from working as efficiently as they might, but critics on the left often view more state intervention as a necessary corrective to markets that generate high inequality and instability. A practical implication of such a view is that we can compare capitalist systems by looking at the size of the state. The story of twentieth-century capitalism is largely the story of the growing state. A special version of this kind of argument is the 'logic of industrialism' which regards the growth of the welfare state as a consequence of the shift from traditional agrarian to modern industrial societies, inducing convergence pressures over time as economies develop and their welfare states grow (Wilensky 1974). The rise of neoliberalism and market liberalization in recent decades has dented this growth somewhat, although the significance of these changes has been controversial (Pierson 1996; Hacker 2004). Whilst this perspective is appealing and very intuitive, it has several limitations. First, it is not clear whether there is such a sharp contrast between states and markets. Certain kinds of state activism, such as the maintenance of law and order and a legal system that secures contracts, are essential to well-functioning markets. More generally, it is hard to distinguish between the effects of different kinds of state activities in a framework that looks at total spending. Whilst the seminal studies in this area have provided important insights into the logic of welfare state expansion, the economic effects of spending on innovation or infrastructure may be quite different from transfers and benefits.

Another approach also focuses on the state, but on its *capacity* in terms of facilitating economic modernization and transformation (Shonfield 1969). Shonfield's (1969) classic volume is widely regarded as the starting point for the modern debate on capitalist diversity and the foundational work within comparative capitalism (Baccaro, Blyth and Pontusson 2022; Schwartz and Tranøy 2019). Shonfield's account of successful economic modernization of France in that volume, and Chalmers Johnson's (1982) theory of the developmental state in East Asia highlight the central role that the state can play in economic governance and modernization. Understanding the role of the state remains an important task for students of political economy and capitalism and has arguably experienced a revival of sorts in recent years. Many studies have demonstrated that market liberalization may be associated with a reconfiguration of the state, but not necessarily its weakening (Gamble 2002; Vogel 1996). In the aftermath of the global financial crisis beginning in 2008 or the Covid-19 crisis, states often played a central role in economic adjustment (Kumar 2021), but this is not necessarily reflective of their actions at other times. Much market activity takes place at the level of individual consumers and producers, financial market actors and households, so it is important not only to consider the role of the state in directly steering the economy, but also its general role in shaping markets (Vogel's 2018).

The third approach shifts the focus away from the state and considers the strength and structure of *organized interests*. This debate has analysed the structure of especially employers and trade unions, and explored their role and influence over policymaking. The most famous example of this kind of approach is the pluralism-corporatism debate which dominated the comparative capitalism literature for much of the 1970s and 1980s (Schmitter 1974; Schmitter and Lehmbruch 1979; Goldthorpe 1984). This literature has contributed to a nuanced understanding of industrial relations and labour market conflicts across Western Europe, and how variation in corporatist practices affected wage setting, inflation and the recovery from the economic crisis of the 1970s. Whilst this continues to be an important debate, the focus on wage setting and industrial relations implies that it may not paint a complete portrait of capitalism in general, especially at a time when union membership is falling in most countries.

Fourth, the social systems of production framework addresses some of the shortcomings of the above-mentioned approaches, though it is effectively a family of approaches, including the French regulation school (Aglietta 1979; Boyer and Saillard 2002), which played a central role in the debates on comparative capitalism, especially for much of the 1980s and 1990s. What all the theories grouped under this heading share is a concern with the social underpinnings of economic activity, including the structure of innovation systems and collective institutions, often at the sectoral or regional level. The French regulation theory (FRT) has developed a sophisticated account of institutional interactions, for example, between labour markets, central banks and monetary policy, competition policy, financial markets and state-society relations. FRT has explored how different institutional configurations constitute distinctive growth regimes and sought to account for differences in the degree of coherence and success of such regimes.

The debates surrounding social systems of production have also focused on the evolution of regimes for organizing production, such as Fordist mass production and the shift towards post-Fordism (Amin 1994; Piore and Sabel 1984; Hollingsworth and Boyer 1997) and the influential research programme on comparative business systems (Whitley 1992, 2007).

These literatures are wide-ranging and still have a lot to teach students of comparative capitalism today, but the most obvious starting point for an introduction to the contemporary debate is the Varieties of Capitalism approach, which integrates elements from all the four above-mentioned approaches and has been the most influential framework for studying comparative capitalism in the twenty-first century.

Varieties of Capitalism: Key ideas

After this introductory chapter, Chapters 2–7 discuss the Varieties of Capitalism (VoC) framework, which is arguably the most influential approach to understanding capitalist diversity. It is the culmination of extensive scholarship by many people, both on new institutionalism and comparative capitalism. The seminal volume edited by Peter A. Hall and David Soskice and published in 2001 could be viewed as the core statement of this approach. It is a major milestone in the academic literature on capitalist diversity and has generated extensive debate across a variety of academic disciplines (Coates 2005; Goodin 2003; Howell 2003; Feldmann 2019).

The VoC framework has five core features. First, VoC is a *firm-centred* theory that is primarily applied to *economies at the level of nation states*. The focus on firms in VoC reflects the central role of enterprises in a market economy. It is clear that governments, regulators and other actors shape economic activity, but we cannot develop a full understanding of capitalism without analysing firms given that most production, hiring and investment decisions are made at the firm level. Whilst it also considers subnational and supranational (regional and global) institutions, the theory focuses on institutions, policies and conflicts at the national level, which remains the main foundation for democratic politics. This means that the theory analyses *national* institutions, but it also explores the effects of these institutions on economic activity on the ground at the firm level.

Second, the VoC framework focuses on *economic coordination*. Every form of economic activity confronts numerous *coordination problems*. Production processes are very complex, as firms need to secure access to a variety of resources, such as labour, finance, raw materials, intermediate inputs, distribution networks etc. If any one of these coordination problems is not resolved, firms may face considerable difficulties which could result in delays or a breakdown in the firm's activities. The VoC framework builds on a key insight of organizational theory and institutional economics, namely that such coordination problems can be resolved in several different ways or by means of different *coordination mechanisms*.

Oliver Williamson (1975) famously focused on two – markets and hierarchy, or decentralized allocation by market mechanisms and centralized allocation by means of state directives or managerial decision-making within companies. Adler (2001) identifies three – in addition to markets and hierarchy, he also discusses trust as a distinct coordination mechanism. Trust could also serve to underpin relational contracting (Williamson 2010). By contrast, Streeck and Schmitter (1985) highlight four different coordination mechanisms – in addition to community, market and state, which are quite similar to Adler's categories, they also focus on associations – or the possibility of achieving negotiated solutions to coordination problems by means of bargaining among key actors, such as employers' associations or trade union federations, that make long-term agreements on wages, training programmes and labour market regulations. This creates the possibility of developing what Schmitter and Streeck call 'private interest government' (Streeck and Schmitter 1985).

The VoC framework emphasizes two coordination mechanisms, namely market-based arrangements based on contractual agreements on the one hand and long-term negotiated agreements based on informal or implicit contracts on the other. This choice has important consequences, perhaps most obviously that market-based contracts can be easy to adjudicate and terminate and therefore facilitate flexible and rapid adjustment. By contrast, negotiated agreements and implicit contracts are likely to require more trust between key actors and may be harder to establish (Hall and Soskice 2001; Goodin 2003), but they also facilitate long-term planning. Longer time horizons are often said to be a key strength that enables long-term strategic planning, but this may also make rapid unilateral adjustment to shocks harder to achieve.

Third, economic activity – and the choice of a particular coordination mechanism – is shaped by *institutions*. As Hall and Soskice (2001a: 33) put it, 'we are suggesting that it can be fruitful to consider how firms coordinate their endeavours and to analyse the institutions of the political economy from a perspective that asks what kind of support they provide for different kinds of coordination'. Institutions can be defined as a 'set of rules, formal or informal, that actors generally follow, whether for normative, cognitive or material reasons' (Hall and Soskice 2001a: 9). This definition shows that institutions are complex phenomena, and there are several important distinctions of note. Institutions can be either formal (usually enshrined in law, as in the case of bankruptcy law or competition law), or informal rules (such as norms). Such institutions shape not only firm behaviour but also many other activities throughout society. The existence of institutions underpins the choices firms make about coordination mechanisms to mobilize resources. In addition, as the above quote indicates, institutions can be rooted in several distinct logics. The most influential distinction is between three kinds of institutionalism – rational choice, historical and sociological institutionalism (Hall and Taylor 1996). This highlights the fact that rules can be seen as deliberate and rational choices to address certain problems, as reflections of historical decisions and processes or as social or cultural norms.

Fourth, and building on the previous points, another key VoC concept pertains to *institutional complementarities* (Hall and Soskice 2001a: 17–21) – this captures the fact that similar institutional logics tend to prevail across multiple domains. Hall and Soskice provide the following definition: 'Two institutions can be said to be complementary if the presence (or efficiency) of one increases returns from (or the efficiency of) the other' (2001b: 17). The original VoC framework considers institutions across a number of key domains – industrial relations, education and training, corporate governance, inter-firm relations, whilst also analysing the internal structure of the firm. Later formulations have sometimes defined the domains in a slightly different way, and the welfare state or social policy is often included as an additional category (Estévez-Abe et al. 2001; Iversen 2005). To illustrate the operation of institutional complementarities it is useful to consider an example: if a long-term bargained approach is used to secure patient capital, Hall and Soskice suggest that it may make sense to have long-term agreements with workers as well. Guaranteed access to both skilled workers and to long-term finance ensures a stable planning horizon. In addition, other aspects of the economy, notably social and macroeconomic policy, are often related to these institutions as well (Iversen 2005; Hall and Franzese 1998). This concept may be the most controversial element of the VoC framework. Whilst some VoC research has sought to demonstrate that economies with complementary institutions outperform hybrid economies lacking such tight complementarities (Hall and Gingerich 2009), critics have suggested that the concept may be too rigid. They have suggested that a looser concept, such as coherence of institutional arrangements, especially since there are situations when hybrid institutions or combinations of very different kinds of institutions, may outperform configurations of more similar institutions (Crouch 2005). Similarly, it is not entirely clear what kind of political process generates complementary clusters of institutions: is it a quest for economic efficiency that induces countries actively to choose complementary institutions, or do similar institutions reflect enduring social norms or historical legacies (Thelen 2004)?

Fifth, another idea underlying VoC analysis relates to *comparative institutional advantage*, or the idea that a given web of institutions is particularly conducive to certain kinds of economic activity or innovation. If a certain kind of coordination mechanism is particularly useful for some economic sectors, but not for others, then comparative institutional advantage implies that countries tend to specialize in sectors that thrive under certain kinds of institutions.

The classical VoC framework focuses on two sets of countries – liberal and coordinated market economies (Hall and Soskice 2001b). There are systematic differences between these two groups with respect to all of the above-mentioned issues. In liberal market economies (LMEs – see Chapter 2), market coordination is the key form of economic coordination. This group primarily includes the main English-speaking countries, Britain, the United States, Canada, Ireland, Australia and New Zealand.

Coordinated market economies (CMEs – see Chapter 3) are characterized by strategic coordination, that is, negotiated and bargained agreements between economic actors. CMEs can be found in Western Europe and include countries, such as Germany, the Netherlands, Belgium, Austria as well as the Nordic countries of Finland, Sweden, Norway and Denmark.

The VoC framework has made a number of key contributions to the understanding of capitalism. The most important one may be that it provides a systematic account of differences in economic institutions. It explains the distinctive logic and functioning of different kinds of institutions and does not interpret them merely as deviations from best practice. As both groups of countries considered by Hall and Soskice are among the most prosperous in the world, the systematic differences across their institutional arrangements and economic coordination mechanisms provides strong support for Hall and Soskice's key claim that there is not just one path to economic success.

However, there are also important differences, for example, in terms of economic specialization. LMEs tend to specialize in sectors relying on rapid innovation, such as biotechnology or software development (see Chapter 2), whereas CMEs specialize in sectors relying on incremental innovation, such as high-quality manufacturing including consumer durables, cars and transport equipment and machinery. There are also key differences in terms of labour markets and inequality, which means that institutional arrangements may be associated with different trade-offs and distributional consequences.

Why global Varieties of Capitalism?

Although the VoC framework has been influential and arguably the dominant approach to comparative political economy for quite some time (Bermeo and Pontusson 2012), it remains controversial. This book argues that a global perspective can enrich the VoC debate and address some of the issues that critics have highlighted. There is already an emerging literature that tries to extend the VoC debate beyond the traditional OECD countries, and this book builds on those writings (Nölke and Vliegenthart 2009; Schneider 2013; Walter and Zhang 2012b; Nölke et al. 2015; Witt et al. 2017). This is one of the first attempts to synthesize the wide-ranging literature on VoC across various continents (Feldmann 2019). Let us consider two of the most influential criticisms of VoC.

First, one of the main concerns relates to the focus on just two varieties of capitalism. Given that not even all Western European countries can be classified as LMEs or CMEs, this binary typology may be too restrictive. France and various Mediterranean countries cannot be classified as either LMEs or CMEs (Culpepper 2008; Molina and Rhodes 2007; Schmidt 2003). Since there is also considerable variation even within these two groups (Pontusson 2005; Konzelmann, Fovargue-Davies and Schnyder 2012), the question arises whether the framework can fully capture even these two groups of countries, especially if we also want to understand change over time.

This book argues that a global approach is a compelling strategy to address such concerns. By exploring a wider range of countries, we can get a better sense of capitalist diversity on a global scale. The countries considered in the original VoC volume may not be representative of the full range of capitalist diversity, as Hall and Soskice (2001b) themselves acknowledged. If we want to understand capitalism in the twenty-first century, it is not enough to look at Western Europe and North America. To make sense of capitalist institutions and their effect on the contemporary global economy, it is essential to adopt a wider lens and to consider more countries and further models and varieties of capitalism (see Chapters 4–7).

Second, some critics have suggested that the VoC framework is excessively focused on economic efficiency and successful economies. Even casual observation of capitalist systems around the world demonstrates that there are big differences between countries in terms of economic performance and that even the most advanced economies are vulnerable to economic crises and other problems, such as high unemployment.

The incorporation of more countries allows us to examine economic performance more systematically. The early VoC literature argued that both liberal and coordinated market economies were equally successful, but that hybrid or mixed market economies, such as the Mediterranean economies, were less successful as they did not have complementary economic institutions of the kind that the coherent VoCs did (Hall and Gingerich 2009; Molina and Rhodes 2007). By considering variation in economic performance across a wider range of capitalist models, it is possible to go beyond the focus on economic efficiency that characterized the original VoC volume and ask more general questions about the effects of institutions on economic performance, including both successful and less successful outcomes.

This can also shed light on the political underpinnings of capitalist diversity. The lack of a detailed political theory of capitalist diversity in the original volume, coupled with a focus on successful economies (Hall and Soskice 2001b), has led many critics to interpret the framework at least as an implicit endorsement of functionalism or that institutions can be explained as a result of their function and success (Streeck 2009). By exploring more countries and not only economies that are regarded as successful in terms of growth rates or levels of GDP, we can consider the political determinants of capitalist diversity from a comparative perspective. A global perspective can provide a better understanding of capitalism in the current age of globalization, when more countries from various parts of the world are active participants in international markets.

In addition to enriching the VoC framework itself, such a global agenda can also make an important contribution to debates about global development. There is an emerging consensus among many economists that institutions are crucial to economic growth and development (Acemoglu and Robinson 2013; Rodrik, Subramanian and Trebbi 2004; Persson and Sharp 2015). However, most cross-country studies are based on relatively simple notions of institutional quality – countries with good institutions succeed and catch up with higher-income economies, whereas countries that do not have such institutions fail to grow and converge (Knack 1996; Barro 2015). The globalized VoC framework offers important additional insights. First, by shifting the attention away from institutional quality to different *types* of institutions, we are better placed to move beyond simple notions of a single path to economic success. And even if first-best institutions can sometimes be identified, they may not be achievable in practice. This also helps us explore a wider array of economic outcomes and trade-offs between different desirable objectives, such as how some countries grow fast whilst maintaining low levels of inequality, whereas others have higher inequality. Second, there is also a growing appreciation that a particular kind of institution may work well in one setting, but less well in others. This means that it is very important to consider contextual factors. Such factors include the broader socio-political context and the constraints it imposes, and also complementary economic institutions (or institutional complementarities). Careful applications of a global VoC approach provide a more nuanced account of such contextual factors, which are crucial to the success and feasibility of economic reform.

A global perspective is also important given the increasing interdependence of national economies. As global trade, foreign investment and global financial markets are increasingly important, economic ties between countries and firms merit more attention. Firms cannot be understood only with respect to their home country, if much of their production takes place elsewhere in the world. The same may be true of countries – heightened interdependence in terms of trade, FDI or borrowing imply that the performance of the economy is at least partly determined by developments beyond national borders. This book explores the significance of such interdependence for understanding capitalism at the national level.

How to globalize the VoC debate

After making the case that the VoC debate should be globalized, we now turn to the question of how this could be accomplished. Some observers have expressed some scepticism about this. As Clift rightly notes, the VoC literature on the BRICs has been limited, for example – and he suggests that there may be good reasons for this (Clift 2021: 114). Other scholars have made similar points even more emphatically and argued that it is necessary to develop new approaches or at least to draw on different kinds of approaches for understanding capitalism beyond the traditional OECD. They have suggested that extending VoC beyond the OECD is misguided: 'But to assume that these models can be readily applied to less developed market societies seems far too much of a stretch' (Bohle and Greskovits 2012: 11). Bohle and Greskovits are certainly correct to highlight that the applicability of a particular theory beyond its original remit cannot be taken for granted – but neither can we generally make any *a priori* assumption about the lack of applicability. Additional research is required to test the applicability of a theory and, if appropriate, suggest necessary modifications or alternatives.

A growing literature on this topic suggests that it is possible to extend the VoC debate to various economies beyond the traditional OECD. As Hall and Soskice themselves suggest about the VoC framework, 'the point of this analysis is not simply to identify these two types, but to outline an approach that can be used to compare many kinds of economies' (2001a: 33). Part II of this book builds on these insights from the original VoC volume, the emerging VoC literature on other regions, and insights from other approaches to synthesize the emerging global VoC literature.

The approach of this book has several components. First, as noted earlier, it is clear that the distinction between LMEs and CMEs does not exhaust the full range of capitalist institutions in the world and that it is not possible to shoehorn all political economies into this binary typology. However, we can use the basic building blocks, such as notably coordination mechanisms, to identify other logics of economic organization and other varieties of economic systems. In addition to market and strategic coordination in LMEs and CMEs (see Chapters 2 and 3), this book analyses four alternative coordination mechanisms that predominate in four additional varieties of capitalism: trust in networked market economies (NMEs – Chapter 4), hierarchy in hierarchical market economies (HMEs – Chapter 5), dependency in dependent market economies (DMEs – Chapter 6), and the state in statist market economies (SMEs – see Chapter 7). See Table 1.1 for an overview of the key models.

Second, it adopts a flexible approach to comparative institutional advantage and regards the efficiency of particular varieties as a question that needs to be evaluated. Given that political

Table 1.1 Varieties of Capitalism: A Comparison of Six Models

	Liberal Market Economies	**Coordinated Market Economies**	**Networked Market Economies**	**Hierarchical Market Economies**	**Dependent Market Economies**	**Statist Market Economies**
Key logic of coordination	Market	Strategic	Network	Hierarchy	International hierarchy: dependence on intra-firm hierarchies in multinational corporations	State: interpersonal reciprocity, loyalty and private–public alliances
Share ownership	Dispersed	Blockholding	Blockholding and cross-ownership	Family blockholding	Significant foreign ownership	Significant state ownership and/or control
Financial system	Stock market-based	Bank-based	Bank-based	Bank-based (often within group)	External finance (FDI or foreign banks)	Bank-based (often state-owned or state-funded)
Corporate governance	Outsider control: minority shareholders	Insider control: concentrated shareholders	Insider control and cross-holdings; family ownership common	Group control (and multinational headquarters)	Control by headquarters of multinational corporations	Insider control by national capital, not by transnational investors
Corporate finance: primary source	Domestic and international capital markets	Domestic bank lending and internally generated funds	Domestic bank lending	Group lending	Foreign direct investments (FDI) and foreign-owned banks	Family capital and state-owned banks, limited foreign finance
Employment system	Pluralist, market-based, few collective agreements; limited employment protection	Corporatist, rather consensual, sectoral or nationwide agreements; strong peak organizations of business and unions; strong employment protection and codetermination	Traditionally lifetime employment; long job tenure and seniority pay; loyal company unions	Segmented (insiders vs. outsiders on informal employment); very short job tenures; weak peak organizations of business and labour	Appeasement of skilled labour, company-based agreements; relatively limited role of peak organizations	Low-wage regime, selective enforcement of worker rights, often limited in practice; often state-dominated labour relations

(*Continued*)

Table 1.1 (Continued)

	Liberal Market Economies	**Coordinated Market Economies**	**Networked Market Economies**	**Hierarchical Market Economies**	**Dependent Market Economies**	**Statist Market Economies**
Welfare system	Liberal welfare state	Conservative or social democratic welfare state	Productivist	Stratified/segmented	Compensatory	Productivist
Education and skill system: key focus	General skills, significant private provision of education, limited vocational skills	Specific skills system (industry or sector-specific), public education	Segmentalist skills system (firm-specific skills); public primary/secondary, but often private college/university	Limited skill investments (universalizing, dual academic-oriented, dual vocational education and training-oriented [VET] and exclusionary)	Vocational and key general skills	Broad-based secondary education, but more limited access to further education
Specialization	Rapid innovation: biotechnology	Incremental innovation (manufacturing)	Incremental innovation (manufacturing)	Commodities, simple manufacturing	Assembly platform for manufacturing	Assembly of medium-tech manufacturing
Key examples	United States, United Kingdom	Germany, Sweden	Japan, South Korea, Taiwan	Most of Latin America, e.g. Chile, Mexico	Hungary, Poland, Slovakia, Czechia	China, India, Brazil

Source: Schneider, p.23, 25, 28, 29; Nölke et al., p. 546; author's adaptations.

economies may not be equally efficient and successful, it is *distinctive* rather than successful performance that is seen as the defining characteristic of a particular capitalist variety. It is also important not to put too much emphasis on success, as such assessments are frequently prone to fads. In the 1950s and 1960s the French model was viewed as superior, whereas Scandinavian corporatism was the flavour of the month in the 1970s. Then attention shifted to Japan in the late 1970s and early 1980s when there was considerable debate about the advantages of introducing elements of the Japanese economic system elsewhere (Boyer 2000). Subsequently analysts embraced the previously criticized US model of capitalism. By focusing on the distinctiveness rather than the success of specific varieties, we avoid hostages to fortune and are able to consider a wider array of countries as well as trade-offs between performance indicators across economic systems and over time within particular political economies.

Third, following the advice offered by several analysts (Becker 2007; Morgan 2007), this book accepts that models of VoC can also be seen as ideal types in the sense defined by Max Weber. This has a number of important implications. In particular, it is important not to conflate the theoretical concepts with the empirical reality of the economies they speak to or try to squeeze every feature of that reality into these concepts. However, the ideal type constitutes a useful benchmark that the empirical reality can be assessed against (Swedberg 2018: 184). This formulation implies we should not expect every or indeed any country to fit this logic in every respect. However, it can be used to analyse actual political economies, and we can assess how close a particular country's economic institutions come to a particular type and whether changes over time move countries closer to or further away from a given ideal type. This also implies that there could be subnational or sectoral variation within a given economy. Such variation will be mentioned in the book, but the main emphasis is on understanding the main national varieties. In other words, there is no presumption that VoC analysis can explain every aspect of these economies or the changes they undergo over time, but the chapters will demonstrate that it can be a useful framework for analysing many key features of these political economies.

This book draws on this framework and argues that economic institutions are complex social-political configurations that are often best understood by means of comparative case study analysis, which highlights the complex interactions that underpin such institutions. Table 1.1 summarizes the main varieties of capitalism analysed in this book. It should also be noted that whilst the book adopts a global perspective, there are inevitably some limits to its coverage, and it would have been desirable to cover an even wider range of economies. The book does not examine quantitative studies of country clusters in global samples (Fainshmidt et al. 2018; Witt et al. 2018) or consider the debate about hybrid models of capitalism or the so-called 'mixed market economies' (MMEs) of Southern Europe except in the context of the discussion of the eurozone crisis in Chapter 10.

Beyond Varieties of Capitalism: The case for pluralism

Whilst the VoC approach remains influential and the most obvious starting point for students learning about contemporary capitalism, it has also attracted criticism that it is less easy to address merely by globalizing the approach. For a number of years even scholars who are sympathetic to the VoC approach have been reflecting on the need to go 'beyond varieties of capitalism' in various respects, for example, by considering the role of the state (Hancké, Rhodes and Thatcher 2007). This book discusses several alternative approaches to comparative capitalism that could be regarded as either complements or alternatives to VoC analysis, and each of these approaches speaks to particular weaknesses associated with the VoC framework.

An influential line of criticisms suggests that VoC pays insufficient attention to change over time in capitalist institutions and to the pervasiveness of economic instability. Throughout its history, capitalism has been associated with regular crises – some have been relatively mild, but others have been severe and even sown seeds of doubt about the viability and survival of capitalism as a system. These criticisms have stimulated refinements of the VoC approach that consider processes of institutional change (Hall and Thelen 2008) and also the causes of financial crises and economic instability (Iversen and Soskice 2012). However, they have also inspired the development of alternative perspectives, notably the analysis of growth regimes, financialization and growth models.

Growth regimes can be used to characterize successive models of economic governance. Scholars have identified three (or more) growth regimes from the mid-twentieth century until the first quarter of the twenty-first century. Each of these regimes has been based on particular institutional arrangements and involved distinctive engines of economic growth. The political underpinnings of these regimes have varied as well. Chapter 8 considers the development of capitalism over time and analyses the contribution of growth regimes to a better understanding of these trends and the diversity of capitalism.

A second challenge to VoC analysis relates to the rapid growth of financial markets and their impact on the global economy and on national economies. This implies that it could be essential to rethink the core logic of capitalism if financial pressures increasingly dominate economies and may overshadow the mechanisms related to institutions in the production regime that the VoC literature has focused on (Davis 2009).

Financialization has become an important research programme in the social sciences that speaks to such concerns, but it is a vast debate with many distinct strands. In one approach financialization could be regarded as a new growth regime or stage of capitalism (Arrighi 2010; Boyer 2000), in which the financial sector has acquired a very central role. Scholars of financialization explore how these developments have transformed the logic of capitalism and reduced the importance of the production regime. To the extent that finance has become increasingly central and operates more autonomously within capitalist economies, key changes in capitalism may be primarily determined by developments in the financial economy. Chapter 9 provides an introduction to financialization and its key dimensions, and it reflects on its impact on capitalism and capitalist diversity.

A third challenge to VoC relates to the role of the macroeconomy in comparative capitalism. VoC largely mirrors key trends within the economics profession of moving away from Keynesian approaches that examine the role of macroeconomic stabilization policy to manage the business cycle. To the extent that VoC analysis considers macroeconomics, it does so through the lens of new Keynesian economics, and it tends to focus on the ways in which a macroeconomy interacts with key institutions in a given capitalist system. In later VoC research such insights have been deployed to analyse key features of the global financial crisis of 2007–8 and of the eurozone crisis as well.

However, many critics argue that the macroeconomy or economic instability pose a much more profound challenge to VoC analysis. Chapter 10 introduces the debate surrounding growth models. Baccaro and Pontusson (2016) have drawn on post-Keynesian economics to revive interest in growth models in comparative political economy, and they argue that this approach provides a more compelling account of capitalism than VoC, since it can also capture distributional concerns and the significance of economic instability. Chapter 10 compares this approach to VoC and discusses recent attempts to analyse *growth regimes* as a synthesis of VoC and growth model analysis.

Table 1.2 summarizes the five alternative approaches to comparative capitalism discussed in Chapters 2–10.

A fourth challenge to VoC relates to its political underpinnings. The focus on economic efficiency that is central to much of the literature has invited interpretations of the theory as functionalist or implying that the existence of these institutions can be explained by their function and successful operation. As institutions are not necessarily successful or efficient and often result from power struggles, appeals to functionalism are generally regarded as problematic in political economy. Whether VoC is necessarily functionalist is disputed (Hall and Thelen 2008), but the emphasis on efficiency has certainly led to a neglect of the political contestation and conflicts that typically surround capitalism and markets.

Chapter 11 examines a key example of political contestation, namely the rise of populism in the 2010s, which has evoked comparisons with earlier periods of turmoil when capitalism and democracy have been under threat. The collapse of capitalism seemed likely in the interwar period as Soviet communism sought to eliminate it altogether and fascism reshaped it in profound ways. Just like the Great Depression strengthened support for alternatives to capitalism and made its collapse seem less unlikely than before, many observers have asked whether the rise of populism in the twenty-first century represents a similar threat to capitalism. Chapter 11 considers the ways in which different capitalist systems have contributed to the rise of populism. It also considers the impact of populism and business responses on these developments.

Overview of the rest of the book

The remainder of the book is divided into two parts – Part II and Part III. Part II explores global VoC by analysing a particular variety in each chapter – first the two classical VoC outlined by Hall and Soskice (2001a) (Chapters 2 and 3) and then the new types of VoC that have been developed to analyse other parts of the world (Chapters 4–7). In each of these chapters I begin by discussing the core logic of that particular variety, including the dominant coordination mechanism and related institutions (finance, including financial systems and corporate governance; labour, including industrial relations, skills and welfare) as well as patterns of comparative institutional advantage. After that each chapter considers case studies to illustrate these institutions and to discuss the political underpinnings of these varieties and change over time as well. It should be noted that these are relatively short and stylized case studies – each of the country cases would merit a book in its own right, so these brief case studies are inevitably incomplete. The main purpose of these case studies is to illustrate how VoC analysis can be applied to analyse capitalist diversity, but the case studies often highlight contemporary or historical features of these economies that fit less well. Each economy has some unique features, and the VoC models are best seen as ideal types that provide a baseline for understanding actual economies whose fit with the model is never perfect. Like a map that helps hikers navigate a complex terrain, the VoC models highlight some salient features of economic institutions that can help us make sense of the complexity of capitalist systems.

In Part III the book introduces other approaches to comparative capitalism that go beyond the VoC debate. Chapter 8 considers change over time by focusing on the evolution of growth regimes. Chapter 9 analyses financialization, whereas Chapter 10 discusses the role of the macroeconomy in comparative capitalism and introduces growth model analysis to study macroeconomic instability. Chapter 11 discusses the relationship between globalization, capitalist diversity and the rise of populism and its implications. The final chapter concludes

Table 1.2. Comparing Approaches

	Varieties of Capitalism	**Growth models**	**Financialization**	**Growth regimes (over time)**	**Growth regimes (at any one time)**
Unit of analysis	Firm/institutions	Structure of demand and growth	Financial sector	Structure of demand, growth strategies and institutional framework underpinning production (including welfare state)	Institutional framework (related to demand and supply side of the economy) underpinning economic activity
Key varieties	LME, CME, NME, HME, DME, SME	Export-led, consumption-led, balanced, investment-led (FD), investment-led (state), commodity-led	Degree of financialization (high to low), degree of financial subordination	Modernization, Liberalization, Knowledge economy	Dynamic services/ export-led, high-quality manufacturing/ export-led, FDI/export, Finance/demand, public finance/demand
What it can explain?	Specialization and performance	Nature of growth and its distributional effects	Impact of financial sector on real economy	Evolution of capitalism over time	Nature of growth, production and welfare
Focus on Instability?	Not central	Yes?	Yes	Not central, but could be integrated	Yes
Focus on sectoral specialization?	Yes	Not central	Not central	Yes	Yes

Source: Author's compilation.

the book with a discussion of the broader lessons of studying comparative capitalism and some implications for future debates.

Discussion questions

- What are the key features of a capitalist system?
- Why might it be important to compare capitalist systems in different countries?
- What are the strengths and weaknesses of the Varieties of Capitalism approach?
- What does a global approach add to the debate about Varieties of Capitalism?
- What are the main reasons for considering alternative theoretical perspectives on comparative capitalism?
- To what extent does comparative capitalism relate to common political controversies about capitalism?

PART II

Global varieties of capitalism

2

Liberal market economies

Introduction

This is the first of six chapters that introduce different types of capitalist systems. This chapter discusses the liberal market economy (LME) model and highlights its key characteristics and associated outcomes by drawing on the VoC framework developed by Hall and Soskice (2001b). It discusses the political underpinnings of the model, notably why it has been closely associated with countries in the English-speaking world, as well as the debate about global convergence on the LME model. The importance of the LME model relates to the fact that the countries associated with it are the most canonical market economies. The United States became the dominant economy in the world in the twentieth century, much like Britain as the first industrializer and modern capitalist economy had previously been. Therefore, these two economies have been a key reference point for much of economic theory and political economy, and this makes it very important to understand how these economies operate. The goal of this chapter is to provide an overview of the logic of the LME model as a distinctive form of capitalism and to shed light on what it can teach us about the US and British economies.

Understanding the LME model

The distinguishing feature of the LME model is the centrality of *market coordination* within a given market economy. Market coordination refers not just to the existence of markets for final goods and services, which exist in all types of capitalist economies, but also to markets as a coordination mechanism that helps firms mobilize key resources for economic activity. In other words, market coordination is central to the ways in which firms access such resources. A key prerequisite for successful market coordination is that there must be well-functioning markets for the key resources that firms rely on, notably labour, capital and skills.

Market coordination has a number of distinctive features. If firms manage key relationships via markets, transactions are generally based on well-defined formal contracts. Other kinds of coordination mechanisms that are discussed later in the book, such as strategic bargaining or networks, may also exist, but they play a less important role in a typical LME than in other kinds of market economies. This has important implications for understanding the role of the state in LMEs. First, the state plays an important role as a guarantor of law and order, property, and contract, but it does not generally exercise any active role in reshaping the sectoral structure of the economy in the way that the state does in statist market economies (see Chapter 7). In LMEs, a strong state helps underpin the functioning of markets (Gamble 1994). This is consistent with the arguments made by classical liberals that more activist states are weakened by overreach. Such overreach occurs if they aim for socio-economic goals that undermine the state's ability to act as an impartial arbiter of the rule of law (Sally 1998). Second, the reliance on market coordination and formal contracts increases the significance of laws and regulations. Market coordination does not emerge automatically. As Vogel (2018) has shown, whilst the US economy is characterized by some of the freest markets, it also has the largest number of rules and regulations governing these markets. Finally, given that business is weakly organized and has limited capacity for coordination, government decisions often play a greater role than in CMEs, where businesses can agree on binding industry standards in business associations (King and Wood 1999). For example, a minimum wage law may act as a wage floor in the same way that collective wage agreements do in economies where unions and employers' associations bargain about wages.

The best-known LMEs are among the most prosperous countries in the world. The LMEs have generally been perceived to be very successful, not least since the two most prominent examples, Britain and the United States, have played a very central role in the world economy. Whilst their influence reflects a long history of high economic growth, their performance varied over time, and at times there has been intense debate about the viability and future prospects of their economic models. In addition, market coordination of the kind that is prominent in LMEs tends to generate higher-income inequality, at least compared to CMEs in Western Europe (Pontusson 2005). This results both from higher wage inequality and from more limited redistribution.

It should be noted that markets are central to the LME model, but in a more specific way than the popular association of the United States and the United Kingdom with free markets suggests. For much of the twentieth century the United States had iconic status as the symbol of free markets and capitalism in the Cold War standoff against the Soviet bloc. A commitment to markets, international trade and limited government are widely regarded as central features of the US economy. The historical association between Britain and free markets goes back even further. The abolition of the Corn Laws in 1832 moved Britain very close to unilateral free trade and signalled a strong commitment to free markets not only domestically but at the international level as well. At the time, free-market ideas were propagated by Britain throughout the British Empire and in various international contexts, much like the United States was seen as the strongest advocate and guarantor of open markets, especially in the second half of the twentieth century.

Corporate governance and financial systems

Corporate governance and financial systems relate to two central and closely related challenges for every firm, namely how it can raise investment funds and how the firm's owners (and sometimes other stakeholders) can ensure that the firm's management acts in the interest of the firm rather than their own self-interest. This relates to the question of how corporate performance is assessed and what kinds of goals firms pursue.

In LMEs, market coordination plays a central role in this regard and manifests itself primarily in the centrality of stock markets. Stock market capitalization, or the total value of the shares traded on stock markets, as a share of GDP, is typically very high in LMEs, which reflects a high percentage of listed companies.

The coordinating role of stock markets operates in several ways. First, share prices are a prime indicator of economic success, and much of a firm's activity is focused on responding to market signals in order to maintain high share prices and to maximize shareholder value. With deep financial markets in place, there are limited incentives to invest in in-depth knowledge about firms that is independent of publicly available information. Ensuring a good return to shareholders is important for maintaining high share prices, as many investors actively seek to maximize the return on their investment. Investors are usually fickle and expect high earnings relatively quickly.

In Albert Hirschman's (1970) terminology, investors respond to unfavourable developments by choosing to exit rather than exercising 'voice', or raising their concerns about the need to address the situation. This contrasts with the responses that would be common in some other types of market economies that are characterized by patient capital, such as CMEs or NMEs (see Chapters 3 and 4). LMEs score low on indicators of patient capital (Culpepper 2011: 47). These features also contribute to an active market for corporate control, which means that mergers and acquisitions are common in LMEs (Culpepper 2011: 1). The threat of takeovers serves as a further source of discipline on firm performance and induces managers to act in ways that maximize share prices. There is generally a market that makes mergers, acquisitions and takeovers easy to implement, which enhances the importance of maintaining a high share price, as undervalued firms face a greater risk of takeover.

Stock market performance is also important to the ability of firms to secure investment funds. First, stock markets are an important source of financing. Second, stock market performance also operates as a sign of creditworthiness, which affects the ability of firms to raise funds in other ways, for example, by issuing bonds or borrowing from financial institutions.

The significant role of short-term financing also enhances the role of top management, which tends to be dominated by the chief executive officer (CEO), who has extensive power and influence over the organization, including the board. Unlike some other types of capitalist systems (notably CMEs), there is a single board. Such CEO dominance is usually justified by the need for rapid responses to market signals. In the absence of other coordination mechanisms or a significant role for negotiations with other stakeholders, such as trade unions or even the state, CEO dominance is reflected in a relatively hierarchical internal structure of firms.

Whilst strong and decisive leadership is often regarded as a strength, critics have suggested that limited accountability to other stakeholders also poses risks to these economies. They point out that some of the most egregious corporate scandals have taken place in LMEs, where companies that competed aggressively and sought to maximize their share prices ignored other concerns. In their quest to cut costs and maximize the share price, Boeing was reported to have neglected quality and safety standards, which contributed to several crashes (Bloomberg 2020). Another dramatic example relates to the Grenfell disaster in London, where sub-standard and flammable building materials had been used in the cladding of apartment buildings, leading to many deaths in a fire that might have been preventable if the construction company had spent more on safer materials. Whilst some members of parliament had advocated stricter rules in the past, regulators had resisted such calls, with a leading regulator suggesting that 'requiring only noncombustible exteriors in residential towers 'limits your choice of materials quite significantly' (Kirkpatrick et al. 2017). Given that the LME vests great authority in CEOs and privileges shareholder interests, there is a risk that other stakeholders' concerns (including effects on employees, customers and the wider community) could be neglected.

Labour markets

In a typical LME, market coordination is also central to the functioning of labour markets. Given the prevalence of market coordination and market adjustment, labour markets tend to be relatively fluid, with comparatively high rates of job turnover, as workers can be easily hired and fired in response to changing conditions.

Industrial relations are generally fragmented and decentralized (Hall and Soskice 2001b). Trade unions and employers' associations are relatively weak, as reflected in low rates of unionization and especially low membership rates in employers' associations. However, perhaps even more importantly, there is limited coordination between unions and employers' associations, which means that it is difficult to reach explicit agreements or to coordinate across firms or sectors. To the extent that there are formal negotiations between unions and employers' representatives, such bargaining takes place at the firm level. The extent of such bargaining and the coverage rates of such agreements are typically low, in that they only cover a relatively small share of firms and of the labour market.

Market competition and decentralized labour market decisions are the primary determinants of wages rather than collective bargaining or negotiated agreements. To the extent that bargaining takes place, it is generally decentralized and at the level of the firm. Other forms of worker involvement with firm governance, such as codetermination or employee representation on corporate boards, are very rare. In this model, relations between employers and workers are often conflictual, with employers worried that higher wages will translate into lower competitiveness.

Given that it is relatively easy for employers to hire and fire workers, and workers often choose to move between jobs, the average job tenure is lower in LMEs than in coordinated market economies (CMEs – see Chapter 3).

This also has important effects on the education and training system, which is closely related to labour market institutions (Iversen and Stephens 2008). Given this fluidity, LMEs place heavy emphasis on general skills which can be deployed in many kinds of jobs across a range of sectors. This is reflected in the significance of post-secondary university and college education in these economies, where enrolment rates are very high by international standards. In 2022, five LMEs were in the global top ten of the countries with the highest share of the population between 25 and 64 with a tertiary educational qualification according to OECD statistics (OECD 2023). Canada was in first place with a 63 per cent share, Ireland in third, Australia in fifth, and the United Kingdom and United States in eighth and ninth with 51 per cent and 50 per cent respectively. When turnover in labour markets is high, neither firms nor workers have any incentive to make big investments in specific skills that might not be useful if a worker transfers to another job. General skills are also useful in a range of service professions, and the emphasis on them is one of the reasons why LMEs have generally been successful at stimulating the expansion of the service sector and jobs within it. Apprenticeships and vocational training systems play a limited role. This means that there are limited opportunities for the less academically inclined to acquire additional skills. This is why the education and skill system has highly inegalitarian features, in that it tends to favour the middle class and the higher end of the income distribution, which also has access to private education (Iversen and Stephens 2008).

This kind of labour market dovetails with a relatively small or residual welfare state that stresses self-reliance – a liberal welfare state in Esping-Andersen's (1990) classic model. This means that there are relatively few benefits and services that are universally available, as most of the support provided by the welfare state is means-tested and targeted to the neediest groups. VoC analysis implies that there are limited economic incentives for a large welfare state. Given the fluid nature of labour markets and the importance of general skills, moving between jobs is relatively easy, so there is less demand for social policy insuring against labour market risks (Iversen 2005). The comparatively short job tenures also imply that employers are generally unwilling to fund big investments in firm-specific skills. They do not know whether they will reap the benefits from such training as the workers will not necessarily stay with the firm. As a result, firms are also unlikely to support high public spending on training or related social expenditures. Firms in LMEs typically regard higher welfare spending or higher spending on training schemes negatively, as it that could undermine their cost competitiveness (King and Wood 1999).

Complementarities and economic outcomes

VoC scholars have also shown that LME institutions are associated with distinctive economic outcomes.

First, highly coherent LME institutions should provide a comparative institutional advantage associated with high rates of economic growth. Whilst patterns of economic growth in LMEs vary over time and across countries, most of these countries are among the most prosperous in the world. VoC analysis sees the success of LMEs as associated with a distinctive form of comparative institutional advantage that is based on the web of complementary institutions in these economies, such as the mutual reinforcement of general skills, a flexible labour market and a stock market-based financial system that makes it easy to raise capital quickly. The basic prediction of the VoC framework is that economic performance in terms of high output growth and low inflation will be strong, at least over longer periods of time. Competitive markets for inputs as well as goods and services should promote efficient resource allocation. The strong economic performance is also based on specialization in sectors in which LMEs have a comparative institutional advantage. LME institutions tend to promote rapid innovation, inducing LMEs to specialize in sectors such as biotechnology or financial services. Ample supply of venture capital and the relative ease of raising capital for new investments promote such patterns of specialization (Hall and Soskice 2001b).

On the other hand, there has been great controversy surrounding the LME model, which has been criticized for excessive short-termism and inadequate skill investments (Finegold and Soskice 1988). At various times, there has been extensive debate about the success of these economies, especially when other models were widely seen to be more successful. For example, the rapid growth of the Japanese economy generated great interest in the United States, and Ezra Vogel's (1979) bestseller *Japan as Number One* captured the ways in which Americans were hoping to draw lessons from Japanese success. Similarly, some of the debate about the British economy in the 1950s and 1960s stressed the importance of strong strategic direction by the state, which suggested that the French economy provided better governance for modernization (Shonfield 1969). At various times arguments for reforming institutions to promote a greater stakeholder orientation (Kelly,, Kelly, and Gamble 1997) or more activist industrial policies by the state to support less prosperous parts of the country (Lee 2010) have come to the fore. Such proposals are typically designed to address the perceived weaknesses of the LME model, including excessive short-termism or regional inequalities.

Another reason why the LME model is controversial relates to relatively high inequality by comparative OECD standards. As a result of decentralized labour markets and a small welfare state, there are few mechanisms to compress wages or to introduce redistribution by means of taxes and subsidies. The decline of manufacturing and other changes associated with the neoliberal era have also contributed to rising inequality, which, especially since the 1990s, has also been underpinned by financialization and great reliance on asset-based welfare (Chapter 9). Although these trends occurred in different types of economies, they have been particularly pronounced in LMEs. Whilst such forms of welfare can provide some insurance at the individual level, they also tend to reinforce inequality as high-income households are best placed to take advantage of the opportunities provided by financial markets.

The United States as an LME

It is hard to overstate the centrality of the US economy to global capitalism. After effectively being a developing economy for much of the nineteenth century, the United States has been the largest economy in the world since the early twentieth century, and it accounted for between 20 and 25 per cent of the world's GDP in the early twenty-first century. The United States features prominently in almost all discussions of VoC analysis, and it is the key example of an LME in the original *Varieties of Capitalism* volume (Hall and Soskice 2001b).

If we consider the core elements of the US political economy, it is easy to see that they fit well with the LME model, especially since the 1980s. First, the United States has a financial system in which stock markets play a very important role. The role of banks was more significant in the nineteenth century, but key legislative and regulatory changes in the twentieth century reduced their importance, notably the Clayton Anti-Trust Act of 1914 and the Glass-Steagall Banking Act of 1933. The Clayton Anti-Trust Act outlawed interlocking directorships between banks and trusts and acquisitions of shares in another company if they reduced competition in an industry, whereas the Glass-Steagall Act enshrined a sharp separation between investment banking and commercial banking. The cumulative effect of these acts was to weaken the role of banks, including investment banks, as sources of financing for firms, which increased the importance of the stock market (Hollingsworth 1997: 138). Whilst stock markets have been more influential in the United States than in most other countries for a long time, this role was further enhanced by trends towards greater financialization in the US economy since the 1980s (Krippner 2005; see also Chapter 9). This includes the growing importance of ideas and practices related to the maximization of shareholder value (Lazonick and O'Sullivan 2000).

The stock market capitalization of the US economy as a share of GDP is one of the highest in the world – according to World Bank statistics, it was 158 per cent in 2022. The importance of the stock market is also reflected at the firm level. The share price is an important metric of corporate success, and it affects companies' ability to raise funds and protects them against hostile takeovers. The existence of a thriving corporate takeover market serves to discipline managers. Within the firm, the organization is generally hierarchical, with greater powers vested in the CEO, although the importance of external factors, such as financial market pressures, has become more significant (Davis 2009). For much of the twentieth century the United States was characterized by a form of managerial capitalism, in which top management enjoyed considerable autonomy (Chandler 1984). In 2002, the Sarbanes-Oxley Act enhanced external reporting requirements and introduced new rules related to board structure that reinforced such trends as well (Cioffi 2010).

Industrial relations also fit the LME model well. The unionization rate is among the lowest in the OECD. According to the Bureau of Labor Statistics, it was 11.2 per cent in 2023, with 6.9 per cent in the private sector. Trade unions face greater legal barriers to organizing in the United States, especially across workplaces, than in other comparable countries (Thelen 2019). Although the Democratic Party developed closer ties with the labour movement in the twentieth century, the political influence of the union movement has traditionally been hampered by the absence of a social democratic or labour party. In addition to business hostility, the judiciary also played a key role in weakening the political organization of labour (Archer 2013). Collective representation of business interests through business associations plays a relatively limited role, although many individual businesses exercise great influence on politics by lobbying and campaign contributions (Drutman 2015).

Whilst total welfare spending is high in some spheres, such as healthcare, the welfare state is largely organized based on a market logic, making public provision mostly residual. A key example of this is Medicaid, which provides healthcare for adults and children on low incomes. Beginning in the 1980s, changes to the welfare state have also tended to contribute to a 'privatization of risk', whereby individuals incur a greater share of life-course risks than previously (Hacker 2004). This is reflected in the move from pensions based on defined benefits to defined contributions. Key reforms that have contributed to these trends include the Personal Responsibility and Work Opportunity Act of 1996 (Eisner 2014: 150). Therefore, the welfare state can be described as liberal and residual, with entitlement programmes mostly targeting groups that are not covered by private provision (Esping-Andersen 1999). Such features have become more pronounced since the 1980s (Hacker 2004), and the United States stands out in comparative perspective in terms of very high rates of in-work poverty and precarity, including limited access to paid sick leave or other kinds of benefits, paid annual leave or parental leave (Thelen 2019).

The skill system is complementary to labour market institutions in that it privileges general skills, with high school and college/university education being the principal sources of education. The university system produces excellent general skills that underpin the US innovation and business systems. More specialized technical and vocational training programmes are integrated into formal education, including community colleges, and training at the company level is voluntary. There is no national system of apprenticeships and vocational training, as federal involvement is limited and restricted to some subsidies for state-level programmes, which may vary considerably (Deeg 2012: 1255).

There are many factors that underpin US exceptionalism. Hacker et al. (2022) argue that the functioning of the US political economy is largely shaped by what they call meta-politics, or processes of institution shaping, agenda setting, and venue shopping. Institution shaping

> refers to the ways in which institutions that embody and influence power relations are forged through political contestation over time. The legacies of previous conflicts set parameters on current politics in ways that are highly consequential yet virtually invisible, as institutions that were previously contested become accepted features of the political landscape. (Hacker et al. 2022: 200)

Given the role of agenda setting and venue shopping, many important issues are largely determined outside the realm of electoral politics and influenced by powerful interest groups and other elite actors who can shape which issues make it onto the political agenda and in what context. Hacker et al. (2022) highlight the centrality of federalism, the nature of the legal system and racial inequality as key factors underpinning these processes. Both federalism and the legal system tend to strengthen business influence in various ways. These institutions facilitate venue shopping. A classic example of venue shopping is the fact that many companies have traditionally chosen to incorporate in Delaware as a result of its business-friendly corporate law and tax system. The centrality of the legal system also provides businesses with many opportunities to advance key priorities effectively, whereas it tends to complicate the exercise of power by labour (Rahman and Thelen 2021; Hertel-Fernandez 2021).

VoC theory can also account for US specialization in key sectors relying on radical innovation. For example, the United States has enjoyed considerable success in biotechnology and other sectors that rely on radical innovation, including software development. The United States has been at the forefront of three economic revolutions since the nineteenth century – what Soskice (2021) has referred to as the scientific, Fordist and information and communication technologies (ICT) revolutions. Soskice highlights the importance of the research/market/finance complex and the legal/political/lobbying complex in underpinning innovation in the United States. The former governs relations between research, universities and high-skill labour markets and finance, whereas the latter determines the relations between parties, courts and lobbying activities. Soskice argues that the decentralized and weakly regulated nature of these two complexes creates a framework that promotes radical innovation by facilitating easy access to critical human and financial resources. The innovation system is also increasingly underwritten by the state. Although the US political and economic rhetoric stresses a strong commitment to free markets and a small state, the state plays an important role in some sectors, especially defence, but to some extent also health-related industries (Owen and Hopkins 2016: 13; Mazzucato 2018). State funding, for example as provided by NIH, has been of great importance in promoting innovation and product development in biotech. In these sectors, the centrality of the state as a risk-taker and also as a funder of both basic and applied research functions effectively as a form of the 'entrepreneurial state' (Mazzucato 2018; see Chapter 7). Given the strong emphasis on free markets in US political discourse, the connection between industrial policy and the defence sector helps legitimate these policies (Weiss 2014). Other forms of government support for innovation operate as a kind of 'hidden developmental state' as they might not otherwise garner as much support given the dominance of free-market ideas in the United States (Block 2008; see also Chapter 7).

However, there are some aspects and organizational features of the US economy that fit the LME model less well. Above all, there has been considerable change over time. In the aftermath of the New Deal reforms of the 1930s, the government played a more activist role in some spheres of economic policy (Weir and Skocpol 1983; Eisner 2014). In the post-war era, governments embraced Keynesian economic ideas, unions played a greater role, and product market regulation was more significant (Deeg 2012). For much of the twentieth century, the United States had a form of managerial capitalism in which large corporations played a central role, and the LME characterization of US business would be an incomplete representation of its functioning (Chandler 1984). These large businesses retained a certain independence from financial markets, and especially in the post-war era, corporate welfare provisions reflected greater concern for stakeholder interests than after the 1980s (Davis 2009; see also Chapters 8 and 9).

Even if one accepts that the LME model characterizes the contemporary US economy quite well, it should be noted that there is considerable internal diversity. Morgan (2009) argues that this relates to weakly institutionalized solutions to coordination problems, which means that the US model of capitalism may be more accommodating to a wider range of institutions and actors than some others, like Japan or Germany (see Chapters 4 and 3). This factor also makes it relatively open to foreign direct investment (Morgan 2009). More generally, such internal diversity implies that there are several features that cannot be straightforwardly explained by the LME model.

First, some observers have highlighted the importance of trust and dense networks underpinning the Silicon Valley model of venture capital and the close university-industry relations that help promote innovation and ensure a pool of human capital (Adler 2001). This is partly an agglomeration effect, which highlights the importance of a particular ecosystem of institutions and actors that are conducive to economic activity by providing access to key skills, resources and infrastructure (Iversen and Soskice 2019).

Second, family-owned firms have historically played a significant role in the US economy (Schmitz 1995), and they are still an important element of contemporary American capitalism. The influence of the founding family is based on several mechanisms, notably dual-class shares, disproportionate representation on corporate boards and special voting agreements (Villalonga and Amit 2009). Some of these firms are part of larger business groups, which share many features with dominant corporate structures in HMEs (see Chapter 5). Many family-controlled firms are not listed on stock markets, and the trend towards privately held firms is also increasing as a result of financialization and the rise of the platform economy (see Chapter 8; Davis 2016b). These developments imply that US capitalism is evolving in various ways that are reshaping firms (Davis 2016b) and the economy as a whole (see Chapters 9 and 10). If the trend towards increasing rates of delisting continues (Martinez and Serve 2017) the importance of widely held firms to the US economy is likely to decline very considerably.

Finally, as noted earlier, the fact that the United States can be regarded as an LME does not mean that the state is unimportant. In addition to funding research and innovation, the role of the state as a regulator is also very important. Market coordination does not emerge automatically, but rather as a result of 'marketcraft' in which the state plays a crucial role. This can account for the seeming paradox that the US economy is simultaneously one of the freest and most regulated economies (Vogel 2018).

The United Kingdom as an LME

The British political economy has played a very important role in debates about capitalism and its diversity, not least given that the Industrial Revolution first took place in Britain. This section demonstrates why the UK is generally viewed as a good example of an LME, but it also highlights a few features that fit the model less well.

Consistent with the LME model, the main feature of the British political economy is market coordination. Other forms of coordination, for example, by the state or based on negotiated agreements between employers and workers of the kind that is common in CMEs (see Chapter 3), are rare. Employers' associations are relatively weak and have a limited capacity to promote employer coordination. The most important peak organization, the Confederation of British Industry, was founded in 1965, which is later than most of its counterparts in other countries. The most successful instances of cooperation between British employers have tended to occur only in times of crisis (Ingham 1984: 233). Processes of financialization and structural change since the 1970s have further weakened the coordinating capacity of employers and businesses in the British political economy (Feldmann and Morgan 2021; see also Chapter 9). At various times, the lack of employer coordination has posed an obstacle to key government initiatives, such as the National Economic Development Council (1960–4) a flagship initiative to promote the modernization of industry (Wood 2001). Business associations have evolved and sought to identify new roles related to lobbying, service, negotiating and standard setting as the scope for traditional bargaining has become more limited (Gooberman, Hauptmeier, and Heery 2020). The role of trade unions is also relatively limited. Even when unions have been influential, there has been a strong emphasis on the autonomy of company unions, thereby weakening the potential for coordination across firms and sectors. This has undermined attempts to develop corporatist-style arrangements in the UK in the past (King and Wood 1999).

The financial system and corporate governance are features of the British economy that fit the LME model particularly well. Financial markets have long been highly developed in the British economy, and even historically operated in a relatively decentralized way (Gerschenkron 1962). The City of London, the core of the British financial sector, is an important economic and political actor, a trend that has been further accentuated by the financial sector reforms since the 1980s. These reforms led to an influx of foreign banks and weakened the role of many traditional actors in the City and contributed to further growth of the financial sector. These developments have also sparked a substantial debate about whether the financial sector has become too big and whether this has harmed the development of industry (Ingham 1984; Baker, Epstein and Montecino 2018).

Labour markets fit the LME model well, in that they are relatively flexible and decentralized. Especially compared to Northern European economies, unionization is low (23.5 per cent in 2019). Whilst union membership is still higher than in some other European countries and in the United States, unionization is concentrated in the public sector. The coverage rate of bargaining agreements in the public sector (60.1 per cent in 2019) is much higher than in the private sector (15.1 per cent in 2019). However, the decentralized nature of labour markets was less clear before the 1980s, as unions played a greater role and participated in policy discussions and collective bargaining. Notwithstanding this, the fact that British unions have traditionally been organized primarily at the firm level and put a high premium on local autonomy has complicated attempts to develop coordinated solutions based on negotiated agreements with social actors. This is clearly demonstrated by the challenges associated with attempts to build corporatist arrangements as part of the Social Contract by the Callaghan government in 1978 (Hay 2010).

More generally, if one considers labour markets in conjunction with the welfare state or the broader social model of the UK, the picture is more mixed (Mayhew and Wickham-Jones 2014). On the one hand, welfare spending as a whole, for example, on labour market support or training, fits quite well with the LME model and Esping-Andersen's liberal welfare state model in that it mostly plays a residual role. On the other hand, compared to other liberal market economies, Britain has long been an outlier with respect to some key aspects of social policy, principally due to the comprehensive National Health Service (NHS), which is an example of a universal social programme more reminiscent of social democratic welfare systems that can be found in some coordinated market economies (see Chapter 3). Britain was a first mover in terms of establishing the welfare state and had the most generous and universalistic welfare state regime in the 1950s. The welfare state has evolved considerably over time, and market elements and quasi-markets have become increasingly important within the health system (Bartlett 1991; Powell and Miller 2016).

The education and training system has privileged general skills, and the expansion of the university sector in the second half of the twentieth century has been a crucial element of the growth of advanced sectors, such as the high-tech and biotechnology cluster around Cambridge as well as service industries. The emphasis on comprehensive education has also primarily contributed to general skills at the primary and secondary school levels, though market logics related to testing, competition and the establishment of academies have increasingly shaped the system. Many studies have regarded the lack of investment in vocational skills as a weakness of the British economy and even regarded this as a source of a 'low-skill equilibrium' (Finegold and Soskice 1988). Despite some attempts to devise policies that could have addressed such weaknesses, the provision of vocational training has been based on voluntarist principles or treated as a matter for employers and employees rather than public policy (King and Wickham-Jones 1998). In the LME context, there have been limited incentives for employers and unions to develop or coordinate any joint initiatives in this area.

There has been great controversy surrounding the performance of the British political economy. In the nineteenth century Britain was the leading economy in the world. Although the British economy grew in the twentieth century, at times at high rates, much of the debate has focused on 'relative decline' associated with the deteriorating relative position of the British economy in international comparisons, with other economies growing faster and overtaking Britain in GDP rankings in the decades following the Second World War (Alt 1979; Gamble 1994). The literature on relative decline has highlighted various potential weaknesses of the British economy, ranging from the under-provision of skills and training (Finegold and Soskice 1988), the problem of 'too few producers' (Bacon and Eltis 1978), to the lack of strategic direction and excessive international commitments (Shonfield 1969) or conflictual industrial relations. There is no agreement on the relative importance of these factors or on the degree to which governments in the 1980s and 1990s were successful at reversing this relative decline (Crafts 2012; Gamble 2002).

As in the American case, there is some controversy surrounding the development of the British political economy over time. In particular, this debate questions whether it is accurate to view Britain as an LME throughout the twentieth century. A VoC perspective would tend to highlight elements of continuity of the kind discussed in this section and stress the predominance of market coordination, even if some aspects of the policy regime did change. Similarly, Runciman (1993) has argued that the British economy has displayed considerable continuity since the First World War, thereby questioning the relevance of other alleged turning points, such as the post–Second World War era (Fulcher 1995) or the rise of Thatcherism (King and Wood 1999). However, others have argued that the most striking feature of the British economy is institutional change, and by implication, the LME label is only appropriate from the 1980s onwards (Howell 2007). Such contributions suggest that the ascent of the Thatcher government with the move to heightened globalization constituted a major transition from a model with many social democratic and even some CME features. Most observers would agree that the period since the early 1980s could be viewed as a neoliberal era and that the thirteen years of New Labour governments (1997–2010) did not change the underlying structure in any fundamental way (Glyn and Wood 2001; Mayhew and Wickham-Jones 2014). In summary, whilst the UK fits the LME model somewhat less well than the US economy, this model captures the structure of British economic institutions, especially since the 1980s.

The politics of LMEs

The political underpinnings of this model are complex. The original VoC volume focused on explaining why different varieties of capitalism have generated successful outcomes and did not devote much attention to the political underpinnings of economic institutions, but the existing literature on the core LMEs suggests a range of possible explanations.

The key feature of LMEs is the centrality of market coordination. This means that economic coordination operates in a decentralized way and mostly at the firm level. The coordinating capacity and collective representation of employers are relatively weak, and the Confederation of British Industry or the US Business Roundtable do not have the same kind of collective capacities that business organizations, notably in coordinated market economies (Chapter 3), do. Whilst the labour movement has been able to mobilize successfully at times, the union movement in both Britain and the United States has operated in a decentralized fashion, making inter-firm or inter-sectoral coordination or mobilization much more difficult.

Another factor that scholarship on VoC has highlighted is the importance of the electoral system, which was already mentioned in the original VoC volume (Hall and Soskice 2001b). Later work by Iversen and Soskice (2006a) has elaborated on this factor and highlighted how majoritarian electoral systems reinforce LME institutions, notably by making centre-right governments introducing more limited redistribution more likely. They have also shown that the roots of these arrangements can be traced to historical legacies. The early decline of the guilds (in Britain) and the lack of a guild tradition (in the United States) is another historical factor that has been mentioned as a determinant of the trajectory of LME capitalism and its decentralized nature based on market coordination. Such historical legacies were associated with the weakness of specific and particularistic interests at the time of democratization and the early development of capitalism (Cusack, Iversen and Soskice 2007).

Much of the literature perceives the distinctiveness of the British economy as bound up with unique historical legacies, such as Britain's position as the first industrializer (Gerschenkron 1962) or the common law tradition (La Porta et al. 1998; La Porta et al. 2008). Scholars have suggested that these factors have predisposed the British economy to a decentralized financial market-based corporate governance system where the state or large banks play a less important role than in many other economies. The early growth of the financial system that followed the Glorious Revolution and reflected a stronger state commitment to secure property rights is another factor that has been regarded as a deeper historical determinant of key institutions (North and Weingast 1989; Hodgson 2023). The role of empire, and especially the role of the City of London as a source of international finance, meant that the financial sector developed relatively independently from industry in the UK and did not establish as close ties as these sectors did in much of Continental Europe (Ingham 1984). The emphasis on the common law system, which is also used throughout the former British Empire, can also help to explain why LMEs are clustered in the English-speaking world. The legal system is also a key factor highlighted in accounts of contemporary US exceptionalism (Hacker et al. 2021).

Other variants of the historical explanation focus on social factors. Kahl (2005) attributes the distinctiveness of LMEs to the importance of reformed Christianity and the ways in which it has conditioned societal views on poverty and social justice. She argues that this has contributed to a culture of self-reliance that is consistent with residual welfare states. In another attempt to identify deeper social roots, Dobbin's (1994) study of the industrial policy related to railways in the nineteenth century develops a cultural theory that helps explain the distinctiveness of Britain and the United States compared to France. In the British case, the political culture stressed the importance of key elite actors who operate under a small state as an engine of progress, whereas the American political culture puts greater emphasis on Tocquevillean associations, which also reinforced the case for decentralized market coordination of railway construction. The clustering of LMEs within the English-speaking world also strengthens the prima facie argument for the importance of common historical roots, including the British colonial tradition and associated legacies, such as the legal system, as key determinants of LME institutions.

Debating the LME model

The influence of the economies associated with the LME model has spurred extensive debate about the potential convergence of other economies on this model. Given the economic and political influence of the United States in particular, the US economy has often been viewed as a key reference point for other countries, and there has been an expectation that the greater success of the LME model (as predicted by its advocates) would induce other economies to emulate it. To some extent, the changes that have occurred across much of the world since the 1980s, or during the era of neoliberalism, would seem to confirm the widespread appeal of market liberalism among policymakers. However, whilst most economies have embarked on some liberalization (see Chapter 8; Baccaro and Howell 2017), there is very limited evidence of full convergence on the LME model.

There are several reasons for this. First, diffusion processes usually operate in complex ways and may not lead to perfect emulation. It is likely that the transmission may be conditioned by local conditions and pre-existing institutions, thereby leading to new kinds of hybrid institutions (Woywode 2002). Second, if such convergence processes are enforced by external actors, such as credit rating agencies or international organizations, then local actors may resist full implementation and instead opt for 'mock compliance' with such rules (Walter 2008). Third, if institutions have deep roots, then continuity and path dependence may be more likely. In particular, if LME institutions are bound up with social and political preconditions, such as specific legal traditions, then it may not be possible to transpose them to countries with other legal systems and institutional arrangements. More generally, if the core premise of the VoC approach is correct, namely that different institutional forms have distinctive comparative advantages, then there may not be any reason to expect general convergence on the LME model.

It is less clear whether there has actually been convergence on the LME model in practice. Some reforms that could be regarded as consistent with convergence, such as far-reaching liberalization of financial markets and deregulation, have taken place in many parts of the world. On the other hand, there is very limited evidence of wholesale adoption of LME institutions, as, for example, most corporate structures and governance arrangements have not spread to the Global South (Fligstein and Choo 2005).

There are only a few cases that are sometimes mentioned as potential examples of convergence, of which two will be considered here. The first and arguably most important case is Israel, which had a heavily regulated economy with some CME and collectivist features until the 1980s, but adopted radical liberalization in the 1980s (Zilberfarb 2005). Many analysts argue that the growth of the financial sector and the start-up economy in Tel Aviv have acquired features that are comparable to US economy in particular and that Israel can be viewed as a hub of rapid innovation that operates very much like an LME (Davis and Kim 2015: 14; Devore 2015). In the case of Israel, these changes have many idiosyncratic features and reflected very dramatic market reforms. The innovation system is also shaped by close ties between innovation clusters in Israel and Silicon Valley (Soskice 2022).

Another example discussed in the literature is Estonia, which has been classified as an 'emerging LME' (Feldmann 2006). Feldmann (2006) shows that Estonia can be viewed as an emerging LME on key dimensions in light of the predominance of market coordination. This is perhaps most striking in the context of labour markets, where wage setting is highly decentralized. To the extent that collective bargaining does occur, this tends to be at the firm level, and the coverage rate is very low. Whilst the traditional welfare state has been regarded as rather small and residual, even by Central and East European standards (Bohle and Greskovits 2012), there has been greater emphasis on social investment, notably in terms of education and relevant public services, which has contributed to the growth of the ICT sector, digitalization and the knowledge economy in Estonia (Avlijaš 2020a). More generally, given that social policy is distinguished by a stronger emphasis on general skills, it has been more favourable to female employment than some other models in the Central and East European region (Avlijaš 2020b; see also Estévez-Abe 2006), which have put more emphasis on specific skills in conjunction with their FDI-led manufacturing focus (see Chapter 6). The emphasis on fostering general skills aligns well with leading LMEs. In terms of economic structure, the Estonian economy has also seen an expansion of the service sector, including real estate, finance, and especially ICT, which is a particularly important element of successful upgrading (Kalanta 2024a). Whilst corporate governance and financial systems institutions fit the LME model less well, some studies have suggested that the main deviations, notably the limited role of the domestic stock market and the reliance on external sources of finance, could be viewed as functional equivalents of LME institutions in a new market economy that is relatively capital-scarce (Buchen 2007). In a similar vein, Kuokštis (2011) suggests classifying the Baltic economies as 'flexible market economies' or as a distinctive variety of capitalism that bears a strong resemblance to the LME model but achieves flexibility in a slightly different institutional context. The size of the financial sector and relatively high levels of financialization broadly fit the patterns of leading LMEs (Feldmann 2013). Other studies have preferred to classify Estonia simply as a neoliberal (Bohle and Greskovits 2012) or free-market economy (Feldmann and Sally 2002). Estonia differs from some other countries in Central and Eastern Europe, such as Hungary or Slovakia, in that there has not been any comparable boom in manufacturing of the kind that those countries have experienced, not least in car production (see Chapter 6).

There are two important lessons from this discussion. First, even if we accept that these economies can be classified as LMEs, it is obvious that the number of new candidates for inclusion in the LME category is relatively small, and there is some debate surrounding the degree of fit. Second, both the Israeli and Estonian economies are exceptional in several respects. Israel benefited from close ties to US venture capitalists, and some leading investors relocated there. US influence on institutional design, legislation and regulation has also been significant, with leading executives frequently educated at US universities or possessing professional experience from the United States. Estonia is also exceptional in many respects. Even compared to the generally far-reaching and rapid market reforms elsewhere in Central and Eastern Europe after the collapse of communism, Estonia stands out as a particularly radical reformer that introduced unilateral free trade after re-establishing independence in 1991 (Feldmann 2018). Similarly, the monetary policy regime operated much like a currency board in that it tied policymakers' hands and quickly committed Estonia to current and capital account convertibility (Feldmann and Kuokštis 2017). Estonia was also a first mover in the region in terms of introducing the flat tax – at the time, one of very few economies with such a tax system, although the policy later spread to other countries in the region (Appel and Orenstein 2018). The political preconditions for such radical market reforms are very stringent, and it is not clear whether such reforms could be implemented elsewhere (Feldmann 2013).

Given how rare convergence on the LME model has been and that the traditional LMEs have been concentrated in the English-speaking world, namely, Britain, Ireland, the United States, Canada, Australia and New Zealand, it seems reasonable to conclude that the model is less universal in its application than in its appeal to free-market advocates.

Another challenge relates to institutional diversity within the LME group. The preceding discussion has highlighted some key differences between the United Kingdom and the United States. If we consider other economies within the LME category, further contrasts become apparent. Two differences are worth highlighting here. First, unlike Britain and the United States, Canada and Australia did not liberalize their financial sectors to the same extent, which also protected them from some of the worst consequences of the global financial crisis (Konzelmann, Fovargue-Davies and Schnyder 2012). This also relates to the unique characteristics of the British and US economies that are bound up with their positions as (former and current) leading economies in the world. This has increased their importance to the global financial system and led to the growth of financial centres in London and New York. Second, Canada and Australia are also more reliant on natural resources, which has led some observers to classify them as a sub-category of resource-led LMEs (cf. Hall 2018: 6).

The global financial crisis prompted further debate about the prospects and viability of the LME model, and especially the great reliance on the financial sector and on borrowing to maintain consumption in the British and US economies (Chinn and Frieden 2011; Hay 2011; Crouch 2009). Whilst these debates evoke many of the issues raised by earlier generations of scholars concerned about training or productive investments in these economies (Lazonick 2014), the main conclusion from this experience was that liberal capitalism was (perhaps unexpectedly) resilient in these economies (Crouch 2011; Hay and Smith 2013; Schmidt and Thatcher 2013).

Conclusion

This chapter has provided an overview of the LME model, one of the two core VoC models identified by Hall and Soskice (2001a). It has highlighted the importance of market coordination and discussed key institutions underpinning economic activity, notably stock market-oriented financial systems and decentralized labour markets. It has examined to what extent the model can shed light on the United States, the United Kingdom and other economies. Given the importance of the US economy, the LME model tends to be viewed as a canonical market economy and an implicit benchmark for many debates about capitalism. Additionally, there has been considerable debate about the prospects for international convergence on the LME model. However, other strands of the debate have also raised concerns about the potential overreliance on the financial sector and its adverse effects on other sectors and on the potential for economic instability.

Discussion questions

- What are the main features of the LME model? Why has it been such an influential reference point in global debates about capitalism?
- How does the interpretation of the United States and United Kingdom as LMEs differ from labelling them as free-market economies?
- What are the main strengths and weaknesses of the LME model?

- What is the role of the state and of the political system in underpinning LMEs?
- How likely is it that the LME model will spread to other parts of the world?
- Some critics have suggested that the global financial crisis demonstrates that the economic model of leading LMEs, like the United States and the United Kingdom, is not viable. Would you agree with this assessment?

3

Coordinated market economies

Are there any alternatives to free-market liberalism of the kind associated with the LME model that could also generate economic success? This is one of the key questions animating much of the VoC literature. The coordinated market economy (CME) model, commonly associated with many countries in Northern and Western Europe, is the second of the two original VoC models identified by Hall and Soskice (2001b). This model has played a very big role in this debate, and it has provided theoretical underpinnings for one of the core claims of the VoC literature, namely that there is more than one path to economic success.

This chapter introduces the CME model by focusing on its core features, notably the importance of strategic coordination, and by discussing its implications for economic performance as well as its political underpinnings. After introducing the general formulation of the CME model, as outlined by Hall and Soskice (2001b), the chapter discusses the examples of Germany and Sweden to distinguish more carefully between the Continental European and Scandinavian versions of coordinated market economies. It evaluates current controversies about the viability of the model and whether it is more appropriate to view it as two separate models. It also considers the ability of CMEs to generate both growth and equity, as well as pressures for convergence on liberal capitalism.

Key features

The CME model is designed to capture the functioning of what has also been described as a form of non-liberal capitalism, or market economies that do not operate based on the market liberal logic which is commonly associated with LMEs. As in the case of the LME model discussed in Chapter 2 and VoC analysis more generally, the CME model is firm-centred and focuses on the key relationships that firms need to manage as part of their operations.

What distinguishes coordinated market economies is the importance of *strategic coordination* (Hall and Soskice 2001b). This concept captures the centrality of non-market relationships to resolve the coordination problems of firms. In other words, instead of merely relying on markets to secure key inputs and resources for economic activity, firms rely on long-term agreements and negotiations with financial institutions, other firms and with their employees. The coordination that these relations rely on can be described as strategic in the sense that economic actors make decisions strategically by factoring in their understanding of what other key actors are expected to do. Given the complexity of these issues, it is not generally possible to formulate such understandings in formal contracts. In other words, they reflect implicit contracts or informal agreements. Such strategic coordination is of central importance to the dense relationships between firms and their stakeholders, such as creditors, workers or other firms (Soskice 1999).

The prevalence of strategic coordination has some important implications for the nature of the relationship between the firm and key stakeholders. First, the relationship between firms on the one hand and creditors, workers and other firms on the other tends to be relatively long-term. Since these stakeholders are committed to the firm, the main mechanism used in these long-term relationships to raise concerns is based on what Albert O. Hirschman (1970) called *voice*. In other words, stakeholders tend to raise (or voice) any concerns they have with the firm to change the situation rather than exit or disinvest, as shareholders in LMEs typically do.

Second, key stakeholders who engage in strategic coordination are usually very well informed. Information is essential for stakeholders to monitor the firm and to raise any concerns, and much of this information is tacit and reflects the familiarity that results from long-run involvement and frequent interactions. For example, the information available to creditors is based on a deep understanding of the firm that goes beyond the metrics that stock market analysts in LMEs necessarily tend to focus on given their large portfolios. It is not possible to acquire such deep familiarity and tacit knowledge about all the firms that are part of a large and diversified investment portfolio.

Third, stakeholders are also well organized. In particular, the membership rates of employers' associations and trade unions tend to be higher than in LMEs. Such associations play a more important role in policymaking and in bargaining about economic outcomes. Therefore these kinds of market economies have also been classified as 'organized market economies' (Soskice 1999), and others have described the role of such actors as a distinctive form of 'associational coordination' (Streeck and Schmitter 1985). Such organizations play an important role in facilitating coordination and in monitoring the implementation of agreements. Employers' associations, in particular, play an important role not only in representing business interests vis-à-vis the government or society at large but also as a key actor facilitating strategic coordination among firms, as inter-firm organization is important for underpinning the provision of skills and the training system in CMEs. Trade unions tend to play a similar role. In other words, their role is not only political in the sense that they aggregate workers' interests and amplify their influence but they also have the 'strategic capacity' to play an important role in coordination, for example, in the context of wage setting, social policy and various other outcomes that affect the performance of the firm in the short and medium term (Iversen 1999).

Given the importance of institutional complementarities or the interdependence of different institutions, strategic coordination prevails across a range of institutional fields. For example, from a VoC perspective it is no coincidence that both labour relations and finance are determined by strategic coordination (Höpner 2005). If some of the key relations were governed by a different logic, such as a more short-termist LME logic, then it is likely that the long-term relations in other institutional spheres would not work well or even break down altogether (Culpepper 2005). Strategic coordination also occurs among firms within a given sector, for example, in relation to standard setting and training to certify industrial skill qualifications (Soskice 1999). This includes relations to suppliers as ensuring a steady supply of key inputs whilst also facilitating any necessary changes to product specification is essential, but also relations to other firms in a given industry.

This also implies that processes of change and adjustment in the face of crises tend to be based on negotiations and bargaining (Feldmann 2017). Many critics have described this as a weakness of the CME model, as it may make it harder to respond very quickly to shocks or unforeseen developments. Others have suggested that it should be regarded as a strength, as the CME model tends to foster a higher degree of consensus among managers, employees and other stakeholders. Hancké, Van Overbeke and Voss (2022) have shown how Germany's response to Covid-19 was strengthened by CME institutions that helped facilitate a negotiated response and preserve skills, jobs and medium-size manufacturing service firms that are central to the German economy more effectively than in the UK. Similarly, the German 'mini-jobs' also helped keep unemployment down in the aftermath of the global financial crisis of 2007–8. This ensures that any response enjoys widespread support and makes it more likely that any reforms are sustainable.

Financial systems and corporate governance

Instead of the shareholder model of corporate governance that predominates in LMEs (see Chapter 2), traditional CMEs come closer to a stakeholder model of corporate governance. This means that companies are not merely focused on maximizing the share price but rather on satisfying the interests of a wider range of stakeholders, including shareholders, and also employees, suppliers, customers and the local community. CMEs are characterized by more limited reliance on stock markets or 'exit' as a mechanism of corporate governance (Hirschman 1970). Key stakeholders regard voice as the best governance mechanism as they perceive their long-term interests as bound up with the firm. In other words, stakeholders use their influence to control and nudge the firm to introduce certain kinds of changes, if necessary. This kind of influence by creditors is often described as 'patient capital' given that it is oriented towards the long-term success of the firm (Vitols 2001).

Institutions of patient capital relate first and foremost to the financial system. Whilst many investments are funded by retained earnings, companies may also rely on external sources of financing. In this regard CMEs are generally categorized as bank, rather than stock market-based. Traditional CME firms have long-term relationships with banks that provide patient capital. This means that external financing does not dry up in downturns as creditors are patient and base their assessments of the firm not on short-run indicators, such as movements of the share price, but on a holistic assessment of the firm's medium- and long-run prospects. As noted, this places great demands on the availability of information, which also reflects the key stakeholders' close ties to the firm and access to inside information about it.

In addition, there are other features of the corporate governance system that enhance stakeholder influence on the firm and constrain CEO decision-making. CMEs tend to have a dual board system, that is, both a management board and a supervisory board. The management board is responsible for decisions related to business operations, whereas the supervisory board's role is to oversee the management board and consider some strategic decisions (Tricker 2019). The supervisory board ensures that wider stakeholder interests are considered and predisposes firms to consensual decision-making, as employee representatives, key shareholders and sometimes bank representatives are also members of the supervisory board.

Another common feature of corporate governance in CMEs is cross-shareholdings, or a situation where different firms (and sometimes firms and banks) hold each other's shares. This creates interdependence between firms and facilitates information sharing and inter-firm coordination, for example, with respect to standard setting and skill provision. This complements the important role of employers' associations in this regard, which often play a central role in industry-wide training regimes and help ensure that there are clear rules in place preventing free riding or poaching.

Labour market institutions and skills

Labour market institutions in CMEs differ considerably from the LME model. As noted earlier, associations representing workers and employers, such as trade unions and business associations, tend to play a significant role and engage in collective bargaining or regular negotiations about a variety of issues, including pay, work conditions, social provisions and sometimes more general issues related to the economy.

To the extent that such negotiations take place in LMEs, they tend to occur at the level of the firm or workplace. By contrast, in CMEs bargaining at other levels plays an important role. This could include sectoral bargaining – establishing pay levels and increases for workers across firms within a given sector – or even national bargaining where peak associations representing all unions and employers within a given economy negotiate about wage setting for the economy as a whole. National bargaining has been common in countries like Sweden, Finland, Belgium and Austria. There are also various intermediate forms of coordination. An important example of this is pattern bargaining, which helps coordinate wage setting across sectors, as in the German model (Thelen 2001). In such cases there is a lead sector, typically an important export industry, which first reaches a pay agreement that is accepted by employers and workers within that sector and that also helps maintain the competitiveness of its exports on international markets. This agreement then serves as a reference point for other sectors that then seek to mirror or follow the pattern established by the lead sector, possibly with some adjustments to reflect their specific circumstances. The main advantage of pattern bargaining is that it helps coordinate wage setting across the economy in a way that helps maintain competitiveness, counteracts inflationary pressures, and enjoys the support of both employers and unions. Successful pattern bargaining presumes that there is a clear consensus on the significance of the lead sector in the economy.

Centralized wage bargaining has a number of important consequences. Firstly, Calmfors and Driffill (1988) found a hump-shaped relationship between the degree of centralization of wage bargaining and unemployment. In other words, both decentralized and highly centralized wage setting are conducive to good performance, whereas intermediate levels of wage setting generate higher unemployment and inflation. The reason for this is that there is a coordination problem at intermediate levels of wage setting. Unions are strong enough to bargain for significant wage increases for their own sector, but not sufficiently encompassing (or representative of the economy as a whole) to consider the effects of the wage agreement on inflation in general (see also Lange and Garrett 1985). Such practices ensure that wage setting can maintain the competitiveness of firms, thereby contributing to employment and growth. However, as the example of pattern bargaining demonstrates, the most important factor is not the formal degree of centralization, but rather the degree of effective coordination across sectors.

Secondly, centralized wage setting is also associated with more egalitarian wage distributions and lower inequality. There is extensive evidence to show that centralized wage bargaining and higher unionization rates tend to lead to more solidaristic wage setting, which leads to smaller wage differentials within and across firms (Rueda and Pontusson 2000). For advocates of the CME model and of centralized collective bargaining and wage setting more generally, this is an important argument for such practices as it implies that such arrangements can help reduce both inflation and inequality, and thereby facilitate the simultaneous pursuit of efficiency and equity.

More generally, strategic coordination of industrial relations and in labour markets is also bound up with the nature of the welfare state and skill system in these economies. CMEs share a number of key features. First, their welfare states are more generous and social spending is higher than in LMEs. Second, their labour markets and welfare states are more conducive to promoting the acquisition of specific skills than LMEs are (Estevez-Abe et al. 2001; Iversen 2005). The reasons for this are twofold. First, given the specialization in sectors based on incremental innovation, such as sophisticated engineering, there is a greater demand for specific skills. In light of the strategic coordination in the financial sphere and the availability of patient capital from associated banks, firms are willing to invest in their labour forces and in developing specific skills, both as part of structured apprenticeships and continuous on-the-job training. Second, especially in Continental European CMEs, inter-firm cooperation on training also facilitates skill provision and certification. CMEs also have more generous welfare states, esp. in the case of the Nordic CMEs and social democratic welfare regimes. A more generous welfare state makes investments in specific skills less risky, as the welfare state provides a safety net in case of job losses and unemployment (Iversen 2005).

However, these commonalities mask considerable differences between the main Continental European CME and the Nordic CMEs in terms of their welfare and skill systems, which also have important consequences for inequality and other labour market outcomes. Following Esping-Andersen (1990), these two groups of countries can be classified as having different welfare regimes. The Nordic countries have social democratic welfare regimes that are based on the principle of universalism and are highly egalitarian. The Continental CMEs have conservative welfare states that are also very generous, but they are based on principles of social insurance, which means that they tend to preserve status differentials. Many welfare state entitlements reflect prior contributions, which means that they do not have the same kinds of egalitarian effects as the policies adopted in social democratic welfare regimes.

These differences are also reflected in the education and skill systems. The social democratic welfare states have comprehensive systems of education, and vocational education has been integrated into the secondary school system in what has been called an integrationist skill regime (Busemeyer 2009). This means that these educational systems transmit both general and vocational skills, and there is typically a significant general skills component as part of the technical and vocational education in these countries. As a result educational inequalities in terms of attainment in maths and literacy are relatively small. This general skills component is also likely to have facilitated the growth of service employment in the Nordic countries.

By contrast, conservative welfare states have differentiated skill regimes (Busemeyer 2009). In many of these countries a tracking system separates children before the age of twelve into more and less academic tracks (in the German case, the more academic *Gymnasium* on the one hand, or the less academic *Realschule* or *Hauptschule* on the other). Such tracking is widely perceived to reproduce inequalities, as children of highly educated parents tend to attend the more academically oriented schools. However, the most distinctive feature is the elaborate vocational skill and apprenticeship system in Continental CMEs. This is a career path that has traditionally provided access to reasonably well-paid jobs. As these jobs require specific skills, they are relatively well remunerated, especially compared to those that workers without academic qualifications have in leading LMEs, like the United States. This means that the vocational system in Continental CMEs has a complex impact on inequality. On the one hand, tracking in secondary schools contributes to early segmentation, but vocational training has traditionally provided a career path with good and relatively well-paid jobs for the less academically oriented segments of the labour force and has been a key determinant of relatively low levels of inequality in CMEs.

Performance

The CME model is the second core VoC model that was analysed in the seminal *Varieties of Capitalism* volume (Hall and Soskice 2001a). The best-known CMEs include Continental European countries like Germany, Austria, the Netherlands and Belgium as well as Nordic economies, like Sweden, Denmark, Norway and Finland. These are widely perceived as exceptionally successful economies, especially during the twentieth century, when most of them grew very fast and achieved very high levels of GDP per capita (Pontusson 2005).

Compared to the key LMEs, these economies have also generally been associated with lower income inequality. This has prompted much debate about whether this experience demonstrates that CMEs have found a way of promoting both efficiency and equity at the same time. It should be noted that the traditional CME institutions are not gender-neutral in their effects. As demonstrated by Estévez-Abe (2006), education systems that privilege specific skills have gendered effects, given that employers may worry about career interruptions and therefore prefer to train men. Women may also prefer not to invest in specific skills for similar reasons, given that such investments entail greater risks and lower returns in the context of career breaks. In that sense the specific skill system may also have reinforced the male breadwinner model in Germany and other kinds of gender inequality, such as vertical segregation, which makes it harder for women to achieve higher-level managerial positions. The work by Mandel and Shalev (2009) has shown that the gendered effects of different VoC are also conditioned by class – LMEs may be most favourable to women on high incomes, who are able to purchase childcare on the market and thereby combine work and family, whereas women on lower incomes with families find it easier to enter the labour market in the Nordic CMEs, given the availability of publicly subsidized childcare and a relatively large number of public sector jobs. The fact that many of them work in the public sector contributes to relatively high horizontal segmentation of the labour market where women are disproportionately represented in some professions (Estévez-Abe 2006). Given that the specific skills system typically privileges insiders, it may also make it harder for other types of new entrants, such as many immigrants, to enter attractive professions that rely on such skills, though existing research on this topic shows that such effects vary greatly across different professions and categories of migrants (Guzi et al. 2022).

The VoC literature also argues that CMEs are associated with distinctive comparative institutional advantages – in other words, the institutional environment of CMEs is conducive to economic specialization and success in certain sectors. These sectors include industries relying on incremental innovation and a skilled workforce with extensive specific skills. Key examples include advanced manufacturing, such as car production, that rely on high-level engineering skills that facilitate incremental innovation, as in the development of new and improved models of cars and other engineering products (Hall and Soskice 2001a).

A key feature of the success of CMEs is that they tend to thrive in a globalized economy, in that they are among the most successful exporters in the world. Many sceptics expected these economies to succumb to convergence pressures in an era of globalization, implying that they might have to adopt LME institutions instead. Whilst the jury may still be out on the future prospects of CME, as discussed in more detail below, it seems clear that globalization has contributed to their success for a long time. Given that exports are integral to their success, access to foreign markets is very important and facilitates the kind of specialization that their export performance is based on. Such specialization would be impossible in the context of a closed economy.

The rise of the post-industrial service economy might be a greater challenge to CMEs (see also Chapter 8). The core logic of VoC analysis, especially in relation to CMEs, relates primarily to manufacturing. This includes the reliance on many kinds of specific skills (especially of a more technical kind) and on many of the political underpinnings. For example, unionization rates tend to be considerably lower in the private service sector. As discussed in more detail later in the book, different CMEs have adopted different strategies in response to these changes (see Chapter 8). Whilst many CMEs, notably Germany, have retained their comparative advantage in traditional advanced manufacturing industries, some CMEs have also been successful at generating new employment in services industries. However, the success achieved by CMEs, like the Netherlands, Denmark and Sweden, has prompted great debate on the future of CMEs and the adjustment processes that have contributed to these outcomes (Thelen 2019b, see also Chapter 10).

Germany as a CME

The VoC literature has traditionally viewed Germany as the canonical CME (Hall and Soskice 2001a, 21–27). Various other studies have highlighted Germany, alongside Japan, as the main alternative to free-market liberalism (Dore 2000; Streeck and Yamamura 2001). This section begins by identifying the core features of the German political economy that inspired much of the debate about its distinctiveness, before briefly discussing some of the pressures for change and the extent to which the German economy can still be viewed as a traditional CME (Streeck 2009).

Corporate governance and finance have been based on patient capital, not least the centrality of banks, a core feature of the industrialization experience in the nineteenth century. Yet the German economy has also been characterized by a dual structure, with a large share of relatively small businesses dependent on close ties with regional banks for financing, alongside large firms with close ties to Germany's universal banks (Herrigel 2000). The dual structure was also underpinned by the development of German corporate law in the late nineteenth century which provided a legal foundation for these corporate forms (Fannion 2016). In both cases the relationship between firms and banks was close, and stock markets have played a much more limited role than in LMEs, especially given that a large proportion of German companies have been privately held and not listed. The so-called 'Hausbanken' (house banks) provided patient capital to firms which insulated them from a variety of short-term pressures, with hostile takeovers being very rare. Banks played a central role in the expansion of German firms and in the process of industrialization (Gerschenkron 1962; Schmitz 1995).

Labour markets are underpinned by negotiations and collective bargaining at the sectoral level and relatively high coverage rates of collective agreements. Industrial relations have traditionally been less centralized than in Sweden, for example, given that bargaining at the national level has not been a component of the German model. Instead coordination is based on pattern bargaining, where the metal-working industry serves as a model to the rest of the economy. This means that the agreements that dominant export industries reach with a view to maintaining competitiveness on global markets then also serve as a reference point for the entire economy. Germany's welfare state has long been relatively generous and associated with high levels of social spending. Germany is usually classified as a conservative welfare state that is primarily based on a social insurance logic and therefore largely maintains social differentiation and stratification unlike the more redistributive and solidaristic social democratic models (Esping-Andersen 1990). Policy reforms since the 1990s have contributed to the liberalization of family, unemployment and pension policies and arguably moved Germany closer to a liberal welfare state that increasingly resembles the British model (Seeleib-Kaiser 2016).

The German economy has also been exceptionally successful over long periods of time. During the Cold War era the West German economy was praised for combining high growth with success in export markets, high wages and low inequality (Streeck 1997b). Key German manufacturers, including producers of cars (such as Volkswagen, BMW and Mercedes-Benz) or chemical (BASF) and electrical engineering firms (Siemens), have developed worldwide reputations thanks to their high-quality manufacturing and continuous incremental innovation. A key controversy surrounding the German economy relates to the underpinnings of the traditional model of capitalism. Whilst most observers agree that the economic success and the positive complementarities between these outcomes are underpinned by business interests in maintaining key elements of the model (Thelen 2001, Wood 2001), others have pointed out that it also relies on a more coercive institutional logic. Streeck (2011) regards these institutions as more 'Durkheimian' or based on a certain degree of coercive enforcement, as they make firms do things they would not have independently chosen to do. Such pressures had traditionally contributed to 'beneficial constraints' that in turn promoted upgrading and the emphasis on production strategies based on quality and innovation rather than cost-cutting (Streeck 1997a).

For some time the costs and pressures related to German unification led many observers to question the viability of the German model, but many of these concerns have subsided (Carlin and Soskice 2008, Fratzscher 2018). Whilst financialization has been more limited than in many other countries, it has led to some decline in patient capital (see Chapter 9). Many large German banks, notably Deutsche Bank, have become more interested in investment banking activities and withdrawn from providing patient capital. Stock markets have become more significant over time. Corporate governance has also been reshaped by other changes, such as reforms of voting rights, which have limited the influence of banks by reducing their ability to use proxy votes to shape corporate governance. Bank ownership of shares has fallen, and foreign ownership has increased over time, reaching 56 per cent of shares by 2011, whereas domestic ownership had amounted to two thirds of shares as late as 2000 (Schröter 2018: 208). Many large companies have devoted greater attention to the maximization of shareholder value.

There has been some fragmentation of industrial relations and decentralization of wage bargaining, with the company level becoming increasingly important. The coverage of collective bargaining has also fallen as a result of sectoral shifts – whilst manufacturing still plays a more important role in Germany than in many other OECD countries, the relative importance and employment share of the service sector has also grown here (Jackson and Sorge 2012). There has been considerable liberalization of industrial relations in Germany since the 1990s, but there are still mechanisms for coordination between export-oriented firms and core workers and for ensuring that wage setting is consistent with the competitiveness of key sectors (Hassel 2014). Labour market coordination is also underpinned by codetermination in works councils. These arrangements also facilitate training and the provision of sector-specific skills. Although codetermination has also been affected by some liberalization, there have been some countervailing trends as works councils and trade unions have developed novel collaborative strategies to enhance the influence of labour (Haipeter 2021). Another key trend in labour markets relates to dualization, where new inequalities between core and casual workers have emerged and grown (Hassel 2014). Changes in employment law have increased the importance of casual or agency work, which has become more significant even within manufacturing.

There has also been some weakening of the traditional training system, not least since employer interest has fallen, especially during economic downturns (Jackson and Sorge 2012: 1151). Vocational programmes also contain a significant general skills component, which is why almost half of those who have acquired vocational qualifications work in different occupations (Busemeyer 2009). In another set of developments, there have been attempts to scale back welfare state commitments, in large part as a result of German unification, which put great strains on public spending. Many of these changes are bound up with dualization, which has led to the growth of precarious or casual agency work associated with less generous welfare provisions, but without greatly impinging on core workers' entitlements (Palier and Thelen 2010).

Yet the debate often has the feel of the old question as to whether the glass is half-empty or half-full, and neither the most optimistic nor the most pessimistic assessments may be warranted (Fratzscher 2018). As this brief overview demonstrates, there has obviously been significant change, but it is less clear whether this has undermined the German model (Streeck 2009) or actually helped consolidate it, by injecting greater flexibility at the margins (Palier and Thelen 2010, Thelen 2014). More generally, these changes do not necessarily mean that Germany is less distinctive, as change does not equate to convergence on the LME model.

Sweden as a CME

The Swedish case has long attracted great attention, partly given the exceptional political dominance of the Social Democratic Party, which was in government for over seventy years from 1932 until 2006 (with only a two interludes of centre-right governments from 1976–82 and 1991–4), The Swedish model was seen as the leading symbol of a political and economic alternative to free-market liberalism. Whilst Sweden is generally perceived as a good example of a CME, the Swedish political economy has also been distinctive in many ways, and many scholars have distinguished between Continental CMEs, like Germany, and Nordic CMEs, of which Sweden is a key example. Like Germany, Sweden also experienced some institutional change beginning in the 1990s, and this section considers the fit of the Swedish model in the twentieth century with the CME model and the impact of subsequent changes as well.

First, in terms of the financial system and corporate governance, the Swedish model could traditionally be described as bank-based and as a good example of CME institutions. Yet Sweden has always exhibited some distinctive features, most notably the prominence of a small number of diversified business groups (see also Chapter 5 on hierarchical market economies). These groups have dominated the Swedish economy and included key banks as well. For most of the twentieth century the Swedish economy was dominated by two large cross-sectoral business groups – Investor (controlled by the Wallenberg family) and Industrivärden (centred on the Swedish bank Handelsbanken). During that period there were considerable limitations on foreign ownership of firms and real estate (Collin 1998; Henrekson and Jakobsson 2003).

Labour markets have corresponded very well to the CME model. Unionization remains very high – the membership rate was 67.7 per cent in 2013, which represents a decline compared to the membership rates in the 1990s, when they were over 80 per cent. Employer organizations are also strong with high membership rates among firms which were at 82 per cent in 2012. Similarly, the coverage rate of collective agreements has been very high as well (it was 89 per cent in 2013, down from 94 per cent in 2005), and the high concentration of business ownership also facilitated coordination between employers, workers and the government. For many years wage bargaining was highly centralized at the national level, and wage setting was effectively based on the Rehn-Meidner model, which was designed to promote both egalitarian outcomes and efficiency. Egalitarian wage setting – where pay depended on the characteristics of the work, and not on the profitability of the firm – effectively acted as a subsidy to the most efficient producers and exerted more pressure on less competitive ones (Erixon 2018). Since the 1980s the sectoral level has been most important, which effectively means that the Swedish model has become more similar to Germany in this regard (Iversen 1996, Ibsen 2016). Whilst the new model is less egalitarian than the traditional one, it still contributes to coordinated wage bargaining (Pontusson 2011).

A key foundation of Swedish labour markets and the Swedish economy more generally relates to the large public sector and a generous welfare state of a universalistic kind (Esping-Andersen 1990). The public sector has also contributed to high rates of female labour force participation, as subsidized public childcare has made it easier for women to enter the labour market, with many of them working in the public sector. By contrast, apprenticeships have played a smaller role in the Swedish economy than in Germany, and most of the vocational education that was integrated into the secondary school system has placed an emphasis on general skills (Pontusson 2011).

In the 1990s many observers spoke of the end of the Swedish model, often suggesting that the state was overstretched and that welfare provisions would have to be rolled back (Lundberg 1985). There was significant liberalization and deregulation in the late 1980s and 1990s. Yet in the early twenty-first century, Sweden was arguably 'once again a model' (Pontusson 2011). The economy has become much more international as a result of increases in foreign direct investment, which has led to a diversification of investment finance and greater influence for institutional investors. Whilst the groups have given up some of their golden shares (the equivalent of 1,000 ordinary shares), largely in response to pressure from international investors (Reiter 2003), they still play a central role in the Swedish economy and in many leading companies (Henrekson and Jakobsson 2012; Larsson and Petersson 2018). Economic performance was strong in the early twenty-first century, and many perceived a commitment to egalitarianism coupled with an emphasis on knowledge-based development and stimulation of high-tech sectors by high R&D spending as essential to this model. Sweden has been more successful at avoiding high unemployment and dualization tendencies than most of Continental Europe (Pontusson 2011).

However, others are more sceptical, highlighting what they see as the increasing neoliberalization of the Swedish economy, which is also associated with higher levels of inequality and the growth of financial markets (Belfrage and Kallifatides 2018). Swedish stock market capitalization is one of the highest among CMEs, and private shareholdings began growing very fast in the 1990s (Henrekson and Jakobsson 2012). Whilst this has led to some pressure to increase yields, the role of dominant block holders is still great (Henrekson and Jakobsson 2012). In the Swedish case financialization has been shaped by pension reform, which has had a profound effect on the Swedish welfare state and also increased the role of institutional investors in the economy (Belfrage and Ryner 2009). Financialization is also closely bound up with developments in housing markets, and critics worry about the sustainability of financialization in this area (Belfrage and Kallifatides 2018). Others see Sweden as an example of a balanced growth model that ensures export success without repressing domestic consumption (Baccaro and Pontusson 2016; see Chapter 10). Yet some other careful studies of the Swedish economic model find that whilst the role of financial markets has grown, they do not shape the economy to such a significant degree (Erixon and Pontusson 2022). Marketization has also permeated the public sector, as education and care services have increasingly been outsourced to private providers.

Whilst this has generally been done in a relatively egalitarian way (Gingrich 2011), there are some concerns about distributional effects and excessive profits – and also about the quality of care and its availability – with media reports mentioning that some Swedish cancer patients were receiving radiation treatments and some mothers were sent to give birth in Finland (Koskinen 2016, SVT Nyheter 2018). An important development is the growth of the market in domestic services, which has also led to an increase in the size of the low-wage labour market, which may lock in women and immigrants in low-paid jobs in a way that counteracts the traditional egalitarian values of Swedish society (Schnyder 2012).

The politics of CMEs

There has been extensive debate about the politics of CMEs, with controversies surrounding both the origins and persistence of the CME model. As Thelen's (2004) seminal study has demonstrated, the reasons for the persistence of certain institutions are not necessarily the same as the factors that initially led to their emergence, and she has shown how many German institutions have been reinvented and modified as circumstances have changed. This also implies that it is futile to look for a grand design of the CME model. The development of CME institutions is more likely to be a gradual process, involving some unintended consequences, but also layering and drift, as new institutions are added to old ones and existing institutions are redefined, displaced or marginalized. Whilst the political origins and persistence of institutions may be related in some respects, this section will consider them separately.

The debate about origins has stressed several explanations, and three of the most influential ones will be discussed here.

First, perhaps the most influential account of origins relates to the balance of class power or simply power resource theory (PRT). This framework analyses the contestation surrounding economic institutions as a form of class conflict (Korpi 1983; Esping-Andersen 1985). Business and capitalists generally favour freer markets, which may contribute to economic growth, but also increase the vulnerability that workers face. In Esping-Andersen's (1990) phrasing, the expansion of markets leads to the commodification of workers. However, if the working class is strong and well organized, it is capable of wielding class power and of extracting concessions from business. In the cases where labour has the greatest power resources, as in the social democratic countries of Northern Europe, such concessions can amount to a high degree of decommodification. However, PRT could be used to develop a similar argument about Germany. In the German case the growing strength of the working class prompted Bismarck's government to engage in anticipatory reforms, notably to expand social policy provisions, as a way of reducing the risk of socialist mobilization and even a workers' revolution. The key achievements of this mobilization are a generous, comprehensive and universalist welfare state and centralized wage bargaining, where workers' interests are represented by strong and encompassing trade unions. As union membership has fallen everywhere, even in countries like Sweden where it still remains high by comparative standards, further decline might potentially raise doubts about the viability of the CME model.

Second, an alternative approach to capitalist diversity is employer-centric and sees business as a key determinant of capitalist institutions. One of the most influential accounts from this perspective is associated with Peter Swenson (1991), who shows that Swedish export industries lobbied for centralization of wage bargaining as a way of containing wage and cost increases in the non-tradable construction industry. A similar argument can be made about other features of the CME model, such as the welfare state and skill system. Employer-centred accounts imply that business may favour such institutions and policies and not resist them, if they reinforce firm strategies and help secure investments in specific skills. Whilst the employer-centric approach remains controversial (Korpi 2006), it can account for the fact that CMEs have been economically successful. If CME institutions constitute a concession extracted from very hostile business actors, then one might expect profits to fall and businesses to reduce investment activity. By contrast, if business was an active contributor to establishing these arrangements, then these institutions may serve them well and help account for the comparative institutional advantage and economic success of these economies. Whilst some of the earlier studies indicated that businesses in CMEs were strongly committed the countries' economic institutions, more recent evidence paints a more complex picture implying that business support is more conditional and shaped by contextual factors (Paster 2013). Various studies have shown that German businesses increasingly favour liberalization (Streeck 2009, Kinderman 2005, 2016), which does not bode well for the prospects of maintaining the CME model in its traditional form given that it relies on the support or at least acceptance of business.

Third, and related to the previous two approaches, some studies have highlighted the importance of electoral systems to capitalist diversity. This is related to the (almost perfect) fit between electoral systems and varieties of capitalism. CMEs tend to have proportional representation (PR) electoral systems, whereas LMEs have majoritarian (first past the post) electoral systems. However, what is less clear is why exactly this correlation exists and whether there is a causal connection between these two sets of institutions. There are several possible explanations. Two connections stand out. PR systems tend to be conducive to consensual decision-making and coalition governments, as it is exceedingly rare for any one party to gain a majority. This means that there is often a greater consensus on key policies that persists even if there is a change of government, as it also reflects greater input by interest groups. Another connection relates to Iversen and Soskice's (2006a) analysis of the effects of electoral systems. In particular, they show that PR is associated with a greater likelihood of centre-left governments, which in turn are more likely to support higher levels of redistribution. Higher levels of redistribution also help protect investments in specific skills. Nevertheless, whilst this provides a good account of the persistence of distinct varieties of capitalism, it is less clear how the differences emerged in the first place, and basically this explanation comes in two guises. On the one hand, it could be understood as reflecting a PRT logic. As most OECD countries had majoritarian electoral systems in the early twentieth century, the ones that moved to PR did so as a result of pressure by the rising working class. In particular, a more divided centre-right feared losing to a strong and unified political left. On the other hand, employer-centred explanations see business as a key actor in this process. In the countries that introduced PR the legacies of guilds and crafts implied that there was a greater reliance on specific skills, and businesses saw PR as a way of protecting them, given that such an electoral system would make it easier for specific and regionally-based interests to gain representation than in a majoritarian system (Cusack et al. 2007). In a similar vein it could be argued that banks played a more central role in mobilizing investments and directing economic change, given that key CMEs, such as Germany and Sweden, were late developers compared to Britain as the first industrializer. In Germany the role of banks – either regional or universal banks – was paramount in providing patient capital in the nineteenth century, given the limits of private savings (Gerschenkron 1962). The imperatives of industrialization then contributed to the emergence of an organizational form that persisted with some adaptation over the twentieth century, as a result of path dependencies associated with prevailing production strategies and corporate forms. The surrounding controversies are bound up with different interpretations of the historical record and of who the main protagonists initiating these reforms were (Korpi 2006).

Finally, another explanation sees the CME institutions as based on a set of social constraints – or what Streeck (1997a) has referred to as 'beneficial constraints' that shape business activity. For Streeck the roots of these constraints are socio-political, and they were initially imposed largely for non-economic reasons. This is why he believes that they will continue to unravel as businesses seek to expand the reach of a narrower market-based business logic and roll back the constraints on their autonomy. Unless these institutions can be enforced by means of social and political means, which is increasingly difficult, the process of liberalization can be expected to continue and lead to the end of the traditional German model of capitalism, and by extension other forms of non-liberal capitalism, including other CMEs. This explanation makes a very strong prediction about further liberalization, though this framework still leaves open the theoretical possibility, also presaged by Polanyi (1944), of a counter-movement or the growth of social forces that seek protection against free markets. Such pressure could strengthen social forces that might seek to rein in markets or constrain economic actors.

Debating the CME model

The CME model remains very important to debates about capitalist diversity, but there are a number of controversial questions about its nature. A key question relates to the scope and applicability of this model. For example, some scholars have classified Japan as a CME, but this book follows other scholars in defining it as a networked market economy (NME – see Chapter 4). Whilst the NME model is similar in some respects to the CME, there are also considerable differences, which justify treating it as a separate model.

Another important controversy relates to the differences between the Nordic and Continental European CMEs; given that there are substantial differences between them, one might ask whether they ought to be classified as separate varieties of capitalism, just like Esping-Andersen's (1990) canonical model of welfare regimes distinguishes between Conservative welfare regimes in Continental Europe and social democratic welfare state regimes in the Nordic countries.

As in the case of the LMEs discussed in Chapter 2, the geographical clustering of CMEs in Western Europe, either in the Nordic countries or on the continent raises the question of whether CMEs can be found elsewhere. We are leaving aside the debate about Japan and some other East Asian countries, which are sometimes viewed as CMEs, but which this book refers to as networked market economies (NMEs) – these cases will be discussed in Chapter 4.

A series of studies have examined the case of Slovenia, a former Yugoslav republic, which established a market economy after the collapse of socialism in the 1990s. There is widespread agreement in the literature that Slovenia did develop into a CME (or at least that it was converging on many key features of a CME, notably in terms of industrial relations) (Feldmann 2006, Crowley and Stanojević 2011; see also Buchen 2007). However, it is also clear that Slovenia is exceptional among the former socialist economies in Central and Eastern Europe in that it is the only one that developed these kinds of institutions. There are a number of reasons for Slovenian exceptionalism related to relatively favourable economic legacies, including relatively high integration with world markets compared to the rest of Yugoslavia and the communist bloc as a whole, historical traditions from the Austro-Hungarian Empire that may have predisposed Slovenia to embrace its corporatist history. Feldmann (2014) argues that many of these contextual factors facilitated this outcome, but that the main factor contributing to the establishment of these institutions is related to the network-preserving negotiated transition that organized labour and senior business leaders helped negotiate. This process helped maintain insider influence in the economy and facilitate a gradual transformation that preserved many pre-existing companies and networks. Whilst this model was widely perceived as very successful and one of the reasons for Slovenia's successful economic performance, it has increasingly come under pressure as the coalition underpinning it has been weakened and a competing flexibility coalition has grown in strength (Feldmann 2017; Stanojevic 2014).

Finally, there is considerable debate about the future viability of the CME model. In particular, many observers have asked whether CMEs should be expected to converge on the LME model, especially given the traditional focus of CMEs on manufacturing. The emphasis on specific skills is complementary to high-quality manufacturing. Some studies have identified a common trend towards greater liberalization affecting most economies (Baccaro and Howell 2017). Whilst not disputing the trend to liberalization, other studies have argued that the liberalization processes vary greatly across countries and that CMEs tend to remain distinctive despite these changes (Thelen 2014). This would imply that liberalization does not necessarily lead to convergence.

However, some of the most striking changes in CMEs are arguably related to dualization, which has affected Continental CMEs much more than Nordic CMEs (Emmenegger et al. 2012; Palier and Thelen 2010). Especially in some of the Continental European economies, dualization has effectively led to increasingly segmented labour markets, with different employment regulations and welfare provisions for core and temporary workers and a growing divide between these categories of workers. Whilst generous welfare provisions associated with the CME model still remain in place for core workers, the growing number of non-standard (temporary or precarious) workers are not covered by these provisions. The impact of these changes is very controversial. Some suggest that such dualization should be welcomed because it injects some additional flexibility into CMEs and thereby helps maintain the CME model, whereas others argue that dualization weakens it by undermining conceptions of solidarity in labour markets. If the CME model can no longer deliver growth with equity for more than a narrow and privileged sub-set of labour force, the case for the model would seem to be considerably weaker, especially in the case of CMEs that struggle to generate growth in advanced service sectors (see also Chapter 10).

More recently, the Nordic economies have widely been regarded as more successful in transitioning to a service-based economy and in promoting growth in knowledge-intensive sectors (see also Chapter 10 and Pontusson 2011, Baccaro and Pontusson 2016). However, the lessons from the Nordic experience and their implications for the CME model are contested. For many observers, the success of Nordic economies represents a more fundamental reorganization of their CME institutions. As a result of such changes their distinctiveness compared to Continental CMEs has become more pronounced in the era of the knowledge-based service economy. For Ornston (2013) a new model of 'creative corporatism' has replaced the traditional form of 'conservative corporatism' that had previously facilitated incremental innovation in long-standing industries. The new arrangements still involve close cooperation between social partners and the state, but there are also novel elements that are conducive to innovation and the development of high-tech industries, notably related to information and communication technologies (ICT). Innovation is also central to Kristensen and Lilja's (2011) analysis. Whilst their account places great emphasis on differences between the Nordic economies, they also highlight that these economies share a commitment to an experimental process that is underpinned by key elements of an enabling welfare state. The welfare state provides a safety net that allows economic actors to take risks related to innovation and the development of new products and processes.

Pontusson (2011) argues that the social democratic aspects of the model are the most important elements of Nordic success. This includes the welfare state, notably the emphasis on education spending and egalitarianism, which have supported the transformation and growth of the Nordic economies and ensured that these countries have not experienced the same degree of dualization as Continental Europe. He argues that such policies do not necessarily depend on CME institutions and that they could work in LMEs as well, though high unionization rates may be a necessary political prerequisite, which would make it harder to implement them in practice in LMEs. What his analysis underscores is how different the Nordic trajectory was from the Continental CMEs, many of which still specialize in traditional industries that rely on incremental innovation (see Chapter 10).

Conclusion

This chapter has considered one of the two core VoC models identified by Hall and Soskice (2001a), namely the CME model. This model is widely seen as the main alternative to liberal capitalism and as a model that could simultaneously deliver high growth and low inequality. There has been extensive debate about its future viability in a more global era in which manufacturing is in decline. This chapter has also highlighted key differences between the Continental and the Nordic CMEs. These differences raise important questions about how to interpret these cases and whether they are best regarded as different models of capitalism (Pontusson 2005, 2011). Whilst the economic performance of Continental CMEs has generated extensive debate, including both praise and criticism, there is no agreement on how to understand the success that the Nordic economies enjoyed in the early twenty-first century and on the significance of economic liberalization or reforms to the social democratic welfare regime in these economies. The answers to such questions may hold important lessons for understanding the future of the CME model and under what circumstances it is conducive to low inequality.

Discussion questions

- To what extent does the CME model show that capitalist economies can simultaneously achieve both high growth and low inequality?
- Can the CME model explain the functioning of post-industrial economies that rely more on services?
- Are the differences between Continental and Nordic CMEs so big that it does not make sense to regard them as examples of the same model?
- Assess the strengths and weaknesses of the CME model.
- Some analysts have suggested that the CME model is no longer viable in the post-industrial economies of the twenty-first century and that it is likely to disappear. Do you agree?

4

Networked market economies

The twenty-first century is often described as a networked age, as various forms of social networks have become very important features of people's lives. This includes domestic, transnational and virtual networks, some of which are facilitated by the internet and new forms of media. Nevertheless, network ties are not a recent phenomenon, and various forms of networks have been shown to shape economic activity and political mobilization in a wide range of historical and cultural contexts, including fifteenth-century Florence (Padgett and Ansell 1993). Ultimately who you know does matter. Many people find out about job opportunities via personal or professional networks. Research has found that 'weak ties' to more distant actors in the network are usually more important than the closest friendship ties (Granovetter 1983). Whilst such networks play an important role in every market economy, this chapter focuses on networked market economies (NMEs), a variety of capitalism in which network coordination can be viewed as the central coordination mechanism. It spells out the core logic of NME institutions and discusses the applicability of this model to Japan, Taiwan and more generally as well.

Understanding the NME model: Networks and trust

As in the case of other VoC models, the defining feature of an NME is the centrality of a particular coordination mechanism, in this case network coordination. This is sometimes called 'relational coordination', which highlights the importance of interpersonal and inter-organizational relations and ties within a network (Sako and Kotosaka 2012: 132). Schneider stresses the role of informal norms, trust and reciprocity as the central components of network coordination (Schneider 2013: 24). Networks are one of the most common logics of economic coordination that have received extensive attention from scholars of capitalist systems (Adler 2001; Granovetter 1983).

This definition implies that there could be some variation between networks, depending on which of these factors is most central. For example, as demonstrated in this chapter, community norms have traditionally been central to the Japanese case, whereas trust is often underpinned by family or kinship ties in Taiwan, where the Chinese concept of *guanxi* is crucial to the functioning of networks.

In other words, compared to other VoC, the role of networks in NMEs is qualitatively different, and they play a more fundamental role in the governance of the economy. A particular manifestation of such networks can be found in business groups, like the Japanese *keiretsu*, where a group of firms are formally or informally connected via close economic and social ties.

It should be noted that business groups are also prominent in hierarchical market economies (HMEs) (to be discussed in Chapter 5). Whilst there are some similarities between NMEs and HMEs in this regard, the main difference relates to the dominant mode of coordination within business groups. In NMEs trust, common norms and network coordination predominate, whereas business groups in HMEs have a more hierarchical structure (Schneider 2009). As noted by Schneider (2013), these concepts are ideal types, and many economies could be seen as hybrids in practice, given that they may contain some elements of both network and hierarchical coordination.

The social embeddedness of the firm and economic activity is reflected at many levels of the economy (Dore 2000: 45). For example, network ties with suppliers are very common and integral to the successful production strategies of firms, in particular when they are heavily reliant on specific inputs that are not widely available. Network ties with other firms are also common and an important foundation of industry standards. Whilst such ties are often informal, they can also be formalized in cooperative activities of industrial associations (Walter and Zhang 2012a: 17) or in institutional interlocks, such as cross-ownership (where firms have reciprocal holdings of shares which facilitate exchange of information and coordination). However, such network ties could also exist within enterprises. Most famously, the Japanese term *sha-in* refers to the enterprise community, which highlights the existence of close social ties both among workers, but also between workers and the firm. This has traditionally been associated with important norms and practices, such as lifetime employment (Dore 2000: 10).

The comparative institutional advantage of NMEs tends to be quite similar to coordinated market economies (CMEs), in that these institutions are conducive to high-quality manufacturing (Schneider 2013: 29). Stable supplier relations and long-termism promote investments in specific skills and incremental innovation in existing industries. The fact that both the leading CME (Germany) and NME (Japan) are world leaders in car manufacturing is an important case in point.

It should be noted that the NME category has some affinity with other VoC models and that some NMEs have also been classified differently. The main points of tangency are with HMEs (Chapter 5), SMEs (Chapter 7) and CMEs (Chapter 3). As noted above, the main commonality between NMEs and HMEs is the prominence of business groups, though the internal organization of such groups tends to differ across these two models and other countries as well (Granovetter 2010). The relationship between the NME and SME models is primarily historical. Some of the most prominent examples of NMEs, such as Japan and Taiwan, two cases discussed later in this chapter, were previously typically regarded as developmental states (Johnson 1982; Wade 2004; see Chapter 7). However, the role of the state is no longer as prominent as it was during the heyday of the developmental state. Different kinds of network ties and co-governance by business and state actors are widely perceived as more central to the functioning of these economies (Walter and Zhang 2012b). The overlap with the CME model is perhaps even greater – in fact, some analysts have classified these economies as CMEs (Estévez-Abe 2008; Song 2014), albeit with some distinctive features. For example, Hall and Soskice (2001a) speak of two forms of CME, namely industry and group-based CMEs, and Thelen distinguishes between solidaristic Western European and segmentalist Japanese CMEs (Thelen 2009). Whilst these distinctions speak to the differences between these models and the role of organized interests, this book argues that such differences make the use of the CME label for NMEs rather misleading, as Pontusson (2005: 18–19) points out as well. The underlying political underpinnings are also different in key respects. For these reasons, this book follows other scholars (e.g. Schneider 2013; Walter and Zhang 2012b) in identifying NMEs as a distinct

VoC rather than as a sub-type of CME, despite some parallels and similarities between these models.

Financial systems and corporate governance

Network coordination has a profound impact on the functioning of the financial systems and corporate governance in NMEs. Networked governance of financial systems bears considerable resemblance to the CME model in that it can also be described as bank-based and insider-dominated (Schneider 2013: 25).

First, relational banking is a common feature of NMEs (Dore 2000: 34). Relational banking refers to the close relationships that firms have to financial institutions, such as the traditional main bank system, in which firms rely on one bank as the main source of finance and this close relationship helps underpin the supply of credit. Whilst the importance of stock markets and foreign capital has increased in NMEs, the main source of financing for firms tends to be bank capital (Ahmadjian 2014). This means that there is patient capital in the sense that banks are more likely to be patient or take a long-term view of the firm and to exercise voice rather than exit by divesting if they perceive any problems (Walter and Zhang 2012a: 17).

Second, other features promote the kind of long-termism commonly described as 'patient capital' (Zysman 1983; Vitols 2001). This includes 'cross-ownership', or reciprocal ownership stakes of multiple firms, and 'block holdings', which refer to the existence of strategic investors who have large ownership shares and who are hence in a position to exercise a very significant role in corporate governance. In other words, key stakeholders such as banks, other creditors or other firms with ownership stakes are less likely to focus only on maximizing shareholder value on the stock market in the short run.

Such reciprocal ownership ties also relate to the existence of informal business groups, which are a key characteristic of NMEs. This includes informal ties within and across sectors and with suppliers within sometimes hierarchically organized markets (Dore 2000: 37). As discussed below, examples of such networks include the famous Japanese *keiretsu* conglomerates, the Taiwanese *guanxi* capitalists and to a lesser extent the South Korean *chaebol*, which are generally viewed as more hierarchical organizations than the conglomerates in the other two cases (Whitley 1992).

Finally, corporate governance is also shaped by network ties between firms and the state. Such ties were significant even during the era of the developmental state. Samuels (1987) shows that the relationship between the state and big business at the time could be characterized as 'reciprocal consent', and Evans has referred to the state's role as 'embedded autonomy' (Evans 1995). These analyses highlight that the state was strong and autonomous, but also that it was embedded in society and that it had close ties to business, with regular meetings with key industrialists a common practice. This relates to what has been described as a business culture based on regular informal consultations that are not understood as lobbying in the traditional sense. Examples of this include the *shingikai* (deliberative councils) in Japan (Zhang and Whitley 2013: 309). In Japan such state-business interactions are commonly viewed as based on the notion of *wa* (harmony) (Hamada 2010: 331–3). Such ties are also reflected in the traditional Japanese practice of *amakudari* (descent from heaven), which enables retired civil servants to take up senior positions in business (Colignon and Usui 2001).

Labour markets

In NMEs, network coordination is also central to the functioning of labour markets. Such coordination plays a significant role both within the firm and beyond it. There are at least four ways in which network ties tend to be important.

First, as in other economies, networks play a role in employment practices. In NMEs network ties are likely to shape the odds of securing employment or a leadership position in a firm, perhaps especially when family or kinship networks are of central importance. In such cases, a high share of senior management positions is likely to be filled by members of such networks.

Second, strong network ties between firms and employees generally make labour markets less fluid. A special case of this is the practice of lifetime employment, which is likely to be associated with strong social ties between employees and employers. Whilst this practice is less common than in the past, it has long been an important feature of the NME model. It increases employees' sense of loyalty and commitment to the firm and promotes investments in on-the-job training as well as experimental approaches to continuous organizational improvements (Hashimoto 1979; Jaeger and Baliga 1985; Aoki and Dore 1996). The flipside of such arrangements is that employees have been closely tied to the firms and had fewer alternative employment options than in many other economies. There are differences across NMEs in this regard. These practices have played a much greater role in Japan than in Korea, where job tenures have also fallen more dramatically since the Asian financial crisis (Song 2020). Unionization rates are generally low. Especially in the Japanese case unions have operated at the firm level and often collaboratively with management.

Third, network ties may also be associated with various collaborative work practices, such as an emphasis on teamwork. This facilitates regular communication between production units and work levels, and many analysts have shown that this has enhanced the efficiency and organizational resources of car manufacturers in Japan (Clark and Fujimoto 1989).

Fourth, close network ties at the firm level are likely to have an impact on collective interest representation. To the extent that such networks contribute to a sense of a specific enterprise community, it is likely to be associated with enterprise unions or sometimes even the absence of strong unions altogether. This is particularly likely if there are strong community norms or if the firm is very small, in which case the sense of community between the firm and its employees is so strong that it makes it harder to create unions that might be regarded as disloyal. Network ties between firms often promote some informal coordination across enterprises and even industry associations, but generally wage coordination tends to be more informal than in Western European CMEs (Thelen 2009; see also Chapter 3). More generally, as noted above, the wider influence of associations is more limited than in CMEs. This has a number of important consequences. Whilst NMEs are relatively egalitarian, especially compared to LMEs or HMEs, the role of negotiations between peak associations of employers and workers typically plays a smaller role in bringing about such outcomes. Welfare states are less generous and typically have a 'productivist' bent that is designed to promote economic activity and labour force participation, typically with inducements to ensure that workers put aside savings to fund entitlement programmes (Holliday 2000). However, whilst NMEs are egalitarian by international standards, they also tend to be highly segmented by occupational category, in that benefits and welfare entitlements vary greatly by occupation and professional categories.

The education systems of NMEs have high-quality primary and secondary education systems, which typically score very high in international comparisons. The university sector has expanded over time and led to a growing, if increasingly unequal, higher education sector, in which private providers have become more significant. Technical and vocational education and in-house training within conglomerates helps support specific skill acquisition in larger conglomerates, especially in Japan. Busemeyer (2009) describes the Japanese skill system as 'segmentalist', as there is a heavy emphasis on firm-level training, but there is limited vocational content in secondary education, which tends to privilege general skills, including mathematics.

Similarly, on-the-job training mostly takes place within large firms, which promotes firm-based skills tailored to the internal structure and career trajectories within enterprises as opposed to the kinds of industry standards common in CMEs (Thelen 2009: 480; Thelen 2004). There are often stark differences between core workers and those on more insecure contracts, and such contrasts have become sharper as a result of greater dualization (Song 2014; Thelen and Kume 2006). There are obvious parallels with the trend towards dualization in the West European CMEs (see Chapter 3; Palier and Thelen 2010). More generally, the provision of general skills and tertiary education has grown significantly over time, and the market for private colleges and universities has expanded considerably. Whilst this has contributed to higher enrolment rates it has also resulted in weaker demand for vocational education.

Complementarities and economic outcomes

For many years, key NMEs were among the most successful economies in the world. Japan, Taiwan and South Korea have gone through some of the most rapid transformations in world history. Their success relates to the general debate about the East Asian miracle and the developmental state, including the role of statist economic coordination in particular (see Chapter 7). However, as noted above, networks played an important role even in the heyday of the developmental state, as captured by the term 'embedded autonomy' (Evans 1995). This section considers the contribution of the network coordination to their economic performance.

The roots of economic success in NMEs have much in common with CMEs. Indeed, Germany and Japan are often viewed as the two main examples of non-liberal, stakeholder or welfare capitalism (Streeck and Yamamura 2003; Dore 2000). Such similarities include the role of patient capital in supporting long-term investments in specific skills and a comparative advantage in incremental innovation and high-quality manufacturing, including the world-leading role in car manufacturing enjoyed by both Germany and Japan (Schneider 2013: 29).

It has been shown that network governance is particularly useful under conditions of demand uncertainty, when there is a great reliance on specific skills and when core tasks are relatively complex and frequent (Jones et al. 1997: 918). Under such conditions network coordination has many advantages, as it contributes to a number of mechanisms to reduce such uncertainty, promote specific skill investments and maintain cooperation by means of monitoring and sanctions. This facilitates teamwork, cooperative supplier relations and just-in-time manufacturing and incremental innovation that characterize high-quality car production. Many car producers in other countries have sought to emulate Japanese production techniques, though not always successfully (Saka 2004; cf. Elger and Smith 2010).

Since the 1990s the merits of network coordination have been more controversial. This is partly related to the slowdown in economic growth, especially in Japan, which experienced what was widely perceived as a lost decade of sluggish performance in the 1990s. This followed a prolonged financial crisis in the aftermath of a finance bubble driven by liberalization initiatives in the 1980s. The causes of the lost decade are controversial. Whilst many analysts view macroeconomic causes as paramount, others have argued that the roots lie in the unique institutions themselves. This prolonged downturn empowered some critics of the Japanese model to argue for the adoption of Anglo-American economic institutions. Some critics have suggested that network coordination could have significant disadvantages and promote crony capitalism. In the view of such critics, rather than fostering trust, cooperation and efficiency, the main effect of network ties is corruption (Kang 2002). Weaknesses in the financial systems of these countries are commonly attributed to these factors. However, such conclusions are controversial. First, the Japanese economy grew faster than the US economy in the first decade of the twenty-first century, thereby casting doubt on the inevitable demise of the Japanese model (Witt 2014a: 100). Whilst Taiwan's growth rates have fallen since the Golden Age of the East Asian miracle, this was inevitable given how successful the catch-up process had been. Perhaps more importantly, Taiwan is still a very successful economy. Second, the evidence of convergence is very mixed. Whilst there has been some reform and liberalization, resulting from international commitments, but partly from changing preferences of domestic actors, it is ultimately not clear whether the functioning of the NMEs has changed in a transformative way (Walter 2006; Zhang and Whitley 2013). Even the response to international pressures to reform the financial sector and financial regulation has often amounted to what Andrew Walter calls 'mock compliance'. In other words, formal rules have been overhauled in some respects, but actual behaviour remains largely unchanged (Walter 2008). It is also not clear whether selective liberalization has led to a declining role of the state or rather to a transformation of its role associated with more rules (Vogel 1996).

Japan as an NME

The Japanese case is very important for studies of comparative capitalism. As Japan was the first non-Western country to develop and to achieve both high levels of industrialization and prosperity, the Japanese case has been of great interest to scholars, analysts and policymakers in many parts of the world, both in East Asia (especially in Taiwan and South Korea) and across the Global South, where the prospect of emulating the Japanese experience of getting rich has served as an important source of inspiration. There has been great interest in Japan even in the Global North, perhaps above all in the United States in the late 1970s and 1980s. The bestselling book *Japan as Number One*, authored by the Harvard sociologist Ezra Vogel and published in 1979, captured the mood of the times and the widely held perception that Japan had developed a superior form of capitalism. A key implication of such analyses was that, unless countries like the United States managed to learn from this experience, they would be destined to fall behind Japan.

Much of the traditional literature about Japan focuses on the centrality of activist industrial policy and characterizes Japan as a developmental state (Johnson 1982). These writings see the Japanese development experience as largely state-led and highlight the central role of state intervention since the Meiji restoration in the late nineteenth century as well as the catalytic role of MITI, the legendary Ministry of the International Trade and Industry in the post–Second World War era. However, these arguments have been qualified by later studies. Samuels (1987) characterizes this relationship as a form of 'reciprocal consent', where the effectiveness of state intervention arises 'not from its own inherent capacity but from the complexity and stability of its interaction with market players' (Samuels 1987: 262). Okimoto (1989) highlights the extensive and dense ties between MITI, leading companies and the Liberal Democratic Party that dominated Japanese politics in the second half of the twentieth century. This has also been tied to the idea of *ie*, or traditional family norms that have played a similar role to corporatist ideas in Germany (Streeck 2003).

Much of the VoC-related literature on the Japanese economy has classified it as an NME, especially since the 1980s (Walter and Zhang 2013; Schneider 2013; Lincoln and Gerlach 2004). Key characteristics of the Japanese economy fit the NME model very well. The most famous element of the Japanese corporate landscape is the horizontal *keiretsu* conglomerates. These are business groups usually centred on a bank that involves extensive cross-holdings by its members. The firms that are part of the *keiretsu* are connected via an extensive web of network ties. The *keiretsu* have emerged via two distinct pathways. The first type has its roots in the classic *zaibatsu* that were family-controlled holding companies controlling highly diversified business groups, but that were dissolved at the instigation of the US occupation authorities after the Second World War. However, the constituent firms retained informal ties and gradually reconstituted themselves as groups centred on a main bank. The classic cases are the Mitsubishi, Mitsui and Sumitomo conglomerates (Witt 2014a: 111). The second form of *keiretsu* only emerged after the Second World War, partly as a result of MITI pressure (Johnson 1982: 206), and these groups were also centred on banks. Fuyo, Ikkan and Sanwa are the key examples (Witt 2014a: 111). In addition, there are also vertical *keiretsu*, denoting close network ties between producers, suppliers and distribution networks (McGuire and Dow 2009). More generally, the economy is characterized by high levels of cross-shareholdings and ownership stakes held by banks, which is conducive to patient capital and long-term relations between firms and their stakeholders. It should be noted that such shareholdings began to fall in the 1990s, but they still remain relatively high by international standards. In 2009 the shareholdings by corporations and financial institutions stood at 51.9 per cent (Witt 2014a: 103). There is an extensive debate about the effects of the *keiretsu* organization and its future viability. The six horizontal *keiretsu* became four as a result of corporate transformations in the late 1990s and early 2000s, but the network coordination still plays an important role in the Japanese economy.

Several recent changes have affected corporate governance in other ways. First, there has been an increase in foreign shareholdings, which rose from 5.8 per cent in 1980 to 26 per cent in 2009 (Witt 2014a: 103). Whilst foreign shareholders have pushed for greater transparency and protection of minority shareholders, there are still various safeguards protecting strategic owners, it is ultimately not clear whether the changes in financial regulation have genuinely transformed regulatory practice (Walter 2006, 2008). Similarly, attempts to promote venture capital funding or to launch new stock exchanges have only had relatively limited effects on the financial systems (Sako and Kotosaka 2012: 137–45).

Therefore, the Japanese financial system is still predominantly bank-based. Although the importance of the stock market and foreign direct investment has increased over time, this has not undermined the centrality of banks as the main source of credit (Witt 2014a: 102). However, whilst the system is overall closest to being bank-based, it is more accurately viewed as syncretic or internally diverse, in that various coordination mechanisms co-exist. Whilst many traditional elements of the financial sector remain, including key features of the postal saving system as well as the regional banks, a variety of new actors have entered the Japanese financial market (Kushida and Shimizu 2013). This includes foreign firms offering a variety of new products based on financial strategies that are very different from the traditional Japanese model. These include stock brokerages and trading in new financial instruments, such as derivatives and convertible bonds (Morgan and Kubo 2005).

Japanese labour markets have had a number of characteristic features that fit very well with the NME model. Network ties within firms have been very strong, and they have often been described as constituting an enterprise community (*sha-in*) (Dore 2000: 10). Such network ties have manifested themselves in various related practices, such as lifetime employment, firm investments in workers' skills and great emphasis on teamwork. Given the prevalence of enterprise unions that are organized by firm and not by sector or industry, the main locus of worker representation is in the firm itself, unlike in the European coordinated market economies where strong union movements operate at the sectoral or sometimes even national level and play an important role in wage bargaining and social dialogue (see Chapter 3).

Yet there has been some coordination of wage setting across firms and sectors in Japan. The most important element of this is the so-called 'Shunto', or annual spring offensive, which amounts to an elaborate wage bargaining system. It was originally established in 1955 as a result of pressure for greater solidarity by some union leaders. Whilst official negotiations take place at the firm level, the Shunto system has been seen as the functional equivalent of encompassing organizations and centralized wage setting that exist in CMEs (Song 2012). Sako and Kotosaka identify three factors contributing to this. Unions and export-oriented manufacturing companies played the role of pattern setters, and these settlements also affected wage setting in the public sector. The peak associations of workers (Rengo) and business (Nippon Keidanren) also issued guidelines for non-inflationary wage settlements. The pay settlements also took place at a specific time in the spring, which prevented deviations and leapfrogging (Sako and Kotosaka 2012: 146)

Beginning in the late 1990s after almost a decade of slow growth, there has been considerable change in labour markets, including some decline in traditional practices, such as lifetime employment and also in the Shunto system. However, the most important change may be the trend towards dualization or the increasingly stark divide between core employees with generous benefits and more peripheral workers on precarious or short-term contracts (see Chapters 3 and 8). Whilst there are long-standing differences between core employees and more casual non-regular workers, they seemed less significant before the 1990s. In particular, in the era of high growth many improvements in work conditions, pay and pensions were also extended to non-regular workers. From the 1990s the contrasts between these worker categories have become sharper, as a variety of labour market reforms have been introduced that have weakened employment protection, pensions and other benefits for non-regular workers, whilst also strengthening the protection of core workers (Song 2012: 422; 429). The importance of non-regular and precarious work has also risen (Gagné 2020). . By contrast, the position of core workers has been protected in large part thanks to a strong alliance between core workers, large firms and conservative policymakers (Song 2012).

The sharpening dualization in labour markets bears some resemblance to the syncretism of financial markets and highlights that the Japanese political economy retains many of its traditional features. The core of the Japanese economy remains networked, but there has been a process of liberalization that has occurred in parallel with the consolidation of these core features. Whether this is a stable equilibrium or whether further reforms might eventually transform the economy in an even more profound way is an open question.

Taiwan as an NME

From the 1960s to the 1980s Taiwan was widely perceived as a key example of the developmental state model (Wade 2004; Amsden 1979, 1985; Hsueh, Hsu and Perkins 2001) (see also Chapter

7). However, the role of the state has been different after the 1980s, and many scholars regard Taiwan as an NME (e.g. Schneider 2013) or as a co-governed market economy (effectively a networked market economy in which state coordination is also significant) (Walter and Zhang 2012a).

Whilst the Taiwanese economy was influenced by the Japanese experience, both as a result of Japanese colonial rule (1895–1945) and the general influence of the Japanese growth experience, the case of Taiwan is complex and in many ways quite different from Japan. After the Chinese Revolution in 1949, the Republican Chinese leadership fled to Taiwan and subsequently dominated Taiwanese politics until the late twentieth century, including much of the democratic era from 1988. For much of the post–Second World War period the Taiwanese economy could be divided into two segments. The first segment consisted of big firms, often related to heavy industry. This part of the economy was generally state-owned or at least had very close ties to the government. In many cases these firms had been run by the Japanese state during the colonial period, and then the Taiwanese KMT government simply nationalized these assets and ran them as state-owned enterprises (SOEs). The activities of SOEs reflected core government priorities. The other part of the economy consisted of small and medium-sized enterprises (SMEs), which were always private, but the institutions of the developmental state influenced the private sector as well. As late as the 1980s Taiwan could be regarded as a state-led market economy, and even after that the role of the state has in some respects been greater than in Japan, as highlighted by the label 'co-governed' discussed above and favoured by some authors (Zhang and Whitley 2013).

The SME sector has traditionally been characterized by dense network ties, often based on family relations. Such family ties are also important within Taiwanese business groups. Official statistics often underestimate the importance of this phenomenon, as pyramidal structures and more diffuse kinship ties that need not be reported sometimes obscure the full scale of such connections. It has also been estimated that up to 80 per cent of listed companies in Taiwan are controlled by families (Lee and Hsiao 2014: 254). Family ties matter within the so-called 'inner circle' that tends to control the management of companies and business groups (Hamilton 1997; Lee and Hsiao 2014: 246). Cross-holdings and pyramid structures also facilitate family control within business groups. Compared to business groups elsewhere in East Asia, social ties are more important to the management of Taiwanese groups than in the more hierarchical *chaebol* in South Korea or the role of community norms in the Japanese *keiretsu*. Taiwanese capitalism has often been called *guanxi capitalism*, where *guanxi* refers to traditional interpersonal relationships and kinship ties associated with Chinese culture. Whilst there is some evidence to suggest that the role of family ties has fallen slightly, it remains very high by comparative standards.

Some of these networks have also become transnational as a result of Taiwanese foreign investment in other countries and thereby embedded in regional or global production networks (Hsu and Saxenian 2000; Jou and Chen 2006). Over time Taiwan's regional role has become more significant as Taiwanese investments in mainland China and Southeast Asia have increased. This has been to the extent that such ties involving ethnic Chinese businesses across multiple economies in Southeast Asia, and not necessarily just Taiwanese businesses, are sometimes also referred to as the 'China Circle' (Yeung 2007).

The Taiwanese economy has also become increasingly sophisticated, in part thanks to the successful catch-up process and the high economic growth from the 1960s to the 1980s. Over time there has been a shift in sectoral specialization, as the economy has proceeded from labour-intensive to capital-intensive industries and increasingly to advanced knowledge-intensive industries as well, including the rise of electronics, IT and even biotechnology in the 1990s and 2000s. Especially since the 1980s, the role of the state has changed and taken on a more indirect role, such as the promotion of research institutes, science parks and funding private research and development initiatives instead of more direct guidance (Zhang and Whitley 2013: 314; Wade 2004). This transformation is associated with important changes in economic coordination in Taiwan.

The Taiwanese financial system was dominated by the state-owned banks until the early 1990s, but it has changed considerably since that time. The financial system is still bank-based, and close relationship ties and size facilitate access to credit. Relational finance is important, in that network ties make it easier for firms to borrow. Smaller firms tend to be at a structural disadvantage in terms of accessing credit. Whilst a large part of the financial system is still controlled by the state (Lee and Hsiao 2014: 242), the stock market became more important in the 1990s and early 2000s as a result of financial liberalization (Zhang 2013). The share of equity finance as a source of corporate funds increased during this time period. Yet this has not undermined the centrality of family dominance. Typically a relatively small ownership stake of about 15 per cent is often sufficient to ensure family control.

Employment relations are quite different from Japan, in that turnover is generally higher for many workers, and there is very limited on-the-job training. However, employees with close personal and network ties to the owners tend to have longer job tenure and a greater commitment to the firms that they work for. In the heyday of the developmental state the union movement was dominated by the Taiwanese ruling party, the Kuomintang (KMT), and relations between workers and employers tended to be peaceful and deferential. However, since Taiwan democratized in 1988 unions have played a greater role in society. Given the dominance of small and medium-sized enterprises (SMEs), unions tend to play a small role in much of the economy outside the SOEs, where they play a greater role. In the late twentieth century Taiwan's university enrolment expanded rapidly, but the provision of vocational skills that used to be important in earlier decades has fallen.

The Taiwanese economy was one of the most successful in the world in the second half of the twentieth century, and it was one of the economies associated with the East Asian miracle (Perkins 2013). Once the country shifted from a more inward-looking strategy of import substitution to export orientation in the early 1960s, the economy grew very fast and rapidly caught up with the high-income economies. The position of vulnerability to conflict with mainland China and the associated support from the United States as well as access to American markets was also an important component of this success (Amsden 1979; Doner, Ritchie and Slater 2005). From the 1990s onwards growth has slowed, which tends to be inevitable once countries have caught up, but the Taiwanese economy has continued to do well in terms of economic growth and is a high-income economy.

The politics of NMEs

This section considers the distinctive political underpinnings of NME institutions by first discussing their origins and then examining the factors accounting for continuity and change. This discussion considers economic incentives related to rational goal-seeking behaviour, social norms and historical legacies (Hall and Taylor 1996).

Whilst there was no grand design underlying the creation of the NME model or any other VoC (cf. Thelen 2004), and there has also been considerable change over time in these models, strategic considerations affected the creation of many key elements of the NME model. For example, Japanese firms started to extend cross-holdings of shares in the 1960s to prevent hostile takeovers (Witt 2006, 2014a: 103). Relationship banking was originally a feature of large firms and conglomerates, but it was extended to smaller firms when large firms began to draw on alternative sources of finance as well and the banks sought out new customers (Takahashi 2012). Similarly, the emergence of Shunto wage bargaining in 1955 attempted to counteract some perceived drawbacks of enterprise unions (Sako 1997; Sako and Kotosaka 2012: 145). Once such arrangements are put in place, there are a variety of firms that benefit from these arrangements. They rely on supply and distribution as well as finance and labour (incl. human capital) facilitated by these institutions. These benefits are also related to classical institutional complementarities or the idea that the benefits accruing from any institution depend on the existence of complementary institutions (see Chapter 1). As NME firms typically develop their economic strategies based on these institutions, many of them have an incentive to retain at least the elements that are integral to the success of their market and production strategies, as in the case of Japanese manufacturing (Witt 2014a). The trend towards syncretism and dualization can be viewed as an attempt to retain the advantages of the traditional model whilst also introducing additional flexibility.

Second, there is the social dimension of institutions (studied by sociological institutionalists) – or the ways in which these arrangements reflect norms, ideas and culture. In the case of East Asian countries, this has traditionally been related to Confucian ideals and strong cooperative norms in society. This includes the concept of *guanxi* in Taiwan or *sha-in* and *ie* in Japan. Such concepts should not be interpreted in an overly rigid fashion, as such values and norms change over time and vary across countries. Indeed, one of the main questions that analysts of Japan and other parts of East Asia have asked is whether changing cultural understandings and greater legitimacy attributed to alternative models, like the US-style LME institutions, will ultimately undermine the viability of the NME model (Dore 2000). Such ideas and understandings are not automatically transmitted, and alternative discourses of reform and liberalization can be used to challenge them, as discursive institutionalists have also shown. As Walter and Zhang (2013) show, foreign discourses and understandings of best practice can be used by policy entrepreneurs to build reform coalitions. In periods of crisis or electoral vulnerability, politicians may exploit such opportunities, as when various scandals in the financial sector empowered governments to undertake financial reforms in Japan in the 1990s (Kushida and Shimizu 2013). However, at the later implementation stage some of these reforms were questioned and partially reversed, in part since especially many of the changes to the postal savings system could be portrayed as illegitimate and ill-suited to Japanese conditions.

Third, the emergence of the NME model also reflects historical legacies and preconditions. In the Japanese case this includes critical junctures when key decisions were particularly significant and had long-lasting effects that generated path dependence. Such critical junctures include the onset of the Meiji Restoration in the nineteenth century (which was shaped both by domestic legacies and a perceived threat from the West – see Fulcher 1988) and also the aftermath of the Second World War, when some aspects of the Japanese economy were profoundly reshaped during the US occupation. In particular, the old economic conglomerates (*zaibatsu*) were broken up, paving the way for the emergence of the *keiretsu*. However, the fact that there was some continuity in the economic administration also facilitated the rise of MITI and the export-led growth miracle of the post-war era. In the Taiwanese case, the impact of the Japanese colonial era was profound, as the KMT government took over firms and practices developed by the Japanese. The effects of political change in the late 1940s and 1980s were equally transformative. Democratization in the late 1980s weakened the commitment to state-owned enterprises and empowered a wider range of economic and social interests, all of which sought to influence economic policymaking in Taiwan. Much like in Korea at the same time, this rendered the exercise of single-minded developmental state policies more difficult, as a variety of objectives and interests had to be taken into account in policymaking (Minns 2001).

Apart from such moments of dramatic change, long-run historical processes and tensions that build up within institutions can generate pressures for change. Four gradual mechanisms of change have been identified by scholars of institutional change, both in Japan and more generally. First, displacement refers to the emergence of new institutions that replace the previous institutional arrangements. Second, layering refers to the emergence of new institutions that exist alongside the old institutions. Third, drift captures the gradual erosion of existing institutions that no longer structure the political economy in the same way as before. Fourth, in the case of conversion old institutions are still in place, but they serve a different purpose from before (Mahoney and Thelen 2009; on Japan, see Thelen 2004 and Sako and Kotosaka 2012). All of these processes have taken place in Japan and Taiwan and facilitated dualization and syncretism, by enabling experimentation without abandoning old institutions. Perhaps most importantly, strategic calculations are shaped by prevailing norms and ideas and by given historical contexts and legacies, which means that the three aspects of institutions are best understood as operating in tandem. Taken together, these mechanisms of gradual change suggest that institutions can develop in a variety of open-ended way, where old elements are recombined with new elements to create new hybrids. Network coordination remains central to these processes and the functioning of these economies.

Debating the NME model

The distinctiveness of the NME model continues to attract a lot of interest, in large part stimulated by the economic success enjoyed by both Japan and Taiwan. However, there are a number of controversial issues associated with this model.

First, as noted earlier, some analysts have simply classified countries like Japan as CMEs rather than NMEs. This raises the question as to whether the NME model is distinctive. This chapter has argued that treating Germany, Sweden and Japan as cases of the same VoC may obscure more than it reveals. More generally, network governance constitutes one of the main coordination mechanisms that can be found in a variety of countries and organizations. As Schneider (2013: 302) has argued, elements of the NME model can be found in many East Asian economies, although it is not clear whether any of them fit the NME model as well as Japan and Taiwan.

Beyond the two cases discussed in this chapter, South Korea (henceforth Korea) is arguably the country that comes closest to being an NME. Walter and Zhang (2012a) classify Korea along with Taiwan as co-governed, and both economies were also regarded as key examples of the developmental state model associated with the East Asian miracle (Perkins 2013). Zhang and Whitley (2013) regard them as converging over time. In many key respects, Korea could be regarded as the economy that is most similar to the Japanese form of capitalism. One of the key similarities that is usually highlighted is the centrality of large business groups, although the Korean conglomerates known as *chaebol* are more hierarchical than the Japanese *keiretsu* and probably more similar to the pre–Second World War *zaibatsu* in Japan (Whitley 1992). The *chaebo*l are family-dominated, and the leading family and norms of generational succession are of central importance.

The financial system is predominantly bank-based, and especially in the heyday of the developmental state the banking system was also state-dominated, with lending reflecting state priorities. In particular, prior to the Asian financial crisis of the late 1990s, many Korean *chaebol* took control of financial institutions, such as insurance companies or security houses, which provided around 50 per cent of credit in the economy at the time. Whilst reforms after the financial crisis were designed to reduce *chaebol* dependence on bank credit and debt by bringing down debt-to-equity ratios, this has only been partly successful. The financial system remains predominantly bank-based (Witt 2014b).

Corporate governance has many distinctive network features, including the centrality of the dominant family within the biggest firms and *chaebols*. In a study of 159 of the largest Korean firms, Carney and Child (2013) find that between 35.8 and 54.5 per cent of these firms were family-controlled, depending on the cut-off used to establish family dominance, and that the role of family ownership had increased since the 1990s. They also show that the impact of these ownership stakes is typically reinforced by weighted voting rights or pyramid schemes of cross-shareholdings within conglomerates.

Whilst various reforms were introduced after the Asian financial crisis (Jun, Rowley and Oh 2022), corporate governance practices are usually regarded as relatively weak in international rankings, especially compared to other leading East Asian economies. The strong insider dominance within firms and *chaebol* is seen to contribute to corruption and cronyism, with considerable scope for insiders to extract rents from these organizations (You 2021).

Employment relations in Korea fit with the NME model to some extent. On the one hand, trade unions are not equally firm-based as in Japan, and job tenures are relatively short, especially for non-core workers. The skill system has put great emphasis on general skills, especially since the late 1990s, when state policies sought to increase tertiary education enrolment, which also led to falling demand for vocational tertiary education (Song 2020). Any remaining commitment to firm-based training and specific skills tends to be restricted to certain core workers in *chaebols*. In combination with a relatively small welfare state and low social spending, this has sometimes been regarded as indicative of patterns that bear greater resemblance to LMEs (Lee, Shin and Lee 2020). On the other hand, both unions and business associations play a greater role in facilitating coordination between firms and *chaebol*, which has prompted others to classify Korea as a CME (Song 2014) or at least as moving in that direction (Schneider 2013).

Another economy that has considerable NME elements is *Thailand*, but these elements have become less pronounced over time. For example, Zhang and Whitley (2013) classify Thailand in the 1980s as networked, when both business associations and the Joint Public-Private Consultative Committee (JPPCC, established in 1981) that operated as a kind of policy network played an important role. However, as network ties both among firms and between firms and the state became less significant, both Zhang and Whitley (2013) and Walter and Zhang (2012a) view the Thai economy as personalized from the 1990s.

Second, another controversy surrounds the viability of the NME model in East Asia. The kind of social embeddedness that underpins patterns of trust and network coordination in NMEs is sometimes perceived as a remnant of a different age that might disappear as marketization continues apace and destroys such social ties (Dore 2000; see also Polanyi 1944). As in the case of the CMEs in Europe, a big debate about the allegedly inevitable demise of the Japanese model emerged during the so-called 'lost decade' of the 1990s when the economy was stagnating. In particular, critics have raised questions about the compatibility of the NME model with globalization and twenty-first-century capitalism more generally. Whilst it is true that some economic actors in Japan have found the US model of capitalism very attractive, especially in the context of the lost decade of slow growth in the 1990s, the evidence of convergence on the US-style LME model is ultimately not conclusive. In contrast to the above-mentioned studies that regard Korea as a CME and using a slightly different system of classification and a quantitative approach to economic institutions and outcomes, a study by Lee and Shin (2021) finds that Korea and Japan have become more similar to LMEs, but that Taiwan has moved closer to the CME model, whilst the erstwhile group of East Asian capitalism that these economies had belonged to is now an empty category.

More generally, the increasing trend towards syncretism and dualization discussed in this chapter may not necessarily imply that these economies are necessarily in the process of converging on the American or any other model. It could simply imply that the Japanese economy and the other East Asian economies are undergoing a range of incremental changes that are making their structures more internally diverse. The recovery of the Japanese economy in the early twenty-first century and the solid economic performance of other NMEs do not confirm claims about any inevitable demise (Witt 2014). This implies that any more significant convergence is more likely to occur in a more gradual fashion and perhaps in a more distant future, if at all. To the extent that these institutions reflect deeper sociocultural roots, key elements may turn out to be quite resilient. Processes of adjustment imposed from without may often lead to 'mock compliance' rather than a wholehearted embrace of foreign models.

Finally, a third controversy relates to the general relevance of the NME model to understanding contemporary capitalism. On the one hand, many analysts of NMEs in East Asia have stressed the cultural specificity of such networks that are related to *guanxi* in Chinese culture or Confucian ideals across the wider region. On the other hand, If we consider subnational and sectoral varieties of capitalism and accept that many economic systems are hybrids of the ideal types of VoC (Schneider 2013: 302), then the NME model can shed light on key features of many other economies. As a result of especially Taiwanese FDI, *guanxi* networks are increasingly transnational and reach into the economies of East and Southeast Asia and perhaps even into the United States. More generally, many accounts of the high-skill ecosystem supporting the biomedical and computer industries in California stress the importance of a supportive environment, including dense ties and high interdependence between key actors that bears some resemblance to the NME model (Adler 2001).

Conclusion

This chapter has explored the NME model of economies in which network coordination – based on trust and social ties – shape the economy. It has highlighted the distinctive patterns of network coordination and how it has shaped the economies of Japan and Taiwan as well as the ways the model relates to other VoC. The chapter has also reflected on the general logic of networks and the debate about their relevance to understanding economic coordination beyond East Asia, especially in the twenty-first century.

Discussion questions

- Some analysts have described networked market economies, notably Japan, but sometimes South Korea as well, as coordinated market economies – how similar are these models?
- To what extent is the NME model a successful way of combining efficiency and equity?
- Some critics have suggested that networks could also be conducive to cronyism and corruption – do you agree? If so, to what extent can countries avoid such pitfalls, whilst still benefiting from the advantages of network governance?
- Why might the NME model be so closely associated with East Asia and Japan in particular? Could it work in other parts of the world too?

5

Hierarchical market economies

As noted in earlier chapters, the two core VoC models – liberal and coordinated market economies – cannot fully capture the range of capitalist institutions beyond the OECD. There have been various attempts to extend this framework and to refine our understanding of capitalism on a global scale (Feldmann 2019). This chapter analyses one of the most important contributions to this debate. It focuses on *hierarchical market economies* (HMEs), a VoC model first developed by Ben Ross Schneider (2009, 2013). Schneider's primary goal was to develop a model to analyse Latin American capitalism, but the importance of this model is potentially much greater. As Hertog (2023) has pointed out, it may well shed light on the functioning of political economies in much of the Global South, given its focus on organizational forms that are prevalent in many parts of the world. Understanding the HME model could thus hold the key to understanding a wide range of economies across various world regions. Beyond Latin America, some of the economies that have been characterized as HMEs include Thailand, Turkey and South Africa (Schneider 2013: 5; Kiran 2018). The segmented market economies (SEMEs) of the Middle East could also be regarded as a special and particularly stark case of similar institutional arrangements, albeit with some distinctive features (Hertog 2023).

This chapter first introduces the core features of the HME model, as developed by Schneider, and then discusses its relevance to the case studies of Chile and South Africa. The final sections discuss the politics of HMEs and some broader lessons, including what this model teaches us about capitalism in Latin America and other parts of the world.

Understanding the HME model

As other VoC models we have encountered in earlier chapters of the book, the HME model is based on a distinctive coordination mechanism. In HMEs this coordination mechanism is *hierarchy*. Hierarchy refers to top-down decision-making within an organization and is therefore different from decentralized market coordination involving price signals that are triggered by general market conditions or strategic coordination involving bargaining between firms and their stakeholders.

The importance of hierarchy as a basic organizational form has been acknowledged by organizational theorists and scholars of institutions. It is one of the basic mechanisms for governing organizations and allocating resources. The most important foundation for comparative institutional scholarship on hierarchy is Oliver Williamson's (1975) classic account of markets versus hierarchies. Building on Coase (1937) who sought to understand why firms exist in the first place, Williamson conceptualizes one of the key decisions firms face as the choice between markets and hierarchies, which relate to external and internal governance processes. For example, a firm can decide whether to buy inputs on the market or whether to create a unit within the organization in order to produce these inputs within a large vertically integrated firm. If the firm buys these inputs from another supplier, the purchase of inputs is an external transaction between two firms. If these inputs are produced within the same firm (or conglomerate), decisions about the supply and availability of inputs become an internal matter for the firm, which is decided hierarchically by the management of the firm. According to Williamson, this choice is primarily related to transaction costs. If securing a steady supply of high-quality inputs via the market is very costly or uncertain (for example, due to the risk of supply disruptions), it is likely that internalization will be beneficial. Williamson has also extended his analysis to other organizational forms, including long-term contracts and implicit contracts of the kind that are important in coordinated market economies (CMEs) and networked market economies (NMEs) (see Chapters 3 and 4) (Williamson 1985). However, given the centrality of hierarchy as one of the two principal coordination mechanisms identified by Williamson as one of the founders of new institutional economics, it is perhaps surprising that VoC analysis initially paid limited attention to hierarchies as a coordination mechanism (apart from the role of internal firm hierarchies in LMEs that are typically centred on CEOs – see the discussion of corporate governance in LMEs in Chapter 2).

Ben Ross Schneider has integrated hierarchies as a core concern into VoC analysis and developed the HME model centred on hierarchy as the core coordination mechanism. Schneider is interested in hierarchies in two kinds of organizations – *diversified business groups* and *multinational enterprises*. It might be possible to view governance centred on the state as a third kind of hierarchy (Carney 2016). Given the distinctiveness of the state as an economic actor, state coordination is discussed in a separate chapter of this book (see Chapter 7).

Diversified business groups (also known as *grupos* in Latin America) have three core characteristics (Schneider 2013: 47–8). First, there is concentrated ownership. In other words, there is a relatively small number of dominant shareholders who have a controlling stake that enables them to exercise influence over decision-making. Second, concentrated ownership is often related to family control. In other words, the entire business group is controlled by an individual family, where the firm hierarchy reflects the internal power structure of the family. Third, these business groups are based on multisectoral diversification. This means that the business groups are active in multiple and often unrelated sectors, such as mining and insurance.

A multinational enterprise (MNE) is 'a firm of a particular nationality with partially or wholly owned subsidiaries within two or more national economies' (Gilpin 2000: 164). The largest multinational enterprises are active in many parts of the world, and their activities are often segmented into smaller components, each of which may take place in particular plants located in different countries. Multinational enterprises have traditionally played an active role in many parts of the Global South, not least in Latin America, and their role has grown in recent years, even prompting some analysts to speak of the 'age of the multinational' (Gilpin 2000).

Business groups and MNEs tend to be the most significant corporate forms across HMEs both in Latin America and also in other parts of the world. Why are both kinds of organizations typically organized in a hierarchical fashion? First, they are often very large organizations containing a variety of units, all of which are subordinated to the top leadership in the corporate headquarters of the MNE or of the business group. In the latter case it is often the head of the family who also maintains control over the leadership of the business group. Second, these organizations are usually independent of many domestic market signals. The multinational is part of a larger global organization, and it is unlikely to draw on local sources of finance for most big investment projects. It will generally be easier and cheaper to raise funds in the home country of the MNE or on international markets. Similarly, since business groups are usually centred on a core owner or even a dominant family, and since they are highly diversified, they are less vulnerable to developments in one particular sector. There may also be banks and financial institutions as part of the group, which means that investment funds can be raised from within the group if retained earnings cannot be used. Whilst such diversification, often across a wide range of unrelated business areas and sectors, goes against the grain of much corporate thinking in the OECD where companies tend to scale back activities and focus on core competencies, diversification may be a valuable insurance mechanism, especially in volatile and uncertain market environments. The following sections outline the key institutions underpinning hierarchical coordination across the core areas of economic governance.

Corporate governance and financial systems

How does the principle of hierarchy manifest itself in corporate governance and finance? The core principle of hierarchy involves top-down decision-making within organizations. This also means that key economic relationships tend to be integrated into the internal structure of the corporate entity rather than external. So unlike LMEs, where firms are highly dependent on stock markets, or CMEs or NMEs, where firms have traditionally been very dependent on banks, the relationship with financial market actors is less close in HMEs. In the case of the two kinds of firms that Schneider considers, the main relationship that matters to managers is with the owners of the firm, usually the family at the apex of the business group, and in the case of the MNEs the key relationship is to the corporate headquarters and the board based there (Schneider 2013: 45). External signals are therefore less important in corporate governance.

This has implications for financing and investment. In particular, it implies that firms rely on internal rather than external sources of finance. This might include retained earnings, funds from another part of the organization that are used to finance new initiatives elsewhere in the organization (cross-subsidies). It should also be noted that there may be banks and other financial institutions within large business groups, which are likely to provide preferential access to finance to other members of the business group. In the case of MNEs, key investment funds are often raised from financial markets or institutions in the home country.

The reliance on internal sources of finance is reinforced by the institutional environment. In a typical HME both the banking system and the stock market are constrained by limited financial development. This is why they are often poorly equipped to provide the kind of finance that large business groups or new firms might require. This also implies that they play a limited role in monitoring firms and that they are less significant corporate governance institutions than those in LMEs and CMEs. The financial institutions and corporate structure are mutually reinforcing. If external sources of finance are scarce or not available on sufficiently favourable terms (perhaps because the market is not deep enough), then firms will choose to rely on internal sources of finance.

This kind of institutional environment and the nature of financial institutions affect the kinds of firms that are most likely to succeed and thrive. As financial markets tend to be less developed than in many other market economies, the firms that are able to mobilize sufficient internal resources to finance investments are most likely to thrive. The two kinds of corporate entities considered by Schneider, business groups and MNEs, are uniquely well placed to do this, which reinforces their dominant market position. By contrast, new firms or domestic firms that are not part of a business group are likely to find it harder to finance their activities.

As noted by many authors (e.g. Fligstein and Choo 2005), family-owned businesses tend to be the most prominent model in much of the developing world. In these firms there is not generally a sharp distinction between ownership and control, as the family owners often play an active role in the management of the firms. In addition to the relatively shallow financial markets, a key factor underpinning this outcome is also risk minimization. Family ownership and control make rapid responses to shocks possible. In uncertain economic environments, diversification also reduces risk, if profits and losses are uncorrelated across the sectors that are part of the business group. This means that a negative shock to one sector within the business group may be offset by stronger performance in another sector.

Multinationals operate in a similar way. As noted above, they are generally relatively independent of local financial markets, as they can draw on other sources of finance. They may in effect sometimes be seen as enclaves in that they are separate from much of the rest of the economy. This is particularly true of firms active in natural resource extraction, which does not rely on a large number of workers or local institutions (see also Chapter 8).

Labour markets: Atomized labour relations and the low-skill trap

Labour markets in hierarchical market economies are also distinctive. Schneider characterizes the system as representing 'atomized labour relations', which differ from LMEs and CMEs in several respects. Schneider highlights five important and interrelated features of HME labour markets (Schneider 2013: 92–7).

First, formal labour market regulation is high, as demonstrated by the scores on many relevant indices, especially related to job security and unemployment protection (Botero et al. 2004; Heckman and Pagés 2000). Several studies have found that dismissal costs are higher in Latin America than in developed countries, including both LMEs and CMEs (cf. Schneider and Karcher 2010: 627–9).

Second, there is significant informality. This means that only a relatively small proportion of workers is covered by formal labour market regulations. It is also associated with high segmentation of the labour market, where a smaller 'labour aristocracy' of workers enjoy secure and relatively well-paid jobs and the benefits of high labour market regulation, whereas others are in a more fragile position. Informality could be viewed as closely related to the high levels of labour market regulation, in that informality offers firms the opportunity to circumvent regulations that are perceived as costly or onerous.

Third, job tenure is very low, indeed even lower than in LMEs. Schneider and Karcher (2010: 630) mention that median job tenure in CMEs was 7.4 years, whereas it was 5 years in LMEs and only about 3 years in Latin American HMEs.

Fourth, unionization rates are also relatively low, and indeed generally even lower than in LMEs. Therefore, unions play a relatively limited role in labour market governance, and to the extent that they have influence, this has generally been channelled into political bargaining, either to extract concessions from the state or to exercise direct influence on policymaking via union-party ties (Etchemendy and Collier 2007). Unions are primarily perceived to represent labour market insiders on formal contracts. Employers' associations have generally been too weak or unrepresentative to engage in bargaining with unions. This is further underpinned by firm strategies that prioritize low-cost production and flexible adjustment, which reduces incentives for cooperation with unions of the kind that is common in CMEs.

Fifth, there is limited investment in education and training. For example, the average years of schooling among adults in Latin America of 5.7 years in 2000 fell well below corresponding figures in CMEs (9.9 years) and LMEs (11 years) (Schneider 2013: 97). The patterns are even starker with respect to vocational training, notably for the unemployed, to which Latin American governments devoted only 0.04 per cent of GDP, compared to 0.23 per cent in LMEs and 0.52 per cent in CMEs (Schneider 2013: 98). Later research has qualified these findings somewhat and distinguished between skill profiles in Latin America by distinguishing between four types of skill supply profiles in Latin America, namely universalizing, dual academic-oriented, dual vocational education and training-oriented (VET) and exclusionary (Bogliaccini and Madariaga 2020). This provides a more nuanced account of the skill systems in Latin America and analyses the political roots of these institutions. This analysis does not necessarily invalidate the core observation of the HME model that strengthening the provision of skills in the economies of the region would be an important policy priority, but it draws attention to the importance of studying variation within the Latin American region. Whilst there has been variation in the degree of generosity, welfare states have generally been highly stratified and segmented, with uneven provision reflecting an urban bias that largely favour the formal sector and insiders (Haggard and Kaufman 2008). Since the 1990s processes of liberalization have transformed welfare states across Latin America to a varying degree, but the early 2000s were a period of expanding social policy provisions and declining poverty and inequality (Holland and Schneider 2017). However, the welfare state generally remains segmented (Ferre 2023).

These five features of labour markets are mutually reinforcing. For example, informality makes it easier for firms to circumvent stringent labour market regulations, and it also makes it easier to lay off workers. This also contributes to shorter job tenure and thereby reduces incentives to train workers, as the returns on such investments are likely to be low if workers leave the firm. This fluidity also reduces incentives for more collaborative industrial relations.

Complementarities and economic outcomes

Whilst these strategies of multinational enterprises and business groups may make sense given the situation they are in, not least as a strategy of risk management, Schneider also demonstrates that there may be negative complementarities. As discussed in Chapter 1, one of the main criticisms of the account of complementarities in the core VoC models is that the concept provides a rather simple view of the relationship between institutions – namely that complementary institutions enhance economic performance. However, we also know that not all economies are equally successful and that institutions may arise for a variety of reasons, such as the pursuit of power or other social or political objectives. One of the key innovations of Schneider's version of VoC theory is that he demonstrates how there may be a self-reinforcing pattern of negative complementarities – in which a web of institutions is maintained over time, despite the fact that they are also associated with suboptimal economic performance in many respects.

There are three closely related outcomes that are worth discussing in more detail. Whilst standard VoC theory as developed by Hall and Soskice (2001a) shows how mutually reinforcing institutions generate distinctive paths to economic success in CMEs and LMEs, Schneider's model shows how complementary institutions can also lock in suboptimal outcomes.

The first one is what Schneider (2013) refers to as the *low-skill trap*. This trap relates to the fact that there are limited investments in education and training, which contributes to locking these countries into relatively low-skill and low value-added sectors. MNEs tend to specialize in activities that do not require an abundant supply of highly skilled workers, as the most skill-intensive activities usually take place in the home country or elsewhere in the Global North. Yet as long as such sectors dominate the economy, it may be rational for individual workers not to invest in further education, training and skill acquisition, given how hard it is to find jobs that provide an adequate return on investments in higher skills. This highlights the need to provide not just an adequate supply of highly skilled workers, but also the importance of ensuring that there is a demand for such skills. In this sense, the economic structure and the skill system are mutually reinforcing, which makes skill-intensive growth difficult to achieve, although there is considerable variation across the region in this regard (Bogliaccini and Madariaga 2020).

The second key outcome is relatively *limited innovation*, including limited investments in research and development, especially by the private sector. Multinational enterprises do not generally conduct R&D in HMEs, and with only a few exceptions, business groups tend not to be involved with R&D activities either. Cemex (Mexico), Techint (Argentina), and Embraer (Brazil) have been some of the most notable exceptions (Schneider 2013: 66). Another important trend across Latin America relates to the fact that the *grupos* that do invest in R&D increasingly do so abroad (Schneider 2013: 67)

Limited innovation also relates to the third key consequence, the *middle-income trap*, which applies to the economy as a whole and which has received extensive attention both in the academic literature and policy debates. The middle-income trap captures the fact that there are many countries that have been categorized as middle-income economies for a prolonged period of time, but that have struggled to graduate to the high-income bracket (Doner and Schneider 2016). It is widely acknowledged that research and development and high skills are crucial to knowledge-intensive production and upgrading. This facilitates specialization in sectors with high value-added, sustainable growth and incomes that rise beyond the middle-income trap. A large proportion of the economies that have been viewed as facing the middle-income trap are hierarchical market economies. This outcome can be related to the negative complementarities discussed in this chapter, not least limited skill investment and innovation, which means that low value-added sectors predominate within these economies. As Doner and Schneider (2016) demonstrate, it is often economically and above all politically difficult to make the investment needed to facilitate this kind of transformation.

Chile as an HME

Chile has long been viewed as a poster child of neoliberalism, as the influence of Chicago economists on economic liberalization programmes during General Augusto Pinochet's time in power in the 1970s and 1980s is well known (Silva 1993; Valdés 1995). During this time a variety of economic reforms ranging from privatization, macroeconomic stabilization, liberalization to pension reform were introduced (Armijo and Faucher 2002). Since the 1970s, Chile's economic policy regime has consistently been characterized by a greater market orientation than other Latin American countries (Mesa-Lago 2003).

Yet these reforms have not turned Chile into an LME. The Chilean economy fits the HME model very well, as it has for a long time. As in the past, large family-led business groups dominate the economy, and many of them are still highly diversified (Lefort 2010; Schneider 2009). It should be noted that only a small number of the groups, notably Matte, Angelini and Luksic, have survived all the transformations of the Chilean economy since the 1960s (Lefort

2010: 392). Yet, whilst there have been some changes in the fortunes of individual *grupos*, the dominance of the business group as an organizational form remains intact. The most prominent business groups tend to fall into two categories. First, many key business groups have prospered thanks to their involvement with the natural resource sector. This includes Matte and Angelini, two of the most prominent and long-standing *grupos* in Chile. Second, other *grupos*, like Falabella or the D&S Group (controlled by the Ibañez family) started out in retail and expanded into other spheres, such as financial services. In addition, it should also be noted that many subsidiaries of multinationals that are active in Chile, such as Santander Chile or ENDESA, have adopted business practices that are very similar to those of domestic *grupos*. This reinforces the general impression that HME institutions shape corporate behaviour and organization in Chile (Lefort 2010: 416), and whilst the market reforms have helped reduce the role of direct state intervention, they have not led to market coordination, but rather consolidated business dominance, especially the role of *grupos*.

Since the economic liberalization programmes also led to a rise in private pension funds and a growth in stock market capitalization, there was a general expectation that liberalization should be associated with a decline in business groups (Fligstein and Choo 2005). Deeper financial markets should have led to more competition and also enhanced the opportunities and incentives to specialize. Alongside the general free-market orientation, this was expected to move Chile closer to LME-style financial institutions and corporate governance practices. However, such liberalization has also created new incentives for family businesses to expand their activities, either by getting involved with the privatization of state-owned firms or by entering new sectors, as retailers have done when they have begun providing financial services to their customers (Lefort 2015: 414–5). Indeed, far from disappearing, business groups seem to have been strengthened and become more numerous as a result of the liberalization process.

However, corporate governance arrangements still correspond to the HME model. Although dual-class shares are rare in Chile, the other key characteristics of HME corporate governance are very common in Chilean business groups. Owners are generally highly involved with the day-to-day management of the firms within the group and also use a variety of tools, including pyramids and cross-holdings to retain control over the company and marginalize the influence of minority shareholders.

The key features of the HME model also characterize Chilean labour markets well. On virtually all the dimensions relevant to such institutions, such as labour market regulation, job tenure and turnover, unionization and skills development, Chile places close to the average level among Latin American HMEs (Schneider 2013). The only exception to this is the degree of informality, which is considerably lower in Chile than elsewhere in Latin America (Schneider 2013: 174). On the other hand, despite several decades associated with neoliberalism, not least under General Pinochet, Chile's labour regulation is still rated as relatively restrictive – and there is a relatively high share of temporary contracts in the economy, in large part to circumvent these regulations.

It should be noted that Chile has been making sustained attempts to break out of the low-skill equilibrium in recent years. These attempts have focused on stimulating innovation, but above all on expanding education. This has been associated with considerable increases in both public and private education spending, especially targeting secondary education, which accounts for about 85 per cent of public spending. However, there have also been dramatic increases in higher education enrolments (Schneider 2013: 175). Improvements in general skill provision associated with expanded secondary and university education might be moving Chile closer to the LME model. Whilst there are some notable successes, such as the improvement in

PISA scores, the outcomes of these reforms and the associated increase in the supply of skills remain controversial (Bogliaccini and Madariaga 2020). On balance they have so far been insufficient to help Chile fully break out of the institutional equilibrium associated with an HME, at least for the time being. Whilst there are many reasons for this outcome, one of the most important factors relates to the increase in inequality in education and skills associated with these reforms (Torche 2005). This is likely to have attenuated the distributional impact one might have expected from such an improvement in skills and education. More generally, this illustrates one of the key insights of the HME model and VoC analysis more generally, namely that changes in one area may fail to generate the intended outcomes if complementary institutions do not change accordingly. Therefore, Chile is still very close to the general regional patterns of labour market institutions and outcomes (Schneider 2013).

In summary, whilst Chile does deviate from the Latin American pattern in some respects, it is a very good example of an HME overall. Whilst the fortunes of individual *grupos* have waxed and waned, the organizational form of the business group has persisted over time and survived radical changes in the policy regime. Given the existence of relatively programmatic parties and a relatively high quality of its public administration and governance practices, Chile may be better placed than many other Latin American countries to overcome the middle-income trap, especially if the recent emphasis on technology policy and education becomes highly institutionalized. However, so far progress has been regarded as somewhat disappointing, in that the qualitative shift in the structure and productivity of the economy that many had hoped for has not materialized (Dingemans 2016).

South Africa as an HME

South Africa is in more ways than most countries a unique society and economy. Long defined by apartheid, a regime based on racial segregation and white-minority dominance of the economy and politics, South Africa has been called a case of 'internal colonization' (Wolpe 1975), in which two economies co-exist: an advanced economy for whites and a developing country economy for others. It has also been shaped by the importance of mining to the emergence and development of capitalism in South Africa (Feinstein 2005). Others have highlighted the centrality of the state, especially in the middle of the twentieth century (Hart and Padyachee 2013), but possibly also in the current era (Nölke and Claar 2013; Nölke et al. 2015). It is clear that a complete account of the nature of the South African case needs to pay attention to these factors, as they continue to shape its capitalist system. In particular, as discussed below, the legacies of apartheid still manifest themselves in contemporary South Africa.

As various analysts have concluded, there are some compelling reasons to view South Africa as a good example of an HME, especially during the apartheid era (Schneider 2013; Nattrass 2014). First, if we consider corporate governance and the financial system, it is clear that South Africa has many features of an HME. This was particularly obvious during the apartheid period when the economy was dominated by a small number of business groups. In most cases the key groups were under family control, including the Oppenheimers (Anglo American and de Beers), Ruperts (Rembrandt), Gordons (Liberty), and the Menells and Hersovs (AngloVaal) (Goldstein 2010: 551; Padayachee 2013a: 263). The biggest groups dominated the economy and cross-shareholdings and pyramidal schemes ensured internal control over the group. 'In 1994, the gold-mining giant Anglo American controlled 43 per cent of the entire Johannesburg Securities

Exchange (JSE) capitalisation – and the top five groups controlled 84 per cent through complex cross-holdings and preferential shares' (Nattrass 2014: 61).

South African labour markets also correspond quite well to many features of the HME model, and though there are some distinctive features related to the legacies of apartheid, post-apartheid reforms and other influences, they can be regarded as a hybrid where various forms of coordination co-exist. There is relatively stringent labour regulation and some collective bargaining institutions in the formal sector, notably Nedlac, which plays a significant role in social dialogue (Nattrass 2014). Labour markets are highly segmented based on the degree of informality and on racial grounds, and unions primarily represent workers in the formal sector (Nölke et al. 2020: 165). Whilst labour market segmentation often has a racial dimension in Latin America, the racial underpinnings of labour market segmentation in South Africa were more explicit and highly institutionalized under apartheid rule. This was also underpinned by a highly fragmented education system, which provided high-quality education for whites and generally low-quality education for other groups, especially Blacks. These legacies shape the contemporary economic system as well. Whilst a more unified education system was introduced after apartheid, the education system does not deliver an adequate level of skill provision, and it remains highly fragmented and unequal. University fees imply that Blacks are underrepresented in higher education due to the costs and more limited financing (Nölke et al. 2020). According to the World Bank's comparative data on inequality of disposable income across countries (based on the most recent observations, as of April 2024), South Africa has the highest rate of income inequality in the world, with a Gini coefficient of 63.

After the collapse of apartheid there were various initiatives that could have moved South Africa away from the HME model. Some of these developments could have been expected to turn South Africa into an LME, especially with respect to corporate governance. Financialization and greater emphasis on shareholder value along with the rise of private equity firms contributed to the unbundling of business groups and facilitated splitting them up into component parts (Karwowski, Fine and Ashman 2018). This has also led to greater internationalization of the South African economy. The influential reports of the King Commission on Corporate Governance led to the introduction of LME-style reporting and transparency standards and the naming of more outside directors. Business groups also control a much smaller share of the stock market (Nattrass 2014).

By contrast, at the end of apartheid many people thought that the political changes might augur the beginning of a more egalitarian form of capitalism that might bear some resemblance to the social democratic CMEs in Europe or even a novel form of Ubuntu capitalism drawing on traditional communal values (Andreasson 2011), notably by strengthening unions and establishing the National Economic Development and Labour Council (Nedlac) (Webster 2013: 213ff.). Such changes could have given rise to a more community-oriented and egalitarian form of capitalism that takes a wider range of stakeholder interests into account. More generally, a programme of Black Economic Empowerment (BEE) was designed to counteract racial inequality in the economic sphere, which includes a range of measures to diversify ownership and improve economic opportunities.

Whilst the cumulative effect of the post-apartheid changes implies that South Africa fits the HME model somewhat less well than in the past, the degree of change should not be overstated. First, there is considerable evidence that informal business groups' ties and influence persist (Padayachee 2013a). Whilst groups have undergone significant change and reduced their involvement with mining, they have not disappeared. For example, Rembrandt has been reconfigured into two largely separate, but still diversified, business groups (Goldstein 2010:

561). Second, whilst there have been some changes in industrial relations that strengthened the role of collective bargaining and improved the representation and influence of unions, the policy impact of social dialogue tends to be modest, partly due to divisions both on the business and union side (Nattrass 2014). Many of the fundamental HME features are arguably intact, and income inequality remains exceptionally high. A factor aggravating inequality is the high level of unemployment, which is also affected by the relatively small informal labour market, a key factor differentiating South Africa from HMEs in Latin America (Nattrass 2014: 62). Critics of BEE argue that the particular reforms that were introduced have amounted to redistribution towards well connected Blacks (and effectively cronyism), but given the role of interlocking directorates this could also be viewed as the emergence of new black business groups. However, BEE reforms have not achieved all the goals its supporters had hoped for; sceptical assessments suggest that they have not created strong small and medium businesses that could have helped create better jobs for Black South Africans, alleviate inequality or stimulate higher economic growth rates (Padayachee 2013b). Ubuntu ideas have often served as a justification for neoliberal policies of market liberalization (McDonald 2010). Others have been more cautious and suggested that the ownership concentration among Black South Africans may not be that high from a comparative perspective, but it remains to be seen how high this concentration may become in the future and whether it will contribute to the emergence of stronger 'black business groups' and better economic performance (Goldstein 2010).

In summary, whilst the HME model characterizes many key features of the South African economy, it does not fit the model in all respects. Especially in light of the key post-apartheid changes many analysts regard the South African economy as a hybrid (Nölke et al. 2020) or as an idiosyncratic version of capitalism (Nattrass 2014; Padayachee 2013b).

The politics of HMEs

What are the political underpinnings of the HME model? Given that the previous sections demonstrated that it does not typically ensure the greatest economic success, one may ask why these institutions persist. Schneider's discussion of Latin America stresses two components in particular.

The first component includes the key actors with a stake in the current arrangements. It is generally the case that any institutional arrangement generates both winners and losers, and winners can be expected to support the arrangement that benefits them. Who benefits from HME institutions? The most obvious winners are the two kinds of firms who tend to prosper in HMEs, namely diversified business groups and multinational enterprises.

As they are well adapted to existing institutions, they may not see any compelling reason to push for change. Whilst some of them could potentially reap even bigger profits from a high-skill equilibrium, there may be several reasons for them not to advocate this. In the short run a move towards a high-skill equilibrium would be associated with considerable costs and uncertain gains. First, it is not clear that groups would be the only actors to benefit – and they might lose their competitive edge if faced with a variety of new entrants. Second, given the interdependences and complementarities of various institutions, change in one area may be undesirable unless accompanied by changes in others. To the extent that firms may have to lobby for reforms in one or two areas at a time, they may abstain from it, given the low likelihood of success and the even lower likelihood of achieving changes across multiple institutional domains at once. In the absence of a wider range of complementary institutions, the return on greater skill investments may be negative, if it generates substantial costs without any corresponding increase in profits.

The second key component focuses on the ways in which the interests favouring existing arrangements are represented politically. It is not sufficient to explore the preferences in favour of a certain set of policies. Unless these interests are articulated and represented in the political system, they are unlikely to have any direct effect on outcomes.

There are many reasons to expect business interests to be well represented in politics. The literature on business power – both in its Marxist and more recent varieties – tends to identify various reasons why business tends to be successful in terms of advancing its interests. In part this is related to the notions of structural power – that is, the structural dependence of the state on business to generate investments and growth (Culpepper and Reinke 2014; Przeworski and Wallerstein 1988). Given that many of the policies that are most important to business are low-salience issues, because of their technical or obscure nature, skilful business lobbies tend to have a further advantage (Culpepper 2011). Business influence is also enhanced by instrumental power, including lobbying, campaign contributions as well as close personal ties. Many of these policies are also likely to enjoy the support of the 'labour aristocracy', i.e. the workers who have secure and well-paid jobs and who are often covered by regular contracts and represented by trade unions (Schneider 2013; Rueda 2007).

In addition to these factors, which exist to a greater or lesser extent in most countries, Schneider and Soskice (2009) highlight another set of political factors that play an important role in augmenting business influence. This relates to the unique combination of a majoritarian presidency alongside legislatures elected by means of proportional representation (PR) that exists in most Latin American countries. Such a system is rare beyond Latin America. Since the president rarely enjoys a majority in parliament, there tends to be a need to build shifting alliances to get the legislative agenda passed. The PR system in turn facilitates the representation of a variety of specific and local interests, which could also include sometimes very narrow business interests (Schneider 2013: 141–2). In many cases such representation is also tied up with clientelism, which refers to 'the direct exchange of a citizen's vote in return for direct payments or continuing access to employment, goods, and services' (Kitschelt and Wilkinson 2007: 2). In such cases it serves particular interests and does not necessarily enhance general welfare. In other words, it is likely to differ from the effects of specific interest representation in CME, which is often perceived to facilitate cross-class coalitions, consensus democracy and a variety of good economic outcomes (see Chapter 3).

However, it should also be noted that political institutions and political regimes do not seem to be the most crucial determinant of HME institutions. In many countries HME institutions have persisted over long stretches of time and survived several regime changes in countries, like Chile, where the role of business groups was significant under General Pinochet, but also under various political systems both before and after Pinochet's military regime. This is consistent with the structural power of business and the ability of these actors to influence politics under any political regimes, given their centrality to the economy. Such powerful economic actors may also adjust their strategies to consolidate their influence under different political and economic conditions. For example, business groups were the dominant corporate form in Chile and Turkey both during periods of import-substituting industrialization and more globally oriented development strategies.

There are a variety of avenues that businesses can pursue to influence policymakers. Some of the most important ones in Latin America are judicial tools, such as challenges to unfavourable legislation, access to the bureaucracy as well as propagation of key policy ideas via think-tanks and the media (Schneider 2013: 145–9). Some of these are funded by business associations, notably in Chile, where they are stronger than in many other parts of Latin America and where direct lobbying of politicians has been harder, especially under the centre-left Concertación administrations in the 1990s and early 2000s. In South Africa leading businesspeople have generally had good access to politicians, as even President Mandela is reported to have met regularly with Harry Oppenheimer (Waldmeir 1997).

Multinationals are generally perceived to be less influential in politics than business groups. Indeed, Schneider even speaks of their mousiness and lack of political activity or active lobbying. They tend not to join business associations, and even if they do, they are usually less active in them. However, by drawing on Hirschman's famous distinction between exit and voice, we can see that the role of multinationals is likely to be more complex. Whilst they may not use 'voice' to influence policymaking in an equally active and structured way as the business groups do, this does not mean that they do not influence politics and economic policymaking. Indeed, the fact that they are less rooted and integrated into the political economy means that the potential threat of exit is potentially more credible. This means that the threat of exit by multinationals may deter the introduction of policies that could adversely affect these companies. Most importantly, given that they have entered HMEs to take advantage of existing conditions, they do not necessarily have any incentive to push for change and can be viewed as a part of a coalition favouring the status quo (Schneider 2013: 86).

Debating the HME model

The HME model is an important extension of the VoC framework and adds a lot to our understanding of capitalist diversity. First, by focusing on the role of hierarchy, it incorporates one of the most important coordination mechanisms that had received limited attention in the previous literature. Given the centrality of hierarchy and of both multinational enterprises and business groups to the functioning of many economies in Latin America and elsewhere around the world, it is possible to expand the remit of the VoC framework well beyond the traditional OECD countries and get closer to a more accurate understanding of the range of capitalist systems at a global level.

Second, it also helps the VoC literature move beyond the focus on economic success. The LME, CME and NME models discussed in previous chapters are generally associated with positive complementarities, which means that they can explain the successful economic performance of many OECD countries in North America, Western Europe and East Asia. Their institutions provide the foundation for economic efficiency based on comparative institutional advantage. This focus on the success and efficiency of different economic models is important and serves to challenge the idea that there is only one path to economic success and that other kinds of institutions should be seen as deviations from best practice. However, it is well known that there is great variation in economic performance across countries. By focusing only on successful varieties, the original VoC model does not provide a comprehensive account of the institutional foundations of economic performance. The HME model provides a detailed analysis of the mutually reinforcing institutions in a wide range of countries. It demonstrates that such complementarities have distinctive effects that can explain suboptimal outcomes in some respects. Given the importance of complementarities and interactions between institutions, it also demonstrates how limited reforms may fail to change the functioning of the system as a whole and why some reform initiatives have been less successful than one might have hoped. This highlights how the institutional framework can also help account for the high levels of inequality in HMEs, especially in Latin America (Hoffman and Centeno 2003; Kaufman 2009). However, this does not imply that all reforms are doomed: even piecemeal reforms could succeed, as long as they are well designed and take the constraints related to the institutional context into account.

The HME model contributes to the institutional turn of development studies (Kingstone 2018), by showing the importance of domestic institutions and the constraints on economic development that result from them. Many accounts of Latin American capitalism tend to analyse the big transformations in the region associated with big shifts in the role of the state, notably the move away from the guiding role it played during the period of import-substituting industrialization (ISI) that lasted from the 1930s until the early 1980s in most countries (the precise timings vary across countries). The subsequent neoliberal era is consequently viewed as a period of globalization and a small state. Yet as this chapter has demonstrated, such a stark juxtaposition of the statist ISI era and the market-oriented period of neoliberal globalization may overstate the degree of change. There are important elements of continuity in firm structure, corporate governance and labour markets. Whilst the fortunes of individual firms have waxed and waned, the centrality of business groups as a corporate form has not been undermined by these shifts, although the role of specific groups has sometimes changed, as some conglomerates have lost their leading role and been replaced by other successful performers. Like dependency theory, the HME model analyses the role of foreign capital and investments and demonstrates the complex ways in which this shapes domestic institutions and growth prospects. This helps clarify why foreign investment may be associated with growth and development, but also with limited upgrading and investments in R&D.

These continuities might also help account for the sometimes disappointing outcomes of market reform, which have not always generated the marked improvements in economic growth or distributional outcomes that many of its proponents had been hoping for (Kaufman 2009; Kingstone 2018). Greater emphasis on the nature and complementarities of these institutions can help explain some of the constraints on reform and development. In particular, the systemic approach shows why reform in one area may not have the desired effect if other related institutions and economic incentives remain unchanged. For example, increasing the provision of education and training may not be sufficient for moving economies away from a low-skill equilibrium if there is inadequate demand for such skills in the labour market.

Another important question related to the HME model relates to its wider applicability. Schneider has shown that it can account for key features of capitalist economies across much of Latin America. In addition, Schneider (2013: 5) has indicated that the model could fit a number of economies across various parts of the world, including Thailand, South Africa and Turkey, and Hertog has suggested that it may apply more widely across the Global South. In principle, this is very plausible, not least given the dominant role of business groups in many economies (Hertog 2023).

Turkey has received systematic attention from the perspective of comparative capitalism. Whilst some studies have emphasized the hybrid nature of Turkish capitalism (Özel 2014), Kıran (2018) argues that Turkey can be regarded as a good example of an HME. Kıran highlights four key features: the dominance of family-owned diversified business groups, state-dominated but weak industrial relations, low skills and the role of foreign direct investment (FDI). This model has complex historical roots, as the business groups grew in tandem with attempts to build a national bourgeoisie in the era of import-substituting industrialization in the mid-twentieth century. The composition of the business sector evolved in the early twenty-first century as a result of the growth of the 'Anatolian Tigers', a set of medium-size firms with close ties to the AK Party. Some of these firms have grown into large businesses. Foreign direct investment grew during a period of liberalization in the late twentieth century. The industrial relations and labour market regime combines strict regulation with a degree of informality, and the union movement is relatively weak and constrained by various legal provisions on protest and organization. The high degree of informality has served as a barrier to skill acquisition in a way that resembles the Latin American cases but the Justice and Development Party governments implemented changes in vocational education and training in the early 2000s that promoted business involvement and skill acquisition and that benefited many small and medium-sized enterprises (Sancak 2020).

More generally, if the HME model captures key features of many economies across the Global South, then it is important to understand differences between economies sharing some of its core features and to explore how different kinds of hierarchies within business groups, the state and multinational enterprises interact with both domestic and global markets in different economies (see also Feldmann 2019; Carney 2016).

Hertog's (2023) model of segmented market economies (SEMEs) is an example of such research. The core logic of the SEME model and the emphasis on labour market segmentation within this model resemble the HME model, so one might regard the SEMEs as special cases or sub-varieties of HMEs or as a separate variety. Hertog devised the SEME model to analyse key Middle Eastern economies, with Algeria, Egypt and (pre-Civil War) Syria fitting the model particularly well, but he also shows that Tunisia, Jordan and Morocco share key features of the model to a considerable extent. This is a very important empirical extension of the VoC debate that helps integrate a region that is often neglected in comparative capitalism scholarship, despite its great significance.

The SEME model has several key characteristics (Hertog 2023: chapter 3). First, it has what Hertog calls an 'overextended state'. This means that public employment rates (usually about 20–40 per cent in SEMEs) are considerably higher than in Latin America and other regions in the Global South (Hertog 2023: 29). In addition, the state imposes stringent regulation of labour markets and plays an active role in other ways, such as by disbursing access to land and imposing protectionist trade barriers. Second, and perhaps most importantly, SEMEs have segmented labour markets. There are three key segments – the formal public, formal private and informal private labour markets, with the public sector playing a dominant role in formal employment. There are marked differences in pay and welfare provisions between these segments, with formal public employment conferring a privileged insider status. There is very limited mobility between segments, which is underpinned by regulation, state employment policies, nepotism and more effective interest representation by insiders in public employment. Third, SEME have segmented business systems, which means that there is a significant insider-outsider divide between privileged large firms, typically with preferential access to the state, and other businesses. Hertog argues that these patterns of segmentation in business and labour markets contribute to inefficiencies and misallocation of resources. Given that insiders are better organized and outsiders are a fragmented set of actors, it is hard to see any strong reform coalition emerging. Fourth, SEMEs have distinctive skill systems. The segmented nature of the labour markets provides very limited incentives for skill acquisition, and employment practices in the public sector tend to put a premium on formal credentials rather than relevant skills. Taken together, these four factors contribute to low growth and dynamism, as key paths to productivity improvements are foreclosed by the barriers that the rigid segmentation imposes.

Whilst the segmentation within labour markets is very similar to the contrast between formal and informal employment in HME, there is a much sharper divide between insiders and outsiders in SEMEs that is associated with greater segmentation of labour markets than in HMEs, and insiders typically enjoy more privileged and stable positions in SEMEs in relative terms. This is why the inefficiencies are typically more marked and economic performance can be expected to be sluggish. The key economies that the model has been applied to manifest low rates of economic growth.

Hertog (2023) demonstrates that a variety of factors contributed to the emergence of this model in the Middle East, including policies related to processes of state building in the 1950s and 1960s, and the public sector and core employees within it played an important part in this process. The persistence of these features is partly attributable to such historical legacies, but also to the political organization of the state, business and labour as key trade unions, like UGTT in Tunisia, largely advocate on behalf of insiders (Hertog 2023: 49).

Conclusion

In conclusion, this chapter has introduced the HME model, arguably the most important extension of the VoC framework beyond the core OECD countries. It has demonstrated that it provides an excellent starting point for understanding the nature of institutions and economic performance in Latin America and across much of the Global South. Unlike much of the VoC literature which has been castigated for being excessively focused on economic efficiency, the HME model highlights the ways in which institutional complementarities may constrain economies and contribute to suboptimal performance or phenomena, like the middle-income trap. The SEME model considers even starker segmentation and deeper insider-outsider divides, where the effects on economic performance are even sharper. Such differences and the nature of the institutions more generally can be traced back to historical legacies and the political organization of the state and the representation of key economic actors. These models show that institutions can interact in different complex ways and serve a range of purposes and should not necessarily be seen as guaranteeing economic efficiency.

Discussion questions

- The HME model is often described as a model that could account for capitalism across various parts of the Global South – how convincing is it as a general model of developing economies?
- To what extent can the HME model explain the middle-income trap?
- What are the main political underpinnings of the HME model?
- How convincing is the SEME model as an account of Middle Eastern economies? Should it be regarded as a separate model or as a sub-type of the HME model?
- To what extent do the HME and SEME models ignore the role of the international economy?

6

Dependent market economies

This chapter discusses an important extension of VoC theory, namely the dependent market economy (DME) model developed by Andreas Nölke and Arjan Vliegenthart (2009). It integrates key insights from classical dependency theory into a VoC model that analyses coordination mechanisms and institutional complementarities. This model extends the VoC literature by developing a model in which international actors play a greater role and key complementarities between firm decisions and institutions have a transnational dimension.

This chapter begins by introducing dependency theory and then discusses the core logic of the DME model as a fusion of dependency theory and VoC analysis. It then proceeds to consider how the DME model can shed light on the functioning of economies that are highly dependent on foreign direct investment (FDI). The primary examples of DMEs are Czechia, Hungary, Poland and Slovakia, four capitalist systems in East Central Europe, but the model has been applied to other economies in the region as well, including Romania (Ban 2019). The chapter then assesses the contributions of this approach and its relevance to understanding capitalist diversity in an age of globalization.

Background: Dependency theory

Dependency theory emerged as a distinctive set of ideas in the Marxist tradition of political economy, in part as a reaction to both mainstream accounts of economic development, notably associated with modernization theory, but it was also inspired by various Latin American traditions of economic analysis, such as the structuralism developed by CEPAL, the United Nations Economic Commission for Latin America and the Caribbean, under Raul Prebisch and Hans Singer in the 1950s and 1960s (Love 1990; Palma 1978). There are considerable differences between authors conventionally labelled as dependency theorists, and

> perhaps the only thing in common which all dependency analyses share is their interest in studying the situation of peripheral capitalist countries from the point of view of the conditioning effects which external forces and structures produce on the internal structures of these countries. (Larrain 1989: 112)

In other words, dependency theorists draw attention to the fact that countries located outside the core of the world economy are dependent, that is, peripheral countries are constrained by developments in the global economy and especially by the most powerful core that dominates it. Dependency theory seeks to explain the functioning of the global economy and its impact on economies in the periphery. In particular, many neo-Marxist strands of dependency theory have been very pessimistic about the prospects of development in the periphery, as captured by references to the 'development of underdevelopment' (Frank 2009). By contrast, the structuralist approach associated with Fernando Henrique Cardoso (Cardoso and Faletto 1979) is more open-ended and focused on analysing the historical forces shaping particular situations of dependency and on assessing their impact on the prospects for economic development, which vary across regions and countries in the periphery. Given the wide range of approaches associated with dependency theory as well as closely related debates, such as World Systems Theory, this chapter follows Kvangraven's (2021: 81) suggestion to regard dependency theory as a research programme with multiple strands that share four key features.

First, dependency theory is characterized by a *global historical approach*. Dependency theorists draw on an interdisciplinary approach that examines how social, economic and political processes unfold over time both at the domestic and global levels to shape patterns of dependency. Second, it draws on economic theorizing to account for the *polarizing tendencies* within the global economy, that is, the tendency for divergence between the centre and the periphery. In other words, it analyses specific mechanisms that contribute to inequality between economies and different regions of the world and that prevent convergence between them. Third, dependency theory analyses *structures of production*, that is, the nature of labour markets, financial markets, leading sectors as well as ownership and state structures. Fourth, the theory examines the *constraints* that economies face if they are located in a peripheral position in the world economy. This includes their exposure to international markets in terms of international trade, investment and financial flows. Some dependency theorists have highlighted extreme volatility, especially if such economies are dependent on the exports of primary products, such as natural resources or agricultural goods, that tend to experience price fluctuations, as well as the possibility of deteriorating terms of trade over time (dos Santos 1970). More generally, if countries are locked into unfavourable positions in the global division of labour and if any profits are repatriated by foreign investors to the benefit of big multinational enterprises in the core of the world economy, then dependent economies may not benefit fully from the economic activities within their borders. And even if they benefit, this merely occurs because it also serves the interests of the economic core or the most advanced economies that play a dominant role in the world economy, which underscores the centrality of such dependency. The dominant role of multinational enterprises and their domestic allies is a key manifestation of dependency.

Each of these four factors has received attention in the academic literature, but Kvangraven (2021) argues that it is the combination of these four features within one approach that makes dependency theory distinctive. She follows Cardoso (2009) in arguing that careful examination of the ways in which these factors interact in particular contexts can explain the prospects for growth and development and also why some peripheral economies, like South Korea, managed to achieve considerable success, whereas others struggle economically. Similarly, Kvangraven (2021) shows how dependency theory can shed light on other aspects of contemporary globalization, including the uneven distribution of gains from trade and investment in the context of globalized production or so-called 'global value chains' (see Chapter 12).

Understanding the DME model: Bridging dependency theory and VoC

The dependent market economy (DME) model was designed to integrate key insights from dependency theory into VoC analysis (Nölke and Vliegenthart 2009: 672). Whilst most contemporary economies are trade-dependent and reliant on the international economy, the DME model draws on dependency theory to analyse the impact of higher degrees of external dependence that are bound up with a position outside the centre of the world economy as well.

Whilst traditional VoC theory does address globalization and shows how economies respond to the opportunities provided by global markets, the relevant institutional framework is primarily domestic. National institutions shape the behaviour of firms and their involvement with global markets, including their ability to take advantage of international trading and investment opportunities. In other words, the global economy is part of the external environment that firms engage with and respond to, but the analytical focus is on the national level – which some critics have labelled as a form of 'methodological nationalism', as VoC analysis tends to pay less attention to sub- or supranational forces (Ebenau 2012).

What the dependent market economy model adds to VoC theory is a framework for understanding economies in which global actors and pressures play a much greater role and shape the functioning of the economy in a more fundamental way. The primary actors in the DME model are multinational enterprises (MNEs), whose headquarters are beyond the borders of the economies in question. This means that the relationship between these firms and the local economy is quite different from typical firms in the LME and CME models, for which national institutions are often paramount.

As in HMEs, the dominant coordination mechanism is hierarchy, in that key decisions are taken at the top of the hierarchies located at the corporate headquarters. The main difference from HMEs is the lack or at least relative insignificance of domestic business groups in DMEs. This means that external dependence and the predominance of international hierarchies within multinational enterprises are much more pronounced in DMEs than in HMEs. This creates a certain disconnect between domestic corporate governance institutions and the key economic actors in the economy that are internationally oriented.

On the one hand, multinational enterprises are much less reliant on the local economy, for example, for investment purposes. Such investment decisions are likely to be a small component of a global strategy that depends on a variety of complex considerations. These multinational enterprises may choose to raise investment funds in their home country, on global markets or draw on retained earnings from the global business. They are rarely listed on the local stock market of the DMEs in which they have invested. There is also a perception that they may be 'footloose' – in other words, they consider a range of possible investment locations and may choose to leave if economic conditions become less advantageous. Whilst domestic firms may also outsource their production, they are traditionally more embedded in their home country and its economy than foreign firms are.

On the other hand, given their importance to the functioning of DMEs, the local economy is very dependent on multinational enterprises. Economic institutions are often created or maintained to attract or at least to retain foreign investment. This might include infrastructure, special economic zones or specific features of the tax system, such as provisions for tax holidays or other inducements. It could also include features of education and training systems, if professional qualifications are designed to meet the employment needs of multinational enterprises. This relates to their importance as investors, employers and producers and may occur in the absence of active lobbying by these firms, if governments themselves seek to attract foreign investment by anticipating the concerns of multinational enterprises (Myant and Drahokoupil 2012).

The main purpose of the DME model is to account for the complementarities between the presence and strategies of MNEs and institutional arrangements in these economies, which can be regarded as mutually reinforcing. In other words, the nature and performance of DMEs are shaped by the centrality of MNEs, but the decision to locate production in DMEs is also determined by key features of these economies, including their institutional arrangements, associated policies and their position within the global economy. The DME model provides an account of these complementarities and their impact on such economies.

Corporate governance and financial systems

The distinctive features of corporate governance and financial systems of DMEs are related to the dependence on foreign capital, notably the centrality of foreign direct investment. For example, according to OECD statistics the stock of inward foreign investment in Czechia accounted for 70 per cent of GDP in 2022. Many of these foreign investors are likely to be multinational enterprises with a global reach or at least with extensive transnational networks and value chains. Whilst other countries have comparable levels of FDI, the importance of multinational enterprises is underscored by their centrality in terms of their important contribution to growth and exports.

Foreign investors bring their own sources of finance and use them to initiate and develop their projects. This makes them relatively independent of the financial markets of the DMEs in which they have invested. As in HMEs, multinational enterprises are likely to draw on retained earnings or access finance in their home country or on international markets. The subsidiaries are unlikely to be listed on the local stock market or to borrow extensively from DME banks.

On the other hand, these governance patterns are also underpinned by what is often a close relationship between the state and foreign investors. Bohle and Greskovits (2012) have referred to this as a form of 'embedded neoliberalism', as market activity is supported and 'embedded' by the state. Others have referred to these states as 'competition states' (Cerny 1997) or even as 'investment promotion machines' (Drahokoupil 2008), where state activity is designed to stimulate foreign investment at all costs, since this is seen as the principal key to economic prosperity. Associated tax breaks and investment inducements also serve to loosen financial constraints and uncertainties faced by foreign investors.

This is also reflected in the general structure of the financial system, as stock markets typically play a relatively limited role in the economy. The domestic banking system could also be undercapitalized, but the scarcity of financial capital is often offset by foreign ownership of banks. This enhances the role of foreign sources of credit in DMEs. Whilst the existence of foreign banks could be regarded as another dimension of dependency, which is likely to constrain the use of activist industrial and financial policy, other research has demonstrated that it has a number of advantages (Epstein 2014). In particular, if foreign banks do not leave in the aftermath of a crisis, their presence can stabilize the financial system and reduce the risk to the public finances associated with financial crises and bailouts.

Over time, the financial and corporate governance systems of DMEs have also been more influenced by international initiatives, such as European corporate governance standards. Some of these international practices have also been introduced by international financial actors, notably the foreign banks that control large market shares of the banking sectors in all DMEs and seek to introduce some of the standards they are familiar with.

Labour markets

Labour markets in DMEs differ from the two canonical VoC models in several respects. As noted by Nölke and Vliegenthart (2009: 684), neither LME-style flexible labour markets (see Chapter 2) nor corporatist arrangements typical of CMEs (see Chapter 3) can be found in DMEs.

Compared to CMEs, industrial relations are decentralized and characterized by weak unions and limited negotiations between organized labour and employers. Membership rates in unions and employers' associations are relatively low, and especially unionization rates fell very rapidly in the decades following the collapse of communism. Out of the four key DMEs, Poland has the highest unionization rate, and it was only 13.4 per cent in 2017 (the most recent year for which OECD/AIAS data are available). Although all of these countries developed corporatist institutions facilitating some negotiations between employers and organized labour in the 1990s, their significance has been limited. Some observers have even labelled these arrangements as cases of 'illusory corporatism' (Ost 2000).

Yet this does not mean that these countries have a system matching the LME model. Labour market regulation and the formal rules regarding layoffs and redundancies are relatively strict, though it is generally easier to circumvent them than in CMEs (Botero et al. 2004).

Multinationals generally seek to avoid the high turnover that is common in many LMEs, as they rely on a stable and relatively skilled labour force. Given that foreign investors seek out such a work force in these economies, some 'appeasement of skilled labour' is common (Nölke and Vliegenthart 2009: 680). This entails paying relatively high wages, and it could also include some collective agreements at the firm level. Drahokoupil and Myant (2012) have shown that labour relations are often less confrontational and more favourable to workers in multinational enterprises than in domestic firms in DMEs, and in that sense FDI protects them from more stringent free-market policies.

However, this does not extend to extensive investments in education and training, as the main appeal lies in a relatively skilled but also inexpensive workforce. The education systems put relatively high emphasis on vocational skills and to a considerable extent already at the secondary level. Greater investments in education and skills could undermine some of the cost advantages that the multinational enterprises see as a key attraction of East Central Europe. Therefore, the model relies to a considerable extent on past investments in education and skill development as well as reasonably good public education systems imparting good foundational skills. A number of studies have questioned whether these systems could support a development strategy based on more knowledge-intensive sectors without very significant new investments and institutional changes in their education and innovation systems (Tarlea and Freyberg-Inan 2018).

Complementarities and economic outcomes

A key difference compared to many traditional accounts of dependent development, which are often quite pessimistic about the prospects for development, is that the DME model has been perceived as relatively successful so far. There is wide agreement that the four Visegrád countries – Czechia, Hungary, Poland and Slovakia – have been more successful than most of the other post-communist economies, such as most of the former Soviet Union (apart from the Baltic States) or South-Eastern Europe, for example.

The roots of the relative success of the DMEs can be related to the core features of the model. The key institutions are relatively coherent and facilitate these countries' comparative advantage in the assembly and production of complex and durable consumer goods, such as cars or electronics (Nölke and Vliegenthart 2009: 672). This turns them into assembly platforms for multinational enterprises that benefit from institutional complementarities between several key elements, as outlined above. First, DMEs have skilled, but relatively cheap labour. Second, FDI facilitates the transfer of technological innovations within multinational enterprises as well as the provision of capital (Nölke and Vliegenthart 2009: 672). In addition to the complementary structure of labour and financial systems, these DMEs are in countries that have other favourable characteristics, notably a geographical location close to important markets that facilitates integration into global production networks. These processes have created some trans-border clusters in East Central Europe given the proximity of the industrial regions in the four DMEs (Hancke 2012). In the East Central European countries, EU membership has been an important element of this process as well, as it has ensured easy access to the common European market.

Whilst this model has contributed to high economic growth since the early 1990s, it has also contributed to economic inequality, especially across regions within these countries. As the FDI-dominated sectors have been the most dynamic ones and tend to be concentrated in specific regions, this has meant that other parts of these countries, such as Eastern Poland and Eastern Hungary, have experienced less growth and prosperity than other parts of these countries.

Although the DME model has been viewed as relatively successful so far, there is more uncertainty surrounding the medium-term prospects of this model (Nölke and Vliegenthart 2009: 674). There are two core concerns.

First, given the dependence on FDI, the risk of losing foreign investment is a potential challenge to the model. This may be a significant concern, especially in successful DMEs, as high growth could lead to higher wages and undermine the advantages based on low costs that these economies have enjoyed. Given that wages and production costs are lower in much of Asia and various other parts of the world, the potentially footloose nature of foreign investment has already received a lot of attention. Whilst foreign investors benefit from other features of these locations, especially their proximity to Western Europe and well-established supplier networks in the region, many other countries also seek to attract investment. Competition for foreign investment within East Central Europe itself is fierce, as countries are trying to outbid each other by offering additional inducements to potential investors.

Second, the other risk associated with the high dependence on FDI relates to the risk of the middle-income trap, as previously discussed in the context of HMEs (see Chapter 5). In the decades following the collapse of communism in 1989, foreign investment was a key engine of growth in East Central Europe. Indeed, most countries that initially put less emphasis on FDI, such as Czechia and Slovakia, eventually changed their economic policies to encourage more multinational enterprises to invest. There were many advantages associated with foreign investment. As these countries had limited investment funds and were undergoing a dramatic transformation of the economy, the investment capital of the multinational enterprises facilitated large-scale projects that would have been hard to implement or finance without their participation. In addition, the multinational enterprises brought new technologies, new forms of organization and marketing skills as well as access to international supplier and distribution networks, which made it easier to reorient economic activity in these countries to Western markets. Whilst this contributed to high growth and a successful transformation of these economies from the socialist systems of the old regime, it is less clear whether this will stimulate high growth in the long term or whether there is a risk of the middle-income trap, especially if there is limited upgrading once the East Central European DMEs no longer maintain their low-cost advantage. The evidence suggests that there is considerable variation in upgrading to more knowledge-intensive sectors, and out of the four economies discussed in this chapter Czechia was particularly successful in this regard in the 2010s (Győrffy 2022).

The lack of emphasis on innovation and on upgrading education and skill systems to facilitate the emergence of new sectors or high-quality jobs has received some attention from academics and policymakers. However, just as in the Latin American HMEs, the main risk is that individual workers or firms making such investments themselves may not be able to secure appropriate returns on these investments afterwards. The high rates of out-migration that some East Central European countries have experienced in the early twenty-first century, especially by young and highly educated workers, has also affected the economy-wide rates of return on public investments in education and skills. Such factors make the development of new high-tech sectors to replace some of the medium-tech sectors that have thrived in East Central Europe since the mid-1990s more uncertain, but there is increasingly an awareness that this is essential to their future economic success.

Hungary as a DME

One of the cases that has been described as coming particularly close to the ideal type of a DME is Hungary. This section looks at the core features of the Hungarian political economy, explores how they emerged and considers the pressures to move away from this model that emerged after 2010.

Foreign direct investment has played a great role in the Hungarian economy since the collapse of communism in 1989. In per capita terms Hungary attracted more FDI than any other country in Central and Eastern Europe in the decade following the collapse of communism in 1989. By 1998 the majority of the twenty top exporters were foreign-owned companies (Mihályi 2002). Key sectors in which foreign investment played a significant role included car manufacturing, telecom, TV/radio parts and receivers as well as data processing. All the top ten exporters in Hungary were at least partly foreign-owned by 2002 (Sass 2004: 82). Germany accounted for the largest share of foreign investment.

In terms of the financial system and corporate governance, Hungary fits the DME model very well. Hungary decided to privatize the banks to foreign investors, and 70 per cent of the banking system was foreign-owned already at the end of the 1990s (Duman and Kureková 2012: 1216). The dominance of foreign investment in the economy means that key governance decisions are made at the corporate headquarters of the multinational enterprises that are central to the Hungarian economy.

Labour markets and industrial relations also correspond to the key features of the DME model. Despite some early attempts to establish tripartism and a number of social pacts in the early post-communist period, industrial relations are fragmented. There is effectively a dual system, with trade unions at the sectoral level and works councils at the firm level, which weakens its effectiveness (Duman and Kureková 2012: 1216).

The Hungarian economy has been among the most successful in East Central Europe. Income and productivity growth have been among the highest in the region, and Hungary has attracted high levels of foreign investment into a variety of sectors, such as car production and electronics. Whilst other countries gradually caught up with Hungary, inward foreign investment stock amounted to 67 per cent of GDP in 2017 (OECD 2018), the second highest share in the region after Czechia. Foreign investors still dominate the most important and export-oriented sectors of the economy.

Whilst there is some evidence of companies shifting at least some R&D activities to Hungary (Sass 2004: 81), no subsidiaries have evolved into strategic independent units (Dörrenbächer 2007). The external dependence of Western multinationals remains high. There was a rhetorical shift associated with the election of Viktor Orbán's Fidesz government in 2010, which put greater emphasis on an Eastern opening and is also associated with high-profile Russian and Chinese investment projects (Rogers 2024). However, this has not eliminated the general dependence on Western European and especially German investments (Bohle and Regan 2021).

Why did Hungary turn into such a good example of a DME? There are two sets of factors that have been particularly important.

First, Hungary had a head start compared to the rest of East Central Europe in that it had gradually opened up to the international economy during the communist period after the launch of the New Economic Mechanism in the 1960s. This meant that there was already some foreign involvement in the Hungarian economy when communism collapsed, and some of the existing investors were interested in expanding their activities. The proximity of Hungary to Western Europe also contributed to making the country a very attractive investment location.

Second, unlike in some of the other East Central European countries, foreign investment played a very big role in the Hungarian reform and privatization programme from the early 1990s. The centre-right government led by Prime Minister József Antall which took office in May 1990 adopted a privatization programme that emphasized the central role of strategic investors, commercial viability and the maximization of budget revenue as part of a gradual approach to privatization with a key supervisory role accorded to the State Property Agency, which in turn was controlled directly by the government (Canning and Hare 1996). This facilitated extensive involvement of foreign capital, as Western companies were particularly likely to meet the criteria of viable strategic investors. There were periodic changes, including moves to reshape the privatization policy to favour 'domestic owners' as well as attempts to stop controversial sales to foreigners and to increase the scope of strategic sectors which should remain in state ownership. Nevertheless, the general direction of reform remained unchanged. If anything, the core principle of centralization was strengthened by new legislation adopted by the centre-left government in 1995, which also sought to accelerate the process of privatization.

Many domestic experts favoured this form of privatization. János Kornai, arguably the most influential Hungarian economist, published a blueprint for the transition process which made the case for gradual privatization to strategic investors (Kornai 1990). There was also fierce popular criticism of the 'spontaneous privatization' initiated by the companies themselves, which had occurred between 1988 and 1990. It was perceived as a corrupt form of self-enrichment and often related to asset stripping in public debates. Profitable parts of companies were siphoned off and turned into joint ventures, whereas the rump of the company remained in state hands (Canning and Hare 1996). This was a key election issue in 1990, and the centre-right parties campaigned against this form of privatization and in favour of strategic sales to outsiders. Much of the managerial and trade union elite supported the Hungarian Socialist Party (MSzP), the ex-communist party, so there were weaker ties between economic elites and the winning centre-right coalition (Körösényi 1999: 76). By contrast, an MSzP-dominated government might have been more inclined to favour privatization to enterprise insiders given such network ties, as in Slovenia (Feldmann 2014; see also Chapter 3). More generally, and very importantly, there was also a severe budgetary and payments crisis. External debt amounted to 56.8 per cent of GDP at the end of 1990 (Hare 1991), which was the highest level in the region in per capita terms – $2,585 in 1990 (Berend 1996: 231). This strengthened the case for privatization to foreign investors, as this would help generate public revenue. Taken together, these factors created strong support for privatization to strategic investors and for attracting foreign investment.

Whilst privatization and the lack of a sizeable domestic business sector were major contributors to the emergence of DME institutions in Hungary, the country's geographical position close to Western European markets also stimulated greenfield investment. As Hungary became increasingly known as an attractive investment location, this also generated agglomeration effects. New entrants benefited from the existence of infrastructure, suppliers and networks in Hungary. The location advantage of Hungary was also further underpinned by strategic government policy to attract foreign investment. This includes tax holidays and other inducements, such as support in identifying facilities (often on favourable terms). Bohle and Greskovits (2012) characterize this kind of economy as a form of embedded neoliberalism. It is neoliberal in that it privileges the expansion of markets, but it is also embedded given that it relies on the state to bring about some market activities and also to compensate some of the losers of these changes, for example by expanding social policy and early retirement.

After the populist turn associated with Orbán's return to power in 2010, businesses with ties to the government, such as Lajos Simicska's business empire, have received favours and support from the state (Szelenyi 2016). This has given rise to concerns about cronyism and its potentially adverse effects on economic performance (Szanyi 2023). Orbán's government has also initiated an 'Eastern opening' aimed at intensifying economic interactions with Russia and China (Jacoby and Korkut 2016). Given the persistent dominance of Western FDI in key sectors (Bohle and Regan 2021), these changes have mostly affected sectors that are less central to the Hungarian political economy, where investment has fallen. However, the populist challenge does highlight greater contestation surrounding some of its core elements and show that the persistence of the DME model cannot necessarily be taken for granted (see also Chapter 11).

Slovakia as a DME

Slovakia's economic policies initially differed from Hungary's and put less emphasis on attracting foreign investment. This meant that Slovakia seemed to be a laggard in terms of attracting FDI for much of the 1990s, this eventually changed. Since the late 1990s, Slovakia has been remarkably successful in terms of attracting FDI. In 2016, the stock of inward foreign investments in Slovakia accounted for 49 per cent of GDP. Thanks to the scale of the car industry, it has come to be known as the new 'Detroit of Eastern Europe' since Slovakia produces more cars than any other country of the world in per capita terms (Bohle and Jacoby 2017: 201). There has also been significant foreign investment in electronics, wood processing and in more traditional sectors, like chemicals and steel, which tend to be concentrated in the Eastern part of the country (Sochulakova and Igazova 2013).

Corporate governance regulations in Slovakia make two-tier boards compulsory as in many CMEs (see Chapter 3). As in Hungary, many changes and reforms to corporate governance regulations were prompted by harmonization with EU standards (Duman and Kureková 2012: 1216). However, these regulations are less important for the FDI-dominated components of the economy, which do not tend to rely on the Slovak economy for financing. As in other DMEs, corporate governance in these enterprises is embedded in the global structure of the multinational enterprises with the corporate headquarters in a dominant position. Banking and financial reform also began at the end of the 1990s. Partly as a result of the process of integrating more closely with the EU and preparing for euro adoption, which occurred in 2009, Slovakia introduced formal corporate governance and banking regulations earlier than many other East Central European countries, such as Hungary (Duman and Kureková 2012: 1216).

Whilst industrial relations are fragmented and less institutionalized than in CMEs, the system has been regarded as more effective than in Hungary, and social partners have played a relatively active role in negotiations about reforms of the vocational education and training system (Duman and Kureková 2012: 1217).

The performance of the Slovak economy during the twenty years following the launch of the foreign investment-led growth strategy in 1998 was impressive. Average annual economic growth rates were about 4 per cent and among the highest in Europe. Whilst inequality is relatively low by international standards, with a Gini coefficient for disposable income of 25 in 2016, foreign investment has led to increases in regional inequality, as most of the multinational enterprises have chosen to locate their activities in the Western part of the country, especially the two most prosperous regions of Trnava and Bratislava (Sochulakova and Igazova 2013). On the other hand, there is very limited evidence of upgrading to higher value-added elements of production. The low levels of spending on education and innovation in Slovakia are a further impediment to such changes. This raises some questions about the growth prospects of the Slovak economy in the medium term (Pavlínek 2016: 588).

As noted, in the early years of the post-communist era, Slovakia would have seemed an unlikely candidate for a country known to attract a lot of foreign direct investment, so this raises the question of how Slovakia became such a good example of a DME. Although there was some foreign investment in the 1990s, Slovakia lagged behind most of the other East Central European countries. When Slovakia became independent in 1993, the core emphasis of the nationalist and populist governments of Vladimir Mečiar was on state building. When he served as Prime Minister he appointed party loyalists to the National Property Fund that was in charge of implementing privatization. The privatization and economic development programme privileged Slovak managers and business people, and in many cases those who were perceived as loyal to Mečiar were seen to get favourable treatment in opaque insider deals (Gould 2003: 295). Slovakia's international status was somewhat uncertain at this time. The Slovak regime was seen to fall short of the democratic standards expected by the international community, and Slovakia under Mečiar has also been classified as a competitive authoritarian regime (Levitsky and Way 2006). Concerns with Slovakia's political system were also seen to weaken the country's prospects of EU accession at the time.

Opposition to Mečiar helped unite a heterogeneous group of political actors, including both market liberals and Social Democrats, whose key goal was economic and political integration with Western Europe. This was seen as a way of strengthening the economy, weeding out corruption and breaking Slovakia's isolation that had been a result of the Mečiar regime before 1998. At the time it seemed likely that Slovakia might not be invited to accede along with the other post-communist countries as part of the first wave of Eastern enlargement, not least since Slovakia, unlike its neighbours, was not invited to begin EU accession negotiations in 1997 (Vachudova 2005).

After a new government came to power in 1998, Slovakia started encouraging foreign investment in various ways. This included some privatization to foreign investors, but also various kinds of economic inducements for new greenfield investments, such as the new investments by Peugeot Citroën and Kia, which entailed a bidding contest with other East Central European countries. The Slovak state subsidized infrastructure as well as the recruitment, training and housing projects for PSA Peugeot Citroën Slovakia's workers, and it even promised to help establish a French school in Trnava (Pavlínek 2016: 582). The government also facilitated the expansion of existing investment projects, like VW Slovakia, which received tax breaks and subsidies to support the construction of a new components factory in 1998 (Pavlínek 2016: 581). As the goal of attracting foreign investment became paramount, spending on the welfare state and support for domestic firms fell (Duman and Kureková 2012). The FDI-led strategy remained a priority for successive governments, though the most generous investment promotion initiatives also faced some resistance from domestic firms (Pavlínek 2016).

The politics of DMEs

This section discusses the political underpinnings of the DME model and the factors that shape FDI dominance in this form of capitalism. It complements Nölke and Vliegenthart's (2009) account to explain why the DME model fits post-communist East Central Europe so well and to analyse both the origins and persistence of such institutions.

The core features of DMEs relate to the dominant role of multinational enterprises and associated economic institutions. Whilst there has been an almost universal trend towards higher levels of globalization and more foreign investment across much of the world, there are important differences in terms of how these processes unfold in different countries. This highlights the fact that globalization is not an automatic process, but that it is politically contested. Many domestic actors, including domestic producers, may be opposed to foreign investment for economic, political or social reasons.

This raises the question of why the post-communist region of East Central Europe as a whole moved so close to the DME model in the 1990s and early 2000s. This region is exceptional in many respects, and there are a variety of factors that made FDI-led development likely.

First, as a result of the Second World War, East Central Europe had ended up in the Soviet bloc and introduced command economies in the post-war period. Private property played a very limited role in these countries given the dominant role of state and collective ownership. Economic activity was directed by central planning and not guided by market forces. Similarly, production patterns did not generally reflect consumer demand as the central planner decided what should be produced (Kornai 1990). Once Communist Party rule came to an end in 1989–91, these countries began introducing market reforms and private property (Lavigne 1999).

This had important consequences as the collapse of communism created a window of opportunity, known as a 'period of extraordinary politics', when radical reform was possible (Balcerowicz 1995; Feldmann 2018). As the old system was largely illegitimate and not perceived to be successful, there was great demand for radical change and the introduction of a market economy. This situation gave policymakers considerable autonomy to introduce radical reform. Perhaps most importantly, market reforms began without a domestic business class. Therefore, the process of introducing a market economy amounted to a process of building 'capitalism without capitalists' (Eyal, Szelényi and Townsley 1999). This created a unique opening for foreign investment. The task of restructuring the economy was immense, and there was a lack of domestic capital and limited experience of producing goods and services targeted to global markets. Foreign investors could provide capital, experience and their own global networks as well. The lack of domestic capitalists also limited political resistance against the entry of foreign firms into these markets.

Second, as discussed above, East Central Europe was also strategically located in close proximity to Western Europe, which made these countries attractive investment targets for Western European firms. As noted above, some of them already had some experience of economic exchanges with these countries. The integration of these economies into world markets also provided new markets and business opportunities for Western European firms, and the geographical proximity also facilitated integration into global production networks (see Chapter 12) as well as access to European export markets.

In short, the capital scarcity in conjunction with great investment needs for restructuring these economies as well as the absence of a strong domestic business class, provided a window of opportunity and strong political demand for foreign investment, as this was seen to facilitate the transformation and modernization of these economies. Given the relative weakness of the domestic private business sector, it was also easier for foreign investors to achieve a dominant position in these economies. Nevertheless, as the two case studies discussed in this chapter highlight, the political processes leading to the emergence of a DME varied across countries. Whilst all the East Central European countries opened up their economies to foreign investment, these processes did not unfold in the same way in all the four Visegrád countries of Hungary, Poland, Czechia and Slovakia.

Hungary developed into a DME more quickly than the other three countries, with Czechia and Slovakia turning into DMEs in the second decade of post-communist reform and Poland being in an intermediate position. This raises questions about the factors that can account for these differences.

Hungary became a DME very quickly, in part thanks to favourable legacies, such as the fact that it had already been quite open before, which helped attract foreign investors. However, there was also a political coalition favouring privatization to strategic outsiders and other policies designed to attract foreign investment. An important factor distinguishing Hungary from what was Czechoslovakia (and then became Czechia and Slovakia) was the high level of external debt. As noted above, Hungary had the highest foreign debt per capita of all the former communist countries. Poland also had a big debt burden, and whilst the Polish privatization debate was complex, Poland effectively followed a similar trajectory in a somewhat more gradual fashion than Hungary. More extensive contestation surrounding privatization delayed the implementation of ownership reform, but ultimately Poland's approach provided extensive scope for privatization to strategic investors and sought to stimulate other forms of foreign investment as well. Somewhat paradoxically, given the emphasis on speed in many debates surrounding post-communist reform, this gradual approach turned out to serve Poland very well, as it facilitated a more careful approach to privatization (Woodruff 2004).

By contrast, Czechia and Slovakia, which were less burdened with foreign debt, developed into DMEs via a more circuitous route. For somewhat different reasons, Czechia and Slovakia sought to stimulate the emergence of domestic business in the 1990s. In the case of Slovakia, the nationalist and populist government of Vladimir Mečiar faced extensive international criticism in the 1990s, and privatization targeted privileged domestic actors. Whilst the Czech government did not face such international pressures and was a strong advocate of free markets, the privatization programme initially contributed to the emergence of a form of 'national capitalism' that promoted domestic capitalists (Myant 2007).

However, neither the Czech nor the Slovak form of national capitalism turned out to be sustainable. As discussed, the change in the Slovak case was dramatic, as a heterogeneous anti-Mečiar coalition gained power in 1998 on a mandate to improve relations with the West and facilitate Slovakia's accession to the European Union. In the Czech case the change was more gradual, as the model privileging domestic firms was perceived as increasingly unsuccessful and over time the demand for attracting FDI grew. The Czech and Slovak cases demonstrate that a more gradual process of globalization can also lead to high levels of FDI and external dependency.

Debating the DME model

The DME model is an important addition to VoC debates and to our understanding of global capitalist diversity. This model helps integrate the market economies of East Central Europe into debates about comparative capitalism and provides a nuanced account of their economic performance. It also introduces the concept external dependence into the VoC debate, which is very important given how highly integrated many economies are into the global economy. This model captures the fact that foreign and transnational actors play an important or even dominant role in many economies and that we cannot understand such capitalist systems by looking merely at domestic actors and institutions.

It seems clear that the post-communist world was a uniquely propitious environment for DMEs to develop, given the lack of a well-established domestic business sector and the great need for investment to facilitate restructuring and transformation of the economy, which would have been hard to finance domestically. This model may be increasingly relevant to other parts of the world if the trend towards higher levels of foreign investment continues and deepens. This could potentially happen in other economies in the longer term, including some HMEs, if higher rates of foreign investment gradually displace domestic businesses and business groups. Schneider has argued that Argentina, at least in the 1990s, may have been moving in this direction (Schneider 2013: 75), though after the left turn under Nestor and Cristina Kirchner this changed. Such an outcome might be most likely in 'semi-peripheral countries' that can be easily integrated into global production networks.

However, there are also issues that the DME model may explain less well. First, one might question how well it captures dependency in general (Ebenau 2012). Whilst FDI is important, there are also other kinds of external dependence, such as the constraints imposed by the reliance on foreign trade and perhaps most importantly international finance. Foreign ownership of banks can be incorporated into the DME model, but other forms of financial dependence associated with high levels of foreign debt and borrowing may have more profound and destabilizing consequences, as captured by the debate on subordinate financialization (see Chapter 9; Kvangraven 2021). The dependence on foreign borrowing imposes a range of constraints on investment and industrial policy, but the risks associated with financial crises are arguably the biggest challenge. In Central and Eastern Europe another form of dependency is on the EU (including EU structural funds and regulations). This suggests that the DME model does not fully account for all dimensions of external dependency. A possible extension to this model could compare the relative significance of different forms of dependency (Myant and Drahokoupil 2012). On the other hand, many other forms of dependency may not be unique to DMEs and perhaps not as central to the functioning of these economies.

Second, one might ask whether the DME model is too focused on foreign investment in these economies. Whilst there is a variation across countries, in some economies characterized as DMEs, domestic firms play a more significant role. This is perhaps especially true of Poland, which is often viewed as a DME and is one of the first economies to which the label 'liberal dependent capitalism' was applied (King and Sznajder 2006). Whilst the economy is highly dependent on exports, the home market is considerably larger than in the other Central European economies. Relatedly, one could also compare the DME model to Bohle and Greskovits's (2012) analysis of 'embedded neoliberal capitalism'. Whilst they agree that these economies are dominated by foreign investment, they argue that these economies are best understood as the result of a state-led process of embedding markets. This includes strategic investment incentives to foreign firms, but also strategic use of welfare policies to mobilize support for FDI-led development. This raises the question of whether these economies are best understood by studying the nature of their states (cf. Feldmann 2019).

Third, it is worth noting that there is some family resemblance to the HME and to a lesser extent also to the SME model (see Chapters 5 and 7) – in both cases, the core coordination mechanism is hierarchy, but the principal difference is the predominance of foreign investment and therefore external dependency in DMEs, which results from the lack of domestically based business groups. Given the centrality of hierarchy in HMEs, DMEs and SMEs (see Chapter 7), one might ask whether these three forms of capitalism should be viewed as sub-types of a general variety of hierarchical capitalism – dominated by diversified business groups (domestic, often family-led conglomerates), multinationals and the state, respectively (cf. Carney 2016). This relates to the discussion about whether NMEs and CMEs should be viewed merely as sub-types of one VoC (see discussion in Chapter 4). Despite certain family resemblances, each of these models has many distinctive features. Therefore this book argues that lumping HMEs, DMEs and SMEs together obscures as much as it reveals and that the functioning and political underpinnings of these economies are best captured by treating them as separate VoC models.

Finally, the main question relates to the future prospects of the DME model. If the dominance of FDI is largely an artefact of the unique features of post-communist transformation, this raises questions about the political sustainability of this model. There are a number of factors that contribute to the resilience of this model, not least the importance of multinationals to growth, exports and job creation in DMEs. This enhances the political influence of multinational enterprises and also the interest of voters as well as national and local governments in attracting and retaining them. The relative weakness of domestic business elites further contributes to this, and both WTO and EU commitments limit the potential for any radical rollback of the openness to FDI (Wade 2003).

On the other hand, there are a variety of factors that could destabilize the DME model. First, the multinationals themselves could decide to relocate elsewhere, especially if production costs increase over time and make the DMEs less attractive as assembly platforms than other countries. Second, dissatisfaction with the DME model could increase, especially if economic performance does not continue to live up to expectations. The aftermath of the global financial crisis of 2007 did spur more criticism of economic policy and some challenges to the status quo (Bohle and Greskovits 2012). The potential challenges associated with the middle-income trap discussed in the context of HMEs (see Chapter 5) could also pertain to DMEs, as MNEs primarily seek cost advantages and refrain from locating higher value-added activities in these countries. Third, forces associated with the populist turn that are critical of foreign influence could lead to attempts to reduce the reliance on international firms and instead promote a domestic bourgeoisie. Therefore, it would be premature to conclude that the DME model is irreversible and entirely resistant to change. As noted above, economic challenges associated with the middle-income trap could potentially lead to pressure for reform. Perhaps even more importantly, as the Hungarian case illustrates, political imperatives may also lead to attempts to roll back foreign influence.

The future prospects of the DME model depend partly on its performance in terms of generating high growth and the political influence of the MNEs as well as the emerging middle class of employees and junior managers in these companies that benefit from it. More generally, it may also depend on the success of governments in terms of 'embedding markets' and compensating the losers of economic change (Bohle and Greskovits 2012). As discussed later in the book (see Chapter 11), the rise of populism in East Central Europe can be regarded as a form of backlash against some aspects of globalization and against key DME institutions as well. Indeed, the former Polish Prime Minister Mateusz Morawiecki explicitly referred to the Nölke and Vliegenthart's DME model to justify the Law and Justice government's economic agenda (Morawiecki 2016).

Conclusion

One of the key questions about the era of globalization relates to how it affects individual economies. This question typically sparks controversy, with some perceiving globalization as the key to economic success, and others worrying about its adverse consequences, especially for smaller countries. This chapter has introduced the DME model, a VoC model that integrates some key insights from dependency theory to explore the impact of globalization on national economies (cf. Cardoso 2009). The DME model considers the role of external constraints and provides a framework for exploring how domestic institutions interact with global economic forces to shape the functioning of capitalist systems that are highly dependent on foreign investment. This chapter has shown how this model can be used to understand the economies of East Central Europe and to analyse the high growth these economies have achieved as well as some of the concerns about external dependence and the future prospects of this model. In that sense these cases capture many of the complex and controversial effects of globalization and the challenges that economies confront when they are highly integrated into the global economy.

Discussion questions

- Why has the DME model emerged in East Central Europe in particular? How important are historical legacies and geography to the emergence of this type of capitalism in this region?
- Under what circumstances, if any, would you expect the DME model to spread to other parts of the world?

- To what extent does the economic performance of East Central Europe imply that the concerns raised by traditional dependency theory are misguided and that globalization and foreign investment are effective tools to advance economic development?
- Does the DME model neglect the importance of financial and political dependence on external actors?
- Some critics have suggested that the DME model is less successful than its advocates would claim and that it is unlikely to be viable in the longer term. What do you perceive as the main challenges associated with this model, and to what extent might governments address them?

7

Statist market economies

A special report published in *The Economist* in 2012 heralded the 'rise of state capitalism', a new form of capitalism in which the state and state-owned companies play a very prominent role (The Economist 2012). This report reflects an active debate, in which various analysts have asked whether the rise of the BRICs is associated with the ascent of a new form of state-dominated capitalism (Kurlantzick 2016) or, given the centrality of China to these debates, even with a new 'Beijing Consensus' replacing the so-called 'Washington Consensus' on economic policy and international development (Beeson and Li 2015; Kennedy 2010). This chapter considers the VoC approach to statist market economies (SMEs) or market economies, in which the state plays a central coordinating role. It discusses what this model teaches us about China, Brazil and about capitalism in the Global South and beyond.

Understanding the SME model

Given the importance of law and order, taxes and subsidies and a general regulatory framework, it is clear that the state is an important actor in all market economies, including LMEs (Chapter 2). However, there is also widespread agreement that the state plays a more important role in economic governance in some countries than in others. This chapter discusses the VoC approach to statist market economies and explores what distinguishes such market economies from other forms of VoC.

Following the approach adopted in previous chapters and throughout this book, we can define a statist market economy as a political economy in which the dominant coordination mechanism is state guidance and where firms look to the state for signals about how to manage uncertainty and resolve coordination problems (Culpepper 2008). However, even where state guidance is paramount, it may come in varying degrees of intensity. The main focus of this chapter is on statist market economies in the twenty-first century, which have also been variously referred to as state-permeated market economies (Nölke et al. 2015), state-enhanced market economies (Schmidt 2003), state-led market economies (Walter and Zhang 2012a) or state-market economies (Carney 2016). This chapter contrasts them with traditional developmental states or the kind of *dirigisme* that attracted a lot of attention in the second half of the twentieth century.

In classical *developmental states*, the role of state intervention was direct and pervasive. Unlike regulatory states, in which 'the state concerns itself with the forms and procedures – rules if you will – of economic competition', developmental or plan-rational states set more detailed and substantive economic goals, for example, about which sectors ought to expand and which sectors ought to contract (Johnson 1982: 19). In developmental states key economic decisions are based on explicit state signals, and economic policymaking is strategic and goal-oriented. Whilst economic actors operate in a market environment both domestically and internationally, their activities are shaped by state signals and reflect state priorities to a very considerable extent. The best examples of developmental states include Japan for much of the twentieth century (Johnson 1982), and South Korea and Taiwan during the East Asian miracle years (Amsden 1989; Wade 2004). France before the 1980s has also traditionally been described as a market economy dominated by the state (Hall 1986; Culpepper 2008; Schmidt 2003; Shonfield 1969). For example, in South Korea under Park Chung-hee, some of these directives were issued by the president himself in meetings with key business leaders. To a lesser extent features of the developmental state model could be found elsewhere in East and Southeast Asia, though in most cases state intervention was either less pervasive and more selective (as in Singapore) or less consistent and effective (as in Malaysia or Indonesia) (Perkins 2013). Successful developmental states also had elements that resemble the NME model (see Chapter 4), in that there were often close network ties between the state and business, but the state was characterized by 'embedded autonomy', so it was familiar with the situation in the economy and key firms, but it also had the autonomy and capacity to enforce key priorities and decisions (Evans 1995).

VoC analysis relates to contemporary statist market economies (or state-permeated or state-led market economies) that have much in common with the classical developmental state model, given the importance of state signals and actions to economic activity and the resolution of coordination problems, but this is not a simple replay of the classical developmental state (Perkins 2001). More generally, these models perceive the role of the state as based on cooperation between the state and business coalitions that are bound together by loyalty and trust rather than 'an all-powerful, centralised, steering bureaucracy' (Nölke et al. 2015: 543). Nevertheless, the state plays a central role in guiding and supporting economic activity. The key examples of statist (or 'state-permeated') market economies that Nölke and his collaborators apply the SME analysis to are China, India and Brazil. An alternative typology of East Asian capitalism developed by Walter and Zhang defines China, Indonesia and Malaysia as 'state-led market economies' (Walter and Zhang 2012a).

The SME models formulated by Nölke et al. (2015) and Walter and Zhang (2012a) have a number of core features. Whilst these coordination mechanisms could be found in a wide range of economies, in practice Nölke et al. (2015) expect it to apply especially to large economies that have sizeable home markets and are less dependent on the global economy. For many other countries deviations from free-market orthodoxy may be less feasible both due to their dependence on global markets and also because of more constraining global norms, or what Wade has referred to as a shrinking of development space (Wade 2003).

Financial systems in SMEs

As in traditional developmental states, the financial system is one of the most important instruments of state influence on the economy in statist market economies. It typically has several distinguishing features (Nölke et al. 2015).

First, the financial systems of SMEs are dominated by national capital. Whilst many SMEs have attracted a lot of foreign investment, foreign capital still constitutes a relatively small share of the economy, especially compared to DMEs or HMEs. Therefore, SME firms are 'relatively independent from short-term volatilities on global capital markets' (Nölke et al. 2015).

Multinational enterprises play a much less significant role in the economy than in DMEs or HMEs. By contrast, state control plays a greater role, either in the form of selective state ownership or more indirect channels of influence, and there is a very limited market for corporate control and hostile takeovers.

Second, state-owned or state-controlled banks are important actors in terms of financing and corporate governance. Whilst these banks may have some independence from day-to-day politics, key investments and patterns of financial support reflect state priorities to a considerable degree. Such access to finance for priority firms may also be complemented with various kinds of preferential treatment, such as credits or tax breaks.

State development banks typically play a central role in financing both domestic economic activity and internationalization and offer important strategic direction for firms. Prominent examples include the Brazilian Development Bank (BNDES) or the China Development Bank, which is also a key funder of large-scale infrastructure projects in China (Gottschalk, Castro and Xu 2022).

Many SMEs also have significant sovereign wealth funds (state-dominated investment vehicles that generally hold large asset portfolios) that are used to enhance state control of domestic business. Whilst these investment portfolios are generally global in outlook, they tend to invest significant proportions of their assets – often over 30 per cent – domestically; this is the case even for the highly profitable Temasek Holdings in Singapore (Kurlantzick 2016: 88).

Labour in SMEs

Labour markets and employment relations in SMEs tend to be dominated by the state. This dominance can manifest itself in multiple ways. In the case of state-owned enterprises the state is directly involved as an employer, but even in other firms the state is frequently a key actor in employment relations, if not de jure, then at least de facto. The state may seek to shape employment relations both in direct and indirect ways, for example, by influencing key labour market actors or by affecting the degree of enforcement of key labour regulations.

SMEs are generally characterized by low-wage regimes and a high degree of segmentation of labour markets. Key worker factions are usually co-opted by the state and offered certain privileges in the form of favourable pay or regulation. The position of such privileged groups of workers is very different from other categories of workers that are paid less or even employed informally. State policy priorities are usually more important than legal provisions, not least since enforcement of labour regulations is often selective and reflective of particular policy goals. More generally, they tend not to apply to informal employment, which is generally a large share of total employment.

Organized labour is often dominated by the state or even somewhat repressed. In a typical SME there are close ties between the state and both unions and employers' associations, which means that the state often exercises a direct influence on all social partners involved in labour market relations.

These labour regimes also relate to the fact that many SMEs have productivist welfare states (Holliday 2000); that is, both labour relations and social policy are subordinated to the core state objectives of stimulating high productivity and growth. This means that they place greater emphasis on investment than on consumption and on keeping wages low to stimulate competitiveness and exports. Education and skill regimes tend to focus on providing standardized primary and secondary education, but with more limited provision of tertiary education beyond a relatively small university sector providing general skills to a sub-set of the labour force.

Institutional complementarities and performance

The appeal of the SME model is tightly bound up with the perceived successes that have been analysed through this lens. The debate surrounding the East Asian miracle – the rapid growth of the East Asian tiger economies – generated much interest in the classical developmental state and in the role of the state as a driver of economic growth more generally.

The rapid economic growth enjoyed by Japan and later by South Korea and Taiwan has strengthened the sense that strong state guidance is central to catch-up. This argument can be made based on the ideas of classical development economists, perhaps most importantly Alexander Gerschenkron (1962). In his famous (albeit somewhat dated) formulation, 'backwardness' confers certain advantages compared to the most advanced economies, in that 'backward' economies can leapfrog the process of development. However, poorer economies tend not to have well-developed financial markets, so in the case of the poorest economies, the state would need to play a central role in facilitating investment and growth.

Whilst there is great controversy in the development literature about the precise contribution of interventionist states to economic development, it seems clear that intervention was compatible with high rates of economic growth in economies, like Japan, South Korea and Taiwan. Strikingly, high economic growth in these countries was also associated with relatively egalitarian outcomes. The record of intervention in other parts of the world is more controversial, though it is ultimately hard to prove whether less successful cases necessarily invalidate intervention as such or whether they demonstrate poor design or implementation of such programmes.

Since the 1980s, many countries have been moving away from interventionist policies, prompting the common view that statism is less suitable to advanced knowledge economies in the context of globalization. Indeed, the failed attempts of the French government under President Mitterrand to reintroduce state intervention in the early 1980s is widely regarded as a key turning point that reinforced the free-market agenda and weakened the case for activist state management of the economy (Culpepper 2005; Schmidt 2003). Taiwan and South Korea also gradually moved away from developmental state institutions, just as Japan had previously done (Perkins 2013).

However, the rise of the BRICs has yet again raised questions about the revival of statism and the sense that the success of China, Brazil and India is at least partly due to strategic state policies rather than to these countries' commitment to freer markets. As in the case of the classical developmental states in the 1950s–1980s, there is a controversy surrounding these interpretations, with some observers stressing that all of these economies have become more market-oriented over time, thereby implying that it is the increasing role of markets that is the main driver of economic growth (Bhalla 2002). By contrast, others see this success as a reflection of a more heterodox policy mix, in which markets co-exist with strategic state intervention.

In particular, in Nölke et al.'s (2015) model, there are institutional complementarities between SME institutions and the strategies of firms that operate in SMEs, and specialize in medium-tech manufacturing goods (Nölke et al. 2015: 556).

China as an SME

The importance of the Chinese economy to current debates about capitalism can hardly be overstated. China's rapid economic growth since the early 1980s has profoundly reshaped the world economy, not least given its profound effects on global growth, inequality and trading patterns. The success of the Chinese economy has also raised a variety of questions about whether the Chinese underpinnings of economic growth should merely be viewed as a form of catch-up growth or whether China has developed a new form of market economy – which given China's growing influence might be exported as a form of 'Beijing consensus' and replace the 'Washington consensus' that had such a profound impact on development thinking in the 1990s.

Any assessment of the Chinese economy is complicated by the fact that it is to some extent a moving target. After the Chinese Revolution in 1949, the following three decades were associated with the construction of a command economy based on very limited private ownership and dominated by the Communist Party. The legacies from this period still loom large in many parts of the Chinese economy and society. Therefore, many studies have analysed the Chinese economy through the lens of post-communist reform (Perkins 1994), including the role of experimentation and incrementalism in ensuring the success of these reforms (Qian 2000; Heilmann 2008; Lau, Qian and Roland 2000). Others have identified China as a case of 'sino-capitalism', a market economy with unique Chinese characteristics (McNally 2012).

Most observers agree that the pace of institutional change slowed down in the early twenty-first century, so it is possible to identify some characteristic features of the Chinese political economy. Some of this debate has focused on comparing the contemporary Chinese model to the developmental states in the heyday of the East Asian miracle (Perkins 2001).

One of the challenges associated with characterizing Chinese corporate governance is the heterogeneity of the business sector, which also underpins financial and governance practices. It is often subdivided into three core categories – state, private and hybrid (Witt and Redding 2014: 16) – but there is a lot of variation within each of them. For example, the private sector includes large and small firms, and both family-owned and foreign companies.

The substantial state sector is a key feature of China as an SME. It was long thought to be in decline, especially in the late 1990s, when the number of state-owned enterprises (SOEs) declined dramatically from about 120,000 in the mid-1990s to just over 34,000 in 2003 (Naughton 2018: 344). This trend also reflected the policy announced at the fifteenth Communist Party Congress in September 1997 by Premier Zhu Rongji of 'grasping the large, letting the small go'. This did not imply that the state sector would disappear, but rather that state involvement should be more selective and focus on the largest enterprises to ensure that they would be as efficient and successful as possible and thereby promote government priorities. SOEs have also begun to play an increasingly important role in China's 'going out policy' of promoting outward foreign direct investment.

The low point for state-owned enterprises (SOEs) occurred in 2003–4, and the importance of state-owned enterprises started growing in the early twenty-first century, leading to a strengthening of the state sector (Breslin 2012: 35). SOEs account for a substantial share of China's growing outward investment and are the dominant players in key industries that are often viewed as the commanding heights of the economy. In 2003 SASAC (State-Owned Assets Supervision and Administration Commission) was created, and it supervises 117 key state-owned enterprises that are considered to be of strategic importance – five sectors account for three quarters of the assets and two thirds of the work force under SASAC control: petroleum and refining, metallurgy, electricity, military industry and telecommunications (Witt and Redding 2014: 13). In addition, there are also provincial and municipal SASACs. Provincial governments and institutions have contributed to the emergence of an 'investor state' given that they play a significant role in the economy by holding minority stakes and being active shareholders in private and listed companies (Chen and Rithmire 2020). According to Pearson, Rithmire and Tsai (2022: 136) the growing role of the state has given rise to a new form of party-state capitalism that has two core features: '1) significant expansion of party-state authority in firms through changes in corporate governance and state-led financial instruments; and (2) drawing political "red lines" to enforce political fealty by various economic actors'.

However, it should also be noted that the state itself is multidimensional. Given that priorities at the central and provincial level are not necessarily aligned, the state does not provide the kind of coherent direction that characterized traditional developmental states. Signals from state actors remain important, and there is also considerable interpenetration of the state (and Communist Party) and business which means that it is not always clear where the border lies. Various kinds of hybrid corporate forms exist, as in the case of the so-called 'Township and Village Enterprises' that played a key role in the early successes of Chinese economic reform (Chang and Wang 1994). Competition between provinces and the opportunities for provincial governments to reap economic gains from business activity in their regions has been seen as a key determinant of economic efficiency in China (Montinola, Qian and Weingast 1995).

There have also been some attempts to foster conglomerates reminiscent of those in South Korea and Japan, either by mergers or by stimulating the creation of industry groups. In some cases this was accomplished by turning an industrial bureau from a government agency into a holding company (Yusuf, Nabeshima and Perkins 2006: 220).

State influence is also reflected in other aspects of the financial system and corporate governance. Whilst stock market capitalization has increased over time, the financial system remains bank-based. The so-called 'big four' state-controlled banks play a particularly central role (Kurlantzick 2016). The allocation of finance often reflects state preferences, with preferential treatment of SOEs very common (Breslin 2012). This also facilitated the resolute Chinese response to the global financial crisis, as part of which funding for local government infrastructure projects played a very significant role in stimulating demand in the aftermath of the crisis (Tan and Conran 2022). The state can also expand or limit access to land as a way of managing economic activity (Rithmire 2017).

The Chinese corporate governance structure of large companies can be viewed as a hybrid of the LME unitary board with some independent outside directors and the German-CME-style two-tier board (Tricker 2019: 300). Yet corporate governance is generally perceived as weak, as independent outside members often play a merely symbolic role and state guidance is inconsistent (Witt and Redding 2014: 17). Dual-class shares are very common, which means that some shares are associated with greater influence than others. This allows the government to control SOEs, even when they are listed on stock markets for the purpose of raising funds (Kurlantzick 2016: 102). The internal structure of firms is very hierarchical (Witt and Redding 2014: 18), with low levels of trust and social capital, which typically reinforce managerial authority. This is also related to a relatively weak rule of law, as the legal system does not operate in a fully autonomous way. The weak legal system strengthens both managerial and political influence (Perkins 2001).

As several studies have noted, the formal tripartite institutions underpinning employment relations in China bear some resemblance to the CME model (Witt and Redding 2014: 19), but in terms of actual practice the Chinese system comes much closer to the SME model (Nölke et al. 2015).

There are several key SME features worth stressing in this context. First, the key organizations participating in tripartism are dominated by the state. The main trade union federation is the ACTFU (All-China Federation of Trade Unions), and it has traditionally been seen as a key transmission belt of Communist Party initiatives to workers, much like in other communist countries, such as the Soviet Union (Harper 1969). Although it has been claimed that unions have taken on a greater role in representing worker interests and mediating between workers and management in recent decades (Zhang 1997), Taylor and Li (2007) show that the ACTFU should not even be seen as a trade union, but as a state organ instead. More generally, given the government's emphasis on pro-business growth policy, the union's positions tend to be well aligned with both managerial and state preferences (Cooke 2016: 299).

A very similar situation applies to the employers' associations. The two main associations are the CEC-CEDA (China Enterprise Confederation-China Enterprise Directors Association), the result of a merger of two associations in 1988, and the ACFIC (All-China Federation of Industry and Commerce). The main distinction is that the former mostly represents state-owned enterprises, whereas the latter mainly covers private firms. Whilst ties between the CEC-CEDA and the Communist Party and state are particularly close, the ACFIC could also be said to represent state interests to a considerable extent (Cooke 2016: 296–7).

Second, whilst tripartism is formally in place, the process of collective bargaining is fragmented across almost 11,000 tripartite bodies ranging from the national to the provincial, local, firm or even street level (Witt and Redding 2014: 19). For SOEs, all participants in the tripartite process are controlled by the Communist Party (Cooke 2016: 303ff.). Given the influence of the state on the other organizations, this also characterizes collective bargaining in general. Several new laws, notably the Labour Contract Law, were passed in 2007 to strengthen employee rights and counteract worker dissatisfaction that was also reflected in strike and protest activity (Remington 2018).

With respect to employment protection, there is a similar contrast between formal institutions, which bear some resemblance to Western European social democracy, and actual practice (Witt and Redding 2014: 20). Employment is characterized by exceptionally high turnover and short-termism, which provides limited incentives to provide in-house training. Informal employment practices are also very common, which adds to the fluidity of labour markets.

During the era of the command economy there was a workplace-based welfare system known as the 'danwei system'. Since the late 1990s the Chinese government has sought to build a more comprehensive welfare system to replace the old system and address growing inequalities in Chinese society, as income inequality has risen dramatically at the individual level but also in regional terms during the economic reform era. The emerging welfare state policies include an expansion of social assistance, social insurance-based pension and medical, unemployment and work-injury insurance programmes that share many features of the conservative welfare state model (Ringen and Ngok 2017: 17). However, the programmes are limited in scope and coverage, with irregular implementation, which renders the impact of the welfare state rather limited and different from the conservative welfare states in many CMEs (see Chapter 3).

The functioning of the labour market is also affected by weaknesses in the education and skills system. In particular, there is a relatively high-skill mismatch and weak vocational training. The high turnover in labour markets affect the very limited incentives to provide in-house training. There are only a small number of initiatives, such as Sino-German Automobile Vocational Education (SGAVE), to develop effective training programmes (Remington 2018: 110).

In the short term this may not be a binding constraint on Chinese development, as the low-wage regime is a key source of comparative advantage in the production of low- and medium-tech products (Nölke et al. 2015: 556). The knowledge intensity of production is not very high and often relies on importing innovation by creatively reinventing imported goods and producing them at lower cost (Nölke et al. 2015: 556). There are also some small-scale production networks, and joint ventures that trade market access for technology transfer, though more recently outward foreign direct investment has become an important way for Chinese companies to access technology and innovation capacities abroad (Fu, Hou and Liu 2018).

Brazil as an SME

Brazil has long been regarded as an example of a statist market economy with activist industrial policy (Evans 1995; Haggard 1990), though in the 1980s and 1990s Brazil undertook a variety of market reforms that were expected to mark the end of statism and the rise of neoliberal and free-market policies. During the Lula presidency many analysts began to ask whether there had been a revival of the developmental state in Brazil, and if the Brazilian success suggested that some form of revised neo-developmentalist state was a viable model in the twenty-first century (Ban 2013). This section will demonstrate that Brazil conforms with many features of the SME model, but that it is less of a good fit than China. In many ways Brazil could be viewed as combining elements of both the SME and HME models (Chapter 5; see also Feldmann 2019).

In terms of ownership and corporate structure Brazil fits the SME model quite well. However, the number of state-owned enterprises (SOEs) is no longer as high as it was before the privatization wave beginning in the 1980s, with the number of federal SOEs falling from about 250 around 1980 to 47 in 2009 and the number of state-level SOEs falling from about 400 in the late 1970s to 49 in 2009. Some of the remaining SOEs play a very central role in the Brazilian economy, including the oil company Petrobras, the water company Sabesp and the electricity companies Cesp, Copel and Electrobras (Musacchio and Lazzarini 2014: 119). State influence remains significant in many privatized companies, especially those in which the state retains so-called 'golden shares'. Whilst the state is a minority shareholder in such companies, the golden shares give the state a strategic role that enables it to influence and even to veto key decisions. A key example of this is one of the great success stories of the Brazilian economy, the aircraft manufacturer Embraer, which is also likely to have helped ensure that the company was not taken over by a foreign competitor (Schneider 2015: 120–1).

However, there are also a few features that are not well aligned with the SME model. First and foremost, compared to China and India, foreign direct investment plays a much greater role in the Brazilian economy (Nölke et al.2015: 548). Brazil was more integrated with the world economy, even in the heyday of import substitution, which never amounted to such a radical turn away from the global economy as the period of central planning in post-revolutionary communist China.

Secondly, as in hierarchical market economies, diversified business groups (*grupos*) have traditionally been central actors in the Brazilian economy. Although some of them, like the Villares Group, are less diversified than they were in the past, they still play a significant role in the Brazilian economy. Votorantim is one of the biggest conglomerates in Latin America and one of the best examples of the kind of diversified business groups discussed in the chapter on HMEs (Chapter 5). It is active in a variety of sectors, including finance, steel, cement, mining, siderurgy, aluminium and agribusiness. Given the centrality of grupos, Schneider (2013) classifies the Brazilian economy as an HME (see Chapter 5).

In many other respects, Brazil fits the SME model quite well. In particular, the state retains great influence over the financial system in Brazil. Several key banks are state-owned and controlled, including the Banco do Brasil, the Banco do Nordeste (focused on regional development), the Banco da Amazônia and the Banrisul. However, the most notable element of state influence over the financial system is exercised by the BNDES (the Brazilian Development Bank), which has played a central role in the Brazilian economy since the 1950s. However, its lending practices have changed over time. Whilst it continues to support many of Brazil's traditional large firms, there is an increasing focus on supporting innovation and internationalization, and many smaller firms also benefit from such loans (Hochstetler and Montero 2013; Hochstetler 2014).

Brazilian industrial relations are still shaped by the legacy of the state corporatist system established under Getúlio Vargas in the 1930s. Whilst much changed after democratization in the late 1980s, some key features remain, such as *unicidade sindical* (the principle that all workers within a professional category and jurisdiction are automatically covered by a particular union), the compulsory union tax and the centrality of labour courts. Whilst unionization fell slightly in the 1990s, it increased again over the following decade, and the membership rate in 2015 was 19.5 per cent (Berg and Schneider 2018: 125). The most dramatic change occurred in the number of trade unions, which increased from about 5,214 in 1990 to over 10,000 in 2013, but it should be noted that there is great variation in the size, representativeness and effectiveness of these organizations, as many of them are not members of any larger union federation . Some of them are often viewed as most interested in securing their share of the union tax and have limited contact with the workers they represent, whereas others play an important role in collective bargaining and in influencing policymakers more directly (Berg and Schneider 2018: 125–6).

These patterns are largely reflected in the nature of the Brazilian welfare state as well. Traditionally, Brazil has had some of the highest levels of income inequality in the world (Signor et al. 2019), although inequality started falling under President Lula. Brazil also has a very high share of informal employment, which means that there is a high degree of dualization in the labour market. These features of the Brazilian political economy also relate to the low-skill equilibrium, where a high degree of informality weakens incentives for investment in training, which in turn contributes to inequality (Schneider 2013).

The Brazilian developmental state of the 1960s and 1970s generated great controversy, with assessments ranging from success to failure. Many analyses have tended to view this as a qualified success (Evans 1995). Brazil enjoyed high rates of economic growth during this period, but a common criticism is that this model was too dependent on external sources of finance and hence vulnerable to shocks, such as that associated with the changes on global financial markets in the aftermath of the second oil shock and the Volcker disinflation in the early 1980s. Brazil was deeply affected by the Latin American debt crisis in the 1980s, which was a period of sluggish performance. In the early 2000s, especially under President Lula's first two terms in office (2003–2010), Brazil was once again touted as a success story that managed to achieve high economic growth along with significant improvements in various social indicators. The impeachment of Lula's successor, President Dilma Rousseff, led to a political crisis and heightened concerns about corruption, and in 2018 the right-wing populist Jair Bolsonaro was elected president, in part thanks to an effective challenge to the status quo.

The ambiguity of the long-run performance of statism in Brazil is also reflected in the mixed record of state-promoted industries. The aircraft producer Embraer is commonly viewed as a major success story, as are some mining and steel firms (and arguably oil, ethanol and flex motor technology as well), whereas intervention in information technology, nuclear energy and coffee is seen as less successful (Schneider 2015: 120–5).

Overall, many features of the Brazilian political economy are well captured by the SME model, although it does not fit it as well as the Chinese economy does. The Brazilian economy is perhaps best understood as a hybrid economy combining both SME and HME features.

Political underpinnings

The political underpinnings of SMEs remain controversial. Most of the literature agrees that there are a number of important political prerequisites for successful SME institutions. First, effective SMEs have highly coherent policy regimes that focus on economic growth and on effective management of the economy. If the focus is exclusively on rent extraction and predatory state action, then it is hardly possible to speak of SME, let alone a developmental state, where state coordination underpins the economy. Second, even if the state is committed to guiding or managing the economy and to the objective of promoting economic growth, it may or may not be able to do this. As the literature on government failure stresses, even good intentions may come to naught if the state does not have the capacity to implement its policies, though seemingly low-quality institutions can sometimes be effective and conducive to high growth (Rothstein 2015). Evans (1995) has described the key features of successful developmental states as embedded autonomy, This concept reflects a combination of strength, notably the ability to resist capture and implement policies, with a structure that is also highly integrated with society and the economy, which enables the authorities to elicit accurate information about planning needs, performance, bottlenecks and so on. This section begins by discussing four influential explanations that are frequently viewed as important determinants of SME institutions.

The first and very influential approach to statism sees it as bound up with what Alexander Gerschenkron's (1962) classical study refers to as the 'logic of backwardness', or the economic gap between a given country and the leading economies in the world, as discussed earlier in this chapter. In his classical study, Gerschenkron shows how England as the first developer had different institutions from Germany and Russia. In Russia, the least developed economy of the three, the state had a crucial role to play in facilitating the funds needed to promote economic growth and investment in the absence of large private savings or well-functioning credit markets. This suggests that statist market economies are more likely in countries with lower incomes or weakly developed capital markets, but since there is no automatic connection here, this raises questions about why and how such a relationship manifests itself. The mere existence of a potential opportunity to promote investment and growth does not explain why some low-income economies develop into successful statist market economies, whereas others do not. Gerschenkron himself stresses various factors, such as key ideas about growth and emulation that could affect political motivations, but the precise mechanisms could be explored more carefully. A second question raised by this framework is whether SME institutions only exist in low-income economies and whether such economies abandon these institutions if they achieve high growth and catch up with more prosperous economies. The decline of the traditional developmental state in East Asia would seem to support this hypothesis, but there could also be some path dependence in institutions that might make such outcomes less likely.

Second, even in the case of a strong state, such institutions could also be attributable to various social and historical factors, such as state traditions. To the extent that markets are embedded in a variety of institutions and a component of political and social life more generally, such traditions may shape the nature of capitalism in profound ways. A good example of this is Zheng and Huang's (2018) theory of China as a 'market in state', which conceptualizes the relationship between markets and the state differently compared to Western thinkers. This work implies that markets are inherently subordinated to the state in China, which also suggests that the Chinese SME institutions effectively reflect a long history and tradition of state primacy that is simply adapted to current conditions. The roots of the modern Japanese state in the Meiji restoration (and earlier features of the shogunate) is another oft-mentioned example of a situation, where historical traditions and norms have shaped subsequent institutional development. Frank Dobbin's (1994) influential work on the roots of industrial policy shows a similar pattern in France, where strong state traditions have influenced the economy in ways that diverge from Britain, the United States or Sweden, for example.

The third explanation is international and highlights the importance of external vulnerability, especially in the context of resource-poor countries. A key question arising from successful SMEs is why a strong state uses its strength to promote economic development and not merely to enrich its own leaders. An influential argument stresses external vulnerability in the form of severe security threats. Such challenges raise the stakes for policymakers, by making successful industrial policy a key determinant of the very survival of the state, especially in resource-poor states that cannot use profits from oil extraction to fund an army (Doner, Ritchie and Slater 2005). For example, the successful post-war developmental states in Taiwan and South Korea faced severe security threats associated with the People's Republic of China and North Korea respectively, and they were resource-poor, which meant that industrialization was perceived as a necessity to secure the country against foreign enemies. The success of these developmental states was also bound up with some more favourable international factors, notably US support and the existence of export markets in North America and Europe that could absorb the output produced in these economies. External factors are also important in the case of the twenty-first-century statist economies, but a favourable geopolitical position that gives them greater leverage to question economic orthodoxy associated with the Washington Consensus may be particularly important, thereby making SMEs particularly likely in large economies (Nölke et al. 2015).

In addition to these three factors, a fourth factor has generated considerable controversy, namely the possible connection of the SME model to authoritarianism. The classical developmental state emerged in authoritarian states, such as Taiwan and South Korea or Japan in the nineteenth century, and a cohesive authoritarian regime could be expected to pursue clear policy priorities. In the case of China, SME institutions co-exist with Communist Party rule. In some of the East Asian miracle economies the heyday of the developmental state era coincided with non-democratic rule, like the leadership of President Park Chung-hee in South Korea, and the decline of the developmental state institutions occurred more or less at the same time as democratization (Minns 2001). Although it is not entirely clear whether there is any causal connection between the two processes, democratization empowered a range of social and economic actors who were able to voice their grievances and lobby for specific policies, thereby arguably weakening the coherence and predictability of state initiatives. On the other hand, post-war Japan and France had democratic systems, albeit with some distinctive characteristics, such as strong and meritocratic bureaucracies that had considerable policy autonomy. In the Japanese case the long-term dominance by the Liberal Democratic Party that was continuously in power from the late 1940s until the 1990s also contributed to policy continuity. Among contemporary SMEs, India has one of the most robust democracies in the Global South, and Brazil has also had a democratic system since 1987. Therefore, there are good reasons to question claims about a necessary connection between SME or developmental state policies and authoritarianism (see also Perkins 2013: 151–2), not least since many authoritarian regimes have not had any developmentalist orientation.

In other words, none of the four explanations discussed here provides a full explanation of the emergence of SMEs, although each of them has been associated with SME institutions in certain contexts. Experience suggests that SMEs can emerge at various times and in different regions, but certain historical and international factors facilitate the emergence of such institutions. Successful statism would seem to require a reasonably meritocratic bureaucracy and consistent growth-oriented policies, but such policies could be compatible with quite different political regimes.

Debating the SME model

How important is the SME model for understanding global capitalism in the twenty-first century? Whilst statism attracted great attention at various points in the twentieth century, towards the end of the century there was a widespread sense that statism was no longer relevant and that any remnants would be swept away by the global tide of neoliberalism. The new democratic leaderships of South Korea and Taiwan, two economies that had had classical developmental states for prolonged periods in the second half of the twentieth century, found it increasingly difficult to address competing demands by various groups that had been weakened under authoritarian rule. Similarly, attempts by the socialist government of François Mitterrand in 1981 to strengthen state intervention in France failed in the face of market pressure, which cast doubt on the viability of statist policy agendas more generally.

Yet, as this chapter demonstrates, the SME model characterizes a number of leading economies very well. Walter and Zhang (2012a) classify Malaysia and Indonesia as state-led. Nölke et al. (2020) view India as the country that fits the SME model best. Like China, India underwent a significant transformation of its economy, and introduced market liberalization and macroeconomic stabilization that have modified the intricate system of state regulation and intervention commonly known as the 'licence raj' (Joshi and Little 1996). Whilst India was never under Communist Party rule in the way China and the Soviet bloc were, Indian policymakers did emulate key elements of central planning inspired by the Soviet experience. Economists from other parts of the Soviet bloc, including Poland, acted as advisers on economic policy and planning (Mazurek 2018). Yet since the early 1990s India has dismantled many traditional regulations. These reforms and the wider liberalization agenda have often been credited as a key part of the success that India has enjoyed in a variety of globally oriented sectors. The famous IT cluster in Bangalore has received extensive attention and become emblematic of India's economic growth and inclusion in the BRICS category of significant rising powers across emerging markets. In addition to IT, there have been many successful private businesses in other dynamic sectors, such as telecommunications and pharmaceuticals. The role of central planning became more limited, and in 2014 the Planning Commission was abolished and replaced with the NITI Aayog (Policy Commission), which is designed to foster cooperative federalism by involving state governments in developing economic policy agendas. However, as several scholars have argued, the growth acceleration predated liberalization. This interpretation suggests that new pro-business policies in the 1980s that helped firms expand domestically in the large home market were the main driver of growth (Nölke et al. 2020: 84).

More generally, the classification of India as an SME highlights the enduring importance of state influence on much of the economy. In light of the liberalization and globalization rhetoric, it has been suggested that 'India's is a state capitalism that dare not speak its name' (Chandra and Chatterjee, p. 702). The state plays a direct role in the economy as a result of a high share of state ownership and control. The number of central public sector enterprises (CPSE) controlled by central government increased in the early twenty-first century from 213 in 2008 to 257 in 2017, which is a larger number than in the pre-liberalization era (Chandra and Chatterjee 2022: 699–700). State-owned enterprises still play a central role, especially in the energy sector and in natural resources more generally, including companies like Indian Oil Corporation, Bharat Petroleum Corporation, Coal India Limited, Oil and Natural Gas Corporation, National Thermal Power Corporation, Gas Authority of India Limited, Steel Authority of India Limited and Power Grid. The central government is the majority owner of these companies (Chandra and Chatterjee 2022: 701).

However, alongside the centrality of SOEs that account for half of the biggest companies in India (Nölke et al. 2020: 92), it is also important to highlight the dominant role of large family-controlled business groups. The largest private businesses are family-controlled, and this explains many key features of their business models and governance practices, including succession strategies. Given the strength of big business in India and the connections between business and government and their influence on economic governance Hu, Cui and Aulakh (2019) classify the Indian economy as co-governed, which they distinguish from the state-led Chinese economy. Co-governed economies refer to capitalist systems in which the state and dominant business actors jointly govern economic affairs. Walter and Zhang (2012a) classify Taiwan and Korea as key examples of co-governed economies (see also discussion of networked market economies in Chapter 4).

The state also plays an important role in the financial system. According to Chandra and Chatterjee (2022: 702), debts issued by public sector banks constitute over 80 per cent of all debt issued in India. Given its centrality to the financial system, the 'state serves as a guardian of indigenous capital' (Nölke et al. 2020: 83). Although stock market capitalization has increased, the stock market serves primarily as a way to raise capital and not as a market for corporate control, which is why increasing numbers of SOEs are also listed. Firms also rely on retained earnings and on transfers to cross-subsidize activities within business groups.

These patterns are also reflected in corporate governance arrangements, where 93 per cent of all firms have a dominant shareholder controlling at least 20 per cent of voting rights. The dominant shareholder is typically either the state or a family. These arrangements often give rise to debate about cronyism, especially in the context of exchanges of favours or 'related party transactions', when funds are exchanged between family members (Nölke et al. 2020: 85). Given the strong position of the dominant shareholder, firms are well insulated from the threat of external takeovers.

Whilst there are close ties between the state and business, the role of organized business and business associations is relatively limited. None of the four national employers' associations engage in collective bargaining with trade unions either at the sectoral or national level. The Confederation of Indian Industry (CII) is generally regarded as the most important business organization, but like the other confederations it is more focused on lobbying activities than on resolving coordination problems among businesses or between business and government (Badigannavar and Ghosh 2020). Employment relations are state-dominated, given that both trade unions and employers' associations are relatively weakly organized. The trade union movement is fragmented into numerous confederations, many of which have close ties to political parties, but unlike most other countries, unionization rates have increased in the twenty-first century, largely thanks to the effective recruitment of informal workers.

Labour law is relatively strict, but with limited enforcement, not least since much of it only applies to a small sub-set of the labour force, mostly in the largest businesses (Nölke et al. 2020). It should also be noted that the state remains the largest employer of workers on regular wages and contracts (Saez 2014). The actual coverage rates of many important employment laws are extremely low and estimated to range between 0.7 per cent and 5.1 per cent for five key employment laws (Badigannavar and Ghosh 2020: 452). This relates to the most important features of India's labour markets, namely segmentation and a high degree of informality. Estimates suggest that about 83 per cent of the Indian labour force works in the informal sector (or even 93 per cent if casual and precarious employment in the public sector is also included), and most of these people are not covered by employment laws or entitled to welfare provisions (Badigannavar and Ghosh 2020).

The segmentation of the labour market also reflects the segmentation of the education and training system. Nölke et al. (2020) emphasize the sharp contrast between the provision of high-quality university education for a small part of the urban labour force and under-investment in vocational skills, which are under-provided both by the state and by firms.

Yet many other countries also fit the SME model quite well – as noted above, such cases include Malaysia and Indonesia (Walter and Zhang 2012a). Singapore is an interesting hybrid case, where a commitment to free trade and other free-market policies co-exists with many statist features (Cheang 2023). The state played a very significant role in establishing dominant firms in various sectors, including Singapore Airlines, the bank DBS or the shipping firm Neptune Orient Lines (Kurlantzick 2016: 195; Carney 2016).

As discussed in Chapter 2, even the United States, the archetype of an LME, has important elements of statism, most notably, in terms of current innovation policies related to the military (Weiss 2014). Other economies with a *dirigiste* tradition, such as France and Finland, have some institutional legacies of state involvement that influence innovation policy, even though the economies as a whole could not be regarded as a SMEs. Whilst various international institutions generally take a negative view of state intervention, the increasing clout of leading SMEs associated with the rise of the BRICs (Brazil, Russia, India, China and South Africa) could lead to a growing influence of statist ideas and policies across other countries and international organizations, not least given the renewed interest in industrial policy in many countries (Mazzucato 2018). This suggests that the SME model could turn out to be increasingly influential and inspire a general revival of state activism and industrial policy (Kurlantzick 2016; see also Nölke et al. 2020).

Another question arising in relation to the SME model is whether it should be regarded as a distinctive VoC model – just as in HMEs, the core logic of coordination in SMEs is hierarchy. The main difference is that the core actors differ – in HMEs they are mostly diversified business groups or multinational enterprises (MNEs), whereas it is the state that plays this role in SMEs. However, as suggested by Carney (2016), both types of economies could be viewed as sub-types of HME, which he calls FMEs (family-market economies dominated by diversified business groups that are often family-led) and SMEs (state-market economies) (see also Feldmann 2019). In practice, as this chapter has also illustrated, SMEs often contain both state-owned or state-dominated businesses and domestic conglomerates, which also turns the distinction between them into a question of degree. This is particularly obvious in the case of Brazil that has been classified both as an HME and as an SME (Feldmann 2019), but this may also apply to other cases, including India given the importance of family-dominated business groups. However, there may be a strong case for considering the state as a distinctive actor whose coordinating role is best analysed as a separate category.

A strong state is also no guarantee for successful SME policies. There are many examples of inefficient and wasteful state interventions, which in turn has inspired many economists' critique of an activist state as contributing to government failure. This is a lively debate where a number of scholars have highlighted the central role of the state in counteracting market failures, whilst others have stressed a more foundational role of the state in every economic system. Whilst there is substantial agreement on the kinds of features that enable a developmental state to function more efficiently, such as a competent and efficient bureaucracy, it is less clear where such institutions come from and when exactly they are successful.

As the previous section illustrates, a variety of factors may contribute to the emergence of SMEs in various contexts. As many scholars have advocated introducing SME-type institutions across a variety of countries, this raises questions about the prerequisites for such institutions. The extent to which such institutions can be crafted or whether certain structural legacies are essential has profound implications for understanding the applicability of this model to other countries.

Another open question relates to the sustainability of the model. On the one hand, the decline of the developmental state in France and East Asia might imply that SME institutions in higher-income countries face certain challenges. Several countries have struggled to maintain developmental state institutions in the face of social demands (Naseemullah and Arnold 2015). Such pressures affected South Korea and Taiwan in the late 1980s as various groups mobilized for greater political influence and democratization. On the other hand, the long-standing success of China in particular has added to the appeal of such a model. Similarly, the role of the state as a strategic investor in innovation and the rise of sovereign wealth funds imply that some SME features retain an enduring appeal across many different countries (Mazzucato 2018).

Conclusion

The rise of China and to some extent that of the BRICs countries has contributed to renewed interest in the role of the state and its potential to guide economies to success. This chapter has discussed the core logic of VoC models of statist market economies. It has focused on contemporary SMEs that loosely fit Nölke et al.'s (2020) principles of identifying relatively coherent state-led economies that are oriented towards promoting economic activity and in which the state signals play a central coordinating role. The VoC perspective highlights the complementarities between the coordinating role of the state, institutions and economic activity in such economies. It has discussed to what extent this model can elucidate key BRICS economies. Whilst the success of these economies prompted debate about state capitalism, some of the challenges they have experienced (including the growth slowdown in China and the crisis in Brazil after 2014) have also strengthened voices of criticism. The core dilemma of state capitalism is captured by Evans's concept of 'embedded autonomy' and the potentially fragile balance between embeddedness and autonomy. An SME that is too embedded may descend into excessive cronyism and rent-seeking, whereas an overly autonomous state may be unaccountable and introduce inappropriate economic policies. The success of SMEs turns on maintaining this balance and updating the policy agenda in response to evolving circumstances.

Discussion questions

- What are the main features of statist market economies? To what extent is the SME model different from the traditional developmental state and other VoC models?
- What are the main advantages of statist market economies?
- What are the potential drawbacks of relying on state direction, and to what extent can such risks be minimized?
- Which economies are most likely to be interested in this model or benefit from adopting it?
- How likely is it that the rise of China will give rise to a 'Beijing consensus' in favour of a greater role for the state in economic governance?

PART III

New challenges and new models?

8

Growth regimes and the evolution of capitalism

One of the most common and important criticisms of the VoC framework is that it does not adequately capture the dynamic nature of capitalism and key processes of change. In particular, some critics have perceived the emphasis on models of capitalism and institutional equilibria as overly static and ill-equipped to capture the dramatic changes that have taken place in the world economy since the end of the Second World War. This chapter provides an overview of key changes, notably liberalization, structural change and the rise of the knowledge economy (other related trends associated with financialization and the macroeconomy are discussed in Chapters 9 and 10). It relates these developments to the nature of capitalism and growth. In addition, the chapter analyses capitalist development from the mid-1940s onwards as a sequence of growth regimes and discusses how they are shaped by political developments, such as the nature of democratic politics and party systems.

Understanding the development of growth regimes

One of the key features of capitalism is the fact that it changes a lot over time. Pre-industrial merchant capitalism was very different from the system that emerged after the Industrial Revolution of the nineteenth century. If we consider the twentieth century, a stark contrast emerges between the interwar period, notably associated with the instability of capitalism and the Great Depression, which led to sharp crises and steep increases in unemployment around the world. These crises were often exacerbated by a commitment to the Gold Standard and fixed exchange rates and further prolonged by increasing protectionism in the 1930s that had a very negative effect on international trade. Against this backdrop, the post–Second World War decades were a period of stability and high economic growth across much of the world (Shonfield 1969). In Europe this era was labelled 'les trente glorieuses', or the thirty glorious years to capture the exceptional nature of this period.

The main challenge arising from these changes is how to understand their impact on the functioning of capitalism. An influential approach to this question relates to the concept of growth regimes. Where Varieties of Capitalism theory was designed to explain differences between economies, growth regimes can be used to analyse variation over time. In a useful summary of these debates, Peter Hall (2022a) defines a growth regime as 'the ensemble of institutionalized practices central to the process whereby a country secures prosperity'. French regulation theory defines growth regimes (or accumulation regimes) in a very similar way as a

Table 8.1 The Evolution of Post-War Growth Regimes in the OECD

Growth regime	Time period	Key features
Modernization	1945–75	Keynesianism, embedded liberalism, manufacturing, Fordism
Liberalization	1980–2000	Monetarism, neoliberalism, post-Fordism, shift to services
Knowledge economy	2000	Deepening globalization and complex value chains, automation and IT, growing knowledge intensity

Source: Hall 2022a, 2022b, Hassel and Palier 2023.

complex institutional infrastructure, in which the relationship between various components, such as the wage-labour nexus, monetary policy regime, competition regime, state-society relations and the position within the international economy, constitute a more or less coherent regime that shapes the nature of economic growth (Boyer 2000). Peter Hall (2022a) distinguishes between three growth regimes associated with the successive eras of (i) modernization, (ii) liberalization and (iii) knowledge-based growth (see Table 8.1; cf. also Hassel and Palier 2023; Hopkin and Blyth 2019).

The era of modernization

The growth regime associated with the era of modernization characterized the early decades after the Second World War, a period often referred to as the 'Golden Age of Capitalism' in Europe and North America. According to Andrea Boltho (1982: 1) this period had four characteristics. First, this was a period of high growth and rapid improvements in living standards. Second, this was a prolonged period of (very close to) full employment. Third, it was a period of structural change, during which agriculture declined and lost its significance as a leading sector. During this period manufacturing was the dominant sector in most countries, but in many countries services were also becoming more significant. Fourth, there was a substantial decline in individual economic risk. The establishment of large and increasingly generous welfare states meant that individuals were well insured against life-course risks, such as unemployment, illness and old age. In addition to the social provision of welfare, it is also worth stressing that especially manufacturing jobs were regarded as good jobs, in that they were stable, well paid and associated with generous benefits. Inequality was relatively low, suggesting that capitalism can be compatible with both egalitarianism and high growth despite the common perception that there is an efficiency-equity trade-off. In most countries this model primarily benefited men and was associated with a traditional male breadwinner model, though female labour force participation started increasing over time.

This period was even more remarkable in some other parts of the world. For example, Japanese economic growth was exceptionally high, and during this period economic growth in the so-called East Asian 'tiger economies' – Hong Kong, Singapore, South Korea and Taiwan – also took off. Their success was widely described as the 'East Asian miracle', given how impressive and unexpected their high growth rates were (Perkins 2013). Whilst growth across various regions was uneven, many Latin American countries also experienced rates of economic growth that seemed quite high at the time, even though they fell short of most East Asian countries and ultimately turned out to be unsustainable once the continent was hit by the Latin American debt crisis of the 1980s. The non-capitalist communist bloc experienced a similar trajectory, as the Soviet Union and other economies led by communist parties also grew very fast for some time in the era of post-war reconstruction, which was a period of resource mobilization for rapid industrialization (Weitzman 1970).

The common characteristic of most economies in this period was the central role of manufacturing, which made a key contribution to growth across the OECD and beyond. Manufacturing accounted for a high share of both employment and economic output. In many parts of the world where industry had previously played a limited role this was a period of rapid industrialization and structural change, as employment shifted from agriculture to industry. This transformation proceeded very fast, especially in the economies that experienced the highest growth rates. By moving workers from low-productivity agricultural and rural employment into high-productivity manufacturing, these economies experienced a big boost to growth and productivity.

The post–Second World War period, especially in Europe and North America, is often characterized as the era of Fordism – an economic system centred on manufacturing and the mass production of standardized products, such as consumer durables, and drawing on modern technology and efficient organization of work (Watson 2019). Fordism also contributed to the rapid growth of both national income and wages. Higher wages translated into higher demand for manufacturing output, such as cars and various consumer durables, thereby boosting output. Higher output led to higher profits and higher wages. This helped create a virtuous circle of rising incomes and rising output, which has been described as a system of wage-led growth (Bhaduri and Marglin 1990; see also Chapter 10), given the importance of rising wages as a source of demand.

Peter Hall (2022a) emphasizes two additional and interrelated characteristics of corporate practice during this period: a drive for economies of scale and especially later in the period, a turn towards diversification in the form of professionally managed conglomerates (Hall 2022a: 6). These corporate practices dovetailed with Fordism, as there were substantial economies of scale in manufacturing, especially of most consumer durables, given the high fixed cost of establishing factories and training workers. The move to professional management was partly a function of scale, but also reflected evolving understandings of corporate best practice and the spread of ideas about scientific management.

In addition, this was also a period when firms showed great concern with the wider community given the centrality of large firms to the localities where they were based. Firms also cultivated stronger bonds with their employees, which were also underpinned by corporate welfare and defined benefit pension plans that tied employees to their jobs and contributed to comparatively long job tenures even in LMEs (Hall 2022b).

This period of high growth was also a period of relatively activist government, including Keynesian demand management to control the business cycle and an expansion of the welfare states across the OECD. Building on the insights associated with the Keynesian Revolution in economics, policymakers tended to agree that the economy could not be viewed as self-adjusting, but that countercyclical monetary and fiscal policies would be needed to prevent both overheating and deep recessions. In terms of the international economy, this era can be described as a system of 'embedded liberalism', as defined by John Ruggie (1982). This system combined managed liberalization of the global economy, notably growth in international trade, with constraints on capital mobility and fixed-but-adjustable exchange rates under the Bretton

Woods system (Eichengreen 2019). Given the limits to capital mobility, governments maintained considerable macroeconomic policy autonomy, especially in larger economies, and there was some scope for macroeconomic policy coordination and exchange rate adjustments to manage international imbalances.

Whilst this system was widely perceived as successful, perhaps especially in hindsight when it has become clear just how exceptional economic performance really was at that time, its core underpinnings were challenged in the 1970s. This was a period of crisis, when growth slowed down, countries faced two oil shocks and the Bretton Woods system underpinning international money and finance broke down. A new term – stagflation – that referred to the combination of stagnation and inflation gained currency. It challenged Keynesian understandings of the macroeconomy, notably the expectations of a relatively stable trade-off between inflation and unemployment, as captured by the Phillips curve. Stagflation, and the period of crisis more generally, led to questioning of the Keynesian orthodoxy and the wider consensus surrounding the mixed economy and the role of government intervention in managing the economy that had underpinned embedded liberalism.

Core features of the growth regime began to change dramatically across much of the world in the late 1970s and early 1980s, though the precise timings and reform sequences varied across countries and regions. The reasons for these changes are complex, and their deeper roots are contested. The immediate drivers relate to the crisis of the 1970s and the emergence of stagflation, which ran counter to dominant Keynesian understandings and made the kind of fine-tuning associated with Keynesian macroeconomic policy virtually impossible (Hall 1993). This reinforced pressures to search for alternative economic policy models and empowered politicians and analysts advocating more radical economic reform, notably to combat inflation. It contributed to the growing influence of monetarism across much of the OECD, an economic theory that implies that the government's ability to control the business cycle is much more limited than policymakers had assumed in the era of modernization. Whilst monetarists accepted that there may be a short-run trade-off between inflation and unemployment, even this was questioned by the new classical school of economics (Dornbusch 1990). These new approaches to macroeconomics regarded attempts to steer the economy by means of countercyclical demand management as counterproductive since it would not have any durable effect on employment and ultimately generate inflation.

The size of the manufacturing sector had also reached its peak, and in many countries, including the UK, leading industries were experiencing a deep crisis in 1970s, raising questions about how to strengthen their performance. At the time it was not entirely apparent what the main sources of the crisis were – and in Britain the Labour Left developed the Alternative Economic Strategy to boost productivity and growth. This strategy involved elements of protectionism and state-led investment and financial control (Wickham-Jones 1996). There were various attempts to support industries in distress, including car manufacturing, but in most cases the support merely prolonged the adjustment process for companies that were in decline instead of helping them recover (Hall 1986). Attempts by Conservative and Labour governments to stabilize the economy by using income policy, including the Labour government's Social Contract, were not successful and culminated in the Winter of Discontent, which emboldened advocates for more radical change (Hay 2010). A similar debate took place in France, where President Mitterrand was elected in 1981 on a socialist agenda and attempted a significant demand expansion (Sachs and Wyplosz 1986). However, after a very negative market response, France moved away from such policies and adopted liberalization, albeit less enthusiastically than Britain and the United States (Hall 1986; Schmidt 2003).

The era of liberalization

The second growth regime relates to the era of liberalization or what many have called the ascent of neoliberalism. This growth regime will be discussed in greater detail, as many of its key features have turned out to be resilient (Schmidt and Thatcher 2013) and to persist even in the era of the knowledge economy. As a result, there is some debate about whether the knowledge economy should be viewed as a genuinely new growth regime or a deepening or further evolution of the neoliberal era. Others regard financialization or the growing influence of finance as the defining feature of a new growth regime (see Chapter 9).

The ensuing transformation of capitalism manifested itself in many ways, and this chapter focuses on the most important processes of change – liberalization, as well as structural change, notably the rise of services and the associated changes in corporate organization.

Liberalization and deregulation

Since the 1980s, market liberalization was a key trend that took place in most economies, although there is some variation in the extent and timings of these developments across countries. This period is often described as the 'rise of neoliberalism' (Centeno and Cohen 2012; Harvey 2007). Although this term is somewhat controversial, as some see it as overly polemical or as too broad, it captures the general trend towards the expansion of markets into more areas of social life. Centeno and Cohen (2012: 318) define neoliberalism as 'an explicit preference for private over public control' that manifests itself in terms of economic policy, ideology and power configurations and represents a sharp break from the era of modernization in each of these respects. Neoliberalism has been associated with deregulation of domestic markets in goods and services and liberalization of financial markets as well (see Chapter 9), with a profound impact on the welfare state, industrial relations and on the role of the state more generally. These trends could be viewed as global, as they have affected most parts of the world, albeit in quite different ways and with uneven effects.

Market reform is sometimes described as a process of shrinking the state, as some previously state-run activities or state-owned firms were privatized, and it has also been associated with other changes. Market mechanisms have permeated the state in various ways, such as public-private partnerships or through the adoption of market logic by public sector actors, as in the case of New Public Management practices or the introduction of outsourcing or quasi-markets within the public sector (Dunleavy and Hood 1994). However, the image of a rollback of the state may be misleading. Another way of thinking about this process is that it is associated with a strengthening of the state. In Andrew Gamble's (1994) account of Thatcherism, a free economy and a strong state were inextricably linked. Other accounts have analysed how market reform entails a reconfiguration of the state's role that results in creating and enforcing new rules (Vogel 1996). The core premise of such interpretations is that a strong state that is capable of enforcing property, contract and other market rules is a prerequisite for strong markets and for underpinning neoliberalism. Advanced markets rely on the existence of sophisticated regulation and a range of complex policy instruments to ensure that they work well (Iversen and Soskice 2019).

Liberalization is also reflected in the role of government. In the field of macroeconomic policy, the decline of the earlier Keynesian consensus meant that governments abandoned attempts to fine-tune the economy and increasingly stepped away from activist monetary policy. Independent central banks with a mandate to focus on maintaining low inflation became common across and increasingly beyond the OECD. The liberalization trend also affected the welfare state, both in terms of its generosity and the way it is organized, as there was a shift from public to private provision even in countries with traditions of very strong public sectors, like Sweden, which saw a big increase in the number of private healthcare and education providers (Gingrich 2011). In other countries, where such services had often featured private providers in the past, like the United States, there have been profound changes that have been described as a 'privatization of risk' (Hacker 2004). Whilst dramatic cutbacks in overall spending levels are rare (spending levels have generally been constant or even risen in many countries), there is a sense of permanent crisis or permanent austerity in the welfare state as entitlement programmes have often failed to keep up with new risks or other developments, such as ageing populations or rising costs of healthcare and medicine. This reinforces the sense that welfare states have become less generous or at least less well equipped to protect households against various market or life-course risks (Pierson 1998).

This process of liberalization has also manifested itself in the organization of work and industrial relations. It has led to increases in non-standard work, including self-employment, part-time work and various forms of precarious work. Such trends are often associated with dualization, or a deepening of the divide between core workers on stable contracts coupled with more generous welfare entitlements and those in more precarious forms of employment (Emmenegger et al. 2012).

There has also been a general trend towards liberalization in the sphere of industrial relations, as documented by Baccaro and Howell (2017). Union membership has fallen in most countries, but there has also been a more general decentralization of industrial relations and wage bargaining. Even in many countries where there used to be national agreements between employers' associations and trade union federations, agreements are now negotiated at the sectoral or even at the firm level. A notable example of this shift is Sweden, once the key example of national-level corporatist agreements (Iversen 1996; Pontusson and Swenson 1996).

Whilst these trends are common to most OECD economies, it should be noted that they do not imply that there has been any complete convergence of all economies on a free-market model or on the LME variety of capitalism, as also acknowledged by Baccaro and Howell (2017) – although there has been a common trend towards greater liberalization, these processes have played out in different ways across countries and not led to full convergence on a uniform neoliberal model (Thelen 2014).

The general institutional context and legacies affect how markets are integrated into a given economy, which means that markets may operate in different ways. As Gingrich (2011) has shown, a general emphasis on market reform and privatization masks considerable cross-national diversity. For example, health and education markets operate in very different ways and generate divergent outcomes depending on particular contexts, and they vary in terms of how they affect consumers and producers or whether they are associated with egalitarian outcomes or how they promote competition. Marketization may involve greater competition between private providers, but if this arrangement is coupled with a funding system that allows people irrespective of income to use private services at a subsidized rate, this could be associated with relatively egalitarian outcomes, especially compared with a system that involves substantial differences in user fees.

In other words, markets play an increasingly important role in most economies and that they often reshape or co-exist (sometimes uneasily) with other coordination mechanisms, and their significance needs to be considered when analysing the evolution of key institutions in particular economies. However, although there is a common direction of travel in terms of the growing significance of markets, many differences persist, which means that fine-grained analysis of particular institutional arrangements and cross-national differences is needed.

Changes in corporate organization and structural change: The rise of services

For much of the twentieth century the OECD economies were dominated by manufacturing and characterized by an economic system that is traditionally referred to as Fordism. This system was largely based on mass production and associated with a period of relatively stable economic growth, rising living standards and moderate levels of inequality. Wage increases contributed to further increases in demand for key manufacturing goods, such as consumer durables. This was also a period of class compromise with corporatism in ascent, in part thanks to a complementarity between low- or medium-skilled workers and for high-skilled workers as Fordist mass production relied on employees with different skill levels (Iversen and Soskice 2019: 104). Beyond the traditional OECD countries, it was also a period of industrialization and rising living standards across various parts of Asia and Latin America.

The era of liberalization affected the way firms operated, and three important shifts in corporate practice can be identified (Hall 2022a: 10). The first shift implies that firms increasingly began to focus on maximizing shareholder value as a key objective of corporate activity (Lazonick and O'Sullivan 2000; see also Chapter 9). The second trend, partly related to the first, was that companies were reorganized to focus on what were regarded as their core competencies. Such a specialization was expected to make them more efficient and to help maximize their share price. This specialization was facilitated by the third trend, namely the move towards outsourcing labour and services that had previously been provided within the boundaries of the firm. The latter process has sometimes been described as the 'Nike-fication' of the firm, given that Nike is a prominent example of this business model. Nike has a relatively small number of employees that mostly focus on design and marketing, whereas everything else, including practically all the production of footwear, is outsourced. In this model the firm itself effectively turns into a 'nexus of contracts' negotiating agreements with its suppliers (Davis 2016a). More generally, this meant that the period of growth in size that had characterized firm structure came to an end. It also contributed to the decline of Fordist mass production. Firms increasingly sought to reorganize their production around *flexible accumulation*, which means that machines and production processes can be used flexibly and for different purposes (Schoenberger 1988). This shift has put a greater premium on skills and technology and contributed to the subsequent emergence of a knowledge economy.

The era of liberalization has also been associated with structural change. Since the 1980s the rise of services has been evident across much of the world, especially in the OECD, as a combination of productivity improvements, outsourcing and the growth of imports has contributed to a decline in manufacturing employment and in manufacturing as a share of GDP. However, the rise of services is increasingly affecting other parts of the world too – the reasons for the gradual shift to services relate to developments both on the supply and demand side. On the supply side, the productivity of manufacturing has increased over time, and therefore the share of manufacturing employment has fallen faster than its share of GDP, freeing up labour and capital for other economic activities, but also contributing to the rising unemployment of former industrial workers. In addition, there are also demand factors related to income elasticities, or the responsiveness of demand to increases in income. Demand for manufacturing goods tends not to grow as fast as demand for services when incomes are rising. As a result, if GDP is increasing, the growth in demand for many manufacturing goods is unlikely to keep up. Rising income levels tend to be associated with growing demand for services as consumption patterns change.

Whilst many governments have celebrated and promoted the rise of services, this has also generated some concern, notably about the impact of deindustrialization on growth. Economic growth rates since the 1980s have generally been lower than during the Golden Age of Capitalism, and one possible explanation for this is that productivity increases may be harder to achieve, at least in many service industries (Baumol 1967; Gordon 1987). This is also one of the reasons why there has been growing concern about premature deindustrialization in the Global South. Dani Rodrik (2016: 21) shows that deindustrialization has begun at lower levels of income per capita since 1990. This is likely to raise complex challenges for economies in the Global South that need to look for alternative sources of growth, but the new industries may not be as conducive to rapid and egalitarian growth as the Fordist model centred on manufacturing.

Governments across the world have been confronted with various challenges as they have sought to respond to these changes. To what extent have economies been transformed as a result of these trends, and how have governments sought to stimulate economic growth and influence the distribution of incomes? An influential early analysis of the trade-offs associated with the rise of the service economy highlighted a trilemma (Iversen and Wren 1998), implying that economies could only achieve two of the following three objectives at a given time: an increase in service sector jobs, low inequality and budget balance. The main reason for this trilemma stressed by Iversen and Wren (1998) relates to the low pay and limited potential for productivity increases in many service-sector jobs, which implied that an increase in low-wage jobs and an associated rise in inequality would typically be a key feature of the expansion of service sector employment. Depending on the choices countries make, which typically reflect their pre-existing welfare state institutions, Iversen and Wren (1998) identify three trajectories. The first is associated with rising inequality and a growth in service-sector jobs, a trajectory most common in LMEs with liberal welfare states (Esping-Andersen 1990). Countries more committed to maintaining low inequality either fail to expand the service sector to a significant extent (as was the case of many Continental European CMEs with conservative welfare states) or seek to do it in a more egalitarian way, usually by expanding the public sector, which puts greater pressure on government finances and tends to increase spending and taxes. This is the response that Iversen and Wren associate with the Nordic CMEs and their large and universalist social democratic welfare states.

In other words, a possible implication of the emerging service economy that is consistent with Iversen and Wren's (1998) analysis is that the changes in economic institutions and performance are still largely shaped by the nature of different VoC and models of welfare states.

Later studies have extended these insights in various ways. First, Wren (2013) has provided a more nuanced account of the nature of the service sector by distinguishing between three kinds of service industries or what she calls dynamic, non-dynamic and welfare services (see Table 8.2). The upshot of her analysis is that both skill requirements and the potential for productivity improvements vary across different parts of the service sector. A further implication of this is that the range of government policies in relation to skills and technology promotion that could affect the growth and productivity of services and also influence distributive outcomes is greater than in the Iversen and Wren model, which increases the scope for social investment and

Table 8.2 Typology of Service Industries

Type of industry	Main characteristics	Key examples
Non-dynamic	Genuine productivity improvements unlikely (serving more customers leads to lower quality)	Hairdressers, waiters, childcare provision
Dynamic	Skill- and technology-intensive – productivity increases likely	Finance, business services
Welfare	Public provision	Education, health

Source: Wren (2013, 2020).

industrial policy. This suggests that there may also be a wider range of adjustment trajectories, as discussed in more detail in Chapter 10.

The era of the knowledge economy

Many observers have suggested that the cumulative effect of various common trends is associated with the emergence of a new growth regime around the year 2000, which has been described as the 'knowledge economy'. This is a form of economy that is characterized by 'skills-based technological progress'. This is a process of rapid technological change that also enhances the importance of skills within the economy.

Three key features stand out (Hall 2022a: 16). The first and perhaps most important element of the knowledge economy is arguably the growth of information technology, whose influence started increasing rapidly around the year 2000 thanks to the spread of these technologies and more widespread use of computers and the internet in the workplace. This has had a profound effect on the nature of work. This process also relates to a second shift which is represented by the growth of intangible investments – this includes skills, but also a growing significance of intellectual property rights to profits and the nature of competition (Schwartz 2022). These two processes have also facilitated a third shift, namely the move towards outsourcing. These new technologies have made it possible to outsource a much wider range of jobs and elements of the production process as it is possible to communicate instantaneously over long distances. As a result, the production process can be segmented and subdivided into components taking place across different parts of the world (see also Chapter 12).

The impact of the knowledge economy has been profound and relates to developments across various sectors, with some of the most notable advances in the 'life sciences and biotechnology, in robotization and artificial intelligence, virtual and augmented reality, as well as in materials and nanotechnology, in sensor technology and mobile and cloud computing, and these have all fed on each other' (Iversen and Soskice 2019: 141). The scale of these changes is enormous, and we may only be at the beginning of this process. In the case of earlier scientific and technological breakthroughs, it took decades before the full impact on the economy and work would become apparent. These processes are likely to affect most sectors of the economy and revolutionize the nature of work and the organization of production by contributing to higher productivity in many professions, including the service sector (somewhat counteracting the trends discussed earlier) – and thereby to economic growth in many parts of the world. However, one of the main reasons why it may take longer for economies to reap the full benefit of these changes is that a variety of organizational changes are needed to take advantage of the new technologies and forms of knowledge (Powell and Snellman 2004).

The complexity of these technologies has increased the role of skills and education. Many of the new sectors and technologies are very skill-intensive and rely on very advanced skill levels as these are crucial not just for innovation, but also for applying complex technologies in flexible ways. To some extent this has defied earlier predictions about sluggish productivity in the post-industrial economy. Nevertheless, although the contribution of these technologies to economic growth has been significant and led to some striking productivity improvements (Jorgenson 2005), they have not fully lived up to the most enthusiastic expectations about their transformative effects on economic performance.

A key reason for this is that the effects of the new technologies are uneven. On the one hand, new technologies can substitute for some low-skilled jobs, as robotization can help reduce the number of workers or even replace them completely in the context of certain tasks. On the other hand, the new technologies are mostly a complement to high-skill jobs. In these cases the high-skilled workers are still needed, but they are increasingly reliant on the new technologies in their work. Whilst the new technologies enhance their productivity, they also increase the skill requirements of these jobs. These trends lead to higher pay for the highly skilled, whilst putting downward pressure on pay for the low-skilled. As a result of these processes inequality is rising across much of the OECD.

It is also likely that these technologies will have a profound effect on the welfare state. In particular, as discussed further in the next section on the platform economy, they facilitate the collection, processing and marketization of information. Health characteristics and health-related behaviours that were unknown or even unknowable in the past can now be measured with greater precision, which could have negative effects on social solidarity and undermine demand for many general and national programmes as it may induce more people to opt out of risk-pooling programmes (Iversen and Rehm 2022).

Towards an era of the platform economy?

In the 2010s the growth of the platform economy was frequently described as a significant transition in the evolution of capitalism, or even as the beginning of a new era of 'platform capitalism' (Rahman and Thelen 2019). This concept refers to the growing centrality of platforms to the business models of influential firms, like Amazon, Uber, Airbnb and others. Their business model is based on maintaining an online platform on which goods and services produced by other firms or rooms or apartments rented out by private individuals on Airbnb can be easily accessed. The rise of this platform model of business has potentially profound consequences for the nature of firms, production and work.

First, this business logic effectively undermines some traditional understandings of firms. In the traditional account based on transaction costs economics and Coase's (1937) seminal analysis of the theory of the firm, firms are created to reduce transaction costs by internalizing certain activities. In the case of large vertically integrated firms most of the production process and many associated activities take place within a single firm. Since the 1980s many businesses have instead sought to focus on their core activities and bought inputs and services from other suppliers and firms that constitute larger supply chains. The rise of the platform model accentuates this process, as the platform firm need not produce anything at all in house. It acts as a matchmaker by facilitating a web of contracts with suppliers or enabling these suppliers to access the market via its platform.

Second, Davis (2016b) argues that the rise of platform capitalism could augur the end of the public corporation. This is the canonical model of firms, especially in LMEs. Public firms are widely held by a large number of shareholders and listed on stock markets with freely tradable shares. Davis (2016b) shows that there has been a trend towards fewer listed firms and a falling number of IPOs (initial public offerings), or attempts to list new firms on the stock market to raise funds. Even among many listed firms dual-class voting rights (previously mostly associated with dual-class shares in CMEs or NMEs – see Chapters 3 and 4) are becoming more common, which weakens the position of minority shareholders. Instead, platform firms tend to be dominated by their founders who are usually also behind the initial innovation. They tend to guard the associated brand jealously, as a weakening of the brand could also undermine the position of these companies. Unlike many traditional firms, they have few assets beyond the brand itself and do not generally produce any goods or services of their own. They rely on what economists call 'network effects', that is, their dominant position in the market place. The more users a particular platform has, the more valuable it is.

Third, platform capitalism also has profound consequences for the nature of work. Platform firms generally have only a small number of core employees on traditional contracts – these employees tend to be well paid and focus on product development, strategy and so on, but the vast majority of people working for many of these firms tend to be contractors or employed on zero-hours contract (paid by the hour or in proportion to the completion of particular tasks). Whilst some accounts view platform work as liberating, by turning workers into contractors who can choose when and how much they work, this progressive potential may often be ephemeral. As the case of Uber drivers demonstrates, the flexibility that comes with the contractor status may well be overshadowed by a dramatic increase in precarity, surveillance and lack of social protection. Uber has argued that standard employment regulation and protections do not apply to its drivers, as they are effectively contractors and not workers engaged in wage labour. Davis (2016a) suggests that this kind of Uberization could lead to a 'dark age' for labour associated with fewer rights and benefits and with precarity, as workers no longer have stable jobs, but perform specific tasks as independent contractors, often under conditions of intense surveillance of their work and of their customers (Zuboff 2019).

Fourth, and related to the previous two points, platform firms are disruptive innovators who often test the limits of existing institutions by introducing new technologies and practices, thereby challenging traditional competitors, such as taxi companies (in the case of Uber), hotels (in the case of Airbnb) and retailers (in the case of Amazon). As a result of these innovations and the creative use of loopholes to circumvent labour law, platform firms are very hard to regulate. Their operations have significant social consequences, not just in terms of work, employment and welfare, but also for housing markets and urban policy, including environmental issues associated with tourism, as in the case of Airbnb. These consequences have prompted intense debate in many countries and led to attempts to use legal or regulatory mechanisms to ban or at least curtail the activities of platform firms in various places.

However, in addition to these broad trends, the rise of the platform economy also raises two other important challenges. First, the political responses have varied considerably across countries. Some economies have been more open to the platform economy than others. In particular, LMEs, and notably the United States, have been at the forefront of these trends. By contrast, European CMEs have been more cautious and often implemented more restrictive regulations limiting the growth of the platform economy. The pioneering work by Kathleen Thelen and her co-authors has shed light on this variation (Thelen 2018; Rahman and Thelen 2019; Culpepper and Thelen 2020). The growth of the platform economy in CMEs is constrained by several factors, including legal systems that are less accommodating of radical disruption. The political influence of employers' associations and trade unions also plays an important role in this context, as this enables workers and other businesses to mobilize more effectively against platform firms.

Second, notwithstanding the differences between countries, it has been surprisingly difficult to regulate and address the social consequences of platform capitalism. This partly relates to their role as disruptive innovators, which means that platform firms deliberately experiment and push the limits of what is legal, and regulators and policymakers have struggled to keep up with these trends and devise appropriate responses. The regulatory response may still be viewed as surprisingly meek as one might also expect traditional firms to support efforts to crack down on platform firms, given the threat that they pose to them. Whilst taxi companies have often opposed Uber and hotels have sought tighter regulations or bans targeting Airbnb, the success of regulation might be viewed as relatively limited.

The puzzling timidity of regulatory responses has been analysed in an influential study by Culpepper and Thelen (2020), who argue that the rise of platform capitalism is also associated with a new form of business power or what they call 'platform power'. This kind of power differs from traditional understandings of business power as either structural (vested in firms thanks to their centrality to the economy) or instrumental (related to the resources they can bring to bear, for example, by lobbying the government and making campaign donations – see also Chapter 9). Platform power relates to the tacit alliance between platform firms and consumers who have grown accustomed to accessing goods and services at low prices and by means of a few clicks on their smartphone. Platform firms have been able to rely on tacit and sometimes explicit support from consumers to stave off any attempts to regulate them in a way that businesses have not traditionally been able to do.

Yet platform firms do not always get their own way. At times there is resistance, even within the LMEs that could be viewed as particularly amenable to platform power for the above-mentioned reasons. Culpepper and Thelen (2020) suggest that variable responses are largely related to framing and priming. As long as platform firms successfully appeal to consumer interests, they are likely to elicit considerable support given how important the speed and convenience of these services are to consumers. However, this permissive consensus underpinning consumer support could break down, for example, due to a loss of trust as a result of quality concerns, privacy issues related to data gathering or reports about manipulation of data, as in the case of Facebook and the US election. In the face of such concerns consumer support may erode. Similarly, if competing appeals to people as citizens gain traction, then concerns related to privacy, democracy or social justice (due to reports of exploitative practices in Amazon warehouses or the adverse effect of Airbnb on housing markets) are more likely to come to the fore and nudge a larger number of people to support more stringent regulation of platform firms. Differences in the characteristics of the products are also likely to affect how effective consumer mobilization is likely to be. For example, Uber caters primarily to local residents and voters, whereas Airbnb caters to tourists who do not vote in the localities where they use the platform.

A key question surrounding the platform economy is how representative it is of trends in contemporary capitalism. Whilst the significance of the key platform firms is considerable, many other parts of the economy have at least so far been less affected by these developments. With some exceptions related to temporary job covers and projects, this includes the public sector, including education and health, manufacturing and many service industries, but it remains to be seen whether the process of disruptive innovation based on platform technologies could affect a wider range of sectors over the coming years and decades. On the other hand, these processes could interact with other technological developments that may have an even bigger impact on the role of business and the functioning of the political economy. The social consequences of these trends, for example, in terms of the 'death of the high street' have a profound impact on communities, especially in smaller cities and towns, though there may also be new opportunities to recast such spaces to cater to a new 'experience economy' (Hughes and Jackson 2015; Orr et al. 2023)

It is also important to emphasize that platform capitalism is increasingly becoming a global phenomenon and also spreading in the Global South. Many influential platforms, like Facebook, already have a foothold and many users across the Global South, and they use a range of tools, including the development of Free Basics, a pared-down version of the platform that was targeted to the Indian market. However, it also encountered fierce opposition and regulatory challenges. Given that the number of internet users is growing fast across much of the Global South, it seems likely that the platform economy will also continue to grow in these regions, often with uneven effects on working conditions and pay (Vallas and Schor 2020). In some cases the platform economy may compare favourably to many alternative informal sector jobs (Cieslik, Banya and Vira 2022).

Politics and the evolution of growth regimes

This section analyses the evolution of growth regimes. A number of factors have contributed to these changes, including new technologies, and competitive pressures that induce firms to look for new profit opportunities. For example, globalization is facilitated by advances in technology, as trade in goods has grown thanks to new modes of transport, and IT facilitates instantaneous financial transactions. Similarly, the rise of platform firms relies on the technology underpinning the platform and the existence of consumers with easy access to the internet. Nevertheless, whilst new technologies facilitate these changes, technological or economic factors are unlikely to provide full explanations of these trends. This is why it is important to consider how their impact on economies is shaped by political factors.

This section explores the political roots of growth regimes by focusing on what Hall (2022a: 6) has referred to as 'representation regimes', which 'reflect conditions in the arenas of electoral and producer group politics that confer influence on specific segments of the population' (Hall 2022b: 1). It also considers a complementary argument about the relationship between growth regimes and party politics developed by Hopkin and Blyth (2019; see also Blyth and Matthijs 2017). Electoral politics is dominated by political parties, but in this context it is not just the partisan composition of government that matters as parties and their platforms evolve over time, largely reflecting the fact that the central cleavage structure in society changes as well. Producer group politics refers to the ways 'in which various segments of labor and capital agitate for policies that benefit them' (Hall 2020: 186). It reflects the influence of trade unions and employers' associations, which provide collective representation for workers and firms. In addition, Hall also considers the role of ideas, which play an important role in shaping common understandings of such interests and help define the range of solutions to key problems that are perceived as viable. This range of ideas constitutes the 'economic gestalt' of a given era (Hall 2020).

Hall (2022b) demonstrates how these factors interact to shape growth regimes. In the era of modernization the political representation regimes across the OECD largely reflected a class divide, which was further reinforced by producer group politics. The active role of unions and employers' associations in this era was conducive to the search for cross-class agreement on economic policy surrounding a mixed economy. In the era of modernization there was a consensus among major parties on Keynesianism ('we are all Keynesians now', as US president Richard Nixon declared) and a mixed economy with a welfare state. To some extent this also reflected the still relatively recent experience of economic crisis in the interwar period and the war-time sacrifices of the working class. In the British context this convergence between left and right gave rise to the idea of 'Butskellism' – implying that the Labour Chancellor Hugh Gaitskell pursued very similar policies to Rab Butler as the Conservative Chancellor. This meant that parties were increasingly operating as what Otto Kirchheimer (1965) called 'catch-all parties' (*Allerweltsparteien*) by developing agendas that could be attractive to a wide range of groups (beyond the core constituencies that had founded them) (Krouwel 2003). In times of high economic growth rates this was often associated with attempts by parties to outbid each other in terms of new policy initiatives (Hopkin and Blyth 2019).

In the era of liberalization the representation regime changed. Hall (2022b) highlights several factors. First and partly as a result of the preceding decades of growth and prosperity and structural change in the economy, notably the growing share of services and white-collar professions, the importance of class had declined. In most countries political competition now operated along two dimensions – a traditional left-right dimension, but also another post-materialist dimension that focused on the environment and a host of social issues. The rise of Green parties across Western Europe is emblematic of these trends. In terms of economic policy these trends were associated with a convergence on more pro-market platforms embracing liberalization, which was also embraced by mainstream centre-left parties, especially in the heyday of the Third Way policies advanced by New Labour in the UK, Gerhard Schröder's Social Democrats in Germany and by other centre-left parties, such as Fernando Henrique Cardoso's Party of Brazilian Social Democracy in Brazil (Power 2001). These policy shifts were underpinned by a weakening of trade unions and growing business influence, in part through channels of quiet politics in addition to traditional producer group politics (Culpepper 2011). Hopkin and Blyth (2019) argue that this led mainstream political parties increasingly to operate like cartel parties, each of which controlled a relatively stable share of the electoral market and engaged in limited oligopolistic competition without significant differentiation on economic policy. As a result, there was weaker representation of economic interests. Peter Mair (2013) has argued that the cumulative effect of this weakening of representation was a 'hollowing out' of democracy.

The emergence of the era of the knowledge economy was associated with changes in economic policy, notably higher spending on social investment, innovation policy as well as policies facilitating outsourcing. To some extent these changes have grown out of the representation regime that emerged during the era of liberalization, including middle-class voters employed in the new knowledge economy. However, they have also created a new cleavage pitting those benefiting from the knowledge economy against traditional working-class constituencies that have not benefited from these changes. This provides an opportunity for populist or anti-system parties to challenge the established party system and the cartel parties, as these constituencies do not feel represented by mainstream parties (Hopkin and Blyth 2019; Iversen and Soskice 2019). This suggests that the political underpinnings of the knowledge economy may be increasingly fragile, which could be a significant challenge for the stability of capitalism (see Chapter 11 for a more detailed discussion of the rise of populism).

The main implication of these debates is that democracy and capitalism evolve in tandem, and the growth regime and representation regime influence and shape each other. A key challenge for research on comparative capitalism revolves around analysing the complex processes by which they shape each other and co-evolve over time.

Conclusion

This chapter has highlighted that capitalism is a dynamic system that it is undergoing dramatic change in a variety of respects. This has important implications for understanding capitalist diversity. In particular, it implies that capitalist institutions should not be understood as rigid or immutable structures. Institutional arrangements change over time, and some of the traditional institutions underpinning manufacturing may acquire new functions or be less significant in a service-based economy. The analysis of capitalism as a sequence of growth regimes – from the era of modernization to the era of liberalization and the knowledge economy – is a useful complement to other strands of comparative capitalism in that it provides a nuanced account of change over time and shows how market institutions and economic structures evolve. It also demonstrates how such changes interact with representation regimes in the sphere of politics and with the evolution of party systems.

Although the changes discussed in this chapter affect most economies, they tend to proceed at different rates and be shaped by national conditions. There were significant cross-country differences during the Golden Age of Capitalism, and the processes of liberalization and embrace of the knowledge economy have varied considerably across the OECD (Thelen 2014). Whilst platform firms are now active in most countries, the regulatory frameworks guiding their operations are not uniform and reflect differences between national varieties of capitalism and their social and political underpinnings (see also Chapter 10).

Discussion questions

- What are the key features of the main growth regimes since the mid-twentieth century?
- What explains the origins of each growth regime? Which factors are the most important determinants?
- Are growth regimes a compelling way of understanding the evolution of capitalism over time?
- To what extent is the evolution of capitalism over time more important than the diversity of capitalism at any given time? Is there any scope for combining these perspectives?
- To what extent can the historical evolution of growth regimes shed light on the options for economic policy in the present?

9

Financialization

The liberalization and deregulation of the financial sector is another trend closely connected to neoliberalism that has attracted great attention since the 1980s. These processes have transformed the role of finance in profound ways in many parts of the world. This transformation is often summarized under the heading of 'financialization', which captures the growing importance of the financial sector. Financialization is often viewed as an alternative general perspective on contemporary capitalism as an era of financialized capitalism. This chapter begins by discussing the relationship between finance, financial crises and capitalism and then examines processes of financialization by distinguishing between the effects of financialization on firms, households and the economy as a whole. The general discussion relates mostly to liberal market economies given that this is where these processes have been particularly pronounced. It then explores the relationship between financialization and VoC and how financialization has affected other types of economies. Towards the end of the chapter attention shifts to the politics of financialization and financial regulation and the significance of these trends for understanding comparative capitalism.

Finance and capitalism: Growth and instability

Finance is an essential feature of most kinds of market behaviour. Indeed, there is a long history of financial intermediation and debt that precedes the rise of capitalism (Ferguson 2008; Graeber 2011).

There are also good reasons to argue that financial markets are essential to capitalism as a system. In Geoffrey Hodgson's (2015) definition 'a developed financial system with banking institutions, the widespread use of credit with property as collateral, and the selling of debt' is a key characteristic of capitalism. For Hodgson (2017), the emergence of capitalism in England in the eighteenth century was largely the result of the post-1688 financial reforms. As a result of these reforms both the use of property as collateral and the market for debt grew, which in turn stimulated capitalist development.

A wide range of economic studies have found that financial development is an important driver of economic growth (Levine 1997). There are many reasons for this. Without access to finance it is hard to establish new companies or for existing companies to invest. Yet seemingly less sophisticated financial systems have also generated high levels of investment, albeit sometimes by other means, as in the context of SMEs, where the state plays a central role in promoting investment (see Chapter 7; Gerschenkron 1962).

Other studies have focused on the importance of finance for innovation, and various schemes have been devised to compensate for the lack of finance in low-income countries and regions. For example, Muhammad Yunus was awarded the Nobel Prize for his contribution to developing micro-finance as a way of alleviating credit constraints for low-income households and especially women (Morduch 1999). There has also been greater emphasis on 'democratizing finance' in terms of promoting access to mortgage finance for low-income households, especially in LMEs. In the United States and the United Kingdom, such schemes have helped boost home-ownership rates. Financial inclusion or granting previously excluded groups access to finance has become a key policy priority in many countries, especially in the Global South, but also in low-income areas of the Global North.

Notwithstanding the contributions of a well-developed financial system, finance is also a contradictory phenomenon. Whilst financial development is closely bound up with economic growth and development, the financial sector is also a source of instability. Most analysts of capitalism – including both supporters and critics – have viewed crises as an endemic feature of capitalism. For Marx this was one of the reasons why capitalism would eventually collapse, whereas Schumpeter viewed crises more favourably, as gales of creative destruction would weed out unsuccessful businesses and reinvigorate the economy. The prevalence of crises inspired Keynes to develop his theory of countercyclical macroeconomic policy as a way of managing the business cycle. Yet financial crises seem to occur periodically in capitalist economies, and the effects of these crises are often devastating. Key examples include the Great Depression of the late 1920s and early 1930s, the Latin American debt crisis of the 1980s, the East Asian crisis of the 1990s, the global financial crisis of 2007–8 and the Great Recession that followed it.

Investors' 'irrational exuberance' tends to trigger excessive borrowing and asset price booms, which subsequently give way to bust, often pushing the entire economy into a deep and sometimes drawn-out crisis (Shiller 2016; Reinhart and Rogoff 2011). Such crises are very disruptive to businesses and households, as people experience job and income losses. Such concerns have prompted much debate about whether regulations can be devised that would enable countries to reap the gains of an advanced financial sector without incurring the risks and potential losses associated with instability and crises. A range of initiatives have sought to address these issues by formulating proposals for governments, regulators and the financial sector itself, in the latter case advocating self-regulation and stronger codes of ethics to eliminate greed and abuse by financial sector professionals. Whilst crises could be regarded as endemic to all kinds of capitalism – indeed, no economy is immune to them – scholars of comparative capitalism have asked whether there is a relationship between capitalist diversity and finance, and this will be examined in the next section.

In addition some critics have suggested that the financial sector could grow too big and even lead to a 'finance curse' that affects the economy negatively, much like abundant natural resources, including oil, have been associated with a natural resource curse. A wide range of studies have found that natural resource abundance is associated with lower economic growth (Sachs and Warner 2001; Baker, Epstein and Montecino 2018). There are several reasons why an oversized financial sector might have similar adverse effects. First, a large financial sector could 'crowd out' other sectors by diverting resources and skilled labour from alternative uses. Second, it may contribute to income inequality and regional disparities. Third, Christensen et al. (2016) argue that a large financial sector may also 'capture' the economy, making it harder for the interests of other sectors to be advanced or for economic challenges to be addressed, given that policymakers prioritize the financial sector as the most important part of the economy.

Finance and VoC

To what extent do financial systems vary, and can the VoC framework shed light on finance? In the canonical VoC model the role of the financial economy is effectively subordinate to what economists refer to as the real economy, namely the production of goods and services. Finance is a tool that facilitates the production and purchase of goods and services and that helps smooth economic activity over time as firms and households can borrow when they are short on cash and then repay their loans in the future when their incomes are higher.

The main contribution of the VoC framework lies in its emphasis on institutional complementarities between the financial system and other institutions, including labour markets institutions and industrial relations, and their impact on the operation of the economy as a whole (Höpner 2005). It highlights the differences between the shareholder model prevalent in LMEs, where the flourishing stock market dovetails with firm strategies in sectors based on rapid innovation. The fast-paced stock market-based model facilitates rapid adjustments and innovation, which is why this financial system has helped these economies thrive in biotechnology, IT and other comparable sectors.

By contrast, CMEs have stakeholder-based systems of corporate governance in which banks play a central role as providers of patient capital. This kind of financial system is well aligned with production patterns in CMEs and facilitates specialization in sectors based on incremental innovation, such as advanced manufacturing, including car production. This kind of financial and corporate governance system also helps firms in CMEs invest in specific skills and weather downturns without shedding their labour force. These arrangements are also underpinned by political foundations. In a series of influential analyses, Mark Roe (2003), and Peter Gourevitch and James Shinn (2005) have shown how the electoral and party systems of CMEs, based on proportional representation and with strong centre-left parties, underpin these corporate governance and financial systems.

This logic can be extended to other varieties of capitalism, including NMEs, SMEs, DMEs and other models discussed in this book and the wider literature. In NMEs the financial system is based on strong network ties between banks and firms, whereas in SMEs, the supply of finance relates to state coordination of the economy and is typically bound up with an activist industrial policy. In DMEs much of the financial system reflects the distinctive form of external dependence that is characteristic of such economies, namely the importance of FDI and also of other foreign sources of finance, including foreign-owned banks. In each case the financial system is complementary to other institutions and to the rest of the economy, in that it facilitates investments, reinforces production strategies and enables the economy to work efficiently by strengthening the dominant logic of coordination in the economy.

This raises two questions, which some critics have viewed as potential blank spots in the VoC framework. First, the emphasis on the financial sector as reinforcing the rest of the economy does not fully acknowledge the contradictory nature of finance and its capacity to disrupt the economy and to trigger financial and economic crises. Second, the basic VoC model pays very limited attention to financialization. As the role of finance has grown over time, one might ask whether it still makes sense to view the financial system as subordinate to the real economy or whether the financial sector has gone from being the oil that greases the wheels of the economy to being its master that increasingly drives economic activity. These questions will be considered in the following sections.

Financial liberalization, deregulation and financialization

The financial sector is subject to various forms of regulation both at the domestic and international level. Domestically, regulations govern the operation of financial institutions, including the kinds of activities each organization is allowed to pursue, the level of reserves it is expected to hold and so on. Internationally, there are a variety of rules that govern convertibility, the degree to which currencies and financial instruments can be traded across borders and under what terms banks and other financial institutions are allowed to operate in other jurisdictions.

For much of the second half of the twentieth century during the era of modernization (see Chapter 8), constraints on the operation of finance were relatively strict, and widely associated with what John Ruggie (1982) has called 'embedded liberalism'. In other words, whilst the financial system was reasonably open and supported the growth of international trade and domestic economic activity, it was subordinated to other goals that were central to the Keynesian era – notably insulating the economy against shocks and facilitating domestic policy autonomy to stabilize the economy. This meant that there were various limits on international capital flows, and domestic financial systems were often heavily regulated. In that sense the financial sector could be said to have supported and been subordinated to the needs of the real economy, or the production of goods and services, much like the VoC framework suggests.

By the end of the twentieth century the role of finance had been reshaped by a range of domestic and international reforms, in many cases promoted by international actors like the OECD or the IMF. These include financial liberalization and deregulation – reforms that limit the constraints on financial institutions and increase opportunities for risk-taking and their autonomy in lending and in issuing bonds and other securities – and corporate governance reforms. Corporate governance reforms affect business practices by reshaping the role of managers, shareholders and financial institutions in the governance of firms.

This has transformed the financial sector in many ways. First, the size of the financial sector has grown in most parts of the world, most strikingly in LMEs. In the United States the financial sector overtook manufacturing as a share of GDP in the early 1990s and exceeded 20 per cent by the early 2000s (Davis and Kim 2015). Second, the financial sector is also increasingly globalized, with a growth in cross-border capital flows, and many banks and financial institutions have become increasingly global. This applies to countries with a long history of involvement in global finance, like Britain, where many banks are globally oriented. For example, a larger share of HSBC's profits arises in Asia than in Britain (Culpepper and Reinke 2014). Similar trends have affected many other countries as well, with Swedish banks dominating the Baltic banking sectors, especially in Latvia and Estonia and with Austrian and German banks playing a comparable role in other East Central European economies. As a result, banks are increasingly transnational in their operations and reliant on markets beyond their home market.

The growth and transformation of the financial sector have generated extensive debate, and much of the controversy surrounding these trends has revolved around the use of the term 'financialization', which started to gain increasing currency in the late 1990s. Fundamentally 'financialization refers to the increasing role of financial motives, financial markets, financial actors and financial institutions in the operation of the domestic and international economies' (Epstein 2005). A complementary definition regards 'financialization as a pattern of accumulation in which profits accrue primarily through financial channels rather than through trade and commodity production' (Krippner 2005: 174). The nature of financialization has varied somewhat across countries, for example, in terms of the relative importance of different types of markets and how it has affected housing (mortgages), pensions and financial markets and particular actors within them (Mader, Mertens and van der Zwan 2020; Schelkle and Bohle 2021).

To make the concept of financialization more specific, it is useful to distinguish between three dimensions of this phenomenon that manifest themselves at the level of the firm, household and the economic system as a whole (van der Zwan 2014; Davis and Kim 2015). The following sections will examine each of these dimensions of financialization and reflect on their significance.

Financialization and the firm

Financialization has led to a big shift in the way firms operate (Davis 2009). The traditional focus of most Anglo-American firms in the post-war period tended to prioritize profits. Profit maximization was justified with reference to economic theory, but it was also beneficial in other ways. In particular, profit maximization facilitated further investments, for example, in new projects or in innovation. It also fed into wage increases and often into corporate expansion as many firms were large conglomerates and expanded through mergers and new activities. However, firms also considered other metrics in addition to profits, such as market share. In highly competitive sectors it was important to keep an eye on competitors to safeguard the relative position of the firm on the market. For listed companies, the share price was also important as a metric of success. The share price determined the cost of borrowing and whether firms would be able to borrow in the first place.

At the level of the firm, financialization is associated with the rise of ideas and practices related to the centrality of maximizing shareholder value (MSV). MSV implies that firms are increasingly focusing on the share price as the core metric of economic success at the expense of other outcomes, such as profits, market share or growth. Ideas about MSV have been described as an ideology or a comprehensive set of beliefs animating all aspects of firm activity (Lazonick and O'Sullivan 2000). Decisions about dividends, investment or hiring and firing are largely taken with the intention of maximizing the share price. The focus on MSV also represents a move away from the kind of 'managerial capitalism' that was prominent for much of the twentieth century (Chandler 1984) and that gave managers considerable autonomy to consider a wider range of issues in decision-making. Under financialization firms are increasingly 'managed by the market', as the evocative title of an influential book on the topic highlights (Davis 2009). Such a focus on MSV ideas has a number of effects on the operation of firms, notably making them more short-termist and focused on factors that may boost the share price in the immediate future. Maintaining high share prices also serves as a protection against takeovers, as seemingly undervalued firms could be a target. As a result managers tend to be wary of investments that might only pay off further down the line, not least since they may no longer be associated with the company by the time when long-term investments bear fruit. The MSV focus has also made financial professionals more powerful within the senior management of firms and weakened the influence of other types of sectoral expertise (Fligstein 1990).

Even non-financial firms devote more attention to finance and sometimes derive more profits from financial transactions than from their core business (Davis 2009). The growth of general financial operations within such firms has been striking. GMAC is an oft-cited example of this process. Originally founded in 1919 to help General Motors finance car sales, it grew considerably over time and achieved $1billion in earnings by 1985, when it also diversified its operations and created GMAC Mortgage, which allowed it to enter the mortgage market (Borghi 2013).

Most scholars of financialization agree that these changes should not only be regarded as a technical shift in the way the firm is governed but also as a profoundly political process that empowers managers and weakens the influence of workers. The main gains from this process accrue to shareholders and senior management who are often remunerated with stock options. In the United States, where financialization has gone furthest, wage increases have not kept up with the very dramatic increases in CEO and senior management pay or even with GDP growth and contributed to a decline in labour's share of income (Lin and Tomaskovic-Devey 2013).

Financialization of the everyday

Financialization has also affected people's lives in a more immediate way at the level of the household. This perspective on financialization highlights the increasing role of finance in people's everyday lives. The financialization of the everyday has two roots – on the one hand it is facilitated by the growth of financial markets and what some analysts have called the 'democratization of finance' (Erturk et al. 2007). As access to financial markets is no longer restricted to a very narrow group of the wealthiest, more people are able to tap into financial markets and find their lives affected by finance.

This perspective looks at individuals and households instead of firms and argues that their lives have been increasingly financialized. People's dependence on finance manifests itself in many ways. At the most basic level finance plays a great role in everyday consumption as people use credit cards or purchase various products and services, notably consumer durables, often based on increasingly complex payment schemes.

More people have invested their savings in mutual funds or shares. Perhaps most importantly, pension systems have changed over time, and defined benefit systems have been replaced by defined contribution systems. This means that people are no longer guaranteed a fixed pension, but the value of their pension entitlement depends on the return on their contribution to the pension fund, thereby exposing them to financial market risk. Another important trend relates to home ownership. Rates of home ownership have increased in many countries, and this has also been bound up with expanding mortgage markets, in some cases including 'sub-prime mortgages', or mortgage schemes created for households that are deemed 'risky' and that would not have been granted a standard mortgage from a bank or building society. These schemes received greater scrutiny in the United States during the financial crisis of 2007–8, as Fannie Mae and Freddie Mac, two organizations providing such mortgages, were in need of a bailout and widely seen to have precipitated the crisis. Other schemes, such as shared ownership programmes of partial ownership, have been promoted in various countries, including the UK, as a way to expand home ownership to groups with lower incomes.

The influence of finance is also buttressed by another set of mechanisms, namely the importance of new narratives and discourses associated with finance. These discourses turn financialization into a world view and an interpretive lens as the model of the 'citizen as investor' has taken on a greater importance (van der Zwan 2014). People increasingly perceive key decisions such as going to university, acquiring a home and perhaps other life decisions primarily as financial decisions. This means that all of these decisions have to be taken very carefully as investment decisions where the individual's responsibility for making the right decision about investments in education, saving for retirement, home mortgages, asset portfolios is great. The cost of servicing student debt has to be borne over the life course, and the return to higher education can be measured as the return on an investment.

This creates an understanding of the 'investing subject', an individual who draws on financial literacy and self-discipline to manage all the key life risks. This creates a strong normative agenda, where dominant discourses serve as tools of self-management, as highlighted by post-structuralist scholarship on financialization. The reliance on credit cards and also credit ratings to access various goods and services, and to secure a mortgage and other goods for which a payment plan may be needed (like cars or other consumer durables), means that individuals are monitored to ensure their compliance with such norms of responsibility. For critical scholars, the main effect of financialization is that it becomes a disciplining device that is used by financial institutions and credit rating mechanisms and increasingly by people themselves who seek to live up to the vision of a responsible person that is embodied in these images.

The prevalence of financialization also relates to a variety of general trends that are often described as the 'privatization of risk' (Hacker 2004). This means that a variety of risks that might have been seen as covered by the welfare state in the past need to be viewed as elements of personal responsibility, but which are no longer covered by contemporary welfare states. Many other investment decisions play an equivalent role, as the purchase of a house is a way to save for retirement and serves as a form of asset-based welfare. More generally, people are also exposed to financial markets via credit cards, mortgages and other types of debt. Housing markets are particularly important in this context as they amount for a very large share of household borrowing, and the purchase of a house is typically the biggest expense people incur in their lives (Ansell 2019). Given the extent to which people's lives are bound up with financialization and shaped by it, there are often only limited possibilities to challenge these processes as households worry about adverse effects on their personal finances (van der Zwan 2014)

The impact of these trends is highly uneven. Wealthier households are likely to benefit from new investment opportunities by expanding their asset portfolios and thereby achieve higher returns. According to Fligstein and Goldstein (2015) about 20 per cent of American households are in a position to thrive and make the most of financialization by actively managing their portfolios. By contrast, poorer households encounter strict policing of their credit card spending and overdrafts, whilst also being the targets of aggressive marketing that could place them in debt traps by encouraging them to spend more as a result of complex payment plans and credit limits.

Financialization and capitalism

The third approach to financialization focuses on the systemic level – how capitalism functions in general as a system of production and accumulation. In this context the main impact of financialization is that finance is increasingly central to the functioning of the real economy – there is evidence that a greater share of corporate profits derives from financial activities, even in the case of non-financial firms (Krippner 2005; Davis and Kim 2015: 205). This includes some car retailers who may profit more from selling payment plans than the actual cars. With respect to capitalism in general, this makes finance more central to the real economy.

This has been described as a new system of accumulation and a quest for new sources of profits in response to slower productivity growth in the real economy (van der Zwan 2014: 1010). For macrosociologists like Arrighi, financialization is a recurring phenomenon in world history and tends to arise in periods of hegemonic transition. Arrighi argues that declining profits in the US economy reflect a decline in the hegemonic status of the United States in the world economy, and US firms adjust to these changes by resorting to financialization, much like British and Dutch firms had done in the past in earlier instances of hegemonic decline. Krippner (2012) analyses the crisis of the American economy in the 1970s and shows how financialization emerged as a solution to declining profits, distributional conflict and balance-of-payments problems that was widely embraced by firms.

The upshot of the greater centrality of finance and of financial practices to non-financial firms is that finance may no longer simply be playing a supporting role to the real economy, but be more of an autonomous and central driver of economic activity. This might imply that we need to rethink theories of capitalism, such as VoC analysis, which suggests that there are institutional complementarities between production regimes and financial systems, with the financial and corporate governance systems underpinning the comparative institutional advantage of key areas of production. Another alternative is to conceptualize financialization as a new finance-led growth regime, in which there are multiple interlocking institutions, but where finance has acquired a more central position (Boyer 2000).

The effects of these trends at the systemic level are controversial, but many scholars have argued that these developments affect the functioning of the capitalist system in profound ways. Three sets of consequences stand out.

First, Lazonick (2014) argues that financialization leads to 'profits without prosperity', given that financialization enhances short-termism and reduces investments in innovation and long-term projects that do not immediately translate into increases in share prices. The emphasis on short-termism leads to the lack of productive reinvestment of corporate profits. Firms instead prefer spending exorbitant amounts on dividends and especially stock buybacks, that is, they buy back outstanding shares of their own company, By buying back stock and thereby reducing the number of outstanding shares, firms are able to boost earnings per share, which is a key metric that investors pay attention to. This can be seen as a way of manipulating the share price and of boosting the earnings of senior executives whose own shareholdings and stock options become more valuable as well. Lazonick (2014) argues that the lack of productive investment leads to a decline in economic growth rates in the medium and long term.

Second, another implication of financialization is that it contributes to a heightened risk of economic instability. The growth in financial markets and financial innovation, notably the growth of securitization, could be regarded as a risk management tool that helps build complex portfolios and hedge the risk of exposure to any individual asset. However, the growth of financial markets also increases systemic risk, notably, the risk of financial crises as a result of shocks that affect the system as a whole and that a diversified portfolio cannot be protected against. The growth of speculative investment in search of rapid returns contributes to greater risk of crises as the emergence of novel and complex securities makes errors in valuation more likely (Sen 2020). The consequences of a crisis are also more severe as the costs of bailing out an oversized financial sector are very high.

Third, financialization also contributes to greater inequality. Whilst financialization has given rise to a debate about the 'democratization of finance' as a result of the fact that exposure to finance is no longer exclusively limited to high-income households, expanding access to finance has had highly uneven effects. There is extensive evidence to suggest that financialization tends to lead to higher-income inequality at the aggregate level. Huber, Petrova and Stephens (2022) show that the main channel by which financialization increases inequality is through higher stock market capitalization (especially for the top 1 per cent) and through higher demand for financial professionals (especially for the 'next 9 per cent', that is the rest of the top 10 per cent). Senior corporate executives who receive stock options and stock awards are particularly well represented within the top 1 per cent of the income distribution, which has a very significant effect on income inequality. They also demonstrate that the effects of financialization are shaped by institutional factors and especially the strength of organized labour. Strong unions counteract the effects of financialization on income inequality to a significant extent. However, the constraints imposed by organized labour on inequality in European CMEs, like Germany, also contribute to wage moderation and German trade surpluses, which are associated with deficits elsewhere, where they may contribute to financialization, inequality and a weakening of labour (Huber, Petrova and Stephens 2022: 448; Oatley and Petrova 2022).

Whilst Huber, Petrova and Stephens's (2022) findings suggest that capitalist diversity conditions the impact of financialization, there are a number of important implications for the VoC debate. Most importantly, to the extent that the financial sector has become more central to contemporary market economies, this raises questions about the nature of economic institutions and institutional complementarities within capitalism. VoC scholars have previously reflected on the centrality of the financial sector to the matrix of complementary institutions, and the changes in the financial sector could therefore have a profound impact on the functioning of capitalist systems. To the extent that financialization increases the importance of the financial sector in its own right, it should not just be understood as a component of a larger web of institutions that underpin the performance of the real economy and the production of goods and service, but rather as a dynamic system with its own internal logic.

Financialization in Western Europe

LMEs are widely perceived as most profoundly transformed by financialization, but these processes have affected countries around the world. This section considers how financialization in Western Europe differs from the Anglo-American LMEs. This section will first consider financialization in Europe. Given the association of Western Europe with the CME model, in which stock markets have traditionally played a less significant role, one might expect economies with bank-based and stakeholder-oriented financial systems to be able to withstand the pressures of financialization to a greater extent.

In Western Europe, significant differences have opened up among countries classified as coordinated market economies (CMEs). Denmark, the Netherlands and Sweden are widely regarded as highly financialized, whereas Germany is seen as much less financialized (Johnston, Fuller and Regan 2021; see also Chapter 10). As Johnston, Fuller and Regan (2021) show, the main driver of high levels of financialization can be found in the mortgage market, and some CMEs have even higher rates of mortgage lending than LMEs. They explain these patterns by showing that traditional CME institutions, such as generous welfare states, contribute to financialization by enhancing the creditworthiness of households, which in combination with liberalized mortgage markets facilitate high levels of borrowing and financialization (Johnston, Fuller and Regan 2021). This implies that CME institutions do not only constrain financialization, they also enable it.

Such contrasts are perhaps most obvious if one compares Sweden and Germany. On many key measures. Sweden has evolved into a highly financialized economy since the early 1990s. The roots of financialization lie in the financial liberalization that began in the late 1980s and opened up the Swedish economy to international capital flows. Liberalization also led to an increase in borrowing, with much of it related to the housing market. Key municipalities, notably including the capital Stockholm, also launched initiatives to privatize public housing. As a result of liberal financial regulation mortgage lending is exceptionally high, and even higher than in financialized LMEs like the UK. In addition to housing, another driver of financialization was the reform of the pension system. As Anderson (2019) shows, pension assets account for a very high share of GDP in Sweden (and an even higher share in Denmark and the Netherlands, whereas the share is much lower in Germany and France). However, the maximization of shareholder value has played a more limited role at the firm level in Sweden than in LMEs like the United Kingdom or the United States, which implies that the importance of other stakeholders persists to a considerable extent in the corporate sphere (van der Zwan 2014: 117)

By contrast, in the German case financialization has been more limited. Germany has not sought to stimulate consumption and credit expansion to the same extent as the LMEs or even Sweden. The differences are also stark in terms of the two key drivers of financialization discussed in the Swedish context. First, real estate markets function in a different way as the mortgage market has not been liberalized to the same extent as in Sweden. Therefore rates of home ownership and mortgage credit as a share of GDP are much lower in Germany than in Sweden (Kohl 2020). Second, pension financialization has not proceeded as far as in Sweden, in part due to resistance by incumbents with a vested interest in the status quo (Röper 2021). These incumbents, including insurance companies, were able to deflect the considerable demand for more financialized pensions by reframing the issue and stressing more conservative understandings of the role of pensions. More generally, the German economy has been more reliant on exports for growth than on domestic consumption, which has also shaped macroeconomic policy and the emphasis on maintaining export competiveness rather than boosting domestic demand (Baccaro and Pontusson 2022).

Whilst limited financialization has sometimes been interpreted as a negative feature of the German economy, as it has contributed to weakening domestic demand and also makes the economy highly reliant on exports to generate growth (Baccaro and Pontusson 2016), limited financialization also means that the German economy is potentially less vulnerable to some of some negative effects of financialization. However, there have been some significant changes, which means that Germany is not fully insulated from global trends towards financialization. Shareholder value has made some inroads into German companies, albeit often more as a statement of aspirations than as an actual strategy. Some of the biggest German banks have moved away from traditional practices of supporting businesses and instead embraced Anglo-American strategies of investment banking. For some observers these changes mark a shift away from the CME model and potentially in the direction of LME institutions. Other studies have found that the outcome is more complex and not entirely successful as organizations, like Deutsche Bank, which pursued these strategies very actively and found itself neither fully aligned with the old CME model nor with the US-style investment banking model (Beck 2022). The investment strategies of some German financial institutions also exposed the economy to some of the risks associated with securitization and risky assets in the US economy.

The more limited financialization in Germany is largely a result of a different kind of regulatory environment, in which there has been less emphasis on financial liberalization, but where some economic actors have embraced elements of financialization, including greater attention to the maximization of shareholder value. This implies that financialization does not proceed in the same way everywhere. Even as practices associated with financialization spread beyond the United States, they are likely to generate new hybrid models, in which American ideas and models are modified and adapted to local conditions and used by local actors to their own advantage (van der Zwan 2014).

Financialization in the Global South and emerging markets

Financialization has increasingly come to be regarded as a global phenomenon as its impact is also felt in emerging markets beyond the traditional OECD, most notably in terms of the growth in financial markets driven by financial liberalization. Such reforms were advocated by economists within the IMF (Chwieroth 2008). The liberalization of capital flows has been controversial and regarded as premature in many cases, as domestic regulatory arrangements were not designed to address the challenges associated with large capital inflows (Porter 2005). However, the nature of financialization has been uneven, with big differences across regions and groups of countries (Karwowski 2022). It should be emphasized that there is great variation not only across, but also within regions. Financialization has had an impact on most economies, but the processes and outcomes have not been uniform, as captured by the term 'variegated financialization'.

There are a few general characteristics that distinguish financialization in the Global South from the cases discussed so far. Most importantly, financialization is shaped by external factors, such as the integration into global financial markets, in which economies from the Global South tend to be disadvantaged. For example, they are not generally able to borrow in their own national currency, a phenomenon often described as 'original sin' by economists (Eichengreen, Hausmann and Panizza 2023). Capital flows are 'fickle' and global factors beyond the immediate control of these economies, such as changes in risk aversion, affect these economies disproportionately (Eichengreen, Gupta and Masetti 2018).

This is why many scholars have referred to this as 'subordinate financialization' (Karwowski 2022) or 'international financial subordination' (Alami et al. 2023). This subordination has several consequences (Alami et al. 2023). It limits the scope for agency by social actors, implies that the distribution of gains from economic activity is uneven between countries, and contributes to unequal prospects for growth and development. Based on a detailed examination of Senegal and Ghana over a 150-year period, Koddenbrock et al. (2022) argue that this is not a new phenomenon in Global South. Whilst some aspects of financialization became more pronounced in the latter part of the period, there was no 'divorce' between the financial and the productive economy, as finance has consistently neglected the needs of domestic production, largely due to its close connection to imperialism.

Karwowski's (2022) detailed comparison of financialization in terms of integration with international financial markets and domestic financialization across emerging economy regions identifies Central and Eastern Europe as the region with the highest share of financialization, followed by Latin America. The VoC literature classifies much of Central and Eastern Europe as dependent market economies, which captures their high level of integration with international markets (DMEs – see Chapter 6). However, the VoC literature has mostly focused on manufacturing (Nölke and Vliegenthart 2009) and not considered the full implications of financial subordination. In these countries foreign investment has also been significant in the financial sector, with very high rates of foreign bank ownership, which has contributed to high financialization and its subordinate nature. High rates of financialization have also had a significant political impact, as high rates of borrowing in foreign currencies has increased opposition to devaluations, even during deep economic downturns (Feldmann 2013). Although financialization has been far-reaching, there have also been unorthodox instances of 'definancialization', notably in Hungary and Romania. In the Hungarian case this led to lasting changes in relations between the state and the financial sector associated with the promotion of domestic banks, partial nationalization and financial repression in mortgage markets (Ban and Bohle 2021; Johnson and Barnes 2015).

The region with the second highest degree of financialization in Karwowski's (2022) study is Latin America, where financial liberalization has been significant since the end of import-substituting industrialization and multinationals have also played a relatively important role, as highlighted by the HME model (see Chapter 5). With the exception of Brazil, the stock market plays a relatively limited role in the financialization process as many business groups (grupos) are not listed.

Asia displays intermediate levels of financialization. Apart from Hong Kong and Singapore that have longer histories of being nodal points for international trade and finance and that are financial centres with very high levels of financialization, the rest of the region is relatively closed to financial flows (Karwowski 2022).

The Middle East and North Africa (MENA region – see Chapter 5) and Africa on the whole display the lowest degree of financialization (Karwowski 2022). Economies in these regions have attracted less foreign investment and more limited inflows of other forms of foreign capital.

In many economies with limited financialization and financial development, there has often been greater emphasis on expanding micro-finance and financial inclusion more generally.

However, there is considerable variation within these regions. The most exceptional case in this context is South Africa (see Chapter 5). Unlike the rest of Africa, South Africa has become highly financialized on many dimensions (Karwowski 2022). With the exception of Hong Kong it has the highest stock market capitalization among emerging markets (Karwowski, Fine and Ashman 2018). A more pronounced MSV orientation has taken hold in many key industries, including platinum, where it has led to financialized practices, such as high dividends and buybacks (Bowman 2018). It has also increased pressure on large conglomerates to unbundle and to reorganize into smaller and more specialized firms (Karwowski, Fine and Ashman 2018). Karwowski (2018) has also analysed the growth of mortgage lending, which is underpinned by excess cash holdings of non-financial firms. These holdings were deposited with banks and then contributed to mortgage lending and significant inflation in real estate markets. This highlights some important parallels between South Africa and key cases of financialization in the Global North, where the housing market has also been a significant mechanism of financialization. The South African experience indicates that financialization has contributed to increasing inequality.

By contrast, in China financialization has reflected greater state influence, and there is some controversy surrounding the use of the concept. Wang (2015) identifies three processes of financialization: state use of shareholder value to manage its assets, the expansion of state asset management bodies and the provision of structured investment vehicles by these bodies. By means of these processes, the Chinese state operates as a shareholder and investor whilst pursuing its objectives in managing its assets and investment projects. Pan, Zhang and Wu (2021) also note that government-guided investment funds (GGIFs) have spread across the country and become increasingly significant. State-owned enterprises play a significant role in the process, and Pan, Zhang and Wu (2021) argue that the Chinese form of financialization has strengthened the state and its capacity to manage the economy in a way that differs from most other countries. For some observers this represents 'financialization with Chinese characteristics' (Petry 2020), whereas others regard the use of the term financialization as misleading. Whilst financial markets may have grown, their main feature is continuity in that banks remain central and the core logic of a state-directed system remains largely intact (Shi 2023). This implies that the economic system has not become subordinated to the financial markets.

As this discussion highlights, financialization has affected the Global South in very different ways. In some countries low levels of financial development are a significant obstacle to growth, whilst other economies have experienced more financialization, but also some adverse effects associated with it. Whilst there is great variation in the degree to which these economies are affected by financial markets, the Global South as a whole tends to be characterized by subordinated financialization.

The politics of financialization and financial crises

Given the centrality of financialization to contemporary capitalism, it is clear that it also has a range of political implications. This section discusses three of the most important political consequences of financialization – its impact on the political power of finance, on the collective capabilities of other businesses and finally on the general public.

First, financialization has been associated with the growth of the financial sector across many countries. As the share of GDP made up of banking and finance has grown, the political influence of the financial sector has increased as well. We can distinguish between instrumental and structural business power. Instrumental power refers to the influence business exercises by lobbying or seeking to exercise influence in other ways; structural power denotes the power that business enjoys thanks to its privileged position within the economy and the government's reliance on business for generating growth and tax revenues (Culpepper 2015).

It has been widely acknowledged that financial institutions seek to wield their considerable influence to promote light-touch regulation and to dilute initiatives that might lead to a tightening of financial regulation. The growth of the financial sector has enhanced its resources to exercise instrumental power and also its structural power given its increasing centrality to the economy. However, the degree to which banks succeed in advancing their agenda varies, and Culpepper and Reinke (2014) have shown that banks' structural power is an important factor. The growth of the financial sector means that policymakers increasingly take it into account in policymaking, given its contribution to the economy. Whilst this is not a new phenomenon – the City has long had an outsized influence on economic policymaking in the UK – financialization has further accentuated this role in many countries. Yet the power of the financial sector has some limits. Culpepper and Reinke (2014) consider the bailouts in the aftermath of the global financial crisis and compare the policy responses in several countries. By comparing bank influence on the bailout packages in the United States and the United Kingdom, they demonstrate that banks were more successful in achieving their goals in the United Kingdom (where banks have more structural power thanks to a more limited reliance on the home market) than in the United States (where banks have greater instrumental power thanks to lobbying and campaign donations).

Secondly, financialization has also had other effects on the political influence of business more generally. In particular, financialization has led to what Mark Mizruchi (2013) calls the 'fracturing of the business elite'. As firms are more focused on maximizing shareholder value, their concerns become narrower and they take less interest in broader concerns of business as a whole. Another manifestation of this could be seen during the Brexit referendum in 2016, when business found it hard to articulate a common position or to influence the referendum in an effective way. This stands in sharp contrast to the 1975 referendum, when both individual businesses and employers' organizations played a very active role (on the role of business in the two campaigns, see Feldmann and Morgan 2021). In the 1970s business faced a different threat, but the organizational structure of business was also different. Business tended to have a wider social and political agenda and they were more closely integrated in social terms, facilitating coordination. By 2016 a range of process – associated in part with financialization, but also with globalization – had transformed the business elite and made such collaboration much harder to sustain as firms tended to focus more on immediate priorities related to the maximization of shareholder value in the short run. This has made business more focused on a narrower set of mostly firm-level concerns and reduced the ability of businesses to act collectively.

Thirdly, financialization has also had a profound impact on popular preferences by generating 'great expectations' (Chwieroth and Walter 2019). As voters are increasingly dependent on financial markets, for example, in connection with mortgages and pensions, their expectations of governments have changed. Before the dramatic increases in financialization, voters tended to prioritize policies that ensured some moderation of the business cycle and employment protection in economic downturns, even if it had negative effects on deficits and interest rates as many voters worried about losing their jobs in a downturn. Bailouts attracted criticism – and many experts favoured so-called 'Bagehot policies' that only target banks which would be solvent under normal circumstances rather than large-scale bailouts of overextended financial institutions (Chwieroth and Walter 2019). Financialization has induced voters to pay more attention to financial markets and to expect bailouts during banking crises. Such bailouts were very rare in the late nineteenth and early twentieth centuries, but became very common towards the end of the twentieth century. However, many voters paid less attention to fluctuations in employment, perhaps because they felt reasonably secure in their jobs, but also because they were worried that countercyclical policies and government borrowing could raise interest rates and mortgages, thereby putting greater pressure on these households. The centrality of the financial sector and the associated great expectations increase the risk of financial crises given that these expectations also fuel moral hazard, or excessive risk-taking by banks, which they feel that can afford given the likelihood of a bailout in hard times. Great expectations also tend to lead to great disappointment as citizens blame governments for slow and unfair bailouts, especially if they are seen to benefit the financial sector or key elites disproportionately. Nevertheless, as increasing numbers of middle-class households perceive their fortunes as bound up with financial markets, significant prudential reforms are hard to implement, not least because popular preferences are asymmetric – favouring financial liberalization in good times, when it is possible to make big gains, and socialization of losses in bad times.

These three sets of factors suggest that there is a strong and potentially robust coalition in favour of financialization which includes not only the financial institutions themselves but also much of the wider public. Their livelihoods and pensions increasingly depend on financialization, which is why they worry about the impact of a financial crisis and of interest rate changes.

Conclusion

This chapter has considered the role of finance and financialization in capitalist systems. Whilst finance and financial crises have a long history that predates modern capitalism, financial systems and corporate governance arrangements have been an integral part of the development of distinct capitalist systems, with significant differences between financial arrangements in various countries. This chapter has also highlighted the ways in which financialization has raised the importance of the financial sector and disrupted interactions between finance and the real economy. These processes may ultimately have an impact on capitalist diversity as well.

Critics have argued that the VoC framework is ill-equipped to address the role of the financialization, as it does not pay sufficient attention to the financial sector as an autonomous actor that may operate independently of developments in the real economy. As discussed in previous chapters, financial systems and corporate governance arrangements are regarded as an integral part of the institutional complementarities considered in the VoC literature. Financialization challenges such institutional arrangements, and VoC scholars would be well advised to reflect more on the impact of financialization. On the other hand, the literature on financialization in general obscures the fact that there are considerable differences between different economies, and VoC approaches can shed light on key feature of the processes of financialization and their impact across countries.

If the process of financialization is more or less universal, as some have claimed (much in the same way as globalization is affecting virtually all economies), then this implies that we need to focus more on the commonalities rather than varieties of capitalism. However, as this chapter has argued, a possible qualification here is that financialization has been more rapid in some cases than in others, but these differences transcend traditional categories – so even though the process has generally been especially rapid in LMEs, some CMEs like Sweden have also experienced very high degrees of financialization.

What these examples show is that financialization has been uneven, and some but not all practices have been disseminated beyond the United States, which means that there has not been full convergence with respect to financialization (Davis and Kim 2015: 14). As van der Zwan (2014: 110) argues, this means that full convergence between economies should not be expected and that various hybrid models are the most likely outcome of financialization on a global scale.

Discussion questions

- What are the main dimensions of financialization?
- To what extent does financialization contribute to economic growth and well-being?
- Why are some economies more financialized than others?
- What does the 'finance curse' refer to, and is it convincing? What are the policy implications, if any, of this concept?
- Does the term 'financialization' adequately describe the role of finance in contemporary societies? To what extent does financialization represent a fundamental shift in the logic of capitalism?
- To what extent has financialization affected politics?

10

Growth models and the macroeconomy

Financialization (Chapter 9) and the structural changes that have taken place since the 1980s (Chapter 8) have given rise to a lively debate about the evolving nature of capitalism and how to study it. In particular, a number of scholars have argued that comparative capitalism needs to devote more attention to the macroeconomy. The first part of this chapter discusses the VoC approach to macroeconomics, including attempts to use VoC to analyse economic instability, notably in the context of the global financial crisis of 2007–8 and the eurozone crisis. However, critics have argued that the VoC framework does not provide a convincing account of the macroeconomy and economic instability. An influential study by Baccaro and Pontusson (2016) has sought to foreground the macroeconomy within the field of comparative capitalism. Their approach has stimulated extensive debate and can be regarded either as an alternative or as a complementary framework to VoC analysis. The latter parts of the chapter introduce the debate about growth models, and about growth regimes as a potential synthesis of VoC and growth models. The chapter concludes by reflecting on the implications of these debates for understanding the macroeconomy and comparative capitalism.

Varieties of Capitalism and the macroeconomy

VoC is largely focused on the supply side of the economy – or what political economists have also called the 'production regime' (Soskice 1999). This is because the competitiveness, productivity and growth of the economy is primarily determined by supply factors, including technology, resource endowments and institutions, which are the key focus of the VoC framework. This perspective allows VoC to explain economic behaviour at the micro-level – in other words, the decisions made and strategies chosen by firms as well as their impact on growth and inequality. The emphasis is on enduring features that shape the long-run performance of the economy and account for the success of different institutional arrangements. This account of the economy also reflects the consensus among mainstream economists since the 1970s that economic performance, at least in the long run, depends on the supply side.

However, VoC analysis has paid less attention to two dimensions that other scholars of capitalism have focused on, namely the macroeconomy and economic instability.

Macroeconomic issues play a relatively limited role in VoC analysis, at least compared to the dominant approaches in the Keynesian era of modernization (see Chapter 8). This reflects a broader trend in political economy since the 1980s, which involved a shift away from macroeconomic concerns about instability (Schwartz and Tranøy 2019). This was also related to the rise of monetarism and new classical economics in macroeconomics which assumed that macroeconomic policy had only short-run effects (in the case of monetarism) or that it was altogether ineffective (in the case of new classical economics). More generally, in the field of macroeconomics the emphasis is on microfoundations or the understanding that macro-phenomena need to be explained in terms of individual incentives and decisions at the micro-level. Keynesian concerns with fallacies of composition, that is, situations in which the macroeconomy follows a distinctive logic and aggregate performance cannot simply be regarded as the sum of individual actions, were no longer central to economic analysis (Stockhammer 2022). For Keynesians, such fallacies of composition increase the importance of the stabilizing role of government, as activist macroeconomic policy can have multiplier effects that ripple through the economy and induce changes of behaviour at the micro-level that magnify the effects of government policy. Such concerns have receded into the background and mostly attract attention from heterodox economists, such as post-Keynesians. Although there was a partial and short-lived revival of 'emergency Keynesianism' during the global financial crisis, even leading centre-left governments later embraced austerity (Bremer and McDaniel 2020).

VoC analyses of the macroeconomy have primarily analysed complementarities between the production regime and macroeconomic policy, notably by exploring the interactions between central bank independence, wage bargaining and labour market institutions. A range of studies have shown that the effects of central bank policies on inflation and unemployment tend to vary depending on the wider institutional context (Hall and Franzese 1998; Iversen 1999; Soskice and Iversen 2000). Such analyses have also highlighted that CMEs tend to adopt rules-based macroeconomic policy regimes, whereas LMEs respond more flexibly to small shocks, a contrast that reflects complementarities with the production regime (Soskice 2007).

The most systematic accounts of macroeconomics in relation to VoC have also stressed the affinity between VoC and new Keynesian economics (NKE) (Hope and Soskice 2016; Soskice 2007). Whilst NKE integrates some assumptions from traditional Keynesian economics, notably the lack of instantaneous market clearing, this approach also adopts key assumptions prevailing in modern macroeconomics. This includes an emphasis on microfoundations (explaining the macroeconomy in terms of individual behaviour and micro-level incentives) and rational expectations. In other words, whilst new Keynesian economics acknowledges the existence of some market imperfections, it sees only a limited role for government intervention in the short run. Traditional Keynesian demand management is likely to be ineffective or even counterproductive from this perspective, though there may still be a significant role for government in promoting micro-level policies that stimulate growth and benefit the economy in the long run (Iversen and Soskice 2006b, 2019). This stands in marked contrast to traditional Keynesianism or contemporary post-Keynesian analyses, which emphasize the inherent instability of capitalism and the importance of macroeconomic policy to stabilize the economy. Post-Keynesians argue that such interventions could also have long-run effects on economic growth as short-run responses to crises often lead to permanent changes in the economy (Stockhammer 2022). These results relate to path dependence in the development of capital stock and employment; capital scrapping may become permanent, and layoffs turn into long-run unemployment through a process that economists call hysteresis (Blanchard and Summers 1986).

However, just like the global financial crisis of 2007–8 prompted soul searching in the field of economics (Blanchard et al. 2012), it also raised questions about VoC analysis. In particular, it triggered debate about whether the VoC account of macroeconomics is adequate and whether it can explain such economic instability. The next two sections consider the VoC account of the crisis.

Varieties of Capitalism and economic instability: The role of global imbalances

One of the most influential VoC accounts of the global financial crisis is a study by Iversen and Soskice (2012). This study seeks to explain why the global financial crisis originated in the leading LMEs, that is, in the United Kingdom and especially the United States, which also play a significant role in global financial markets. Iversen and Soskice regard the crisis as the result of failures in financial and macroeconomic regulation, which jointly contributed to the build-up of risk within the financial system and economic imbalances at the international level. These two sets of failures will be examined in turn.

First, the failures in financial regulation contributed to excessive risk-taking which increased systemic risk and the fragility of the financial system. Lighter regulation stimulated lending and financial innovation, notably the development of new financial instruments, such as derivatives. These instruments are ostensibly tools for managing risk, as they combine different types of assets, helping investors hedge against certain kinds of risks, whilst simultaneously contributing to greater systemic risk. High levels of systemic risk increase the likelihood and potential severity of a crisis. This is because minor shocks to the system can lead to loss of confidence or even financial panics that may put both risky and solvent financial institutions at risk and even bring down the financial system as a whole.

Whilst most analysts agree that inadequate regulation contributed to the crisis, the distinctiveness of the VoC approach to these issues relates to the way it connects regulatory failures to the comparative institutional advantage of LMEs in the financial sector. Both the United States and the United Kingdom have big financial sectors and dominant financial centres in New York and London. Governments in both countries have generally been supportive of the financial sector and promoted liberalization since the 1980s. In the British case the original 'big bang' of financial liberalization took place under the Conservative Thatcher government, but the New Labour governments of Tony Blair and Gordon Brown maintained a commitment to 'light-touch financial regulation' and sought to gain the support of the financial sector. This could also be seen as a key reason why financialization has advanced so far in both the United States and the United Kingdom (Chapter 9). The VoC approach developed by Iversen and Soskice (2012) relates these policies to the comparative institutional advantage of these economies as governments take a great interest in the success of the economy and its leading sectors (Iversen and Soskice 2012). However, even if light-touch regulation was intended to promote growth and the success of a key industry in these economies, it also had other unintended effects, and the inattention to the potential consequences of increasing systemic risk constituted a regulatory failure.

Second, Iversen and Soskice (2012) also argue that LMEs are structurally predisposed to generate large deficits. Large imbalances increase the risk of macroeconomic instability and financial crises, which could be triggered by speculation against the currencies or heavily indebted financial institutions of deficit economies. Such imbalances create interdependences between economies and can also explain why financial crises spread across borders and generate global economic crises. Although external deficits sometimes generate concern (Chinn and Frieden 2011), financialization and the fact that key constituencies within LMEs benefit from the high levels of consumption that it facilitates imply there is limited demand for tighter macroeconomic policy that would reduce aggregate demand. An ill-timed tightening of macroeconomic policy could also weaken investors' confidence and precipitate a crisis, which tends to make policymakers and central bankers more reluctant to pull the brakes. By contrast, CMEs like Germany are highly reliant on exports, and mechanisms of wage coordination, such as centralized wage bargaining, help maintain the competitiveness of exports on international markets. Workers, firms and governments in these economies rely on the success of these export industries and therefore support policies, including education and training programmes but also wage moderation, that help strengthen the performance of key export industries. Global imbalances result from the fact that CMEs run trade surpluses, much like LMEs tend to be associated with deficits, and it is politically difficult to reduce surpluses in CMEs and deficits in LMEs.

The interdependence of LMEs and CMEs is an example of more general patterns, where some economies generate surpluses and others tend to generate deficits. Another important example of such interdependence is the relationship between the two largest economies in the world economy, the United States and China – sometimes referred to as the G2 (in contrast to the G7 or G20) or even as Chimerica (Ferguson and Schularick 2007). Taken together these two countries account for about 40 per cent of global GDP, and their trade, financial and investment ties are central to the functioning of the world economy.

This interdependence manifests itself in multiple ways. First, trade ties between the two countries are extensive and associated with significant imbalances. The United States has run sizeable current account deficits for most years since the 1980s. In 2018 the total deficit on trade in goods and services with China was $419.2 billion, or 47.7 per cent of the total deficit (Kwan 2020: 58). Second, China acquired about $1.1 trillion of US treasury securities and bonds between 1995 and 2010, which helped finance US deficits (Beltran et al. 2013). Third, there has also been considerable Chinese foreign direct investment in the United States, which hit an all-time high of $46 billion in 2016. Total Chinese FDI in the United States from 1990 until December 2020 amounted to $175.52 billion, whereas total US FDI in China during the same period was $284.9 billion (US-China Investment Hub).

There has been extensive debate about the significance of these trends. In economic terms they provide opportunities to both countries. US consumption would be considerably lower if the country did not have access to imports from China and could not borrow as much from China to finance its current account deficits. The United States might be able to borrow elsewhere, but any reduction in global credit would lead to higher interest rates, which would have a negative effect on spending in the United States. Similarly, whilst the trade deficits with China are politically controversial, they reflect high demand for Chinese goods and services that are available at relatively low costs to US consumers. The Chinese economy benefits greatly from exports to the United States, and the holdings of US treasury bills are arguably the best way for China to secure a stable return on its large surpluses.

However, this interdependence has become increasingly controversial over time, perhaps especially after 2015. Chinese policymakers have been concerned about overreliance on exports, especially in the face of harsher rhetoric about China in the United States. In China this has prompted greater emphasis on 'dual circulation' or the idea that growth should rely not only on exports but increasingly also on domestic consumption (Pettis 2021). Security concerns in the United States have prompted calls for 'decoupling' from trade with China (Pearson, Rithmire and Tsai 2022).

To what extent can VoC analysis shed light on these imbalances? The relative surplus and deficit positions are in large part shaped by the specific features of the two economies in question. In the case of China, growth is largely export-led, and economic policy is designed to maintain export competitiveness. High public savings keep consumption down, and an undervalued exchange rate further boosts exports. This is in line with the policies adopted by other SMEs and export-oriented CMEs and NMEs. By contrast, as Iversen and Soskice (2012) show in their VoC account of the crisis, the US economy has a comparative institutional advantage in the financial sector, which stimulates financial innovation and an expansion of lending. Since US growth depends more on domestic demand and real income growth has been slow, especially in the middle and lower half of the income distribution, this has also led to political incentives to promote the expansion of credit to boost consumption, which also contributes to larger deficits.

There are various possibilities for addressing such imbalances. Popular explanations of these outcomes in the United States often amount to a form of China-bashing. They suggest that China is seeking to compete unfairly, largely by maintaining an undervalued exchange rate that makes Chinese exports very cheap and thereby leads to substantial trade deficits in the United States. In principle, an increase in US savings and a fall in consumption could reduce the deficit, as an appreciation of the Chinese renminbi is also likely to do, but each of these adjustment strategies would benefit some groups more than others, and powerful actors have a vested interest in the status quo. Most solutions would either have adverse effects on key economic actors or be politically unattractive for other reasons, and the two countries' governments would probably be unwilling to adopt them. Therefore, it is perhaps not surprising that attempts to forge international agreements to limit deficits and exchange rate misalignments have not achieved any lasting success (Kalinowski 2019).

The imbalances associated with the economic relationship between LMEs and CMEs and in the context of Chimerica are merely some of the most striking examples of interactions between export-oriented surplus economies and deficit-prone economies. VoC analysis can shed some light on the factors generating such imbalances. As Kalinowski (2019) has demonstrated, countries have divergent preferences on financial regulation that are largely shaped by their distinctive capitalist institutions. Therefore, international negotiations about financial regulation or on global imbalances should not be understood as the search for the most effective technical solution, but rather as a very political and conflictual process. This makes it hard to reach international agreements. Whilst imbalances may not be problematic as long as they can be financed and seen to benefit all parties, pervasive imbalances are a key source of potential instability in the international economy.

Varieties of Capitalism and the eurozone crisis

The most important application of VoC analysis to study the crisis has been in the context of the eurozone. The eurozone crisis can even be seen as a test case for VoC analysis, not least given that Western Europe has been a core focus of the VoC literature and inspired much of the debate on capitalist diversity and alternatives to Anglo-American capitalism. Given the depth of the crisis experienced by many countries in the EU, especially the eurozone countries in Southern Europe, an understanding of the factors contributing to it is also very important.

VoC approaches to the eurozone crisis focus on the role of institutional differences and especially on the co-existence of different types of economic institutions within a currency union. It analyses the differences between the CMEs, like Germany, and the Southern European economies that do not fit with either of the two core VoC models. The Southern European or Mediterranean economies are typically classified as mixed market economies (MMEs). They differ from both LMEs and CMEs, but their growth has long been reliant on domestic demand and the export of services like tourism that tend to be relatively price-sensitive. This created significant challenges in the context of the European Economic and Monetary Union (EMU). Traditionally the Southern European economies had experienced higher inflation than Northern Europe and also relied on periodic devaluations to compensate for losses of competitiveness and to adjust in the face of significant imbalances (Johnston and Regan 2016). However, once these economies had adopted a common currency, devaluations in relation to other European economies were no longer possible.

Whilst the eurozone institutions and associated rules are technically the same for all the countries that have adopted the euro, VoC analysis highlights their uneven effects. Economic institutions in Germany and other CMEs are well aligned with the EMU, and designed to generate wage moderation and help maintain these economies' competitiveness on export markets. The fact that devaluations are no longer possible within the common currency area also implies that the CMEs need not worry that their competitiveness might be undercut by competitive devaluations in other EU countries.

However, the monetary policy for the eurozone as a whole is not necessarily optimal for each member state, including the Mediterranean MMEs, in part because their business cycles are not fully synchronized with the rest of the currency area. In the run-up to the eurozone crisis monetary and fiscal policy was too loose for these economies, as they took advantage of low interest rates to borrow on more favourable terms than they had enjoyed in the past. This was perceived as a key gain from membership of the eurozone as creditors regarded these economies as safer borrowers once they had adopted the euro. However, this borrowing contributed to the build-up of deficits and significant imbalances, and the Southern European countries as well as Ireland found themselves engulfed by a deep economic crisis.

Once the crisis had begun, the institutional framework of the monetary union left few tools for restoring competitiveness in Southern Europe. The expectation of austerity in the face of the crisis to comply with the EU's fiscal rules meant that a deflationary strategy of cutting wages and costs further exacerbated the crisis in the short run. Given that these economies are less export-oriented than the CMEs, these policies further weakened domestic demand, which might have helped them recover.

Various options that could have helped Southern Europe weather the crisis existed. This included a common European fiscal policy with transfers to countries hit by the crisis or Eurobonds – bonds underwritten by the eurozone as a whole – but these options were unpalatable to Germany and also fiercely resisted by others. Northern/Continental European CMEs, like Finland or the Netherlands, were concerned that such instruments might affect their credit ratings, make them permanently fund Southern European deficits and also undermine the shared commitment to common rules in the eurozone.

Whilst the eurozone crisis had many roots, including weaknesses in the design of the monetary union and long-standing challenges in the Southern European economies (Frieden and Walter 2017), a VoC perspective can shed light on key dimensions of the crisis. In particular, a VoC perspective highlights some of the risks of interdependence and common institutions in the absence of institutional complementarities. Eurozone accession was initially heralded as a triumph for Southern Europe, which did not want to be left behind when the new phase of European integration began. The high growth rates these countries initially experienced seemed to validate the adoption of the euro, as these economies attracted investments and were able to borrow on more favourable terms than before. Yet this experience is also a cautionary tale and an illustration of the importance of institutional complementarities. The main insight of the VoC approach is that key eurozone institutions are more compatible with CME institutions than with MMEs, which also reflects unequal bargaining power and the limited clout of the MMEs within the eurozone institutions (Iversen, Soskice and Hope 2016).

Beyond Varieties of Capitalism: Post-Keynesian growth models in Europe and North America

As noted in Chapters 8 and 9, the transformation of capitalism along with its instability raise questions about the ability of the VoC framework to capture the nature of contemporary market economies. Various scholars have been searching for alternatives to VoC since its inception (Coates 2005; Brenner 2005), and this section considers an alternative and increasingly influential approach based on growth models, as defined by Baccaro and Pontusson (2016) and various post-Keynesian thinkers (Stockhammer 2022). These alternative approaches seek to move the macroeconomy to the centre of the analysis, and they imply that the prevalence of instability and crises has profound implications for understanding capitalism.

This approach is widely regarded as a more radical departure from VoC analysis. First, it is focused on the demand side of the economy (especially the key sources of demand for output – domestic consumption, investment or exports). By contrast, traditional VoC analysis focuses on the supply side (or the productive capacity of the economy, including the institutions shaping the supply of labour and finance to firms).

Second, Baccaro and Pontusson's (2016) growth model analysis builds on post-Keynesian macroeconomics, a heterodox tradition that has had a relatively limited impact on mainstream economics. Post-Keynesian research draws on insights from traditional Keynesianism which fell out of favour with economics in the 1970s and 1980s and from other sources, such as ideas associated with Michał Kalecki (1943) which highlight the importance of social forces and power struggles in shaping macroeconomic outcomes. Post-Keynesians reject many core assumptions of traditional economics and regard the macroeconomy as fundamentally unstable, prone to crises and characterized by distributive conflict.

Baccaro and Pontusson's (2016) framework is based on the premise of a profound transformation of capitalism associated with the rise of the service economy and the other changes associated with the era of liberalization (see Chapter 8). The starting point of their analysis is that all the OECD economies were characterized by wage-led growth until the late 1980s. The prevalence of wage-led growth reflects the centrality of manufacturing across the OECD during the Golden Age of Capitalism. During this period there was a virtuous circle between rising wages and increasing demand for consumer durables, such as cars, which in turn helped to boost production and employment in the manufacturing sector (see the discussion of the era of modernization in Chapter 8).

Baccaro and Pontusson argue that no country has experienced this kind of wage-led growth since the early 1990s, which is why the sources of growth can be found in other elements of demand (for a discussion and critique of this assumption, see Stockhammer 2022). They identify four growth models that operate in distinctive ways (see Table 10.1).Table 10.1 Four Post-Fordist Growth Models

The first growth model identified by Baccaro and Pontusson (2016) is export-led, and the main example of this model is Germany. Long known as an export powerhouse, in which leading car producers and engineering companies dominate world markets thanks to their high-quality products, Baccaro and Pontusson (2016) show that Germany can be regarded as having a distinctive export-led growth model. Baccaro and Höpner (2022) argue that the main feature of this model is real undervaluation, which is underpinned by a wage bargaining system that generates wage moderation and lower price increases than in other countries and by conservative macroeconomic policy and a financial system offering few opportunities for financial investments in the domestic economy, thereby predisposing investors to seek higher

Table 10.1 Four Post-Fordist Growth Models

Growth model	Main driver of growth	Key example
Export-led growth	Export of manufacturing	Germany
Consumption-led growth	Domestic consumption	United Kingdom
Balanced growth	Combination of exports and domestic consumption	Sweden
Stagnation	Lack of sustained growth	Italy

Source: Baccaro and Pontusson (2016).

yields abroad. All these factors contribute to the price competitiveness of exports, and in combination with membership of the eurozone they lock in Germany's advantage vis-à-vis other European economies that cannot use devaluations to restore their competitiveness. This growth model enjoys the support of key manufacturing firms and other groups which benefit from the model and which have a shared understanding that high exports are advantageous for the economy as a whole (Baccaro and Pontusson 2022; Baccaro and Höpner 2022).

The second model identified by Baccaro and Pontusson (2016) is consumption-led. It is designed to capture the highly financialized British economy, and it also applies to the US economy. Reisenbichler and Wiedemann (2022) highlight two key mechanisms through which financial markets boost consumption in these economies, namely a housing channel and an income maintenance channel. As noted in Chapter 9, financialization has played a key role in the British and US economies, and these two mechanisms highlight the ways in which it affects consumption. Home ownership and rising real estate prices have a wealth effect and a credit effect, in that they make households feel wealthier and increase their assessment of feasible lifetime spending, whilst also making it easier for them to borrow or increase their credit card spending limits. Reisenbichler and Wiedemann (2022) also analyse the political underpinnings of consumption-led growth, which they relate in the British case to a range of government policies, including policies facilitating greater borrowing (see Chapter 2). This also includes the expansion of home ownership and mortgage markets, where rising house prices have fuelled consumption. These processes have led to a system sometimes described as 'house price Keynesianism' (Hay et al. 2008) or 'privatized Keynesianism' (Crouch 2009), where the concepts capture how the role of responding to shocks that the government was expected to play in the Keynesian era of modernization (see Chapter 8) has become an individual responsibility shaped by financial markets, including house prices given the importance of mortgages. Privatized Keynesianism also relates to the idea that people use financial markets to respond to shocks, unlike the traditional Keynesian model in which it was the government that used countercyclical spending to shield the economy from economic downturns.

In addition to these two models, Baccaro and Pontusson (2016) also highlight the possibility of balanced growth, of which they view Sweden as the prime example. Sweden has managed to grow by simultaneously stimulating both consumption and exports, largely thanks to the fact that Sweden has successfully expanded the production of dynamic services. Baccaro and Pontusson (2016) argue that dynamic services as less price-sensitive than German manufacturing exports. In a more recent refinement of the analysis of the Swedish economy Erixon and Pontusson

(2022) distinguish between two post-Fordist growth models in Sweden. The first one applies to the period before the financial crisis (1994–2007) and the other one after the crisis (2010–). They regard both models as balanced, but in the first period the model is primarily export-led, whereas consumption began to play a more significant role in the aftermath of the financial crisis, partly due to sluggish demand in key export markets, but also thanks to some domestic policy changes that helped boost demand.

The fourth and final model highlighted by Baccaro and Pontusson (2016) characterizes Italy as an example of an economy mired in stagnation as it has not managed to establish a viable growth model based on either consumption or exports. This stands in sharp contrast to the core VoC models of LMEs and CMEs which are regarded as efficient, though some of the other models, like the HME model, do go beyond the efficiency focus of the original VoC volume (Feldmann 2019; see also Chapter 5).

Baccaro and Pontusson's work represents a very important contribution to political economy, not least given the renewed attention this perspective accords to macroeconomic issues. It is an important corrective to the firm-centred and production- and supply-oriented focus of VoC. Some aspects of the growth model framework are still subject to debate and contestation. As Baccaro and Pontusson (2022) note, their growth models are 'descriptive entities and are operationalized through growth decomposition exercises' by examining different sources of economic growth during a given time period. This means that the theoretical foundation of the economic relationships from which these models are derived is not fully developed, and post-Keynesian economists have suggested that the analysis could be strengthened by integrating further theoretical insights from post-Keynesian economics and financialization (Stockhammer 2022).

Growth models in global perspective

The discussion so far has focused on Western Europe and the United States, which raises the question of whether this framework can shed light on economic systems elsewhere in the world. There have been some attempts to extend the growth models debate to the Global South, and Stockhammer (2023) has argued that the growth models of economies in the Global South are constrained to a greater extent by external factors. He highlights two factors in particular – namely structural disadvantages in export markets and what he calls 'subordinate financialization' (see Chapter 9). The structural factors highlight the fact that these economies generally specialize in goods and services that have lower income elasticities, that is, demand for them is unlikely to grow as fast as incomes do in foreign markets. Subordinate financialization refers to their dependence on external sources of financing and the limited ability to borrow in their own currencies, which makes them more vulnerable to international financial market pressure. Taken together, as a result of these factors, economies in the Global South have a weaker position and are more dependent on market pressures, on economies in the Global North and on global financial institutions, as highlighted by dependency theory as well (Kvangraven 2021). On average capital tends to be less abundant, which means that there is a greater incentive to seek external sources of finance to support new investments. Three models have attracted attention in debates about emerging markets beyond Western Europe and North America.

First, much of this literature has focused on FDI-led growth, as discussed by Bohle and Regan (2021). This model is particularly common in the countries that VoC analysis has classified as dependent market economies (DMEs – see Chapter 6). In such economies growth strategies have been oriented towards attracting foreign investment, which is a key source of investment capital and facilitates access to other resources, including relevant technology or access to global value chains (see Chapter 12). These strategies include a variety of inducements, such as favourable tax incentives and other kinds of support (including access to land or real estate), to convince foreign companies to invest in a particular country or region. FDI-led growth is also similar to export-led growth in that a very large share of the output of these industries is exported, partly due to the fact that the home markets of these economies are often quite small. The main difference compared to export-led economies like Germany, where the export industries tend to be 'home-grown', is that the FDI-led growth model is highly dependent on external markets, not only to secure demand for exports, but also to finance investments.

Second, Mertens et al. (2022) have also identified an investment-led growth model, which highlight the role of state investment as a source of demand. In many respects this corresponds to the classical logic of developmental states in which state investment was often a key catalyst for dramatic transformation of the economy and a key source of demand in economies with low private savings and investment rates (see also Chapter 7). A key contemporary example of this growth model is China, in which investment-led growth characterizes the functioning of the Western Chinese economy in particular (Tan and Conran 2022). This investment-led growth model co-exists with an FDI-led growth model, which has characterized the coastal regions in Eastern China, where special economic zones were established early in the economic reform process. Foreign investment in these special economic zones played an important role in the transformation process under Deng Xiaoping's leadership that moved the economy away from the command economy model after 1978. Investment-led growth related to investments in infrastructure and construction has played a significant role, especially in provinces where the external environment has been less favourable, but also at critical times, such as in the aftermath of the East Asian and global financial crises or during the Covid pandemic, when its influence extended to other regions as well and made up for the shortfall arising from low demand on international markets. Nölke (2018) argues that the FDI-based and investment-based growth models (associated with DMEs and SMEs) are the two most viable strategies for economies in the Global South that seek to promote growth.

Investment is also central to the Spanish growth model, especially prior to the euro crisis. Baccaro and Pontusson (2022) characterize the Spanish growth model of that time as *construction-led*, and investments in real estate development were a key driver of growth as construction was the leading sector of the economy along with banking. However, the mechanisms underpinning construction-led growth also display similarities to consumption-led growth models. First, domestic demand has been the key driver of economic growth, and demand was not driven by wage growth or public spending, but principally by credit expansion. Baccaro and Pontusson (2022: 214) argue that the main sources of credit were domestic. This credit expansion financed investment in real estate and significant construction projects. Second, increases in house prices fuelled borrowing and private consumption in addition to investment. Rates of home ownership were exceptionally high – in 2007 it was 87 per cent (López and Rodríguez 2011: 10). This meant that booming real estate prices could be used as collateral to finance private consumption across much of the population, including both high-income and many low-income households (Baccaro and Pontusson 2022: 215).

Third, a large number of economies in the Global South are characterized by commodity-driven or natural resource-led growth (Sierra 2022). This means that much of their income is generated by natural resources and other primary products. Incomes rise in tandem with natural resource prices on international markets and drop when these prices fall, which means that such economies often experience significant fluctuations. The key feature of such economies is the dominant role of the resource sector, which tends to shape economic activity across the whole economy. A particularly striking example of this model is Saudi Arabia, where oil accounted for 90 per cent of export earnings, almost 90 per cent of government revenues and over 60 per cent of GDP in 2006 (Losman 2010: 444). To the extent that other sectors play a role in such economies, they tend to be highly dependent on developments in the resource sector as investment is financed with natural resource revenues. For example, the most systematic attempts to diversify Saudi Arabia's economy in the 1980s took place in years when oil revenues were high. In the late 1980s many elements of this very ambitious industrial policy programme unravelled, as falling oil prices made it hard to fund key initiatives, but even in this period oil revenues constituted at least half of government revenue (Niblock and Malik 2007: 99). The success of the more ambitious Saudi Vision 2030 programme that is designed to promote diversification is also likely to depend on the availability of funds from energy exports (Bradshaw, Van De Graaf and Connolly 2019).

Each of these models has generated high economic growth at certain times, though each of them also faces potential challenges. Natural resource-abundant economies are characterized by lower economic growth on average, which economists have referred to as a 'natural resource curse' (Sachs and Warner 2001). Nevertheless, some oil-abundant economies are among the countries with the highest national income per capita, but as already noted, these incomes tend to be volatile. Such volatility and concerns that oil will run out have stimulated diversification efforts in many resource-abundant economies (Bradshaw, Van De Graaf and Connolly 2019). The investment-led and FDI-led models depend on maintaining high levels of investment, which are generally funded either by mobilizing domestic savings, as in the case of investment-led growth, or high foreign investment inflows in the case of FDI-led growth. Many countries that have had such growth models have sought to develop strategies that increase the importance of domestic consumption. This includes China where the authorities began to stress 'dual circulation' of output (implying that output circulates both in export markets and domestically) in 2020 (Lin and Wang 2022). This concept highlights concerns about the viability of the pre-existing growth model if geopolitical tensions grow and international markets become less accessible to Chinese exports. The dual circulation proposal is designed to strengthen the role of domestic consumption and possibly even shift the Chinese economy towards a consumption-led growth model (Lin and Wang 2022).

Another important feature, especially of large economies in the Global South, is the co-existence of different growth models within one economy, as the above-mentioned contrast between the investment-led growth model in Western China on the one hand and the FDI-led growth model in the coastal provinces illustrates. Whilst the Chinese economy is a particularly stark example of this, the Brazilian economy also displays a contrast between FDI-led, investment-led and even natural resource-led growth, which attests to the size and complexity of the Brazilian economy and the range of sectors and economic actors within it. This can also explain why Brazil has been classified both as an SME (Chapter 7; Nölke et al. 2020) and as an HME (Schneider 2013; Feldmann 2019).

The FDI, domestic investment and commodity-based growth models are useful additions to growth models literature, and they capture key patterns of growth in many economies, especially in emerging markets. It should be noted, however, that there is no consensus on the full range of growth models and how to identify them. Existing studies identify a range of typologies, for example, models and sub-models that differentiate between exports of high-quality and low-quality manufacturing goods within the category of export-led growth models (Kalanta 2024b).

Politics and stability of growth models

If different growth models exist, this raises two important questions that the debate about this topic has not fully answered. First, how stable are the growth models? And second, what explains why a particular growth model operates in a given country?

Many analyses of growth models regard the flexibility of the growth models framework and its ability to account for change and instability as a key advantage compared to the VoC framework that is portrayed as too static. However, it also seems clear that growth models are not infinitely malleable. Several studies have suggested that growth models in high-income OECD countries are relatively stable and that any changes tend to be within the scope of a particular model, such as changes in the nature of exports within an export-led model. Baccaro and Pontusson (2022) argue that growth models are relatively stable in normal times, but that there may be an opening for change in crises or in the aftermath of shocks. By contrast, growth models in emerging market economies could change more easily (Kalanta 2024b). Yet as especially the record of natural resource-led growth models illustrates, shifting from one growth model to another is not necessarily easy. Many countries that have relied on natural resource-led growth have sought to move away from it and shift towards other growth models. As demonstrated by the Latin American experience (Sierra 2022), natural resource dependence persists for the region as a whole despite various attempts to diversity Latin American economies by means of state-led import-substituting industrialization and more recently by increasing exports, especially to China. Yet the countries, like Brazil, that had relied on Chinese demand for natural resource exports found themselves in a more difficult situation when this demand slowed in the 2010s, which did necessitate some adjustment away from commodity exports (Morgan, Doering and Gomes 2021).

In Baccaro and Pontusson's work there are two alternative accounts of the politics of growth models. In early versions of the argument, Baccaro and Pontusson (2016, 2019) speak of social blocs – a concept drawn from Antonio Gramsci's work. The concept of a social bloc highlights the interaction of material factors with hegemony. This implies that there is a powerful economic elite consisting of the most important sectors of the economy that stands to gain from the growth model. In addition, the social bloc is also underpinned by a dominant ideology that justifies narrow and particularistic elite interests as being in the general national interest. This implies that even groups that do not benefit directly from these arrangements may have come to accept that they are desirable.

In later versions of the argument Baccaro and Pontusson (2022) speak of a growth coalition that includes same dominant economic actors, which may also be underpinned by 'quiet politics'. 'Quiet politics' describes a situation where many aspects of economic policy that underpin the growth model are regarded as very technical, and are agreed between business and politicians in negotiations that have a low public salience (Culpepper 2011). Hegemony receives less emphasis in this account. Since key aspects of economic policy are shaped by independent central banks or European fiscal rules, electoral pressures are expected to play a less significant role. Baccaro and Pontusson (2022) place great emphasis on the role of producer group politics, including the strength of unions, which was a key factor ensuring that Sweden did not develop the kind of export-led growth model in the 1980s that is associated with Germany, even though some Swedish export industries would have favoured it (Baccaro and Pontusson 2022: 216–7). This was also a factor contributing to the recalibration of the growth model after the global financial crisis, when the importance of consumption-led growth increased within the Swedish growth model.

Towards a new synthesis: Growth regimes

Whilst the growth model agenda has generated great interest, questions about the political underpinnings of growth models and about their relationship to other aspects of the economy have prompted further debate. A particular concern relates to the importance of not neglecting the supply side of the economy in studies that focus on the importance of demand.

Some studies have identified *growth regimes* as a novel synthesis between VoC and growth models (Hassel and Palier 2020). They are similar to the growth regimes discussed in Chapter 8, but here they are designed to account for differences between capitalist economies rather than the evolution of capitalism over time. Growth regimes represent a synthesis as they incorporate the growth models framework and its focus on the macroeconomy and key sources of demand, but they also draw on the VoC literature to integrate key elements of the supply side of the economy, such as economic and institutional structures related to production. In addition, they also consider government economic policy (or its growth strategies) (see Table 10.2). Other studies have suggested that the French regulation theory provides a more compelling theoretical framework for understanding contemporary capitalism (Amable 2023; see also Chapters 1 and 8). FRT's emphasis on growth regimes or regimes of accumulation overlaps with the analysis developed by Hassel and Palier (2020).

The rationale for seeking such a synthesis is twofold. First, as acknowledged by Baccaro and Pontusson (2016), an exclusive focus on the demand side is likely to give an incomplete account of the functioning of a capitalist regime. Second, there is a clear correlation between the classification of particular economies into VoC and growth models. In particular, it is generally LME and MMEs that are consumption-led, whereas CMEs, NMEs and DMEs are export-led. SMEs and HMEs are more complicated cases, but are often export-led (or hybrids combining different growth models within a single economy, as in the cases of China and Brazil).

Avlijaš, Hassel and Palier (2020) identify five distinct growth regimes that seek to incorporate both the supply and the demand side of the economy (see Table 10.3; also Hassel and Palier 2023). The concept of growth regimes refers to 'a mode of governance for the economy' (Hassel and Palier 2020b: 12), and it incorporates three key components: the engine of growth (the key sectors), economic institutions and the sources of demand (growth model). Within the institutional context the welfare system receives special emphasis.

The first regime is centred on *promoting dynamic service industries*. It is based on significant investments in technology, notably information technology, to help harness productivity improvements that rely on skills and new technologies. This is underpinned by a welfare state regime that fosters social investment or public spending on such skills and technologies. A

Table 10.2 Comparing Growth Models, Growth Strategies and Growth Regimes

	Growth model	**Growth strategy**	**Growth regime**
Key unit of analysis	Macroeconomy	Government policy	Regime defined by institutions, growth model and growth strategy
Key focus	Source of demand	Policies to stimulate growth	Interactions between institutions, growth model and growth strategy

Source: A simplified account based on Hassel and Palier (2023), Hall (2020).

Table 10.3 Five Post-Fordist Growth Regimes

	Dynamic services, export-led growth regime	**High-quality manufacturing, export-led growth regime**	**FDI-financed, export-led growth regime**	**Finance-based, domestic demand-led growth regime**	**Publicly financed, domestic demand-led growth regime**
Demand drivers of growth	Export	Export	Export	Domestic consumption	Domestic consumption
Financialization	High	Low	Low	High	Low
Knowledge-based economy	Strong	Medium	Low	Strong	Low
Welfare state reform	Social investment	Dualization of welfare	Fiscal and social attractiveness	Commodification of welfare	Social protectionism
Example	Netherlands, Luxembourg	Germany, Austria, Belgium, Japan	Central and Eastern Europe	United Kingdom, United States	Southern Europe, France

Source: Hassel and Palier (2023).

good example of a country that has embraced such a strategy is the Netherlands, which has experienced rapid deindustrialization and considerable growth of dynamic service industries, especially in skill-intensive and sophisticated sectors, but most of the Nordic countries fit this model too (Hassel and Palier 2023).

The second path is centred on an *export-led growth model* based on high-quality manufacturing. This model is underpinned by institutions that deliver wage moderation and foster the skills needed to produce the goods and services that are exported and to maintain the competitiveness of exports. It is perhaps most closely associated with Germany in the twenty-first century and with the country's traditional CME institutions that still shape core sectors of the economy, such as high-quality manufacturing in the car and engineering industries. This strategy entails 'doubling down' on traditional areas of strength in the German economy, such as car manufacturing (Thelen 2020), but it is associated with relatively slow growth of the service sector. It is also characterized by dualization or increasing disparities between core workers in manufacturing and more precarious employment practices for other workers.

The third path is an *FDI-based export-led growth regime* underpinned by a government strategy that seeks to attract FDI with a combination of low costs and other inducements. This is the strategy adopted by DMEs (see Chapter 6) and also by many countries in the Global South. FDI-led growth has also played an important role in the Irish economy (Bohle and Regan 2021).

The fourth path relies on *high levels of consumption* to maintain aggregate demand. It tends to be associated with financialization (see Chapter 9). Financial liberalization has contributed to the growth of credit and debt, especially in the post-Fordist era of slower growth, when it has also helped fuel consumption and largely maintain it even in downturns. This model is common in LMEs, like Britain and the United States.

The final path is based on *high levels of public spending* to maintain aggregate demand, either by stimulating employment in the public sector or by providing subsidized public services. It is a key feature of many Southern European economies.

It should be noted that these five growth regimes might be best viewed as ideal types – in practice many countries are likely to combine elements of these regimes in varying proportions. However, Hassel and Palier (2020, 2023) argue that most OECD economies can be fitted into one of these categories. They show that there is a high correlation between VoC and the growth model and argue that the best way to make sense of contemporary capitalism is by combining the insights of both approaches and considering both the demand and production regime.

Conclusion

Much like the Great Depression and the crisis of the 1930s contributed to the Keynesian Revolution and the growth of macroeconomics a field, the global financial crisis and the recession that followed in its wake have prompted greater attention to the macroeconomy and economic instability.

This chapter has shown that these developments raise two important challenges for comparative capitalism and the study of Varieties of Capitalism in particular. First, it raises the question of how the macroeconomy should be incorporated into the study of comparative capitalism – should the diversity of capitalism be studied primarily by focusing on supply-side institutions or should there be greater emphasis on the demand side? And if the macroeconomy is placed at the centre of the analysis, to what extent is the mainstream new Keynesian economic approach suitable for this purpose, as VoC scholars have argued (Hope and Soskice 2016; Soskice 2007)? Do the growth models advocated by Baccaro and Pontusson (2016) that are inspired by post-Keynesian economics provide a more compelling framework for this purpose, notably by highlighting the importance of instability and distributional conflict within capitalism?

The second challenge relates to the status of Varieties of Capitalism as an approach to comparative capitalism. Whilst most VoC scholars have accepted the argument for paying more attention to macroeconomic factors and begun to integrate these issues into the framework in a more systematic way (Iversen, Soskice and Hope 2016; Iversen and Soskice 2006b; Hall 2018), Baccaro and Pontusson (2016) have argued that growth models constitute a more compelling alternative to VoC and even made the case for a 'paradigm shift'. They suggest that growth models are a more flexible framework that takes demand and the macroeconomy seriously, whilst also accounting for economic instability and change.

An alternative interpretation implies that the existence of growth models is largely consistent with VoC analysis. VoC scholars have demonstrated that the patterns identified by Baccaro and Pontusson are highly correlated with the LME and CME model (Hope and Soskice 2016). If so, VoC and growth model analysis should be seen as complements rather than competing paradigms, and they could potentially be combined as part of the study of growth regimes (Hassel and Palier 2023). Another alternative might be to revive earlier traditions of political economy, such as French regulation theory (Amable 2023), which has many similarities to the growth regimes approach.

More generally, this debate raises important questions about the best way to study contemporary capitalism. VoC scholars privilege the production regime, whereas scholars of growth models put the demand regime at the core of their analysis. This suggests that different approaches are useful for different purposes. VoC analysis may be most useful as an account of the enduring features of a country's production regime, whereas growth models provide a compelling lens to study short-run fluctuations in the economy.

Discussion questions

- Does the VoC framework neglect the macroeconomy and economic instability?
- How does the growth models framework differ from VoC? How are the models related?
- Would you expect growth model analysis to displace VoC analysis, as some of its proponents have suggested?
- Discuss whether growth regimes can be regarded as a successful synthesis of VoC and growth models.

11

The populist challenge

Comparative capitalism and the rise of populism

Populism is increasingly seen as a global phenomenon or even as a spectre haunting the world, as some have argued, evoking the words of the preface of the Communist Manifesto in which Karl Marx and Friedrich Engels spoke about the spectre of communism that was haunting Europe. Whilst the election of Donald Trump to the US presidency in 2016 and the Brexit referendum earlier that year came to be seen as emblematic of populism, especially in Anglo-American debates, populism has been used to describe leaders across various parts of the world. This includes Viktor Orbán in Hungary, the Law and Justice-led governments in Poland, the presidencies of Recep Tayyip Erdoğan in Turkey, Jair Bolsonaro in Brazil and Rodrigo Duterte in the Philippines and the Narendra Modi premiership in India, to name just a few examples. In many other countries populists became influential challengers by the 2010s, yet without managing to win power, as in the cases of Marine Le Pen's Rassemblement National (RN, formerly known as the Front National, FN) in France, or the Alternative für Deutschland (AfD) in Germany. In another set of countries, populists became junior members of governing coalitions, as in Norway, Austria, Finland and Estonia, or they provided parliamentary support through confidence and supply agreements to minority governments, as in Denmark (2001–11) or in the more formalized Tidö agreement that was concluded between the centre-right minority government and the Sweden Democrats in Sweden in 2022.

Widely regarded as a challenge to the status quo and the establishment, the significance of the populist tide is fiercely contested. A key controversy relates to its impact – to what extent does populism actually represent a threat to democracy or to global capitalism? This chapter assesses the rise of populism and explores the interactions between capitalist diversity and different models of populism. It is organized in the following way. The next section discusses the concept of populism and different forms of populism. After that the chapter considers the factors that have led to the rise of populism. The following sections of the chapter analyse the interactions between comparative capitalism and different forms of populism, across the Global North and in the Global South. In the final section the chapter discusses the impact of populism on business and the ways in which firms have sought to respond to populism.

What is populism?

Whilst the term 'populism' has been used extensively, notably in the aftermath of the Brexit referendum, the 2016 presidential election in the United States and the rise of populist leaders elsewhere in the world, the concept may sometimes seem elusive as it has also been interpreted and defined in different ways. This complicates any attempt to analyse it.

In particular, some uses of the term are purely polemical, making it seem that analysts use populism to refer to any kind of political movement that they do not like or to something that should be viewed as bad policy or 'bad economics' (cf. Rodrik 2018). For others, populism represents the core of democratic politics and popular mobilization, and it should therefore be seen as an important tool to reinvigorate stale representative institutions. In Laclau's (2005) understanding, populism is an 'empty signifier', so it can be mobilized for a range of purposes, including both progressive and reactionary agendas. Appealing to people and creating a shared sense of a political community and agency is at the heart of democratic politics, and a wide range of political actors could be described as populist in this sense. This debate highlights why populism is controversial. Tormey (2018) has captured its contradictory nature by describing it as a 'pharmakon' that could either have beneficial or detrimental effects on democracy. Given this complexity, some analysts prefer other concepts, like 'anti-system politics' (Hopkin 2020), to capture such phenomena.

This chapter builds on a wide range of studies that see populism primarily as standing in opposition to traditional forms of democratic politics. Based on a very comprehensive review and synthesis of the literature, Mansbridge and Macedo (2019: 60) define the core meaning of populism, as '(a) the people (b) in a morally charged (c) battle against (d) the elites'. It also accepts the heterogeneity of populism, which means that there are several kinds of populism – in particular, the literature distinguishes between right-wing or exclusionary populism on the one hand and left-wing or inclusionary populism on the other.

Alternatively, in Müller's (2016) influential definition, populism could be said to have three core characteristics, namely 'attempts to hijack the state apparatus, corruption and "mass clientelism" (trading material benefits or bureaucratic favors for political support by citizens who become the populists' "clients"), and efforts systematically to suppress civil society' (Müller 2016: 4). Another feature of populism that follows from these core characteristics is the embrace of 'holism' – or attempts to emphasize a form of organic unity of the people that transcends its parts. This is why populism is anti-pluralist: it views the expression of special interests as threatening to the unity of the people, in a way that resembles traditional critiques of political parties as divisive and particularistic (Rosenblum 2008).

However, beyond these general characteristics it is often hard to pin down the precise meaning of populism. A particular feature of the problem is what Mudde (2004) calls the 'thin-centred' nature of populism as an ideology– it has few defining characteristics, and therefore populist appeals and mobilizational strategies can be combined with other ideologies to generate a wide range of policy platforms. Some analysts have suggested that populism is primarily performative – it is a political style that is provocative and associated with 'bad manners', which is regarded as offensive by many people, but as an authentic and unscripted statement of important but inconvenient truths by its supporters (Moffitt and Tormey 2014).

At the most basic level both right-wing (or exclusionary) and left-wing (or inclusionary) populists rally against the status quo, but the two forms of populism conceptualize the people and the elites in different ways. The inclusion/exclusion can involve material resources, affect political representation or be symbolic (Mudde and Rovira Kaltwasser 2013; Filc 2009). Right-wing populism tends to be associated with nativist appeals, efforts to curb immigration and appeals to traditional values related to family, culture, and gender and sexuality. By contrast, left-wing populism is centred on appeals for more radical leftist policies to combat inequality and other forms of social exclusion. It tends to be more inclusive in the sense that it appeals to

Table 11.1 Key Varieties of Populism

	Right-wing populism	**Left-wing populism**
Key features	Exclusionary; welfare chauvinism, nationalistic mobilization typically associated with anti-immigration sentiment	Inclusionary; outflanking of left-wing parties in terms of progressive economic agendas
Key examples	Sweden Democrats, Danish People's Party, Alliance for Germany, Law and Justice (Poland), Trump Republicans (USA)	La France Insoumise (France), Podemos (Spain), Syriza (Greece), Kirchners (Argentina), Left Democrats (Sanders/ USA)

the '99 per cent', as in the case of the Occupy Movement, and it is not generally nativist in its rhetoric (see Table 11.1).

To what extent does populism and anti-system politics translate into policies that actually challenge the status quo? Populist economic policies vary considerably, which means that it is hard to generalize the actual impact of populism on the economy and economic policy. Traditional understandings of economic populism are based on studies of Latin America, especially in the 1970s and 1980s, and they tend to focus on a distinctive form of macroeconomic policy that generates boom-bust cycles (Dornbusch and Edwards 1991; Edwards 2019). Contemporary populism is rarely characterized by the kinds of policies characteristic of Latin America at that time (Feldmann and Popa 2022). Venezuela is arguably the main twenty-first-century case that fits the classical model of a populist boom-bust cycle quite well (Edwards 2019).

Although contemporary populists seek to challenge the status quo, there is considerable variation in the policy areas that they aim to challenge or influence. Whilst some populists have targeted macroeconomic policy, notably central bank independence (Goodhart and Lastra 2018), the main emphasis tends to be on other types of institutions and microeconomic policies related to trade, investment or welfare. Left-wing populist agendas usually have much in common with traditional socialist or social democratic policies, whereas right-wing populism is more ambiguous and diverse, typically incorporating a mix of fairly orthodox pro-market policies with various policies that business actors find more problematic (Feldmann and Morgan 2023d).

General causes of populism

The rise of populism in the 2010s has led to questions about its causes. Whilst the general view is that populists mobilize people who are frustrated with the current political system, three types of explanations of populism have dominated the debate so far. These explanations are cultural, economic and institutional.

The cultural explanation perceives populism as a backlash against rising immigration, globalization and other forms of social change (Norris and Inglehart 2018). This account highlights the fact that especially right-wing populists emphasize traditional understandings of the family and the nation, which often come with xenophobic undertones, and their agendas are typically associated with culture wars, including anti-woke agendas. From this perspective populism is a cultural backlash against various social changes that have occurred across the OECD since the 1970s, and that have contributed to the rise of post-materialist values associated with autonomy and self-expression across societies (Inglehart 1981). This includes greater concern with environmental issues and women's empowerment, increasing female labour force participation, greater ethnic diversity, and expanding rights for sexual minorities.

The economic explanation of populism focuses on growing economic insecurity associated with globalization, changing welfare state policies, and developments in labour markets. In many countries economic growth since the 1980s has not translated into rising real wages, and people have become increasingly worried about stagnant incomes and increasing precarity associated with the risk of layoffs and insecure part-time or even zero-hours contracts that have become more common. Such trends reflect long-run structural change associated with the rise of the knowledge economy and the decline of manufacturing (which provided stable and well-paid jobs to core, often male, workers – see Chapter 8; Grumbach and Collier 2022). Such concerns intensified after the 2007–8 financial crisis, which ushered in a period of austerity and cutbacks in many countries (Blyth 2013).

The third explanation focuses on the nature of political institutions and political parties in particular. This interpretation blames political institutions and mainstream political parties for the rise of populism. It highlights changes in the representation regime (Hall 2022b; Hall, Evans and Kim 2023) or even a 'hollowing out' of democracy (Mair 2013), where political parties are no longer responsive to popular concerns and worries. Even the centre-left, which has traditionally been viewed as the main representative of the working class, has neglected the concerns of the losers of globalization and neoliberalism or adopted market-friendly and technocratic policies that have represented a convergence on the centre-right (Mudge 2011).

Attempts to adjudicate between cultural and economic explanations have failed to generate any consensus on the determinants of populism. As many thoughtful observers have noted, it may ultimately be unwise to try to separate economic and cultural factors, as they are not independent of each other, and it may be more productive to explore their interactions (Berman 2021; Gidron and Hall 2020). It is likely that cultural scripts are activated and also successfully deployed under certain circumstances when economic conditions make citizens particularly receptive to them (Feldmann and Mazepus 2018). As Berman (2021) points out, general attitudes to cultural and other social issues (including immigration, gender etc.) have become more liberal and tolerant over time, but in certain situations their salience increases in a way that benefits populist parties. There have also been various attempts to combine economic and cultural factors as part of an overarching framework, as in Gidron and Hall's (2020) analysis of social status.

Taken together, these debates underscore the importance of economic factors. There is some disagreement on the degree to which they are decisive. Whilst other determinants, such as cultural and institutional factors or the agency of populist leaders, certainly play a role too, their resonance is likely to be influenced by economic conditions.

Varieties of capitalism and varieties of populism

The fact that populism relates to key developments in global capitalism and that it also comes in different varieties, notably left-wing and right-wing populism, raises the question of whether the nature of populism is related to capitalist diversity. As noted earlier, there is no clear correlation between cultural grievances and populist sentiment, which raises the question as to whether differences between capitalist systems can explain differences in populism.

This section draws on the emerging literature that seeks to explain the variation between different types of populism with respect to different Varieties of Capitalism (Roberts 2019), and especially two of the most detailed assessments of this topic (Manow 2018; Hopkin 2020).

Manow (2018) builds on Dani Rodrik's influential analysis of the economics of populism to address these questions. In Rodrik's framework, populism is best understood as a reaction to the impact of globalization, and the diversity of populism reflects the uneven impact of globalization on different parts of the world. In countries where the most controversial aspects of globalization relate to greater competition driven by trade and foreign direct investment, left-wing populists have been successful. They advocate a variety of policies to address concerns about the effects of globalization, either by expanding welfare provisions to compensate vulnerable groups or by intervening more directly by means of industrial policy. Like other scholars (Mudde and Rovira Kaltwasser 2013), Rodrik views Latin America as a whole as the main example of inclusionary left-wing populism along with Southern Europe.

Manow extends this analysis in two important ways. First, he analyses the divide between inclusionary and exclusionary forms of populism in Europe in more detail and demonstrates how the vote shares of right- and left-wing populist parties vary across different parts of Europe (Manow 2018: 41–2). This also relates to Hopkin's analysis of the divide between debtor and creditor countries in the eurozone, where debtor countries have tended to support inclusionary populism and creditor countries have seen the rise of exclusionary parties (Hopkin 2020). Second, Manow also shows how the effects of globalization are largely shaped by national Varieties of Capitalism (see also Roberts 2019). Differences in national economic systems can explain why countries have been affected by globalization in different ways and why certain aspects of globalization are controversial in particular countries. Manow identifies four pathways to populism that relate to particular clusters of countries and can be identified as North, South, East and West in the European context. The core logic applies beyond Europe and can be used to analyse cases in other parts of the world, notably in the Americas (see Table 11.2).

Manow takes issue with the dominant framing of populism as a generalized cultural backlash or resistance by the losers of globalization by focusing on a key observation, namely that there are clear geographical patterns of populism, which cannot be easily explained with reference to varying cultural grievances or differences in cultural intolerance (cf. Berman 2021: 76). In Europe, there are four populist clusters – what Manow calls South, North, East and West. In addition to the European cases, Manow and Roberts also suggest that the United States and key Latin American cases, like Venezuela, Bolivia or Ecuador, can be added to this framework (see also Mudde and Rovira Kaltwasser 2013). The following sections explore the four pathways to populism identified by Manow (2018).

Pathways to right-wing populism

Right-wing populism has attracted the most attention and been most common in much of Europe and some other parts of the world. Manow identifies three pathways to right-wing populism in the European context – what he refers to as North, East and West. This section discusses each of these pathways in turn.

Table 11.2 Varieties of Capitalism and Populism: The Manow (2018) Typology

Varieties of populism	Variety of capitalism	Key features	Key examples
North	CME	Exclusionary right-wing populism; welfare chauvinism	Germany, France, Sweden, Denmark, Norway
South	MME	Inclusionary left-wing populism	Spain, Greece, Italy, France
East	DME	Exclusionary right-wing populism	Poland, Hungary
West	LME	Exclusionary right-wing populism targeting low-wage competition on labour markets	Britain (Brexit), United States (Trump)

Northern Europe

As Manow shows, in Northern European CMEs, notably Germany, the Nordic countries (Sweden, Norway, Denmark and Finland) and the Netherlands/Austria, right-wing populism has become influential. In Finland, Norway and Austria right-wing populist parties have served in government and headed important ministries. Their role in the other countries has also been significant. The Sweden Democrats emerged after the 2022 election as the second-largest party in parliament. Although they did not formally enter government or name any ministers, the three-party centre-right government that took office in 2022 was reliant on the Sweden Democrats to secure a majority in the Swedish parliament. The cooperation between the Sweden Democrats and the government was formalized in the so-called 'Tidö agreement', and the Sweden Democrats appointed their own representative in the cabinet office. The Danish People's Party played a similar (if somewhat less formalized) role in propping up Danish centre-right governments in the period 2002–12. In Germany the AfD achieved some striking successes in the 2010s, and its rise has caused great concern in the German establishment, including some business constituencies (Kinderman 2021).

Populists in these countries have focused much attention on traditional right-wing populist priorities, such as immigration, welfare chauvinism and traditional values. Euroscepticism and criticisms of the EU have also played a significant role, especially in conjunction with the euro crisis.

These economies are successful exporters and highly export-dependent, which means that international trade and competitiveness have been of limited importance in populist agendas compared to many other countries. By contrast, populist mobilization has tended to focus on immigration, with a special emphasis on refugees. This has also been related to 'welfare chauvinism' – as these economies have generous (conservative or social democratic) welfare states. High rates of immigration have prompted concerns about the viability of the welfare state in an era of high migration, often expressed in terms of the cost of supporting rising numbers of beneficiaries and associated pressures on public services, including education and health care. At times such concerns are framed in terms of possible abuses of the system, which are sometimes labelled as 'benefit tourism'. Such sentiments were further heightened by the refugee crisis in 2015 that led to an influx of people and fuelled popular debate and controversy about mass migration in Germany and Sweden. The euro crisis that began in 2009 also fuelled Euroscepticism throughout much of the 2010s that was framed in terms of groups and countries that deserve or do not deserve support. Northern European populists often described the crisis as the outcome of irresponsible spending and rule-breaking in Southern Europe. They railed against bailout packages for Southern Europe, arguing that they would turn Northern Europe into the paymasters picking up the bills to fund Southern profligacy.

A striking feature of the right-wing populist agenda is that it cuts across the traditional left-right divide – they combine support for the welfare state (which is typically associated with the left) with exclusionary policies that limit access to benefits, by introducing tight eligibility criteria (effectively making benefits available only to the country's nationals) and by dramatically reducing immigration (Manow 2018; Röth, Afonso and Spies 2018).

Brexit, Trump and Anglo-American populism

In the two core LMEs populism has manifested itself in very different ways. If we use Iversen and Soskice's (2019) measure of populist attitudes, the LMEs, and especially the United States and the United Kingdom, score very high. In these majoritarian systems the barriers for new anti-system parties to enter parliament and play a central role in politics are much greater than in the Continental European proportional representation systems. So whilst populist attitudes are strong, the opportunities for new parties to arise are more limited than in CMEs where multi-party systems are more open to challenger parties.

In the British case, UKIP and its successors (the Brexit Party and Reform UK) were unsuccessful at gaining seats at general elections until 2024, though UKIP achieved some success in local elections and especially in the European Parliament elections that were based on PR. This is why populism is associated with the Brexit referendum in the UK and to some extent also with growing populist influence over the Conservative Party under Boris Johnson's leadership, which in itself was bound up with the Brexit process. The Brexit campaign followed the populist playbook to a considerable extent – it portrayed EU membership as an arrangement that only benefited the elite and the Remain campaign as an elite-dominated group engaged in 'Project Fear' that did not care about ordinary people and their concerns.

In the United States Donald Trump secured the Republican nomination as the Republican presidential candidate in 2016 after outcompeting a large field of contenders, many of whom enjoyed much greater support from the Republican establishment. Trump won in large part thanks to the support he enjoyed in the so-called 'rust belt' of the United States, that is, in areas where previously successful manufacturing industries were in decline.

Why did populism emerge in LMEs? On the one hand, these are countries where the transformation of the economies has proceeded rapidly and the service sector has grown very fast, both in terms of highly paid and high-skilled jobs in the new economy and low-paid service jobs. Incomes for much of the population have been stagnant for a long time, though financialization and the growth of debt attenuated the impact of wage stagnation. The global financial crisis fuelled resentment when credit dried up and there was a wave of foreclosures (Stout 2019). Inequality is relatively high in these flexible labour markets; there are limited opportunities for lifelong learning, training and for the upgrading of skills in the old middle classes, thereby leading to a deeper divide between old and new middle classes in these countries (Hopkin 2020).

Whilst there are some similarities with the right-wing populism that prevails in CMEs, notably with respect to emphasis on immigration, there are also important differences. As immigration is predominantly work-based, the main mobilization has revolved around low-wage competition in labour markets (Manow 2018). In addition to greater competition for low-wage jobs, immigration was also widely perceived as a challenge to public services since the education and health care sectors were under severe strain during the period of austerity after the global financial crisis. Immigration increased rapidly in Britain, partly as a result of the relatively open and flexible labour market. Similarly, unlike Germany, for example, the UK did not introduce any transition period for the free movement of labour after the EU enlargement in 2004. The US case is similar in the sense that much of the mobilization focused on low-wage immigration, with Mexicans a particular target of Donald Trump's rhetoric and initiatives, including the proposal to build a wall on the Mexican border to stop illegal immigration. However, in Trump's case the rhetoric also focused on international trade and outsourcing (Noland 2018).

The impact of populism on these economies remains contested. The Trump administration was divided on many matters of foreign economic policy, including protectionism (Baltz 2021). Some analysts have suggested that on most fronts Trump governed as a conventional Republican, with the main milestone being the Trump tax cuts (Pierson 2017; Mizruchi and Galăn 2023). Progress on other matters that might have revitalized the economy in the post-industrial areas of the United States has been much more limited, and in the wake of the Covid pandemic President Trump failed to secure re-election. Similarly, in the case of the UK the full impact of the populist turn is unclear. Whilst Brexit did materialize, what exactly post-Brexit Britain might look like was contested, in part since no particular model of Brexit was on the ballot. The Johnson government signalled some commitment to 'levelling up' post-industrial areas in the North of England through regional and industrial policy activism, but other visions, such as Global Britain or Singapore-on-Thames, indicated a stronger commitment to free trade and globalization, albeit with greater restrictions on low-skilled immigration.

Dependent market economies in Central and Eastern Europe

The Central and Eastern European economies represent another striking shift to right-wing populism – whilst these developments have begun to affect a range of countries across the region to varying degrees, this discussion focuses on the two countries where these trends have gone furthest and which are most central to the debate, namely Hungary and Poland. In Hungary Viktor Orbán's Fidesz party won the 2010, 2014, 2018 and 2022 elections and acquired a dominant position in Hungarian politics, which enabled it to transform policymaking and state institutions. A similar process took place in Poland in the period 2015–23 as the Law and Justice Party won both the parliamentary and presidential elections, often explicitly evoking the Hungarian experience as a template by raising the prospect of bringing 'Budapest to Warsaw' (Jasiecki 2017).

To many observers the triumph of the populists in these countries came as a big surprise. Both countries were widely hailed as the most successful economies in Central and Eastern Europe, with Poland also the only EU economy not to experience a GDP contraction during the global financial crisis and the ensuing Great Recession. This raises two questions – why did populism emerge in the first place, especially in the two economies that were widely perceived as very successful, and second, to what extent has populism affected the economic models in these countries?

As in the case of the Northern CMEs, these economies have benefited from globalization in many ways. High rates of foreign investment have turned these countries into dependent market economies (DMEs – see Chapter 6) maintaining FDI-led growth models (Chapter 10). They differ from the Northern CMEs in that they have not received any significant numbers of immigrants or refugees, at least until the outbreak of the war in Ukraine in 2022. By contrast, there has been significant emigration from Central and Eastern Europe. However, the refugee crisis of 2015 was used by populist politicians to mobilize support in Poland and Hungary by evoking the European debate on refugee quotas. Mobilization surrounding concerns about mass immigration was arguably a key factor contributing to the Law and Justice Party's narrow election victory in 2015, and it also helped boost Orbán's popularity in Hungary at the same time (Manow 2018: 38).

However, populism enjoyed the greatest support in areas that have been less successful during the post-communist era. For example, in Poland there is a sharp geographical divide between the prosperous big cities and rural areas, especially in the East of the country, where levels of income are lower and support for the populist Law and Justice Party is much higher. In such regions frustration is directed against the elites in Warsaw, but also sometimes portrayed in cultural tones, by drawing on ethno-religious tropes. The Law and Justice Party has been able to gain votes by advocating social policies that help especially poorer households, but which also resonate with traditional conservative and religious agendas that are typical of right-wing populism and that can be framed as a way of strengthening the traditional family (Manow 2018; Orenstein and Bugaric 2022). However, some groups within the financial sector that might be regarded as beneficiaries of post-communist reform were increasingly frustrated with some elements of economic policy and the limited opportunities to acquire a more active role (Naczyk 2022).

The emergence of populism in these countries relates in large part to controversies surrounding the outcomes of post-communist transformation, but also to specific features of the political system in each country. Although these economies were very successful in terms of standard metrics, such as economic growth, the gains were unevenly distributed. Cities and regions that had been reliant on declining industries, but did not benefit from the process of FDI-led reindustrialization and growth, have been particularly receptive to populist appeals.

Assessments of the impact of populism on these economies vary, largely depending on which aspects of their political economies are the core focus of any given study. Feldmann and Popa (2022) show that macroeconomic policies were relatively orthodox and not associated with the kind of boom-bust cycle that traditional forms of populism in Latin America often exhibited (Dornbusch and Edwards 1991), at least in the first years of populist rule. It also seems clear that many key features of their DME institutions are unchanged, and privileged FDI-based industries, such as notably car manufacturing, retain their centrality within the economy under populist governments (Bohle and Regan 2021). In other parts of the economy there have been more significant changes. Others have focused more on changes in the domestic business structure and on sectors that are less central to their economic models (such as retail and finance) and argued that there has been a big shift towards state capitalism (Szarzec, Totleben and Piątek 2022), or authoritarian capitalism, especially in Hungary (Sallai and Schnyder 2021). Szelényi has argued that this has given rise to a form of prebendalism where property rights are conditional on maintaining the support of the regime (Szelenyi 2016; Rogers 2020). Other analysts have suggested that populism has given rise to a new economic policy model based on economic nationalism and conservatism (Bluhm and Varga 2020; Orenstein and Bugaric 2022). This model fuses more activist economic policy and redistributive elements, such as the Polish

500+ programme that provides more generous child benefits, with a very conservative cultural and social agenda privileging traditional families and religion. In this sense, many populists in Central and Eastern Europe, especially the Polish Law and Justice Party, bridge the traditional left-right divide in a very stark way by expanding welfare entitlement whilst also advancing a traditional cultural agenda.

Pathways to left-wing populism in Southern Europe and Latin America

Left-wing populism has been particularly strong across two regions, namely Southern Europe and Latin America. These two regions have undergone dramatic changes since the 1970s and 1980s. These changes have been both political and economic, as many countries across both regions democratized and liberalized their economies. As a result of the debt crisis of the 1980s, the consensus among policymakers in Latin America shifted away from import substitution and towards embracing markets, globalization and deregulation (Armijo and Faucher 2002). In Southern Europe this period was also associated with European integration, as Portugal, Spain and Greece joined the European Communities/European Union and later adopted the euro as well. As discussed in Chapter 10, the early years of eurozone membership were a period of rapid growth associated with high levels of consumption.

Yet the outcomes of market reform were contradictory and uneven across both regions. Southern Europe was severely affected by the Great Recession and the eurozone crisis, which led to a severe and drawn-out crisis in these countries. In Southern Europe the crisis exacerbated various economic and social challenges, such as insider-outsider divides in labour markets, with very high rates of long-run unemployment, also among young people. As discussed in Chapter 10, these economies were also affected by membership of the eurozone, which removed devaluations as a policy tool. Given the nature of their labour market institutions, they were not able to use coordinated wage setting as a means of restoring competitiveness and exports, as CMEs are able to do (Hancke 2013; Hall 2012). Therefore the crisis was particularly deep in these economies, and the consequences of austerity on the Greek economy contributed to the rise of left-wing populism associated with Syriza. The ascent of Podemos in Spain and the Five Star Movement in Italy reflected similar processes and an anti-austerity agenda that was also critical of the EU's approach to the euro crisis (Hopkin 2020; see also Chapter 10). More generally, left-wing populism enjoys the support of labour market outsiders, many workers on informal contracts and other excluded groups as the inclusionary agenda is seen to provide greater opportunities to these groups (Roberts 2019; Manow 2018).

In Latin America economic performance has often fallen short of the high expectations many people had of the reform agenda of the 1980s and 1990s (Schneider 2013). In particular, growth has not been as high as expected, but above all inequality has remained persistently high across much of the region, in part as a result of key HME institutions and the highly segmented labour markets (see Chapter 5). What unites supporters of left-wing populists across both regions is a sense of disillusionment with the economic policies of their predecessors, especially among core supporters and excluded groups (indigenous populations and people on low incomes). In Southern Europe some of the most radical proposals have been constrained by euro area membership, as the Syriza government had to backtrack on some of its policy commitments once faced with the risk of 'Grexit' or the expulsion of Greece from the euro area (and possibly even the European Union).

These factors and an economic downturn affecting much of the region in the late 1990s contributed to the so-called 'pink tide' in the early 2000s, which brought a number of centre-left or socialist leaders and governments to power. In the case of Argentina this process was particularly dramatic due to the financial crisis of 2002 when the country's currency board arrangement collapsed (Feldmann and Kukštis 2017). Some of the leaders associated with the Pink Tide have been described as left-wing populists, including Rafael Correa (Ecuador), Nestor Kirchner (Argentina) or Hugo Chávez and Nicolás Maduro in Venezuela, and Evo Morales (Bolivia) is often included in this category as well (Mudde and Rovira Kaltwasser 2013). The subsequent election of left-wing populist Andrés Manuel López Obrador as president of Mexico was fuelled by similar concerns, including disillusionment with the two dominant parties, corruption and persistent inequality, and by an inclusionary agenda courting support from marginalized groups in society (Beck and Iber 2022).

The policies adopted by left-wing populists across the two regions have varied and rarely lived up to all the expectations associated with their agenda. As noted above, in Southern Europe Syriza backed down from opposing the austerity policies expected by the EU to secure financial support and guarantee Greece's membership of the eurozone. In the Spanish case some of the most tangible effects occurred at the municipal level, though even here there was disappointment with the progress on promoting equitable housing policies (Feenstra and Tormey 2023).

The Venezuelan experience is the most radical and controversial and has involved a standoff with many private businesses and business associations, except for the *boliburguesia*, that is the bourgeoisie that is loyal to Chávez's 'Bolivarian Revolution' (Cannon 2014). Argentina, Ecuador and Bolivia adopted a mix of populist and more traditional centre-left policies, but with the partial exception of Bolivia, many of these initiatives were swiftly reversed by later governments. Most strikingly, Correa's successor Lenín Moreno, who had served as his vice president, distanced himself from key aspects of his agenda and adopted more orthodox macroeconomic policies (de la Torre 2018).

Left- and right-wing populism within the same country

It should be noted that the neat separation of regions and countries into left- and right-wing populism obscures the fact that left- and right-wing populism often co-exist within the same country. In Italy, the Five Star Movement was (especially initially) regarded as left-wing populist, whereas the Lega was viewed as right-wing populist, like Silvio Berlusconi's Forza Italia and Giorgia Meloni's Brothers of Italy (Fratelli d'Italia, FdI). In France, Marine Le Pen's Rassemblement National co-exists with Jean-Luc Mélenchon's La France Insoumise, and in the US context the rise of Donald Trump coincided with a very strong primary campaign by Bernie Sanders, whom many analysts have characterized as a left-wing populist. Similar arguments have been made about the rise of Corbyn in the UK alongside the Brexit coalition (Hopkin 2020).

According to Manow (2018) the co-existence of different forms of populism within one country relates to internal divides within the country. There is great variation in terms of how globalization affects individuals, households, firms and regions, all of which may contribute to subnational variation. For example, in the Italian case, there is a significant difference between the high-income regions of the North that are the support base of the Lega (initially known as Lega Nord and running on a regionalist platform), and the less prosperous South where the Five Star Movement has been more successful. The North-South divide in Italy mirrors the

North-South divide between right- and left-wing populism in Europe as a whole, and Manow suggests that different parts of the United States are affected in different ways by globalization, giving rise to a mix of anti-immigration and anti-trade sentiment. Such forces translate into a potential support base for either right-wing or left-wing populism, which can co-exist within one country.

Right-wing populism in the Global South

Despite the common association between left-wing populism and the politics of the Global South, especially in the Latin American context, the 2010s gave rise to several successful right-wing populist breakthroughs across various parts of the world. Some of the most striking cases include Narendra Modi's BJP government in India and the presidencies of Jair Bolsonaro in Brazil and Rodrigo Duterte in the Philippines.

In these countries the rise of right-wing populism partly reflected disillusionment with centre-left projects. Heller (2020) has described Brazil and India as cases of 'retrenchment populism', in which middle-class actors have sought to protect their privileges and gain further resources. In the Brazilian case twelve years of Workers' Party (PT) rule under Presidents Lula da Silva and Dilma Rouseff ended against the backdrop of crisis, with the impeachment of President Rouseff and a prison sentence for ex-president Lula. The rise of right-wing populism in Brazil under President Jair Bolsonaro (2018–22) represented a significant political shift. Known as 'the Trump of the Tropics', Bolsonaro ran on a similar platform of exclusionary populism targeting perceived privileges of minorities and women, many of whom had benefited from economic growth and social programmes under the Workers' Party governments in Brazil. The Bolsonaro campaign castigated the PT era as a period characterized by corruption and branded some of its signature social programmes that had helped address poverty and inequality as wasteful and as benefiting the undeserving poor. Whilst Bolsonaro was not the preferred candidate of business, key business interests regarded him as the 'lesser evil' who would be most likely to defend their core economic interests (Evans 2020). This support was further bolstered by his selection of Paulo Guedes as Finance Minister and guarantor of business-friendly policies (Doering et al. 2023).

In the Philippines, socio-economic inequalities might also be seen as a fertile ground for inclusionary populism, and the Estrada presidency (1998–2001) is widely regarded as an example of left populism. Joseph Estrada, a former actor, campaigned on an inclusionary agenda, but his presidency was marred by corruption allegations and ultimately cut short after street protests that led to Estrada's impeachment and resignation in 2001. Rodrigo Duterte, often described as a penal populist due to his reputation as a 'punisher' and his hard line on crime, came to power thanks to an emphasis on law and order, having famously promised to throw thousands of bodies of murdered drug criminals in Manila Bay until the fish grew fat.

Much like in Brazil, where the preceding PT era had been heralded as a period of growth and falling inequality, the Duterte regime was preceded by the Aquino presidency, which was widely regarded as successful on similar grounds, notably in terms of economic growth and stability. However, the liberal reformist regime in Philippines was also vulnerable as various features, including corruption and inequality, remained matters of concern. Duterte used social media to attack the political elite as out of touch and was able to build a new largely middle-class coalition concerned about crime and corruption, which included various groups who felt that they had not benefited enough under the Aquino era (Thompson 2016; Thompson 2020).

In the Indian case the exclusionary populism of Modi's BJP rallied against the long-standing dominance of the Congress Party and against corruption and various spending programmes. The mobilizational strategy targeted 'alien elites', including Muslims, as well as the undeserving poor, who were portrayed as the beneficiaries of wasteful affirmative action programmes. In that sense these cases bear a resemblance to the status concerns among groups in other countries who feel that their status is under threat given that they have not benefited as much as they feel others have. Similar processes have contributed to support for right-wing populism in the Global North, especially among the traditional white and male working class who are worried about status decline (Gidron and Hall 2020).

However, in both Brazil under Bolsonaro and the Philippines under Duterte economic policy remained highly orthodox, with both presidents appointing technocratic finance ministers to assuage business and market concerns about their economic agendas (Takagi 2023, Doering et al. 2023). The Modi government in India was also relatively orthodox on many dimensions, though it also generated uncertainty and concern, notably by criticizing companies like Infosys or exercising political pressure on the Central Bank, which prompted its governor Raghuram Rajan to resign (Wyatt 2023, Jaffrelot 2021).

These cases demonstrate that right-wing populism is not purely a phenomenon tied to the Global North. Much like in the United States, where the rise of Trump coincided with Bernie Sanders' successful primary campaign, large and segmented economies, like Brazil, India and the Philippines, feature a wide range of economic actors and social groups, and right-wing populists may succeed by mobilizing key constituencies that are receptive to its agenda. This shows that economic conditions and capitalist institutions do not fully predetermine which kind of populism enjoys success within a given country and that much of the Global South is potentially fertile ground not only for left-wing populism, but also for right-wing populist appeal.

Populism as a challenge to business and capitalism?

One of the key questions about populism relates to its perceived challenge to business and capitalism. In the neoliberal era business has generally exercised substantial influence on policymaking. There are several reasons for this. In part this reflects the fact that governments of all stripes have tended to adopt pro-market and pro-business policies in the neoliberal era (see Chapter 8). Business was also deeply involved in policymaking, notably through mechanisms of network governance (Stoker 2019). As business was viewed as a key stakeholder with relevant expertise and an understanding of how economic policies and regulation might affect economic activity, they were frequently consulted either formally (as members of expert committees or advisory teams) or informally. Business influence was strengthened by two other factors. First, the technical nature of many key economic policy questions reduced their salience in the public domain, which made it harder to generate interest and public scrutiny. Second, much of this influence reflected what Pepper Culpepper (2011) has termed 'quiet politics' – in other words, this influence occurred away from the spotlight and in meeting rooms. Culpepper's research shows that business influence is at its greatest under conditions of quiet politics – when controversies and policy issues spill over into the public domain, policymakers are less likely to defer to business.

The rise of populism disrupts this cosy relationship in two respects (Feldmann and Morgan 2022). First, populists are less likely to defer to experts or to rely on network governance.

'This country has had enough of experts', as Michael Gove, one of the leaders of the Leave Campaign before the Brexit referendum, declared. Second, populism is associated with noisy politics, and under such conditions it is generally more difficult for business to exercise influence. In such situations the general public is highly mobilized, which makes it harder for business to exercise its influence behind the scenes, and business rarely engages in noisy politics directly given the difficulty to swaying public opinion (Feldmann and Morgan 2021). On the other hand, business attitudes towards populists are often ambivalent, and there is substantial variation between businesses and sectors. Why is this the case, and how can we make sense of this variation?

Existing research has demonstrated that populist agendas vary, as does their political influence. For example, there are substantial differences even within the categories of right-wing and left-wing populism. The impact of populism also depends on the amount of power that the populists wield. If populists are in government, and if their power is entrenched, as in Hungary, business is unlikely to be able to insulate itself from dealing with populism. By contrast, if populists are a small minority within (or outside) parliament, business can generally afford to ignore them, unless they believe that the influence of populism is likely to grow in future.

The differences between the programmes and the influence of populist parties are a key factor shaping business responses. Another important factor shaping business responses relate to the nature of the firms and sectors within which they operate as this also has an important impact on how they might be affected by populist agendas. This raises the question how best to understand business responses. Feldmann and Morgan (2023b) draw on Hirschman's typology of exit, voice and loyalty to identify five types of business responses to populism.

The first possible response is exit or the decision by a firm to leave a particular country. In addition to complete exit, the exit could also be partial: firms may reduce their involvement with an economy, for example, by scaling back their existing activities or reducing future investments. This kind of strategy is only available to internationally mobile firms, such as multinationals, and firms that adopt it may incur substantial costs as they forego business opportunities in this economy.

The next two responses build on Hirschman's analysis of voice. Feldmann and Morgan (2023b) distinguish between two types of voice as a response to the noisy and conflictual environment stirred up by populism – *soft voice* and *loud voice*.

Soft voice relates to many of the usual channels that business traditionally uses to influence policy – lobbying, informal discussions with politicians and contributions to expert committees and other forms of consultation associated with network governance. The main challenge for business is that populists are typically less receptive to business influence than governments have been in the neoliberal era, thereby making it harder for firms to use such channels to modify and influence government policies.

Loud voice, or more forceful criticism and opposition to the populist agenda, tends to be very rare. Not only are such interventions very costly, but they may also backfire. If businesses are portrayed as a part of the privileged elite, then their interventions may be seen as self-serving or as a way for them to advance their own narrow self-interest, perhaps at the expense of wider social and economic concerns. And if populists are entrenched in power, then exercising loud voice could also trigger retaliation. Some of the most striking examples of loud voice can be found in Germany, where many businesses have expressed concern about the impact of the rise of the AfD and mobilized against it, in part for economic reasons, but also given the risk of reputational damage related to associations with the legacy of Nazi Germany (Kinderman 2021). This implies that business may be able to use their financial resources and innovative campaigning effectively to influence public opinion even under conditions of noisy politics, as also demonstrated by business mobilization in Swiss referendum campaigns (Kinderman 2023).

The final two responses relate to loyalty. *Implicit loyalty* is perhaps the most common response. It is adopted by a range of firms, including many businesses that are supportive of the populist agenda and also some businesses that are more critical. Implicit loyalty involves not speaking out and 'keeping one's head down' (Feldmann and Morgan 2022). This approach is attractive to business as it allows them to keep out of politics and not to take a stand on controversial matters.

Explicit loyalty involves taking a stand and actively speaking out in support of the populist agenda. As in the case of loud voice, this strategy is usually rare. There are some examples of overtly pro-Trump business executives in the United States and business leaders who played a very active role in the Brexit campaign in the United Kingdom, but this strategy is usually perceived as costly and risky by businesses. However, once populists are in power or close to power, there is a potential payoff as populists could seek to reward their most loyal and outspoken supporters, as the Orbán regime in Hungary has done (Szelenyi 2016). In such cases explicit loyalty is more common.

In conclusion, business responses to populism in power vary greatly given that populist policy agendas are not uniform. Populists agendas that are pro-business in key respects, as in the case of the Trump tax cuts (Mizruchi and Galǎn 2023), tend to enjoy business support. More importantly, when populist governments embrace a strong commitment to technocratic and market-oriented policy (Doering et al. 2023; Takagi 2023), then fewer businesses are likely to be opposed to populism. When the relative balance between the destabilizing and pro-business elements is less favourable, business may take a more critical stance, but they face the dilemma that many standard tools of influence are harder to implement. To the extent that populism may become a more permanent feature of contemporary politics, business may need to seek novel ways to engage with populist leaders and to shape their policy platforms.

Conclusion: Populism and the end of global capitalism?

This chapter has shown that the populist turn is complex and multifaceted and highlighted the ways in which the rise of populism interacts with capitalist diversity and globalization. Different capitalist systems are more likely to generate right-wing or left-wing populism than others, given that the effects of globalization vary across different types of market economies. However, both forms of populism may co-exist within the same society by appealing to different groups or regions.

Given the complexity and elusiveness of populism, its effects on capitalism are not uniform. Whilst some aspects of populism may constitute a challenge to economic actors, populism is not always unattractive to business, and in some cases right-wing populism is quite consistent with many features of neoliberalism (Doering et al. 2023; Takagi 2023) or with a commitment to a pro-business agenda (Pierson 2017). Similarly, the existing evidence on the economic effects of populism does not suggest that it necessarily leads to poor economic performance or economic crises (Feldmann and Popa 2022; Rodrik 2018). In that sense the current wave of populism seems to differ from common understandings of earlier waves of economic populism in Latin America (Dornbusch and Edwards 1991; Edwards 2019).

Therefore the concern that populism heralds the end of neoliberalism or the end of globalization seems premature. Many populists have adopted anti-globalization rhetoric, but they have usually done so in a selective way. Most populists want to retain globalization, but crack down on particular aspects of it, such as outsourcing or migration, notably under the banner of welfare chauvinism. Similarly, for some right-wing populists and supporters of Brexit, the UK's departure from the European Union represents an opportunity to deepen the commitment to globalization and free market under the banner of 'Global Britain', a vision of a deregulated and free-trading economy that has been relieved of the regulatory shackles associated with EU membership, or a kind of 'Singapore-on-Thames' as this vision has been called. However, this should not be taken to imply that populism is entirely unproblematic for global capitalism. Its rise captures a widely shared frustration among large segments of the populations in many countries, and it is typically associated with great uncertainty and unpredictability (Feldmann and Morgan 2023c).

Discussion questions

1. To what extent is populism associated with a coherent economic model?
2. Does populism represent a challenge to globalization and market-based capitalism?
3. What explains the rise of global populism?
4. What is the relationship between capitalism and populism? Can differences in capitalist models explain the nature of the range of populist movements across countries?
5. How would you assess the future prospects of the populist turn? Are populist movements likely to decline once they have voiced their protests, or would you expect them to become an enduring feature of political systems around the world?

PART IV

Conclusion

12

Conclusion

Comparative capitalism and its prospects

As capitalism has become increasingly dominant around the world, understanding how it operates has arguably never been more important. This book has introduced the field of comparative capitalism as a lens to study capitalism.

The core idea animating this book is that capitalism does not look the same everywhere. Comparative capitalism scholars have highlighted important differences in the way capitalism functions in various contexts (Shonfield 1969). There is significant variation in the role of the state and in the ways that markets are governed and embedded in institutions. Firms adopt divergent strategies and secure access to investment capital and labour in different ways. The book has shown that careful analysis of such patterns can shed light on how economies operate and on many of their achievements and challenges. This final chapter has three objectives. First, it distils some of the main conclusions from the book: it discusses the advantages of adopting a global perspective on comparative capitalism and the importance of pluralism in comparative capitalism, especially in the context of key developments in the twenty-first century. Second, the chapter also looks beyond the topics covered in the chapters of the book to consider two contemporary challenges – the role of global value chains/global production networks and the impact of the climate crisis – and what they imply for understanding capitalism. Third, the chapter concludes by reflecting on the resilience and likely future of capitalist diversity in light of these challenges.

The case for a global perspective on comparative capitalism

Much of the research on comparative capitalism, including the original VoC framework and early work on growth models and financialization, has focused on Western Europe and North America, with some attention to East Asia and Australia. In a sense this is hardly surprising, given the centrality of these regions to the world economy, and such research remains very valuable and indeed essential to the field. Yet if we want to understand capitalist diversity in general, then there is a strong case for going beyond these regions.

One of the core premises of this book is that a global perspective on comparative capitalism can advance the debate. Capitalism can be regarded as a global system, and the growing importance of the Global South to the world economy means that a focus on Western Europe and North America does not fully capture the complexity of contemporary capitalism. Generalizations based on Western Europe and North America are vulnerable to standard criticisms of Eurocentrism (Chakrabarty 1992), and such accounts also generalize from a very restricted sample. Regardless of whether these experiences are exceptional or representative of capitalism in general, the degree of exceptionalism can be best captured by examining them from a comparative perspective. This book has drawn on the growing literature on comparative capitalism in other parts of the world to highlight three points.

First, it has argued that a global perspective has important theoretical benefits. Capitalism takes many forms, and it is necessary to consider a wide range of cases to capture this complexity. For example, much of the Varieties of Capitalism (VoC) debate has focused on comparing liberal market economies based on market coordination and coordinated market economies based on strategic coordination. Much of the world cannot be shoehorned into these two categories. By considering networked, hierarchical, dependent and statist market economies, this book has highlighted the importance of other logics of coordination that shape economies in distinctive ways. As noted in Chapter 1, the book has treated these models as ideal types and highlighted how particular economies relate to them, whilst acknowledging that every economy has some unique features. Similarly, whilst early contributions to the contemporary debate on growth models also focused on Western Europe (Baccaro and Pontusson 2016), later work has begun to consider growth models in emerging markets as well (Baccaro, Blyth and Pontusson 2022). Such work has highlighted that the principal sources of demand vary considerably across economies and that generalizations based on a smaller number of economies do not capture the full range of capitalist models.

This book has taken a step towards globalizing comparative capitalism debate by synthesizing the literatures on the Global North and Global South, which have mostly developed separately. It should be added that there are inevitably gaps in the scope of the book as it is not possible to cover the entire world in one volume. A number of quantitative studies have sought to identify clusters within large samples of countries from most of the world (Fainshmidt el. al. 2018; Witt et al. 2018), but it is clear that more work is needed especially on Africa and on the parts of Asia and Oceania that have not been discussed in this volume.

Second, a global perspective has the potential to contribute to a better understanding of the varying foundations of economic growth. Since the late 1990s academic research on economic growth and the policy advice given by the World Bank has emphasized the centrality of institutions. Most of these studies focus on institutional quality that is understood to be high or low (Aron 2000; Acemoglu, Johnson and Robinson 2005). This renders some 'economic miracles' or cases of high growth in the context of low-quality institutions puzzling (Popa 2021). The range of countries that were originally studied by VoC scholars meant that the focus was mostly on successful economies, which is why critics have suggested that the theory is excessively oriented towards the study of economic efficiency. The main contrast in early VoC research was between the highly successful LMEs and CMEs on the one hand and the somewhat less successful Mediterranean mixed market economies. The MMEs were regarded as less successful as they were hybrids that lacked the complementary institutions of either LMEs or CMEs (Hall and Gingerich 2009).

By integrating the Global South and a wider range of economic institutions, the global perspective on VoC can account for cross-country differences in economic performance, such as the prevalence of the middle-income trap in HMEs (Doner and Schneider 2016) or the deeper insider-outsider divides that limit growth in the private sector of segmented market economies (SEMEs – see Chapter 5). Similarly, the literature on the more successful DME and SME models highlights key dilemmas confronting economies in emerging markets and across the Global South, as these models are closely related to the two principal growth models in these regions, namely FDI-led growth and state-led growth (Stockhammer 2023). Therefore these models hold important lessons for understanding the impact of global economic integration on economic growth and the economic policy choices emerging market economies face with respect to state involvement in the economy and external liberalization as well as the associated opportunities and risks (Nölke 2018).

Third, a global approach also reflects a growing need to consider globalization and interactions between different VoC and growth models. For example, the DME model depends on investors from abroad. An export-led growth model is only viable if there are other economies that are prepared to buy these exports. Whilst individual economies can run surpluses and deficits for long periods of time (as long as they can be financed), the world as a whole needs to be in trade balance. Other kinds of interactions pertain to the central role of the Global South in global value chains and global production networks (see below) and increasingly not only as a recipient, but also as a provider of credit and foreign investment are becoming more important. This is why it is particularly important to study VoC, growth models and other perspectives on comparative capitalism in a wider international or even global context (cf. Baccaro, Blyth and Pontusson 2022).

Finally, one might ask whether the models covered in this book represent any theoretical closure in terms of identifying all the relevant varieties of capitalism. Schneider (2013: 22) argues that his identification of four VoC models – LMEs, CMEs, NMEs and HMEs – provides an opportunity to achieve such closure given that each of the four varieties corresponded to a basic logic of coordination. Whilst he makes a compelling argument for a limited number of varieties on these grounds, he also acknowledges that some state-dominated economies might warrant a separate category. Given that he also regards the models as ideal types, many economies are best classified as hybrids, as many East Asian economies combine elements of the CME, NME and HME models (Schneider 2013: 30–2).

This book does not claim to have achieved any theoretical closure. On the one hand, there are a range of economies especially in Africa, the Middle East and Asia that this book has not analysed, and it is likely that further models could be identified in those regions. For example, by drawing on Breckenridge (2021), Karwowski (2022: 942) specifies a special category of Constrained Market Economies (CoME) to analyse African economies, but notes that there is no agreed categorization of these capitalist systems. On the other hand, it is not clear whether the theoretical categories can be made so clear that analysts can agree that theoretical closure has been achieved. For example, as noted earlier in this book, many analysts classify NMEs as a form of CME, though other scholars are more sceptical of such a classification. Similarly, there is a certain affinity between the HME, DME and SME models, as well as the SEME model (which was discussed as a sub-type of the HME model in Chapter 5). Hierarchy plays an important role in each of these varieties, but the key actors and impact of hierarchy vary across these models (Carney 2016). This makes it difficult to assess whether they are genuinely distinctive varieties or sub-types of one variety, especially since there are virtually always hybrid elements in the relevant empirical cases.

Pluralism and comparative capitalism

As discussed in Chapter 1, the field of comparative capitalism has featured a variety of approaches and theories (Schwartz and Tranøy 2019), and at times there has been lively debate between scholars advocating particular theories. Whilst such debate is healthy and even essential to progress in the field, this book has adopted a pluralist perspective and suggested that theoretical pluralism is a key strength of comparative capitalism. The field is strong if scholars have many theoretical tools at their disposal.

Chapters 2–7 of this book were devoted to a global perspective on varieties of capitalism, as VoC analysis has exerted a profound influence on comparative capitalism since the late 1990s. Even scholars who seek to go beyond this framework tend to begin their analysis by positioning their work vis-à-vis VoC literature (Baccaro and Pontusson 2022; Baccaro, Blyth and Pontusson 2022). By synthesizing the VoC debate about different parts of the world and developing a global perspective on it, the book has sought to show that VoC theory provides a nuanced and theoretically grounded account of the diversity of capitalist institutions in various parts of the world.

However, the book has also highlighted that there are important features of capitalism to which the VoC framework pays insufficient attention. The pluralist commitment of the book is particularly central to Chapters 8–11, where alternative perspectives are considered to address such issues.

First, capitalism is a dynamic system that evolves over time. The emphasis on cross-country differences in VoC analysis and some other strands of research on comparative capitalism implies that the dynamic nature of capitalism tends to recede into the background (Deeg and Jackson 2007). This is why research on comparative capitalism is enriched by the study of growth regimes, which provide a framework for analysing the evolution of capitalism over time. Chapter 8 introduced growth regimes by discussing key changes to capitalism since the mid-twentieth century. The chapter focused on three growth regimes – associated with the era of modernization, the era of liberalization and the era of the knowledge economy – and discussed the implications of the emergence of platform capitalism as well. As VoC analysis places great emphasis on manufacturing, the discussion of growth regimes also provides an important complementary perspective that can account for structural change, including the growing importance of the service economy (Hassel and Palier 2020a). Ultimately a nuanced understanding of capitalist diversity requires paying attention both to cross-country differences and to change over time.

Second, the growing importance of the financial sector has potentially profound implications for capitalism. These changes have stimulated a rich debate on financialization (Chapter 9). This concept and the associated theoretical literature capture a range of processes that began in the last quarter of the twentieth century, primarily in the United States, but gradually spread across the world. A key question animating these debates is whether financialization has fundamentally changed the nature of capitalism and whether scholars of comparative capitalism need to shift their gaze from the production regime to finance and consider financialization as the principal driver of contemporary capitalism. It is clear that a detailed understanding of financialization and the role of the financial sector in contemporary market economies is of great importance to comparative capitalism, and more research is needed given the importance and rapid pace of change in global finance.

Third, much of the comparative capitalism literature in recent decades has prioritized the production regime and paid limited attention to the macroeconomy and economic instability. Chapter 10 asks whether the supply-side focus of VoC can account for these issues and introduces post-Keynesian growth models as an alternative (or complementary) perspective. It discusses the application of growth model analysis to traditional OECD countries in Western Europe and North America and to other parts of the world, including the Global South. The research programme on growth models is a valuable corrective to the supply-side focus of much of the literature on comparative capitalism.

Finally, in order to consider the political contestation surrounding capitalism and debates about whether 'global capitalism will fall again' (Frieden 2006), the book examined the populist tide of 'anti-system politics' that began in the 2010s. Whilst this does not constitute a distinctive model of comparative capitalism, Chapter 11 considered to what extent populism relates to capitalism and discussed the ways in which differences in capitalist institutions shape the nature of the populist challenge in various countries. It also considered the impact of populism on capitalism and the ways in which business, a key actor in capitalist systems, has sought to respond to populism. The discussion of populism shows the importance of considering the influence of groups that seek to challenge the status quo in various ways.

Taken together, these chapters have highlighted the potential for fruitful dialogue between various perspectives on comparative capitalism. Whilst theories are essential to making sense of comparative capitalism, any theory, and especially a dominant one, may also run the risk of being a straightjacket. The scholar and student of comparative capitalism may be best served by having more than one theoretical perspective in their toolbox as this makes it easier to choose the most appropriate one for any particular research question. There may also be scope for combing the theories creatively and eclectically and thereby refining the analysis of particular research questions or contributing to further theory development. For example, growth model analysis might be strengthened by integrating more insights from studies of financialization (Stockhammer 2022) or French regulation theory (Amable 2023). There are also potentially important connections between VoC and growth models (Hope and Soskice 2016). VoC analysis would also benefit from more systematic engagement with financialization and growth regimes. For example, the DME model has focused on dependency in the context of investments by multinationals in manufacturing, but greater attention to the role and management of financial subordination would contribute to a more nuanced understanding of the operation of these economies. More generally, further engagement with the revival of dependency theory could enrich debates about comparative capitalism (Cardoso 2009; Kvangraven 2021).

Looking ahead: Current challenges

If the past is any guide, it seems clear that capitalism will face numerous challenges in the years and decades to come. Capitalism has always been characterized by crises and transformation, and its future seems destined to be as turbulent as its past. One of the key premises of the comparative capitalism debate is that capitalisms come in multiple forms or at least that it is helpful to study capitalism in that way (Hay 2020). However, if common pressures are strong, could they challenge capitalist diversity or capitalism itself? This section considers two key challenges that are likely to shape the future of capitalism, and it reflects on the significance of these trends and their impact on capitalism and capitalist diversity.

Global value chains, production networks and the end of national models of capitalism?

Globalization has often been described as a significant challenge to capitalist diversity. In particular, arguments based on the so-called 'efficiency hypothesis' have stressed that the growing competitive pressures associated with globalization could lead to convergence by weeding out less successful forms of capitalist organization. VoC scholars have generally been sceptical of such arguments as different models could be efficient and instead predicted that globalization could facilitate greater specialization and differentiation (Soskice 1999). More generally, as outlined in the alternative 'compensation hypothesis', globalization could also be associated with greater public spending to offset some of the risks and dislocation associated with globalization, including trade and outsourcing, thereby maintaining political support for global market integration (Garrett 1995).

However, a potentially more fundamental challenge to capitalist diversity relates to the transformation of global production. This goes beyond the traditional model of foreign direct investment in which multinationals simply replicate their production model abroad. Instead, the production process is 'organizationally fragmented and spatially dispersed' (Coe and Yeung 2015). In other words, it is broken down into smaller components that take place in different localities across various countries, and many firms contribute to the production of particular goods and services. In some cases virtually the whole production process is outsourced, and only a few elements, such as marketing and sales, are the direct responsibility of the lead firm (see Chapter 8). There are several closely related frameworks that seek to capture these shifts, and the two most influential frameworks are *global value chains* (GVC) and *global production networks* (GPN) – *global commodity chains* (GCC) is another alternative concept. These approaches are closely related, in that all of them capture the complex transnational structure of production, but there are some key differences of emphasis.

Research on GVC (and on GCC) analyses the ways in which various stages of production add value to the product and explores how each stage is organized and why it is based in a particular country or location (Gereffi et al. 2005). The main emphasis is on the product or commodity itself – how it is created and how each stage of the process adds value to the product as it moves through the chain.

By contrast, Global Production Network (GPN) analysis focuses more on the network relations between actors that are involved in the production process, notably the relationships between lead firms and their suppliers and the geographical structure of networks within and between firms, but also the relationships between firms and their workers and other stakeholders (Henderson et al. 2002). Although Coe et al. (2008) point out that power may rest in different parts of the network and not be constant, key decisions affecting the entire network are often taken by the lead firm (often a multinational or leading global company) within a given network of firms. The network includes a range of actors, including suppliers of inputs, producers of components and intermediate outputs, assembly and logistics companies, and also in a wider sense governments, unions and other actors that have an impact on the production process. The lead firm tends to be the most powerful and may often reap disproportionate gains, but it may also be heavily dependent on key suppliers and producers within the network, which creates vulnerability, especially in the short run if alternatives are not readily available. Gereffi's (2014) typology of producer-dominated and consumer-dominated chains captures the fact that product and market characteristics also matter – for example, in the cases of textiles and clothing or large supermarkets in the Global North, consumer demand is a very important factor, whereas producer power tends to be greater in cases when production is shaped by high capital requirements and economies of scale or by complex technology.

To what extent does the growth of GVCs and GPNs affect comparative capitalism? In the classical VoC model key national institutions of the political economy are closely bound up with the nature of the firm and patterns of production. National institutions relate to the relationships that firms need to manage in order to secure the key resources that they draw on – such as labour, skills or financial capital. These relationships are perceived as institutionally embedded at the national level, as the firm's activities are shaped by the national financial system, industrial relations system or skill system.

GVCs and GPNs represent a challenge to the model of the firm described above. First, the GVCs span multiple jurisdictions, which means that different parts of their activities are embedded in different national systems and institutions. This raises questions about the association between distinct national systems of capitalism and comparative institutional advantage. If the components constituting a widget were produced across multiple countries, it is not clear whether any particular country has a comparative institutional advantage in a given sector. As the production process is fragmented into small components, it is more plausible to argue that comparative institutional advantage relates to specific tasks or elements of the production process, but the GPN as a whole is multiscalar (operates on multiple scales) and largely dis-embedded from the national context (Coe and Yeung 2015: 208). Such trends are likely to make patterns of specialization and comparative institutional advantages less stable (cf. Schneider and Paunescu 2012), but they could also give rise to 'creative incoherence' in institutions as institutions play different and potentially productive roles in relation to a variety of production processes (cf. Crouch 2005).

An institutionalist perspective on production remains valuable, but the national Varieties of Capitalism model may need to be modified given that firms, industries and production processes transcend national borders. In practice, multinational enterprises often engage in 'institutional arbitrage'; that is, they compare institutional frameworks in various countries and choose the location and, in the case of outsourcing, the firm that is most suitable for a particular part of the production process. This allows firms to take advantage of location-specific advantages and choose locations and suppliers or partners that have a comparative institutional advantage in particular components of the value chain. Core competencies, such as innovation, design, product strategy and some of the highest value-added components of the production process, are often concentrated in the lead firm's home country (Gereffi et al. 2005), if the requisite skills and expertise are abundant there. Elements of the production process that are cost-sensitive are located in low-cost settings, whereas the tasks that rely on certain key resource inputs are usually located in places where such inputs are available. This means that local conditions and institutions shape economic activity and largely determine which elements of the production process are located where.

GPNs may also create greater regional differentiation both between and within economies, as regions or cities differ with respect to their integration into global markets and production networks. This may make generalizations about entire economies increasingly problematic, especially in the case of large and complex economies. For example, in China the differences between the coastal regions, including Guangdong province, and the less globally integrated inland regions are one of the important dimensions of sub-regional variation, which have become an important focus of study related to the Chinese political economy (Rithmire 2017). As discussed in Chapter 10, different parts of the Chinese economy are also reliant on different growth models as the coastal regions are primarily export-led, whereas many inland provinces in the West of the country are investment-led (Tan and Conran 2022).

These patterns demonstrate why the institutional context still matters, as each part of the value chain is embedded in local, regional and/or national institutions. From a VoC perspective this might imply that there should not necessarily be any convergence pressures as GPNs will help accentuate differences between countries and facilitate specialization in particular types of processes. However, such claims may understate the impact of globalized production on comparative capitalism, especially in the longer run.

First, activities in different parts of the GPN/GVC are not independent of each other. For example, outsourcing may have spill-over effects on institutions in the home country. As shown by Lane (2007), the outsourcing of textile production from Germany has had an impact on the German skills and training systems as well. If outsourcing affects the demand for certain types of skills in the multinational's home countries, then this is likely to affect the supply of these skills as well, especially if similar processes occur across many firms and sectors. Such processes could affect other institutional arrangements as well and gradually lead to the erosion of institutional complementarities and the distinctiveness of the national model of the country from where production is outsourced.

Second, even if economies manage to retain their comparative institutional advantages in certain products (or processes and activities), much will also depend on the demand for these particular processes. As Pontusson (2011) has noted in relation to national economies, if demand for goods and services produced by LMEs that rely on radical innovation increases faster than demand for goods and services produced in CMEs that rely on specific skills and incremental innovation, then this will have an adverse effect on CMEs. Similar processes may operate within global value chains. From an economic perspective countries and firms participating in GPNs can be expected to favour upgrading or taking over parts of the value chain that generate more value-added than others. Whether firms and economies succeed in doing this depends on many factors, including the nature of institutions and the factors that are most central to such upgrading. In practice, the growth of GVCs may also lock countries and regions into labour-intensive and relatively low value-added activities, as highlighted by dependency theorists (Kvangraven 2021).

Third, the growth of FDI and GPNs/GVCs could also have profound effects on the political underpinnings of capitalist systems. Traditional understandings of capitalism are premised on a stable relationship between business and the state. It is in the state's interest to maintain an attractive business environment, given the structural dependence on capital (Przeworski and Wallerstein 1988). Similarly, comparative capitalism has also emphasized that business preferences are conditioned by the institutional framework and may vary across countries depending on the ways in which firms operate (Wood 2001). Whilst the lead firm is often particularly influential, power may vary in more complex ways, and these relationships within GPNs may evolve over time. Chinese suppliers of car parts have gradually acquired a more significant role within value chains, and some of them, like Wanxiang Group, have even taken over US car part producers (Kurlantzick 2016: 106). As key hubs emerge in other parts of the world (for example, Bangalore in India), it is likely that they will also be increasingly attractive to business. Iversen and Soskice (2019) argue that the state is more powerful than businesses in the most advanced economies given that businesses are so heavily reliant on access to key resources and the ecosystems of skills, networks and other key businesses that are available in key hubs, such as Silicon Valley in the United States. Culpepper and Reinke (2014) also demonstrate that the structural power of big banks varies depending on their dependence on the home market, with big American banks more dependent on the US market than British banks are on the UK market. However, in the context of most GVCs it is unlikely that any single hub is completely irreplaceable. Therefore governments have some leverage over firms, though it is likely to vary across countries (Iversen and Soskice 2019). If alternative locations are available, then firms may still be able to relocate. In many cases the relationship of business and government is best understood as one of mutual dependence given that both sides rely on each other.

Fourth, the political effects of multinational enterprises and lead firms within GPNs go beyond their influence on individual governments. As global economic governance has become more important, the significance of international or supranational rules and regulations has also grown. Bartley (2018) has shown that multinational enterprises have profound effects on economic governance, and he distinguishes between three forms of influence exercised by them, corresponding to three distinctive roles as sponsors, inhibitors and direct providers of global governance. For example, in their role as sponsors they have successfully advocated neoliberal trade rules, whilst inhibiting labour and environmental regimes advocated by some governments and non-governmental organizations. The third role highlights how they have also provided private rules and standards that are often binding for leading firms, as they become international industry standards for safety, finance or sustainability (Bartley 2018). GVCs have led to an increase in private governance and rule-making, and this trend is likely to continue.

Finally, given their complexity GVCs are often fragile, and bottlenecks or logistical challenges can create shortages (Dayen and Mabud 2022). As evidenced by the Covid-19 pandemic, GVCs could collapse altogether in the face of shocks, which could bring about processes of 'globalization in reverse' (Gong et al. 2022). GVCs are vulnerable to economic, logistical and technological shocks in addition to health crises.

The impact of such shocks is also mediated by political forces, which determine how countries respond and whether and on what terms the GVCs can be re-established. As long as nation states serve as the primary locus of political representation and a substantial number of regulations remain national, national actors and national institutions will play a central role in shaping the governance of GVCs. Political and business concern with the vulnerability of supply chains led to some initiatives to bring about reshoring (especially in the case of some critically important goods and services) and to discussions about making other GVCs more resilient. However, given how widespread GVCs are and how integral they are to the business models of firms across the world, they are likely to persist and also to reshape national systems of capitalism.

Capitalism and the climate crisis: Green growth or degrowth?

The most fundamental challenge to the future of capitalism is arguably the climate crisis. Much of the early debate on this topic focused on the role of markets in addressing environmental concerns. Whilst most environmentalists favoured strict regulations to curb pollution and environmental problems, many environmental economists regarded markets as a very important part of the solution to the climate crisis (Anderson and Leal 2001). They saw environmental problems as related to missing markets – if the reach of markets could be extended, then a solution would be more likely. This idea is based on a key concept in economic theory, namely that of economic externalities. These are effects of economic activity that are not directly considered by economic actors as they are not part of the profit and cost calculation of individual firms. For example, economic production may cause pollution that destroys the environment, but there is no price tag on it and if the firm can maximize its revenue and profits by using a polluting technology, then it will usually choose to do so. To the extent that pollution generates any costs, they may affect other firms or society at large, perhaps even in other countries. This is why the standard economic solution to such problems is to internalize the externality – in effect, by assigning property rights or at least a price to environmental resources and ensuring that the cost of pollution is factored in by the firm. Such proposals were met with a lot of scepticism, but since the 1990s, market-based solutions have become well established. A key example of this is carbon trading, which has become a very important element of environmental policy. However, there are still limits to market solutions. In some situations they are widely regarded as unethical or ineffective (Sandel 2012).

Ultimately the impact of the climate crisis on capitalism is more profound and complex, primarily as a result of its connections to economic growth and consumption. Capitalism as a system is based on the pursuit of profit and economic growth which has historically led to the depletion of the world's natural resources and to environmental degradation. In particular, the car industry has been central to economic growth since the heyday of Fordism. It has been a key employer, and governments have supported car producers in various ways and also helped consumers buy cars as a way of maintaining high economic growth and living standards. By the same token, this focus on the car industry has served as a disincentive against investments in public transport. It is only in the 2010s that more significant investments were made to support the development of electric cars. Paterson's (2000) critical political economy research on the car industry highlights some of the key processes and complementarities pushing countries into a vicious circle of production and consumption. Given the importance of the auto industry for job creation and growth, governments are wary of reining it in. This explains why governments have often stimulated the demand for new cars, which in most cases have polluted the planet. Widespread car ownership makes it harder to marshal support for other alternatives, such as the expansion of public transportation systems. In any case, very considerable investments in public transportation would be needed to dissuade people from driving. Achieving this is generally easier in larger metropolitan areas than in provincial cities and towns or in rural areas, where there are fewer potential passengers and often longer distances to cover, which makes it harder to finance an elaborate public transportation system.

As capitalism is oriented towards profits and growth, which in turn fuel consumption, it is not surprising that many environmentalists regard capitalism as a root cause of the climate crisis. Given the profound changes that would be needed to meet the climate targets, this raises critical questions about the implications for capitalism. For some critics these challenges imply that capitalism itself is doomed. However, capitalism has reinvented itself in the past and evolved through a variety of growth regimes, so it is worth considering whether capitalism could be adapted to address these concerns. The assessment of this question will proceed in two steps – by considering the role of economic growth and then capitalism and capitalist diversity.

The idea that the climate crisis can be addressed without sacrificing economic growth is contested. A number of organizations have outlined visions of 'green growth', and whilst the concept is sometimes used in a vague way, it generally implies that the nature of economic growth could change in such a way that it no longer harms the climate. The core concept underlying green growth is decoupling, which refers to the process of separating growth (economic value creation) from the use of natural resources and any impact on the climate. It is important to distinguish between relative and absolute decoupling. Relative decoupling refers to efficiency improvements so that each unit of output is created using less energy and a smaller amount of raw materials, whereas absolute decoupling refers to an overall decline in the use of resources in the economy. Relative decoupling implies that the production processes are greener or less resource-intensive, but even if resource efficiency improves, material use could still be increasing overall if the growth rate of output is very high. For example, even if new cars emit less, total pollution could still go up if more cars are produced. This means that even though new technologies are less polluting and use fewer material and energy resources per unit produced, there may not be any absolute decoupling if an overall increase in output leads to more pollution.

Most of the available evidence indicates that decoupling is very difficult to achieve. Studies that focus on 'domestic material consumption' (DMC) suggest that key OECD countries have made significant progress on relative decoupling, but if one considers the 'material footprint' that also includes the material impact of imported goods, then there is no evidence of decoupling (Hickel and Kallis 2020: 471). Absolute decoupling is much more difficult to achieve.

Whether it might be possible to achieve absolute decoupling in the future depends on many factors, perhaps most importantly on the scope for developing new and energy-efficient technologies. Techno-optimists would see enormous untapped potential to transform production and make it more sustainable than people could even imagine. Such trends might be reinforced by further development of the circular economy, which refers to 'a regenerative system in which resource input and waste, emission, and energy leakage are minimized by slowing, closing, and narrowing material and energy loops thanks to long-lasting design, maintenance, repair, reuse, remanufacturing, refurbishing, and recycling' (Geissdoerfer et al. 2017: 759). More generally, if consumer demand continues to shift away from manufactured goods towards services, then there could be more of a decline in the environmental footprint.

Techno-pessimists are more sceptical that the impact will go beyond relative decoupling as growth might still be associated with higher consumption overall. They would also note that many services may have a more substantial hidden environmental footprint.

Another key challenge relates to the organization of production and especially the importance of global production networks and value chains, as discussed in the previous section. This dimension is not fully incorporated into key measures of resource efficiency in a given country. The impact of long-distance transport within value chains is very significant, and they make it harder to achieve global sustainability targets. Value chains could complicate the process of implementing the logic of the circular economy, if inputs and final goods were to travel across the world multiple times in loops, thereby adding considerably to the material footprint of the circular economy. If green growth fails to generate absolute decoupling, then a reduction in output and consumption might be needed to address the climate crisis (Hickel and Kallis 2020).

To what extent is it possible to combine environmental sustainability and capitalism? It is not clear whether the climate crisis can be addressed by tinkering with capitalism and markets, for example, by imposing new regulations or by taxing pollution heavily, which increases the cost of production and may induce the firm to look for other technologies that are associated with less pollution. Economists generally favour other more market-confirming solutions. This might include assigning property rights for environmental resources or tradable pollution permits, as in the case of carbon trading. The advantage of such tools is that firms can buy and sell such permits, which means that the firm that values them most highly or is most reliant on such technology has access to it, whilst controlling the total amount of pollution. The case of electric cars and other innovations relates to another area of contention. For advocates of capitalism and market solutions, such examples illustrate the strengths of capitalism as an engine of innovation and growth. If business incentives can be made to reflect the imperatives of addressing the climate crisis, then the profit motive could be a powerful inducement to develop new technologies and products that will help save the planet in the most cost-effective way.

However, many analysts would agree with the techno-pessimists that green growth is unlikely to bring about the kind of shift in the economy that would be needed to address the climate crisis. This has contributed to the emergence of ideas about degrowth (Kallis 2011) or the need for a permanent reduction in economic output. It is not clear whether this can be achieved simply by tweaking taxes and regulations. Many would argue that achieving such a goal requires shifting the focus of business and national economies away from growth. It would require moving away from consumerism and affect consumption patterns at the level of individuals and households. This scale of the transformation associated with the degrowth agenda calls for a systemic approach.

It seems clear that degrowth could pose a fundamental challenge to capitalism. Can capitalism be reconfigured in a way that creates new incentive structures that induce economic actors not to act in way that promotes economic growth? This would require a profound transformation of the core logic of capitalism, as both producers and consumers would have to pursue different objectives. It is not clear whether such a system could still be regarded as capitalist or whether it would be a new form of post-capitalist system.

Most of the existing proposals to reform capitalism fall short of such ambitions. Tienhaara (2014) discusses the Green New Deal, Green Stimulus and the Green Economy as three influential proposals. She notes that these terms may sometimes overlap in practice or be used in slightly different ways. They vary in the degree to which they use market mechanisms, how they use technology and financial markets and what role they see for economic growth. Some versions of the Green New Deal could be compatible with degrowth (Mastini, Kallis and Hickel 2021), whereas the Green Stimulus and the Green Economy proposals tend to be committed to green growth (Tienhaara 2014). Given the complexity of these challenges and coordination problems, it is very difficult to assess the potential of capitalism to be reinvented in a way that is conducive to addressing the climate crisis, in part because much depends on how exactly any necessary changes could be embedded in politics and society.

This raises the question of whether the comparative capitalism debate holds any lessons for understanding these challenges. Nahm (2022) shows that growth models that are heavily reliant on exports, such as Germany and China, have the best prerequisites for industry-led decarbonization. 'Crucially, and tellingly, in both economies, the first far-reaching national climate legislation was passed after an export-driven renewable energy industry had been established domestically—in 2000 in Germany and 2007 in China' (Nahm 2022: 451). In the consumption-led growth models of the LMEs, it is harder to build the kinds of producer coalitions that are emerging in Germany and China. On the other hand, the shift away from manufacturing has proceeded faster, especially in Britain, which means that emissions have fallen faster there than in many other economies (Nahm 2022). This could also relate to VoC institutions as Hancke, Van Overbeke and Voss (2022) have shown in their analysis of adjustments to Covid. These kinds of differences are significant as market-based solutions to the climate crisis need to address both supply conditions – the availability of technology, skills and investments in green tech firms – and demand conditions, or the existence of market demand for their output, either domestically or internationally. These challenges have also prompted interest in a more activist role for the state – or even green or eco-developmental states (Lin and Wang 2023). Such a model could emulate key elements of the classical developmental state and perhaps also the contemporary SME model (see Chapter 7). It would entail more activist and strategic direction by the state to bring about a green transition. Instead of using such state institutions and policies as a tool to promote economic growth, green developmental states could use these tools to induce firms to move towards environmentally sustainable practices and to develop new green technologies and products (Thurbon et al. 2023).

The wider implication of this discussion is that the climate crisis represents a profound challenge to capitalism that all economies will continue to struggle with, but comparative capitalism suggests that the potential path to sustainability is likely to vary across different countries. Even though it is likely that any international agreements may impose similar kinds of obligations to promote decarbonization, a country's economic institutions, growth models and pre-existing economic structure will affect the range of feasible policies and strategies for transforming the economy.

It remains to be seen whether any changes take place fast enough to address the climate crisis before it is too late. It is unclear whether capitalism will reinvent itself successfully as part of this process to ensure that firms and households or producers and consumers adjust their behaviour in response to price and other market-based incentives or whether this adjustment will depend on more decisive state action to reform capitalist institutions in a more profound way. If green growth does not achieve these goals, then degrowth and or even a process of scaling back consumption may be on the agenda. Such dramatic transformations would have a profound impact on capitalist systems.

The resilience and future prospects of global capitalism

The downfall of capitalism has been predicted many times in the past, but capitalism has generally turned out to be resilient (Iversen and Soskice 2019). For Karl Marx the vulnerability of capitalism to periodic crisis was one of the reasons for predicting its ultimate downfall. To what extent are the dramatic changes discussed in this book likely to bring about the end of capitalism or at least the end of capitalist diversity? Many analysts and pundits expected the global financial crisis of 2007–8 and the subsequent Great Recession to be a moment of momentous change, but at least in the short run economic arrangements were relatively resilient (Schmidt and Thatcher 2013). The subsequent rise of populism might be regarded as a backlash against the status quo, but as discussed in Chapter 11, the degree of this challenge is variable and the ultimate impact on capitalism remains uncertain.

Part III of this book has highlighted significant changes in contemporary capitalism, notably in relation to the knowledge economy and financialization, which could pose significant challenges for capitalism. What do such trends along with the rise of global value chains and the climate crisis discussed in this chapter imply for the prospects of capitalism and capitalist diversity?

Capitalism relies on economic factors, notably its ability to generate growth, but also on political support or at least consent. Each of these trends raises profound political challenges.

First, the evolving growth regimes, including the development of the knowledge economy, financialization and the platform economy have reshaped capitalism in profound ways and are likely to continue to do so. However, whilst they have generated new opportunities for productivity improvements, they have also had deeply inegalitarian consequences. The new technologies have been mostly complementary to high-skilled work, whereas they often replace low-skilled work. These trends have led to higher inequality, and the declining complementarity of low-skill and high-skill jobs (Iversen and Soskice 2019) poses significant challenges for social solidarity. The effect of financialization is similar in that it also tends to increase inequality.

Rates of inequality have traditionally varied across capitalist economies, but the key question is whether these trends are opening up new and deeper divides in society. If there is not only inequality, but an increasingly large number of people feel that such divides cannot be bridged and that there is no place for them in the knowledge economy as a result of permanent unemployment, then this could lead to a backlash against capitalism. It remains to be seen whether capitalism can be adapted to forge an updated social contract that enjoys popular support. If stable work is not available for everyone (or even a sizeable majority) of the population, then it is likely that proposals to institute some form of universal basic income (UBI) or a negative income tax will become more central to debates about capitalism (Kelly 2023).

Second, the growth of global production networks has added to these challenges. Whilst it has provided some opportunities for economies to grow by taking advantage of the potential of a segment of a large value chain, this also associated with uncertainty as these networks could be reconfigured. More generally, political agency may be more diffuse and upgrading is difficult, especially if the lead firm controls technology. Another key question relates to the resilience of these value chains, as the Covid pandemic of 2020–1 showed their vulnerability in the face of lockdowns. It also led to more public concerns and political debate about 'reshoring' to make sure that economies are more resilient in the face of crises.

Third, the climate crisis is the most fundamental challenge for capitalism. One of the main challenges is that the task of adapting capitalism to address the climate crisis is global. Whilst each economy can make a contribution, it is unlikely to be sufficient if others do not. This raises at least three problems beyond identifying a way of modifying capitalism (which is already a big challenge) – policy coordination, enforcement of agreements and a fair distribution of costs.

It is clear that each of these three trends could pose a severe challenge to capitalism and lead to pressure for change or possibly even its downfall. At the very least, these trends could fuel a further globalization backlash. Given that the primary locus of political authority remains at the level of the nation state, people tend to look to national governments for solutions when they seek to 'take back control', as the key slogan of the Brexit campaign put it. The populist tide highlights the potential for anti-system mobilization, which could come in various forms, including challenges to capitalism (see Chapter 11).

What does this imply about comparative capitalism? In practice, these challenges are likely to vary greatly across countries. The key actors are different, and their coordinating capacity varies as well. In some cases the state or unions play a more central role. Since the dominant sectors vary, the growth coalitions and power of particular sectors vary too. Such factors shape the impact of the challenges that these three trends pose, and they also affect the range of feasible solutions. Therefore comparative capitalism can be a valuable tool for understanding how economies might craft solutions to the great challenges of the twenty-first century.

Discussion questions

1. How valuable is a global perspective on comparative capitalism?
2. What are the main strengths and weaknesses of alternative approaches to comparative capitalism?
3. To what extent does the growth of global value chains render the focus on national models of capitalism obsolete?
4. How significant is the challenge to global capitalism and to capitalist diversity posed by the climate crisis?
5. How resilient is capitalism in the face of contemporary challenges? Are these challenges uniform, or would you expect them to affect some forms of capitalism more than others?

BIBLIOGRAPHY

Acemoglu, D., Johnson, S. and Robinson, J. A. (2005), 'Institutions as a Fundamental Cause of Long-run Growth', in P. Aghion and S. Durlauf (eds), *Handbook of Economic Growth*. North-Holland: Elsevier, 385–472.

Acemoglu, D. and Robinson, J. A. (2013), *Why Nations Fail: The Origins of Power, Prosperity, and Poverty*. Paperback edn. London: Profile Books.

Adler, P. S. (2001), 'Market, Hierarchy, and Trust: The Knowledge Economy and the Future of Capitalism', *Organization Science*, 12(2), 215–34. Available at: https://doi.org/10.1287/orsc.12.2.215.10117.

Aglietta, M. (1979), *A Theory of Capitalist Regulation: The US Experience*. London: NLB.

Ahmadjian, C. L. (2014), *Corporate Governance and Business Systems in Asia*. Oxford: Oxford University Press.

Alami, I., Alves, C., Bonizzi, B., Kaltenbrunner, A., Koddenbrock, K., Kvangraven, I. and Powell, J. (2023), 'International Financial Subordination: A Critical Research Agenda', *Review of International Political Economy*, 30(4), 1360–86.

Allison, G. T. (2017), *Destined for War: Can America and China Escape Thucydides's Trap?* Melbourne London: Scribe Publications.

Alt, J. (1979), *The Politics of Economic Decline Economic Management and Political Behaviour in Britian since 1964*. Cambridge: Cambridge University Press.

Amable, B. (2023), 'Nothing New Under the Sun: The So-called "Growth Model Perspective"', *European Journal of Economics and Economic Policies Intervention*, 20(3), 444–60.

Amin, A., ed. (1994), *Post-Fordism: A Reader*. Oxford; Cambridge, MA: Blackwell (Studies in urban and social change).

Amsden, A. H. (1979), 'Taiwan's Economic History: A Case of Etatisme and a Challenge to Dependency Theory', *Modern China*, 5(3), 341–79. Available at: https://doi.org/10.1177/009770047900500304.

Amsden, A. H. (1985), 'The Division of Labour is Limited by the Rate of Growth of the Market: The Taiwan Machine Tool Industry in the 1970s', *Cambridge Journal of Economics*, 9(3), 271–84. Available at: https://doi.org/10.1093/oxfordjournals.cje.a035581.

Amsden, A. H. (1989), *Asia's Next Giant: South Korea and Late Industrialization*. New York: Oxford University Press.

Anderson, K. M. (2019), 'Financialisation Meets Collectivisation: Occupational Pensions in Denmark, the Netherlands and Sweden', *Journal of European Public Policy*, 26(4), 617–36.

Anderson, T. L. and Leal, D. R. (2001), *Free Market Environmentalism*. New York: Palgrave Macmillan US. Available at: https://doi.org/10.1057/9780312299736.

Andreasson, S. (2011), 'Understanding Corporate Governance Reform in South Africa: Anglo-American Divergence, the King Reports, and Hybridization', *Business & Society*, 50(4), 647–73.

Anievas, A. and Nisancioglu, K. (2013), 'What's at stake in the transition debate? Rethinking the origins of capitalism and the "rise of the west"', *Millennium: Journal of International Studies*, 42(1), 78–102.

Ansell, B. W. (2019), 'The Politics of Housing', *Annual Review of Political Science*, 22(1), 165–85.

Aoki, M. and Dore, R., eds. (1996), *The Japanese Firm: The Sources of Competitive Strength*. Repr. Oxford: Oxford University Press.

Appel, H. and Orenstein, M. A. (2018), *From Triumph to Crisis: Neoliberal Economic Reform in Postcommunist Countries*. Cambridge: Cambridge University Press.

Archer, R. (2013), 'The State and its Unions: Reassessing the Antecedents, Development, and Consequences of New Deal Labor Law', *Labor History*, 54(2), 201–7. Available at: https://doi.org/10.1080/0023656X.2013.773145.

Armijo, L. E. and Faucher, P. (2002), '"We have a Consensus": Explaining Political Support for Market Reforms in Latin America', *Latin American Politics and Society*, 44(2), 1–40. Available at: https://doi.org/10.1111/j.1548-2456.2002.tb00204.x.

Aron, J. (2000), 'Growth and Institutions: A Review of the Evidence', *World Bank Research Observer*, 15(1), 99–135.

Arrighi, G. (2010), *The Long Twentieth Century: Money, Power, and the Origins of Our Times*. London : New York, NY: Verso.

Avlijaš, S. (2020a), 'Beyond Neoliberalism? Revisiting the Welfare State in the Baltic States', *Europe-Asia Studies*, 72(4), 614–43.

Avlijaš, S. (2020b), 'Growth Models and Female Labor in Post-socialist Eastern Europe', *Social Politics: International Studies in Gender, State & Society*, 27(3), 534–61.

Avlijaš, S. (2022), 'Explaining the Contrasting Welfare Trajectories of the Baltic and Visegrád Countries: A Growth-Strategy Perspective', in J. L. Garritzmann, S. Häusermann and B. Palier (eds), *The World Politics of Social Investment: Volume II*. New York: Oxford University Press, 209–28.

Avlijaš, S., Hassel, A. and Palier, B. (2020), 'Growth Strategies and Welfare Reforms in Europe', in S. Avlijaš, A. Hassel and B. Palier (eds), *Growth and Welfare in Advanced Capitalist Economies*. Oxford University Press, 372–436.

Baccaro, L., Blyth, M. and Pontusson, J., eds. (2022), *Diminishing Returns: The New Politics of Growth and Stagnation*. New York, NY: Oxford University Press.

Baccaro, L. and Höpner, M. (2022), 'The Political-Economic Foundations of Export-Led Growth: An Analysis of the German Case', in L. Baccaro, M. Blyth and J. Pontusson (eds), *Diminishing Returns*. New York: Oxford University Press, 238–67.

Baccaro, L. and Howell, C. (2017), *Trajectories of Neoliberal Transformation: European Industrial Relations since the 1970s*. Cambridge University Press.

Baccaro, L. and Pontusson, J. (2016), 'Rethinking Comparative Political Economy: The Growth Model Perspective', *Politics & Society*, 44(2), 175–207.

Baccaro, L. and Pontusson, J. (2019), *Social Blocs and Growth Models: An Analytical Framework with Germany and Sweden as Illustrative Cases*. Genève: Université de Genève. Available at: https://hdl.handle.net/21.11116/0000-0003-5ACB-4.

Baccaro, L. and Pontusson, J. (2022), 'The Politics of Growth Models', *Review of Keynesian Economics*, 10(2), 204–21.

Bacon, R. W. and Eltis, W. (1978), *Britain's Economic Problem: Too Few Producers*, 2nd edn. London: Macmillan.

Badigannavar, V. and Ghosh, D. (2020), 'India', in C. Frege and J. Kelly (eds.), *Comparative Employment Relations in the Global Economy*. London: Routledge.

Baker, A., Epstein, G. and Montecino, J. (2018), *The UK's Finance Curse? Costs and Processes, SPERI report*. Available at: http://speri.dept.shef.ac.uk/2018/10/05/uk-finance-curse-report/ (Accessed: 14 October 2023).

Balcerowicz, L. (1995), *Socialism, Capitalism, Transformation*. Budapest: Central European University Press.

Baltz, M. J. (2021), '"Americanism Not Globalism Will Be Our Credo!": An Analysis of the Economic Nationalism(S) of Trump's Administration and an Agenda for Further Research, *Nations and Nationalism*, 27(3), 797–815.

Ban, C. (2013), 'Brazil's Liberal Neo-Developmentalism: New Paradigm or Edited Orthodoxy?' *Review of International Political Economy*, 20(2), 298–331.

Ban, C. (2019), 'Dependent Development at a Crossroads? Romanian Capitalism and its Contradictions', *West European Politics*, 42(5), 1041–68.

Ban, C. and Bohle, D. (2021), 'Definancialization, Financial Repression and Policy Continuity in East-Central Europe', *Review of International Political Economy*, 28(4), 874–97.

Barro, R. J. (2015), 'Convergence and Modernisation', *The Economic Journal*, 125(585), 911–42.

Bartlett, W. (1991), 'Quasi-markets and Contracts: A Markets and Hierarchies Perspective on NHS Reform', *Public Money & Management*, 11(3), 53–61.

Bartley, T. (2018), 'Transnational Corporations and Global Governance', *Annual Review of Sociology*, 44(1), 145–65.

Baumol, W. J. (1967), 'Macroeconomics of Unbalanced Growth: The Anatomy of Urban Crisis', *The American Economic Review*, 57(3), 415–26.

Beck, H. and Iber, P. (2022), 'The Contradictions of AMLO', *Dissent*, 69(2), 108–17.

Beck, M. (2022), 'The Managerial Contradictions of Extroverted Financialization: The Rise and Fall of Deutsche Bank', *Socio-Economic Review*, 20(4), 2017–40.

Becker, U. (2007), 'Open Systemness and Contested Reference Frames and Change. A Reformulation of the Varieties of Capitalism Theory*', *Socio-Economic Review*, 5(2), 261–86.

Beeson, M. and Li, F. (2015), 'What Consensus? Geopolitics and Policy Paradigms in China and the United States', *International Affairs*, 91(1), 93–109.

Belfrage, C. and Kallifatides, M. (2018), 'Financialisation and the New Swedish Model', *Cambridge Journal of Economics*, 42(4), 875–900.

Belfrage, C. and Ryner, M. (2009), 'Renegotiating the Swedish Social Democratic Settlement: From Pension Fund Socialism to Neoliberalization', *Politics & Society*, 37(2), 257–87.

Beltran, D.O., Kretchmer, M., Marquez, J. and Thomas, C. P. (2013), 'Foreign Holdings of U.S. Treasuries and U.S. Treasury Yields', *Journal of International Money and Finance*, 32, 1120–43.

Berend, T. I. (1996), *Central and Eastern Europe, 1944-1993: Detour from the Periphery to the Periphery*. Cambridge: Cambridge University Press.

Berg, J. and Schneider, E. (2018), 'Industrial Relations and Inclusive Growth in Brazil: The Swinging Pendulum', in S. Hayter and C. H. Lee (eds), *Industrial Relations in Emerging Economies: The Quest for Inclusive Development*. Cheltenham: Edward Elgar, 115–50..

Berman, S. (2021), 'The Causes of Populism in the West', *Annual Review of Political Science*, 24(1), 71–88.

Bermeo, N. G. and Pontusson, J., eds. (2012), *Coping with Crisis: Government Reactions to the Great Recession*. New York: Russell Sage Foundation.

Bhaduri, A. and Marglin, S. (1990), 'Unemployment and the Real Wage: The Economic Basis for Contesting Political Ideologies', *Cambridge Journal of Economics*, 14(4), 375–93.

Bhalla, A. S. (2002), 'Sino-indian Growth and Liberalization: A Survey', *Asian Survey*, 42(3), 419–39.

Bhambra, G. K. and Holmwood, J. (2018), 'Colonialism, postcolonialism and the liberal welfare state', *New Political Economy*, 23(5), 574–87.

Blanchard, O., Romer, D., Spence, M. and Stiglitz, J. E. (2012), *In the Wake of the Crisis: Leading Economists Reassess Economic Policy*. Cambridge, MA: MIT Press.

Blanchard, O. J. and Summers, L. H. (1986), 'Hysteresis and the European Unemployment Problem', *NBER Macroeconomics Annual*, 1, 15–78.

Block, F. (2008), 'Swimming Against the Current: The Rise of a Hidden Developmental State in the United States', *Politics & Society*, 36(2), 169–206.

Bloomberg, J. N. (2020), 'News Analysis: Boeing Sacrificed Quality on the Altar of Shareholder Value', *Los Angeles Times*. Available at: https://www.latimes.com/business/story/2020-01-17/nocera-boeing (Accessed: 14 April 2024).

Bluhm, K. and Varga, M. (2020), 'Conservative Developmental Statism in East Central Europe and Russia', *New Political Economy*, 25(4), 642–59.

Blyth, M. (2013), *Austerity: The History of a Dangerous Idea*. Oxford: Oxford University Press.

Blyth, M. and Matthijs, M. (2017), 'Black Swans, Lame Ducks, and the Mystery of IPE's Missing Macroeconomy', *Review of International Political Economy*, 24(2), 203–31.

Bogliaccini, J. A. and Madariaga, A. (2020), 'Varieties of Skills Profiles in Latin America: A Reassessment of the Hierarchical Model of Capitalism', *Journal of Latin American Studies*, 52(3), 601–31.

Bohle, D. (2014), 'Post-Socialist Housing Meets Transnational Finance: Foreign Banks, Mortgage Lending, and the Privatization of Welfare in Hungary and Estonia', *Review of International Political Economy*, 21(4), 913–48.

Bohle, D. and Greskovits, B. (2012), *Capitalist Diversity on Europe's Periphery*. Ithaca: Cornell University Press.

Bohle, D. and Jacoby, W. (2017), 'Lean, Special, or Consensual? Vulnerability and External Buffering in the Small States of East-Central Europe', *Comparative Politics*, 49(2), 191–212.

Bohle, D. and Regan, A. (2021), 'The Comparative Political Economy of Growth Models: Explaining the Continuity of FDI-Led Growth in Ireland and Hungary', *Politics & Society*, 49(1), 75–106.

Boltho, A., ed. (1982), *The European Economy: Growth and Crisis*. New York: Oxford University Press.

Borghi, R. A. Z., Sarti, F. and Cintra, M. A. M. (2013), 'The "Financialized" Structure of Automobile Corporations in the 2000s', *World Review of Political Economy*, 4(3), 387–409.

Botero, J. C., Djankov, S., LaPorta, R., López-de-Silanes, F. and Shleifer, A. (2004), 'The Regulation of Labor', *The Quarterly Journal of Economics*, 119(4), 1339–82.

Bowman, A. (2018), 'Financialization and the Extractive Industries: The Case of South African Platinum Mining', *Competition & Change*, 22(4), 388–412.

Boyer, R. (2000), 'Is a Finance-led Growth Regime a Viable Alternative to Fordism? A Preliminary Analysis', *Economy and Society*, 29(1), 111–45.

Boyer, R. and Saillard, Y., eds. (2002), *Regulation Theory: The State of the Art*. London; New York: Routledge.

Bradshaw, M., Van De Graaf, T. and Connolly, R. (2019), 'Preparing for the New Oil Order? Saudi Arabia and Russia', *Energy Strategy Reviews*, 26, 100374.

Breckenridge, K. (2021), 'What Happened to the Theory of African Capitalism?' *Economy and Society*, 50(1), 9–35.

Bremer, B. and McDaniel, S. (2020), 'The Ideational Foundations of Social Democratic Austerity in the Context of the Great Recession', *Socio-Economic Review*, 18(2), 439–63.

Brenner, R. (2005), 'The Capitalist Economy, 1945–2000: A Reply to Konings and to Panitch and Gindin', in D. Coates (ed.), *Varieties of Capitalism, Varieties of Approaches*. London: Palgrave Macmillan, 211–41.

Breslin, S. (2012), 'Government–Industry Relations in China: A Review of the Art of the State1', in A. Walter and X. Zhang (eds), *East Asian Capitalism*. Oxford University Press, 29–45.

Buchen, C. (2007), 'Estonia and Slovenia as Antipodes', in D. Lane and M. Myant (eds), *Varieties of Capitalism in Post-Communist Countries*. London: Palgrave Macmillan, 65–89.

Busemeyer, M. R. (2009), 'Asset Specificity, Institutional Complementarities and the Variety of Skill Regimes in Coordinated Market Economies', *Socio-Economic Review*, 7(3), 375–406.

Calmfors, L. and Driffill, J. (1988), 'Bargaining Structure, Corporatism and Macroeconomic Performance', *Economic Policy*, 3(6), 13.

Canning, A. and Hare, P. (1996), *Political Economy of Privatization in Hungary: A Progress Report*, 1–49. Available at: https://citeseerx.ist.psu.edu/document?repid=rep1&type=pdf&doi=d6b1cb7600d6d3f3fac736fe5ce97a1c0a7e354d.

Cannon, B. (2014), 'As Clear as Mud: Characteristics, Objectives, and Strategies of the Opposition in Bolivarian Venezuela', *Latin American Politics and Society*, 56(4), 49–70.

Cardoso, F. H. (2009), 'New Paths: Globalization in Historical Perspective', *Studies in Comparative International Development*, 44(4), 296–317.

Cardoso, F. H. and Faletto, E. (1979), *Dependency and Development in Latin America*. Berkeley: University of California Press.

Carlin, W. and Soskice, D. (2008), 'German Economic Performance: Disentangling the Role of Supply-Side Reforms, Macroeconomic Policy and Coordinated Economy Institutions', *Socio-Economic Review*, 7(1), 67–99.

Carney, R. W. (2016), 'Varieties of Hierarchical Capitalism: Family and State Market Economies in East Asia', *The Pacific Review*, 29(2), 137–63.

Carney, R. W. and Child, T. B. (2013), 'Changes to the Ownership and Control of East Asian Corporations between 1996 and 2008: The Primacy of Politics', *Journal of Financial Economics*, 107(2), 494–513.
Centeno, M. A. and Cohen, J. N. (2012), 'The Arc of Neoliberalism', *Annual Review of Sociology*, 38(1), 317–40.
Cerny, P. G. (1997), 'Paradoxes of the Competition State: The Dynamics of Political Globalization', *Government and Opposition*, 32(2), 251–74.
Chakrabarty, D. (1992), 'Provincializing Europe: Postcoloniality and the Critique of History', *Cultural Studies*, 6(3), 337–57.
Chandler, A. D. (1984), 'The Emergence of Managerial Capitalism', *Business History Review*, 58(4), 473–503.
Chandra, R. and Chatterjee, E. (2022), 'State Capitalism in India', in M. Wright et al. (eds), *The Oxford Handbook of State Capitalism and the Firm*. Oxford: Oxford University Press, 697–718.
Chang, C. and Wang, Y. (1994), 'The Nature of the Township-Village Enterprise', *Journal of Comparative Economics*, 19(3), 434–52.
Cheang, B. (2023), *Economic Liberalism and the Developmental State: Hong Kong and Singapore's Post-War Development*. Cham: Springer International Publishing.
Chen, H. and Rithmire, M. (2020), 'The Rise of the Investor State: State Capital in the Chinese Economy', *Studies in Comparative International Development*, 55(3), 257–77
Chinn, M. D. and Frieden, J. A. (2011), *Lost Decades: The Making of America's Debt Crisis and the Long Recovery*, 1st edn. New York: W.W. Norton & Co.
Christensen, J., Shaxson, N. and Wigan, D. (2016), 'The Finance Curse: Britain and the World Economy', *The British Journal of Politics and International Relations*, 18(1), 255–69.
Chwieroth, J. M. (2008), 'Normative Change from Within: The International Monetary Fund's Approach to Capital Account Liberalization', *International Studies Quarterly*, 52(1), 129–58.
Chwieroth, J. M. and Walter, A. (2019), *The Wealth Effect: How the Great Expectations of the Middle Class have Changed the Politics of Banking Crises*. Cambridge: Cambridge University Press.
Cieslik, K., Banya, R. and Vira, B. (2022), 'Offline Contexts of Online Jobs: Platform Drivers, Decent Work, and Informality in Lagos, Nigeria', *Development Policy Review*, 40(4), e12595.
Cioffi, J. W. (2010), *Public Law and Private Power: Corporate Governance Reform in the in the Age of Finance Capitalism*. Ithaca: Cornell University.
Clark, K. B. and Fujimoto, T. (1989), 'Lead Time in Automobile Product Development Explaining the Japanese Advantage', *Journal of Engineering and Technology Management*, 6(1), 25–58.
Clift, B. (2021), *Comparative Political Economy: States, Markets and Global Capitalism,* 2nd edn. London: Red Globe Press.
Coase, R. H. (1937), 'The Nature of the Firm', *Economica*, 4(16), 386–405.
Coates, D., ed. (2005), *Varieties of Capitalism, Varieties of Approaches*. New York: Palgrave Macmillan.
Coe, N. M., Dicken, P. and Hess, M. (2008), 'Global Production Networks: Realizing the Potential', *Journal of Economic Geography*, 8(3), 271–95.
Coe, N. M. and Yeung, H. W. (2015), *Global Production Networks: Theorizing Economic Development in an Interconnected World*. Oxford University Press.
Colignon, R. and Usui, C. (2001), 'The Resilience of Japan's Iron Triangle', *Asian Survey*, 41(5), 865–95.
Collin, S. (1998), 'Why are these Islands of Conscious Power Found in the Ocean of Ownership? Institutional and Governance Hypotheses Explaining the Existence of Business Groups in Sweden', *Journal of Management Studies*, 35(6), 719–46.
Colpan, A. M. (2010), *Business Groups in Turkey*. Oxford: Oxford University Press.
Cooke, F. L. (2016), 'Employment Relations in China', in G. Bamber, F. L. Cooke, V. Doellgast and C. Wright (eds), *International & Comparative Employment Relations: Global Crises and Institutional Responses*, Sixth edn. London: SAGE.
Crafts, N. (2012), 'British Relative Economic Decline Revisited: The Role of Competition', *Explorations in Economic History*, 49(1), 17–29.

Cronin, J. E., Ross, G. and Shoch, J., eds. (2011), *What's Left of the Left: Democrats and Social Democrats in Challenging Times*. Durham: Duke University Press.

Crouch, C. (2005), *Capitalist Diversity and Change: Recombinant Governance and Institutional Entrepreneurs*. Oxford, NY: Oxford University Press.

Crouch, C. et al. (2005), 'Dialogue on "Institutional Complementarity and Political Economy"', *Socio-Economic Review*, 3(2), 359–82.

Crouch, C. (2009), 'Privatised Keynesianism: An Unacknowledged Policy Regime', *The British Journal of Politics and International Relations*, 11(3), 382–99.

Crouch, C. (2011), *The Strange Non-death of Neoliberalism*. Cambridge: Polity Press.

Crowley, S. and Stanojević, M. (2011), 'Varieties of Capitalism, Power Resources, and Historical Legacies: Explaining the Slovenian Exception', *Politics & Society*, 39(2), 268–95.

Culpepper, P. D. (2005), 'Institutional Change in Contemporary Capitalism: Coordinated Financial Systems since 1990', *World Politics*, 57(2), 173–99.

Culpepper, P. D. (2008), 'Capitalism, Coordination, and Economic Change: The French Political Economy since 1985', in P. D. Culpepper, P. A. Hall and B. Palier (eds), *Changing France*. London: Palgrave Macmillan, 29–49.

Culpepper, P. D. (2011), *Quiet Politics and Business Power: Corporate Control in Europe and Japan*. New York: Cambridge University Press.

Culpepper, P. D. (2015), 'Structural Power and Political Science in the Post-Crisis Era', *Business and Politics*, 17(3), 391–409.

Culpepper, P. D. and Finegold, D., eds, (1999), *The German Skills Machine: Sustaining Comparative Advantage in a Global Economy*. New York: Berghahn Books.

Culpepper, P. D. and Reinke, R. (2014), 'Structural Power and Bank Bailouts in the United Kingdom and the United States', *Politics & Society*, 42(4), 427–54.

Culpepper, P. D. and Thelen, K. (2020), 'Are We all Amazon Primed? Consumers and the Politics of Platform Power', *Comparative Political Studies*, 53(2), 288–318.

Cusack, T. R., Iversen, T. and Soskice, D. (2007), 'Economic Interests and the Origins of Electoral Systems', *American Political Science Review*, 101(3), 373–91.

Davis, G. F. (2009), *Managed by the Markets: How Finance Reshaped America*. Oxford; New York: Oxford University Press.

Davis, G. F. (2016a), *The Vanishing American Corporation: Navigating the Hazards of a New Economy*. Oakland, California: Berrett-Koehler Publishers, Inc.

Davis, G. F. (2016b), 'What Might Replace the Modern Corporation: Uberization and the Web Page Enterprise', *Seattle University Law Review*, 39(2), 501–15.

Davis, G. F. and Kim, S. (2015), 'Financialization of the Economy', *Annual Review of Sociology*, 41(1), 203–21.

Dayen, D. and Mabud, R. (2022), 'How We Broke the Supply Chain', *American Prospect*, 31 January.

De La Torre, C. (2018), 'Ecuador after Correa', *Journal of Democracy*, 29(4), 77–88.

Deeg, R. (2012), 'The Limits of Liberalization? American Capitalism at the Crossroads', *Journal of European Public Policy*, 19(8), 1249–68.

Deeg, R. and Jackson, G. (2007), 'Towards a More Dynamic Theory of Capitalist Variety', *Socio-Economic Review*, 5(1), 149–79.

Devore, M. R. (2015), 'Defying Convergence: Globalisation and Varieties of Defence-Industrial Capitalism', *New Political Economy*, 20(4), 69–93.

Dingemans, A. (2016), 'Trying to stay ahead of the Curve in Chile's Economic Development: Exploring a way out of the Middle-Income Trap through Pragmatic Export Development', *Development Policy Review*, 34(5), 643–69.

Dobbin, F. (1994), *Forging Industrial Policy: The United States, Britain and France in the Railway Age*. Transferred to digital print. Cambridge: Cambridge University Press.

Doering, H., Barros, A., Gomes, M. and Rodrigues Silva, C. (2023), 'Populist "Order and Progress": Authoritarianism and Loyal Business Elites in Brazil', in M. Feldmann and G. Morgan (eds), *Business and Populism*. Oxford: Oxford University Press, 223–42.

Doner, R. F., Ritchie, B. K. and Slater, D. (2005), 'Systemic Vulnerability and the Origins of Developmental States: Northeast and Southeast Asia in Comparative Perspective', *International Organization*, 59(02), 327–61.

Doner, R. F. and Schneider, B. R. (2016), 'The Middle-Income Trap: More Politics than Economics', *World Politics*, 68(4), 608–44.

Dore, R. P. (2000), *Stock Market Capitalism: Welfare Capitalism; Japan and Germany versus the Anglo-Saxons*. Reprinted. Oxford: Oxford University Press.

Dornbusch, R. (1990) 'The New Classical Macroeconomics and Stabilization Policy', *American Economic Review*, 80(2), 143–7.

Dornbusch, R. and Edwards, S., eds. (1991), *The Macroeconomics of Populism in Latin America*. Chicago: University of Chicago Press.

Dörrenbächer, C. (2007), 'Challenges for Foreign-Owned Subsidiaries in FDI-Led Modernization Strategies: The Case of Hungary', *Competition & Change*, 11(2), 179–97.

Dos Santos, T. (1970), 'The Structure of Dependence', *The American Economic Review*, 60(2), 231–6.

Drahokoupil, J. (2008), *Globalization and the State in Central and Eastern Europe*. London: Routledge.

Drutman, L. (2015), *The Business of America is Lobbying: How Corporations became Politicized and Politics became More Corporate*. Oxford: Oxford University Press.

Duman, A. and Kureková, L. (2012), 'The Role of State in Development of Socio-Economic Models in Hungary and Slovakia: The Case of Industrial Policy', *Journal of European Public Policy*, 19(8), 1207–28.

Dunleavy, P. and Hood, C. (1994), 'From Old Public Administration to New Public Management', *Public Money & Management*, 14(3), 9–16.

Ebenau, M. (2012), 'Varieties of Capitalism or Dependency? A Critique of the VoC Approach for Latin America', *Competition & Change*, 16(3), 206–23.

Edwards, S. (2019), 'On Latin American Populism, and its Echoes around the World', *Journal of Economic Perspectives*, 33(4), 76–99.

Efrat, A. (2012), *Governing Guns, Preventing Plunder: International Cooperation against Illicit Trade*. Oxford; New York: Oxford University Press.

Eichengreen, B. J. (2019), *Globalizing Capital: A History of the International Monetary System*. Third edn. Princeton: Princeton University Press.

Eichengreen, B., Gupta, P. and Masetti, O. (2018), 'Are Capital Flows Fickle? Increasingly? And Does the Answer Still Depend on Type?' *Asian Economic Papers*, 17(1), 22–41.

Eichengreen, B., Hausmann, R. and Panizza, U. (2023), 'Yet it Endures: The Persistence of Original Sin', *Open Economies Review*, 34(1), 1–42.

Eisner, M. A. (2014), *The American Political Economy: Institutional Evolution of Market and State*, Second edn. New York, NY: Routledge.

Elger, T. and Smith, C. (2010), *Global Japanization?: The Transnational Transformation of the Labour Process*. Hoboken: Routledge.

Emmenegger, P., Hausermann, S., Palier, B. and Seeleib-Kaiser, M., eds. (2012), *The Age of Dualization: The Changing Face of Inequality in Deindustrializing Societies*. Oxford: Oxford University Press.

Epstein, G. A. (2005), 'Introduction: Financialization and the World Economy', in G. A. Epstein (ed.), *Financialization and the World Economy*. Cheltenham, UK; Northampton, MA: Edward Elgar, 3–16.

Epstein, R. A. (2014), 'Assets or Liabilities? The Politics of Bank Ownership', *Review of International Political Economy*, 21(4), 765–89.

Erixon, L. (2018), 'Progressive Supply-Side Economics: An Explanation and Update of the Rehn-Meidner Model', *Cambridge Journal of Economics*, 42(3), 653–97.

Erixon, L. and Pontusson, J. (2022), 'Rebalancing Balanced Growth: The Evolution of the Swedish Growth Model since the mid-1990s', in L. Baccaro, M. Blyth and J. Pontusson (eds), *Diminishing Returns*. New York: Oxford University Press, 268–92.

Erturk, I., Froud, J., Johal, S., Leaver, A. and Williams, K. (2007), 'The Democratization of Finance? Promises, Outcomes and Conditions', *Review of International Political Economy*, 14(4), 553–75.
Esping-Andersen, G. (1985), *Politics against Markets: The Social Democratic Road to Power*. Princeton, NJ: Princeton University Press.
Esping-Andersen, G. (1990), *The Three Worlds of Welfare Capitalism*. Princeton, NJ: Princeton University Press.
Esping-Andersen, G. (1999), *Social Foundations of Postindustrial Economies*. Oxford: Oxford University Press.
Estévez-Abe, M. (2006), 'Gendering the Varieties of Capitalism. A Study of Occupational Segregation by Sex in Advanced Industrial Societies', *World Politics*, 59(1), 142–75.
Estévez-Abe, M. (2008), *Welfare and Capitalism in Postwar Japan: Party, Bureaucracy, and Business*. Cambridge: Cambridge University Press.
Estevez-Abe, M., Iversen, T. and Soskice, D. (2001), 'Social Protection and the Formation of Skills: A Reinterpretation of the Welfare State', in P. A. Hall and D. Soskice (eds), *Varieties of Capitalism*. Oxford: Oxford University Press, 145–83.
Etchemendy, S. and Collier, R. B. (2007), 'Down but Not Out: Union Resurgence and Segmented Neocorporatism in Argentina (2003–2007)', *Politics & Society*, 35(3), 363–401.
Evans, P. B. (1995), *Embedded Autonomy: States and Industrial Transformation*. Princeton, NJ: Princeton University Press.
Evans, P. (2020), 'Polanyi meets Bolsonaro: Reactionary politics and the double movement in twenty-first-century Brazil', *International Sociology*, 35(6), 674–90.
Eyal, G., Szelényi, I. and Townsley, E. (1999), *Making Capitalism without Capitalists: Class Formation and Elite Struggles in Post-communist Central Europe*. London: Verso.
Fainshmidt, S. et al. (2018), 'Varieties of institutional systems: A contextual taxonomy of understudied countries', *Journal of World Business*, 53(3), 307–22.
Fannion, R. (2016), *Goldilocks and the Three Corporate Forms: Bank Finance and the Creation of the German Economy, 1870–1892* (Working Paper), Stanford: Stanford University
Feenstra, R. A. and Tormey, S. (2023), 'From Social Mobilisation to Institutional Politics: Reflecting on the Impact of Municipalism in Madrid and Barcelona', *Social Movement Studies*, 22(1), 80–98.
Feinstein, C. H. (2005), *An Economic History of South Africa: Conquest, Discrimination, and Development*. New York: Cambridge University Press.
Feldmann, M. (2006), 'Emerging Varieties of Capitalism in Transition Countries: Industrial Relations and Wage Bargaining in Estonia and Slovenia', *Comparative Political Studies*, 39(7), 829–54.
Feldmann, M. (2013), 'From the Ruble Zone to the Euro Zone: The Political Economy of Estonian Macroeconomic Policy', *Post-Soviet Affairs*, 29(4), 354–70.
Feldmann, M. (2014), 'Coalitions and Corporatism: The Slovenian Political Economy and the Crisis', *Government and Opposition*, 49(1), 70–91.
Feldmann, M. (2017), 'Crisis and Opportunity: Varieties of Capitalism and Varieties of Crisis Responses in Estonia and Slovenia', *European Journal of Industrial Relations*, 23(1), 33–46.
Feldmann, M. (2018), 'Extraordinary Politics and Durable Reform: Lessons From Trade Liberalisation in Estonia and Poland', *Post-Communist Economies*, 30(3), 365–81.
Feldmann, M. (2019), 'Global Varieties of Capitalism', *World Politics*, 71(1), 162–96.
Feldmann, M. and Mazepus, H. (2018), 'State-Society Relations and the Sources of Support for the Putin Regime: Bridging Political Culture and Social Contract Theory', *East European Politics*, 34(1), 57–76.
Feldmann, M. and Morgan, G. (2021), 'Brexit and British Business Elites: Business Power and Noisy Politics', *Politics & Society*, 49(1), 107–31.
Feldmann, M. and Morgan, G. (2022), 'Business Elites and Populism: Understanding Business Responses', *New Political Economy*, 27(2), 347–59.
Feldmann, M. and Morgan, G. (2023a), 'Brexit, Populism and Business: The Business Elite Loses Control?' in M. Feldmann and G. Morgan (eds), *Business and Populism*. Oxford: Oxford University Press, 79–97.

Feldmann, M. and Morgan, G., eds. (2023b), *Business and Populism*. Oxford: Oxford University Press.
Feldmann, M. and Morgan, G. (2023c), 'Populism, Risk and Business: Present and Future Prospects', in M. Feldmann and G. Morgan (eds), *Business and Populism*. Oxford: Oxford University Press, 345–64.
Feldmann, M. and Morgan, G. (2023d), 'Business and Populism: The Political Economy of the "Odd Couple"', in M. Feldmann and G. Morgan (eds), *Business and Populism*. Oxford: Oxford University Press, 3–35.
Feldmann, M. and Popa, M. (2022), 'Populism and Economic Policy: Lessons from Central and Eastern Europe', *Post-Communist Economies*, 34(2), 219–45.
Feldmann, M. and Kuokštis, V. (2017), 'Currency Boards, Depoliticization and Macroeconomic Stability: The Political Economy of Institutional Complementarities', *Policy Studies*, 38(4), 356–74.
Feldmann, M. and Sally, R. (2002), 'From the Soviet Union to the European Union: Estonian Trade Policy, 1991–2000', *The World Economy*, 25(1), 79–106.
Ferguson, N. (2008), *The Ascent of Money: A Financial History of the World*. New York: Penguin Press.
Ferguson, N. and Schularick, M. (2007), '"Chimerica" and the Global Asset Market Boom', *International Finance*, 10(3), 215–39.
Ferre, J. C. (2023), 'Social Policy Expansion and Segmentation in the First Two Decades of the 21st Century in Latin America', *International Journal of Social Welfare*, 32(4), 486–505.
Filc, D. (2009), *The Political Right in Israel*. London: Routledge.
Finegold, D. and Soskice, D. (1988), 'The Failure of Training in Britain: Analysis and Prescription', *Oxford Review of Economic Policy*, 4(3), 21–53.
Fligstein, N. (1987), 'The Intraorganizational Power Struggle: Rise of Finance Personnel to Top Leadership in Large Corporations, 1919–1979', *American Sociological Review*, 52(1), 44.
Fligstein, N. (1990), *The Transformation of Corporate Control*. Cambridge, MA: Harvard University Press.
Fligstein, N. and Choo, J. (2005), 'Law and Corporate Governance', *Annual Review of Law and Social Science*, 1(1), 61–84.
Fligstein, N. and Goldstein, A. (2015), 'The Emergence of a Finance Culture in American Households, 1989–2007', *Socio-Economic Review*, 13(3), 575–601.
Foot, R. and Walter, A. (2011), *China, the United States, and Global Order*. Cambridge; New York: Cambridge University Press.
Frank, A. G. (2009), *Capitalism and Underdevelopment in Latin America: Historical Studies of Chile and Brazil*. New York; London: Monthly Review Press.
Fratzscher, M. (2018), *The Germany Illusion: Between Economic Euphoria and Despair*. New York, NY: Oxford University Press.
Frieden, J. (2006), *Will Global Capitalism Fall Again?* Brussels: Bruegel
Frieden, J. and Walter, S. (2017), 'Understanding the Political Economy of the Eurozone Crisis', *Annual Review of Political Science*, 20(1), 371–90.
Fu, X., Hou, J. and Liu, X. (2018), 'Unpacking the Relationship Between Outward Direct Investment and Innovation Performance: Evidence From Chinese Firms', *World Development*, 102, 111–23.
Fulcher, J. (1988), 'The Bureaucratization of the State and the Rise of Japan', *The British Journal of Sociology*, 39(2), 228.
Fulcher, J. (1995), 'British Capitalism in the 1980s: Old Times or New Times?' *The British Journal of Sociology*, 46(2), 325.
Fulcher, J. (1997), 'Did British Society Change Character in the 1920s or the 1980s', *The British Journal of Sociology*, 48(3), 514.
Gagné, N. O. (2020), 'From Employment Security to Managerial Precarity: Japan's Changing Welfare-work Nexus and its Impacts on Mid-career Workers', *Pacific Affairs*, 93(2), 379–400.
Gamble, A. (1994), *Britain in Decline: Economic Policy, Political Strategy, and the British State*, 4th edn. New York: St. Martin's Press.

Gamble, A. (2002), *The Free Economy and the Strong State: The Politics of Thatcherism*. Basingstoke: Palgrave.
Garrett, G. (1995), 'Capital Mobility, Trade, and the Domestic Politics of Economic Policy', *International Organization*, 49(4), 657–87.
Geissdoerfer, M., Savaget, P., Bocken, N. M. and Hultink, E. J. (2017), 'The Circular Economy – A New Sustainability Paradigm?', *Journal of Cleaner Production*, 143, 757–68.
Gereffi, G. (2014), 'Global Value Chains in a Post-Washington Consensus World', *Review of International Political Economy*, 21(1), 9–37.
Gereffi, G., Humphrey, J. and Sturgeon, T. (2005), 'Governance in Global Value Chains', *Review of International Political Economy*, 12(1), 78–104.
Gerschenkron, A. (1962), *Economic Backwardness in Historical Perspective: A Book of Essays*. Cambridge: Belknap Press.
Gidron, N. and Hall, P. A. (2020), 'Populism as a Problem of Social Integration', *Comparative Political Studies*, 53(7), 1027–59.
Gilpin, R. (2000), *The Challenge of Global Capitalism: The World Economy in the 21st Century*. Princeton: Princeton University Press.
Gingrich, J. R. (2011), *Making Markets in the Welfare State: The Politics of Varying Market Reforms*, 1st edn. Cambridge: Cambridge University Press.
Glyn, A. and Wood, S. (2001), 'Economic Policy Under New Labour: How Social Democraticis the Blair Government?' *The Political Quarterly*, 72(1), 50–66.
Godard, J. (2009), 'The Exceptional Decline of the American Labor Movement', *ILR Review*, 63(1), 82–108.
Goldstein, A. (2010), 'Business Groups in South Africa', in A. M. Colpan, T. Hikino and J. R. Lincoln (eds), *The Oxford Handbook of Business Groups*. Oxford: Oxford University Press, 547–72.
Goldthorpe, J. H., ed. (1984), *Order and Conflict in Contemporary Capitalism*. Oxford: Oxford University Press.
Gong, H., Hassink, R., Foster, C., Hess, M. and Garretsen, H. (2022), 'Globalisation in Reverse? Reconfiguring the Geographies of Value Chains and Production Networks', *Cambridge Journal of Regions, Economy and Society*, 15(2), 165–81.
Gooberman, L., Hauptmeier, M. and Heery, E. (2020), 'A Typology of Employers' Organisations in the United Kingdom', *Economic and Industrial Democracy*, 41(1), 229–48.
Goodhart, C. and Lastra, R. (2018), 'Populism and Central Bank Independence', *Open Economies Review*, 29(1), 49–68.
Goodin, R. E. (2003), 'Choose Your Capitalism?' *Comparative European Politics*, 1(2), 203–13.
Gordon, R. J. and Gordon, R. J. (1987), 'Productivity, Wages, and Prices Inside and Outside of Manufacturing in the U.S., Japan, and Europe', *European Economic Review*, 31(3), 685–733.
Gottschalk, R., Castro, L. B. and Xu, J. (2022), 'Should National Development Banks be Subject to Basel III?' *Review of Political Economy*, 34(2), 249–67.
Gould, J. A. (2003). 'Out of the Blue? Democracy and Privatization in Postcommunist Europe', *Comparative European Politics*, 1(3), 277–311.
Gourevitch, P. A. and Shinn, J. (2005), *Political Power and Corporate Control: The New Global Politics of Corporate Governance*. Princeton: Princeton University Press.
Graeber, D. (2011), *Debt: The First 5,000 years*. Brooklyn, NY: Melville House.
Granovetter, M. (1983), 'The Strength of Weak Ties: A Network Theory Revisited', *Sociological Theory*, 1, 201.
Granovetter, M. (2010), '19. Business Groups and Social Organization', in N. J. Smelser and R. Swedberg (eds), *The Handbook of Economic Sociology,* Second edn. Princeton, NJ: Princeton University Press, 429–50.
Granovetter, M. S. (1973), 'The Strength of Weak Ties', *American Journal of Sociology*, 78(6), 1360–80.
Grumbach, J. and Collier, R. B. (2022), 'The Deep Structure of Democratic Crisis', *Boston Review*, 6 January. Available at: https://www.bostonreview.net/articles/the-deep-structure-of-democratic-crisis/ (Accessed: 16 April 2024).

Guzi, M., Kahanec, M. and Kureková, L. M. (2022), 'What Explains Immigrant–Native Gaps in European Labor Markets: The Role of Institutions', *Migration Studies*, 9(4), 1823–56.
Győrffy, D. (2022), 'The Middle-Income Trap in Central and Eastern Europe in the 2010s: Institutions and Divergent Growth Models', *Comparative European Politics*, 20(1), 90–113.
Hacker, J. S. (2004), 'Privatizing Risk Without Privatizing the Welfare State: The Hidden Politics of Social Policy Retrenchment in the United States', *American Political Science Review*, 98(2), 243–60.
Hacker, J. S., Hertel-Fernandez, A., Pierson, P. and Thelen, K. eds. (2021), *The American Political Economy: Politics, Markets, and Power*. Cambridge: Cambridge University Press.
Hacker, J. S., Hertel-Fernandez, A., Pierson, P. and Thelen, K. (2022), 'The American Political Economy: Markets, Power, and the Meta Politics of us Economic Governance', *Annual Review of Political Science*, 25(1), 197–217.
Haggard, S. (1990), *Pathways from the Periphery: The Politics of Growth in the Newly Industrializing Countries*. Ithaca: Cornell University Press.
Haggard, S. and Kaufman, R. R. (2008), *Development, Democracy, and Welfare States: Latin America, East Asia, and Eastern Europe*. Princeton: Princeton University Press.
Haipeter, T. (2021), 'Between Industry and Establishment: Recent Developments in German Collective Bargaining and Codetermination', *Labour & Industry*, 31(3), 204–16.
Hall, P. A. (1986), *Governing the Economy: The Politics of State Intervention in Britain and France*. New York: Oxford University Press.
Hall, P. A. (1993), 'Policy Paradigms, Social Learning, and the State: The Case of Economic Policymaking in Britain', *Comparative Politics*, 25(3), 275.
Hall, P. A. (2012), 'The Economics and Politics of the Euro Crisis', *German Politics*, 21(4), 355–71.
Hall, P. A. (2018), 'Varieties of Capitalism in Light of the Euro Crisis', *Journal of European Public Policy*, 25(1), 7–30.
Hall, P. A. (2020), 'The Electoral Politics of Growth Regimes', *Perspectives on Politics*, 18(1), 185–99.
Hall, P. A. (2022a), 'Growth Regimes', *Business History Review*, 1–25.
Hall, P. A. (2022b), 'The Shifting Relationship Between Post-War Capitalism and Democracy', *Government and Opposition*, 57(1), 1–30.
Hall, P. A., Evans, G. and Kim, S. I. (2023), *Political Change and Electoral Coalitions in Western Democracies*. New York: Cambridge University Press.
Hall, P. A. and Franzese, R. J. (1998), 'Mixed Signals: Central Bank Independence, Coordinated Wage Bargaining, and European Monetary Union', *International Organization*, 52(3), 505–35.
Hall, P. A. and Gingerich, D. W. (2009), 'Varieties of Capitalism and Institutional Complementarities in the Political Economy: An Empirical Analysis', *British Journal of Political Science*, 39(3), 449–82.
Hall, P. A. and Soskice, D. W. (2001a), 'An Introduction to Varieties of Capitalism', in P. A. Hall and D. Soskice (eds), *Varieties of Capitalism*. Oxford: Oxford University Press, 1–68.
Hall, P. A. and Soskice, D. W., eds. (2001b), *Varieties of Capitalism: The Institutional Foundations of Comparative Advantage*. Oxford: Oxford University Press
Hall, P. A. and Taylor, R. C. R. (1996), 'Political Science and the Three New Institutionalisms', *Political Studies*, 44(5), 936–57.
Hall, P. A. and Thelen, K. (2008), 'Institutional Change in Varieties of Capitalism', *Socio-Economic Review*, 7(1), 7–34.
Hamada, Y. (2010), 'Japanese Business–Government Relations', in D. Coen, W. Grant, and G. Wilson (eds), *The Oxford Handbook of Business and Government*. Oxford: Oxford University Press, 330–45.
Hamilton, G. G. (1997), 'Organization and Market Processes in Taiwan's Capitalist Economy', in M. Orru, N. W. Biggart, and G. G. Hamilton (eds), *The Economic Organization of East Asian Capitalism*. Thousand Oaks: SAGE, 237–93.
Hancke, B. (2012), 'Multinational Companies and the Production of Collective Goods in Central and Eastern Europe', in M. Heidenreich (ed.), *Innovation and Institutional Embeddedness of Multinational Companies*. Cheltenham: Edward Elgar, 295–310.

Hancké, B. (2013), *Unions, Central Banks, and EMU: Labour Market Institutions and Monetary Integration in Europe*. Oxford: Oxford University Press.
Hancké, B., Rhodes, M. and Thatcher, M., eds. (2007), *Beyond Varieties of Capitalism: Conflict, Contradictions, and Complementarities in the European Economy*. Oxford: Oxford University Press.
Hancké, B., Van Overbeke, T. and Voss, D. (2022), 'Crisis and Complementarities: A Comparative Political Economy of Economic Policies after Covid-19', *Perspectives on Politics*, 20(2), 474–89.
Hare, P. G. (1991), 'Hungary: In Transition to a Market Economy', *Journal of Economic Perspectives*, 5(4), 195–201.
Harper, P. (1969), 'The Party and the Unions in Communist China', *The China Quarterly*, 37, 84–119.
Hart, K. and Padayachee, V. (2013), 'A History of South African Capitalism in National and Global Perspective', *Transformation: Critical Perspectives on Southern Africa*, 81(1), 55–85.
Harvey, D. (2007), *A Brief History of Neoliberalism*. Oxford: Oxford University Press.
Harvey, D. (2015), *Seventeen Contradictions and the End of Capitalism*. Paperback ed. London: Profile Books.
Hashimoto, M. (1979), 'Bonus Payments, On-the-job Training, and Lifetime Employment in Japan', *Journal of Political Economy*, 87(5), 1086–104.
Hassel, A. (2014), 'The Paradox of Liberalization — Understanding Dualism and the Recovery of the German Political Economy', *British Journal of Industrial Relations*, 52(1), 57–81.
Hassel, A. and Palier, B., eds. (2020a), *Growth and Welfare in Advanced Capitalist Economies: How Have Growth Regimes Evolved?* Oxford: Oxford University Press.
Hassel, A. and Palier, B. (2020b), 'Tracking the Transformation of Growth Regimes in Advanced Capitalist Economies', in A. Hassel and B. Palier (eds), *Growth and Welfare in Advanced Capitalist Economies*. Oxford: Oxford University Press, 3–56.
Hassel, A. and Palier, B. (2023), 'Same Trend, Different Paths: Growth and Welfare Regimes Across Time and Space', *Annual Review of Political Science*, 26(1), 347–68.
Hassel, A. and Wiß, T., eds. (2020), 'Financialisation Meets Collectivisation: Occupational Pensions in Denmark, the Netherlands and Sweden', in *The Political Eeconomy of Pension Financialisation*, 1st edn. Routledge.
Hay, C. (2010), 'Chronicles of a Death Foretold: The Winter of Discontent and Construction of the Crisis of British Keynesianism', *Parliamentary Affairs*, 63(3), 446–70.
Hay, C. (2011), 'Pathology Without Crisis? The Strange Demise of the Anglo-Liberal Growth Model', *Government and Opposition*, 46(1), 1–31.
Hay, C. (2020), 'Does Capitalism (Still) Come in Varieties?' *Review of International Political Economy*, 27(2), 302–19.
Hay, C., Riihelainen, J. and Watson, M. (2008), 'Ireland: The Outlier Inside', in K. Dyson (ed.), *The Euro at 10*. Oxford: Oxford University Press, 182–203.
Hay, C. and Smith, N. J. (2013), 'The Resilience of Anglo-liberalism in the Absence of Growth: The UK and Irish Cases', in V. A. Schmidt and M. Thatcher (eds), *Resilient Liberalism in Europe's Political Economy*. Cambridge: Cambridge University Press, 289–312.
Heckman, J. and Pagés, C. (2000), *The Cost of Job Security Regulation: Evidence from Latin American Labor Markets*. Washington, DC: Inter-American Development Ban, 1–44.
Heilmann, S. (2008), 'Policy Experimentation in China's Economic Rise', *Studies in Comparative International Development*, 43(1), 1–26.
Heller, P. (2020), 'The Age of Reaction: Retrenchment Populism in India and Brazil', *International Sociology*, 35(6), 590–609.
Henderson, J. et al. (2002), 'Global production networks and the analysis of economic development', *Review of International Political Economy*, 9(3), 436–64.
Henrekson, M. and Jakobsson, U. (2003), 'The Transformation of Ownership Policy and Structure in Sweden: Convergence Towards the Anglo-Saxon Model?', *New Political Economy*, 8(1), 73–102.
Henrekson, M. and Jakobsson, U. (2012), 'The Swedish Corporate Control Model: Convergence, Persistence or Decline?' *Corporate Governance: An International Review*, 20(2), 212–27.

Herrigel, G. (2000), *Industrial Constructions: The Sources of German Industrial Power*. Cambridge: Cambridge University Press.
Hertel-Fernandez, A. (2021), 'Collective Action, Law, and the Fragmented Development of the American Labor Movement', in J. S. Hacker et al. (eds), *The American Political Economy*. Cambridge: Cambridge University Press, 103–30.
Hertog, S. (2023), *Locked Out of Development: Insiders and Outsiders in Arab Capitalism*, 1st edn. Los Angeles: Cambridge University Press.
Hickel, J. and Kallis, G. (2020), 'Is Green Growth Possible?' *New Political Economy*, 25(4), 469–86.
Hirschman, A. O. (1970), *Exit, Voice, and Loyalty: Responses to Decline in Firms, Organizations, and States*. Cambridge: Harvard University Press.
Hochstetler, K. (2014), 'The Brazilian National Development Bank goes International: Innovations and Limitations of bndes' Internationalization', *Global Policy*, 5(3), 360–5.
Hochstetler, K. and Montero, A. P. (2013), 'The Renewed Developmental State: The National Development Bank and the Brazil Model', *Journal of Development Studies*, 49(11), 1484–99.
Hodgson, G. M. (2015), *Conceptualizing Capitalism: Institutions, Evolution, Future*. Chicago; London: The University of Chicago Press.
Hodgson, G. M. (2017), '1688 and all that: Property rights, the Glorious Revolution and the rise of British capitalism', *Journal of Institutional Economics*, 13(1), 79–107.
Hodgson, G. M. (2023), *The Wealth of a Nation: Institutional Foundations of English Capitalism*. Princeton: Princeton University Press.
Hoffman, K. and Centeno, M. A. (2003), 'The Lopsided Continent: Inequality in Latin America', *Annual Review of Sociology*, 29(1), 363–90.
Holland, A. C. and Schneider, B. R. (2017), 'Easy and Hard Redistribution: The Political Economy of Welfare Statesin Latin America', *Perspectives on Politics*, 15(4), 988–1006.
Holliday, I. (2000), 'Productivist Welfare Capitalism: Social Policy in East Asia', *Political Studies*, 48(4), 706–23.
Hollingsworth, J. R. and Boyer, R., eds. (1997), *Contemporary Capitalism: The Embeddedness of Institutions*. Cambridge: Cambridge University Press.
Hollingsworth, R. (1997), 'The Institutional Embeddedness of American Capitalism', in C. Crouch and W. Streeck (eds), *Political Economy of Modern Capitalism*. London: SAGE, 133–47.
Hope, D. and Soskice, D. (2016), 'Growth Models, Varieties of Capitalism, and Macroeconomics', *Politics & Society*, 44(2), 209–26.
Hopkin, J. (2020), *Anti-system Politics: The Crisis of Market Liberalism in Rich Democracies*. New York: Oxford University Press.
Hopkin, J. and Blyth, M. (2019), 'The Global Economics of European Populism: Growth Regimes and Party System Change in Europe', *Government and Opposition*, 54(2), 193–225.
Höpner, M. (2005), 'What Connects Industrial Relations and Corporate Governance? Explaining Institutional Complementarity', *Socio-Economic Review*, 3(2), 331–58.
Howell, C. (2003), 'Varieties of Capitalism: And Then There Was One?' *Comparative Politics*, 36(1), 103.
Howell, C. (2007), 'The British Variety of Capitalism: Institutional Change, Industrial Relations and British Politics', *British Politics*, 2(2), 239–63.
Hsu, J.-Y. and Saxenian, A. (2000), 'The Limits of *Guanxi* Capitalism: Transnational Collaboration between Taiwan and the USA', *Environment and Planning A: Economy and Space*, 32(11), 1991–2005.
Hsueh, L., Hsu, C.-K. and Perkins, D. H., eds. (2001), *Industrialization and the State: The Changing Role of the Taiwan Government in the Economy, 1945 - 1998*. Cambridge, MA: Harvard Univ. Press.
Hu, H. W., Cui, L. and Aulakh, P. S. (2019), 'State Capitalism and Performance Persistence of Business Group-Affiliated Firms: A Comparative Study of China and India', *Journal of International Business Studies*, 50(2), 193–222.
Huber, E., Petrova, B. and Stephens, J. D. (2022), 'Financialization, Labor Market Institutions and Inequality', *Review of International Political Economy*, 29(2), 425–52.

Hughes, C. and Jackson, C. (2015), 'Death of the High Street: Identification, Prevention, Reinvention', *Regional Studies, Regional Science*, 2(1), 237–56.
Ibsen, C. L. (2016), 'The Role of Mediation Institutions in Sweden and Denmark After Centralized Bargaining', *British Journal of Industrial Relations*, 54(2), 285–310.
Ingham, G. K. (1984), *Capitalism Divided? The City and Industry in British Social Development*. Basingstoke, Hampshire: Macmillan.
Inglehart, R. (1981), 'Post-materialism in an Environment of Insecurity', *American Political Science Review*, 75(4), 880–900.
Iversen, T. (1996), 'Power, Flexibility, and the Breakdown of Centralized Wage Bargaining: Denmark and Sweden in Comparative Perspective', *Comparative Politics*, 28(4), 399.
Iversen, T. (1999), *Contested Economic Institutions: The Politics of Macroeconomics and Wage Bargaining in Advanced Democracies*. New York: Cambridge University Press.
Iversen, T. (2005), *Capitalism, Democracy, and Welfare*. New York: Cambridge University Press.
Iversen, T. and Rehm, P. (2022), *Big Data and the Welfare State: How the Information Revolution Threatens Social Solidarity*. New York: Cambridge University Press.
Iversen, T. and Soskice, D. (2006a), 'Electoral Institutions and the Politics of Coalitions: Why Some Democracies Redistribute more than Others', *American Political Science Review*, 100(2), 165–81.
Iversen, T. and Soskice, D. (2006b), 'New Macroeconomics and Political Science', *Annual Review of Political Science*, 9(1), 425–53.
Iversen, T., Soskice, D. and Hope, D. (2016), 'The Eurozone and Political Economic Institutions', *Annual Review of Political Science*, 19(1), 163–85.
Iversen, T. and Soskice, D. W. (2012), 'Modern Capitalism and the Advanced Nation State: Understanding the Causes of the Crisis', in N. Bermeo and J. Pontusson (eds), *Coping with Crisis Government Reactions to the Great Recession*. New York: Russell Sage, 35–64.
Iversen, T. and Soskice, D. W. (2019), *Democracy and Prosperity: Reinventing Capitalism through a Turbulent Century*. Princeton, New Jersey: Princeton University Press.
Iversen, T. and Stephens, J. D. (2008), 'Partisan Politics, the Welfare State, and Three Worlds of Human Capital Formation', *Comparative Political Studies*, 41(4–5), 600–37.
Iversen, T. and Wren, A. (1998), 'Equality, Employment, and Budgetary Restraint: The Trilemma of the Service Economy', *World Politics*, 50(4), 507–46.
Jackson, G. and Sorge, A. (2012), 'The Trajectory of Institutional Change in Germany, 1979–2009', *Journal of European Public Policy*, 19(8), 1146–67.
Jacoby, W. and Korkut, U. (2016), 'Vulnerability and Economic Re-Orientation: Rhetoric and in Reality in Hungary's "Chinese opening"', *East European Politics and Societies: and Cultures*, 30(3), 496–518.
Jaeger, A. M. and Baliga, B. R. (1985), 'Control Systems and Strategic Adaptation: Lessons From the Japanese Experience', *Strategic Management Journal*, 6(2), 115–34.
Jaffrelot, C. and Schoch, C. (2021), *Modi's India: Hindu Nationalism and the Rise of Ethnic Democracy*. Princeton: Princeton University Press.
Jasiecki, K. (2017), 'The Nature of Capitalism in Poland. Controversy Over the Economy since the end of 2015: The Prospects of Business Elite and Employer Associations', *Corvinus Journal of Sociology and Social Policy*, 8(3), 171–93.
Johnson, C. A. (1982), *MITI and the Japanese Miracle: The Growth of Industrial Policy, 1925 - 1975*. Reprinted. Stanford: Stanford Univ. Press.
Johnson, J. and Barnes, A. (2015), 'Financial Nationalism and its International Enablers: The Hungarian Experience', *Review of International Political Economy*, 22(3), 535–69.
Johnston, A., Fuller, G. W. and Regan, A. (2021), 'It takes Two to Tango: Mortgage Markets, Labor Markets and Rising Household Debt in Europe', *Review of International Political Economy*, 28(4), 843–73.
Johnston, A. and Regan, A. (2016), 'European Monetary Integration and the Incompatibility of National Varieties of Capitalism', *JCMS: Journal of Common Market Studies*, 54(2), 318–36.

Jones, C., Hesterly, W. S. and Borgatti, S. P. (1997), 'A General Theory of Network Governance: Exchange Conditions and Social Mechanisms', *Academy of Management Review*, 22(4), 911.

Jorgenson, D. W. (2005), 'Accounting for Growth in the Information Age', in P. Aghion and S. Durlauf (eds), *Handbook of Economic Growth*. Amsterdam: Elsevier, 743–815.

Joshi, V. and Little, I. M. D. (1996), *India's Economic Reforms, 1991-2001*. Oxford: Clarendon Press.

Jou, S.-C. and Chen, D.-C. (2006), 'Regionalization of Networked Production: Taiwanese Manufacturing Capital in Southeast Asia and China', *Geography Research Forum*, 26, 9–31.

Joyce, S., Stuart, M. and Forde, C. (2023), 'Theorising Labour Unrest and Trade Unionism in the Platform Economy', *New Technology, Work and Employment*, 38(1), 21–40.

Jun, Y., Rowley, C. and Oh, I. (2022), 'Corporate Governance Reforms Amidst Economic Maturation and Democratization: The Case of the Korean Chaebol since the 1990s', *Asia Pacific Business Review*, 28(1), 1–15.

Kahl, S. (2005), 'The Religious Roots of Modern Poverty Policy: Catholic, Lutheran, and Reformed Protestant Traditions Compared', *European Journal of Sociology*, 46(1), 91–126.

Kalanta, M. (2024a), 'The Political Economy of Economic Upgrading in Central Eastern Europe', *New Political Economy*, 1–17. Published online first. Available at: https://doi.org/10.1080/13563467.2024.2318430.

Kalanta, M. (2024b), 'Growth Model Change in Emerging Economies: Sectorial Loci of Growth and Politics', *Socio-Economic Review*, 1–27. Published online first. Available at: https://doi.org/10.1093/ser/mwae018.

Kalecki, M. (1943), 'Political aspects of full employment', *The Political Quarterly*, 14(4), 322–30.

Kalinowski, T. (2019), *Why International Cooperation is Failing: How the Clash of Capitalisms Undermines the Regulation of Finance*. Oxford: Oxford University Press.

Kallis, G. (2011), 'In Defence of Degrowth', *Ecological Economics*, 70(5), 873–80.

Kang, D. C. (2002), *Crony Capitalism: Corruption and Development in South Korea and the Philippines*. Cambridge: Cambridge University Press.

Karwowski, E. (2020), 'Economic Development and Variegated Financialization in Emerging Economies', in P. Mader, D. Mertens and N. Van Der Zwan (eds), *The Routledge International Handbook of Financialization*. London: Routledge, 162–76.

Karwowski, E. (2022), 'The Regional Distinctiveness and Variegation of Financialisation in Emerging Economies', *Cambridge Journal of Economics*, 46(5), 931–54.

Karwowski, E., Fine, B. and Ashman, S. (2018), 'Introduction to the Special Section "Financialization in South Africa"', *Competition & Change*, 22(4), 383–7.

Kaufman, R. R. (2009), 'The Political Effects of Inequality in Latin America: Some Inconvenient Facts', *Comparative Politics*, 41(3), 359–79.

Kelly, G., Kelly, D. and Gamble, A., eds. (1997), *Stakeholder Capitalism*. Basingstoke: Macmillan.

Kelly, L. (2023), 'Re-politicising the Future of Work: Automation Anxieties, Universal Basic Income, and the End of Techno-optimism', *Journal of Sociology*, 59(4), 828–43.

Kennedy, S. (2010), 'The Myth of the Beijing Consensus', *Journal of Contemporary China*, 19(65), 461–77.

Kinderman, D. (2005), 'Pressure from without, Subversion from within: The Two-Pronged German Employer Offensive', *Comparative European Politics*, 3(4), 432–63.

Kinderman, D. (2016), 'Challenging Varieties of Capitalism's Account of Business Interests: Neoliberal Think-tanks, Discourse as a Power Resource and Employers' Quest for Liberalization in Germany and Sweden', *Socio-Economic Review*, 15(3), 587–613.

Kinderman, D. (2021), 'German Business Mobilization Against Right-Wing Populism', *Politics & Society*, 49(4), 489–516.

Kinderman, D. (2023), 'Business Power, Right-Wing Populism, and Noisy Politics: Lessons from Brexit and Swiss Referendums', *Socio-Economic Review*, Published online on 14 November. Available at: https://doi.org/10.1093/ser/mwad061

Kindleberger, C. P. (1981), 'Dominance and Leadership in the International Economy: Exploitation, Public Goods, and Free Rides', *International Studies Quarterly*, 25(2), 242–54.

King, D. and Wickham-Jones, M. (1998), 'Training without the State? New Labour and Labour Markets', *Policy & Politics*, 26(4), 439–55.
King, D. and Wood, S. (1999), 'The Political Economy of Neoliberalism: Britain and the United States in the 1980s', in H. Kitschelt et al. (eds), *Continuity and Change in Contemporary Capitalism*. Cambridge: Cambridge University Press, 371–97.
King, L. P. and Sznajder, A. (2006), 'The State-Led Transition to Liberal Capitalism: Neoliberal, Organizational, World-Systems, and Social Structural Explanations of Poland's Economic Success', *American Journal of Sociology*, 112(3), 751–801.
Kingstone, P. R. (2018), *The political economy of Latin America: reflections on neoliberalism and development after the commodity boom*. Second edition. London: Routledge.
Kirchheimer, O. (1965), 'Der Wandel des westeuropäischen Parteisystems', *Politische Vierteljahresschrift*, 6(1), 20–41.
Kirkpatrick, D. D., Hakim, D. and Glanz, J. (2017), 'Why Grenfell Tower Burned: Regulators Put Cost Before Safety', *New York Times*, 24 June, Available at: https://www.nytimes.com/2017/06/24/world/europe/grenfell-tower-london-fire.html?_r=0.
Kitschelt, H. and Wilkinson, S., eds. (2007), *Patrons, Clients, and Policies: Patterns of Democratic Accountability and Political Competition*. New York: Cambridge University Press.
Kıran, J. (2018), 'Expanding the Framework of the Varieties of Capitalism: Turkey as a Hierarchical Market Economy', *Journal of Eurasian Studies*, 9(1), 42–51.
Knack, S. (1996), 'Institutions and the Convergence Hypothesis: The Cross-National Evidence', *Public Choice*, 87(3–4), 207–28.
Kocka, J. and Riemer, J. (2016), *Capitalism: A Short History*. Princeton: Princeton University Press.
Koddenbrock, K., Kvangraven, I. H. and Sylla, N. S. (2022), 'Beyond Financialisation: The *Longue Durée* of Finance and Production in the Global South', *Cambridge Journal of Economics*, 46(4), 703–33.
Kohl, S. (2020), 'Too Much Mortgage Debt? The Effect of Housing Financialization on Housing Supply and Residential Capital Formation', *Socio-Economic Review*, 19(2), 413–40.
Konzelmann, S., Fovargue-Davies, M. and Schnyder, G. (2012), 'The Faces of Liberal Capitalism: Anglo-Saxon Banking Systems in Crisis?' *Cambridge Journal of Economics*, 36(2), 495–524.
Kornai, J. (1990), *The Road to a Free Economy: Shifting From a Socialist System: The Example of Hungary*, 1st edn. New York: Norton.
Körösényi, A. (1999), *Government and Politics in Hungary*. Budapest: CEU Press.
Korpi, W. (1983), *The Democratic Class Struggle*. London: Routledge.
Korpi, W. (2006), 'Power Resources and Employer-centered Approaches in Explanations of Welfare States and Varieties of Capitalism: Protagonists, Consenters, and Antagonists', *World Politics*, 58(2), 167–206.
Koskinen, E.-M. (2016), 'Mammor från Sverige tvingades föda i Finland - svenskar risar sin sjukvård'. *Svenska Yle Nyheter*, 29 December. Available at: https://svenska.yle.fi/a/7-1148971 (Accessed: 13 April 2024).
Krippner, G. R. (2005), 'The Financialization of the American Economy', *Socio-Economic Review*, 3(2), 173–208.
Krippner, G. R. (2012), *Capitalizing on Crisis: tThe Political Origins of the Rise of Finance*. Cambridge, Massachusetts: Harvard University Press.
Kristensen, P. H. and Lilja, K., eds. (2011), *Nordic Capitalisms and Globalization*. Oxford: Oxford University Press.
Krouwel, A. (2003), 'Otto Kirchheimer and the Catch-all Party', *West European Politics*, 26(2), 23–40.
Kumar, R. (2021), 'Bringing the Developmental State Back in: Explaining South Korea's Successful Management of COVID-19', *Third World Quarterly*, 42(7), 1397–416.
Kuokštis, V. (2011), 'What Type of Capitalism do the Baltic Countries Belong to?' *Emecon Employment and Economy in Central and Eastern Europe*, 2(1), 1–16.

Kurlantzick, J. (2016), *State Capitalism: How the Return of Statism is Transforming the World*. New York: Oxford University Press.
Kushida, K. E. and Shimizu, K. (2013), 'Syncretism: The Politics of Japan's Financial Reforms', *Socio-Economic Review*, 11(2), 337–69.
Kvangraven, I. H. (2021), 'Beyond the Stereotype: Restating the Relevance of the Dependency Research Programme', *Development and Change*, 52(1), 76–112.
Kwan, C. H. (2020), 'The China–US Trade War: Deep-Rooted Causes, Shifting Focus and Uncertain Prospects', *Asian Economic Policy Review*, 15(1), 55–72.
La Porta, R. et al. (1998), 'Law and Finance', *Journal of Political Economy*, 106(6), 1113–55.
La Porta, R., Lopez-de-Silanes, F. and Shleifer, A. (2008), 'The Economic Consequences of Legal Origins', *Journal of Economic Literature*, 46(2), 285–332.
Laclau, E. (2005), *On Populist Reason*. London; New York: Verso.
Lane, C. (2007), 'National Capitalisms and Global Production Networks: An Analysis of their Interaction in Two Global Industries', *Socio-Economic Review*, 6(2), 227–60.
Lange, P. and Garrett, G. (1985), 'The Politics of Growth: Strategic Interaction and Economic Performance in the Advanced Industrial Democracies, 1974-1980', *The Journal of Politics*, 47(3), 792–827.
Larraín, J. (1989), *Theories of Development: Capitalism, Colonialism, and Dependency*. Cambridge: Polity Press.
Larsson, M. and Petersson, T. (2018), 'Sweden: Tradition and Renewal', in A.M. Colpan and T. Hikino (eds), *Business groups in the West*. Oxford: Oxford University Press, 245–72.
Lau, L. J., Qian, Y. and Roland, G. (2000), 'Reform without Losers: An Interpretation of China's Dual-Track Approach to Transition', *Journal of Political Economy*, 108(1), 120–43.
Lavigne, M. (1999), *The Economics of Transition: From Socialist Economy to Market Economy*. Basingstoke: Palgrave.
Lazonick, W. (2014), 'Profits without Prosperity', *Harvard Business Review*, 4–11.
Lazonick, W. and O'Sullivan, M. (2000), 'Maximizing Shareholder Value: A New Ideology for Corporate Governance', *Economy and Society*, 29(1), 13–35.
Lee, S. (2010), 'Necessity as the Mother of Intervention: The Industrial Policy Debate in England', *Local Economy: The Journal of the Local Economy Policy Unit*, 25(8), 622–30.
Lee, K. and Shin, H. (2021), 'Varieties of Capitalism and East Asia: Long-Term Evolution, Structural Change, and the End of East Asian Capitalism', *Structural Change and Economic Dynamics*, 56, 431–7.
Lee, K., Shin, H.-C. and Lee, J. (2020), 'From Catch-up to Convergence? Re-casting the Trajectory of Capitalism in South Korea', *Korean Studies*, 44, 54–79.
Lee, Z.-R. and Hsiao, H.-H.M. (2014), 'Taiwan: SME-Oriented Capitalism in Transition', in M. A. Witt and G. Redding (eds), *The Oxford Handbook of Asian Business Systems*. Oxford: Oxford University Press, 238–58.
Lefort, F. (2010), 'Business Groups in Chile', in A. M. Colpan, T. Hikino and J. R. Lincoln (eds), *Cover for The Oxford Handbook of Business Groups The Oxford Handbook of Business Groups*. Oxford: Oxford University Press, 387–423.
Levine, R. (1997), 'Financial Development and Economic Growth: Views and Agenda', *Journal of Economic Literature*, 35(2), 688–726.
Levitsky, S. and Way, L. A. (2006), 'Linkage Versus Leverage: Rethinking the International Dimension of Regime Change', *Comparative Politics*, 38(4), 379–400.
Lin, J. Y. and Wang, X. (2022), 'Dual Circulation: A New Structural Economics View of Development', *Journal of Chinese Economic and Business Studies*, 20(4), 303–22.
Lin, V. K. and Wang, J. (2023), 'The Green Energy Transition and Peripheral City Development in China: Towards a Local Eco-Developmental State', *Development and Change*, 54(3), 514–42.
Lin, K.-H. and Tomaskovic-Devey, D. (2013), 'Financialization and U.S. Income Inequality, 1970–2008', *American Journal of Sociology*, 118(5), 1284–329.

Lincoln, J. R. and Gerlach, M. L. (2004), *Japan's Network Economy: A Structure, Persistence, and Change*. New York, NY: Cambridge University Press.
López, I. and Rodríguez, E. (2011), 'The Spanish Model', *New Left Review*, (69), 5–29.
Losman, D. L. (2010), 'The Rentier State and National Oil Companies: An Economic and Political Perspective', *Middle East Journal*, 64(3), 427–45.
Love, J. L. (1990), 'The Origins of Dependency Analysis', *Journal of Latin American Studies*, 22(1–2), 143–68.
Lundberg, E. (1985), 'The Rise and Fall of the Swedish Model', *Journal of Economic Literature*, 23(1), 1–36.
Mader, P., Mertens, D. and Van Der Zwan, N., eds. (2020), *The Routledge International Handbook of Financialization*. London: Routledge.
Mahoney, J. and Thelen, K. (2009), 'A Theory of Gradual Institutional Change', in J. Mahoney and K. Thelen (eds), *Explaining Institutional Change*. Cambridge: Cambridge University Press, 1–37.
McDonald, D. A. (2010), 'Ubuntu Bashing: The Marketisation of "African Values" in South Africa', *Review of African Political Economy*, 37(124), 139–52.
Mair, P. (2013), *Ruling the Void: The Hollowing of Western Democracy*. London; New York: Verso.
Mandel, H. and Shalev, M. (2009), 'Gender, Class, and Varieties of Capitalism', *Social Politics: International Studies in Gender, State & Society*, 16(2), 161–81.
Manow, P. (2018), *Die politische Ökonomie des Populismus*. Berlin: Suhrkamp.
Mansbridge, J. and Macedo, S. (2019), 'Populism and Democratic Theory', *Annual Review of Law and Social Science*, 15(1), 59–77.
Marglin, S. A. (2008), *The Dismal Science: How Thinking Like an Economist Undermines Community*. Cambridge, MA: Harvard University Press.
Martinez, I. and Serve, S. (2017), 'Reasons for Delisting and Consequences: A Literature Review and Research Agenda', *Journal of Economic Surveys*, 31(3), 733–70.
Mayhew, K. and Wickham-Jones, M. (2014), 'The United Kingdom's Social Model', in J. E. Dølvik and A. Martin (eds), *European Social Models From Crisis to Crisis*. Oxford: Oxford University Press, 144–76.
Mastini, R., Kallis, G. and Hickel, J. (2021), 'A Green New Deal Without Growth?', *Ecological Economics*, 179, 106832.
Mazurek, M. (2018), 'Polish Economists in Nehru's India: Making Science for the Third World in an Era of De-stalinization and Decolonization', *Slavic Review*, 77(3), 588–610.
Mazzucato, M. (2018), *The Entrepreneurial State: Debunking Public vs. Private Sector Myths*. London: Penguin Books.
McGuire, J. and Dow, S. (2009), 'Japanese keiretsu: Past, Present, Future', *Asia Pacific Journal of Management*, 26(2), 333–51.
McNally, C. A. (2012), 'Sino-Capitalism: China's Reemergence and the International Political Economy', *World Politics*, 64(4), 741–76.
Mertens, D., Nölke, A., May, C., Schedelik, M., Ten Brink, T. and Gomes, A. (2022), *Moving the Center: Adapting the Toolbox of Growth Model Research to Emerging Capitalist Economies*. Working Paper 188/2022. Working Paper. Available at: https://www.econstor.eu/handle/10419/264891 (Accessed: 26 November 2023).
Mesa-Lago, C. (2003), *Market, Socialist, and Mixed Economies*. Baltimore: Johns Hopkins Univ Press.
Mihályi, P. (2000), 'Foreign Direct Investment in Hungary – the Post-communist Privatisation Story Reconsidered', *Acta Oeconomica*, 51(1), 107–29.
Minns, J. (2001), 'Of Miracles and Models: The Rise and Decline of the Developmental State in South Korea', *Third World Quarterly*, 22(6), 1025–43.
Mizruchi, M. S. (2013), *The Fracturing of the American Corporate Elite*. Cambridge, MA: Harvard University Press.
Mizruchi, M. S. and Gălan, R. (2023), 'The Trump Phenomenon and Right-Wing Extremism: Is Donald Trump a Populist?', in M. Feldmann and G. Morgan (eds), *Business and Populism*. Oxford: Oxford University Press, 39–58.

Moffitt, B. and Tormey, S. (2014), 'Rethinking Populism: Politics, Mediatisation and Political Style', *Political Studies*, 62(2), 381–97.
Molina, Ó. and Rhodes, M. (2007), 'The Political Economy of Adjustment in Mixed Market Economies: A Study of Spain and Italy', in B. Hancké, M. Rhodes and M. Thatcher (eds), *Beyond Varieties of Capitalism*. Oxford: Oxford University Press, 223–52.
Montinola, G., Qian, Y. and Weingast, B. R. (1995), 'Federalism, Chinese Style: The Political Basis for Economic Success in China', *World Politics*, 48(1), 50–81.
Morawiecki, M. (2016), 'The Polish Case for Less Economic Liberalism', *Politico*. 21 October, Available at: https://www.politico.eu/article/the-polish-case-for-economic-illiberalism-stability-development/ (Accessed: 12 April 2024).
Morduch, J. (1999), 'The Microfinance Promise', *Journal of Economic Literature*, 37(4), 1569–614.
Morgan, G. (2007), 'National Business Systems Research: Progress and Prospects', *Scandinavian Journal of Management*, 23(2), 127–45.
Morgan, G. (2009), 'Globalization, Multinationals and Institutional Diversity', *Economy and Society*, 38(4), 580–605.
Morgan, G., Doering, H. and Gomes, M. (2021), 'Extending Varieties of Capitalism to Emerging Economies: What Can We Learn from Brazil?' *New Political Economy*, 26(4), 540–53.
Morgan, G. and Kubo, I. (2005), 'Beyond Path Dependency? Constructing New Models for Institutional Change: The Case of Capital Markets in Japan', *Socio-Economic Review*, 3(1), 55–82.
Mudde, C. (2004), 'The Populist Zeitgeist', *Government and Opposition*, 39(4), 541–63.
Mudde, C. and Rovira Kaltwasser, C. (2013), 'Exclusionary vs. Inclusionary Populism: Comparing Contemporary Europe and Latin America', *Government and Opposition*, 48(2), 147–74.
Mudge, S. L. (2011), 'What's Left of Leftism? : Neoliberal Politics in Western Party Systems, 1945–2004', *Social Science History*, 35(3), 337–80.
Müller, J.-W. (2016), *What is Populism?* Philadelphia: University of Pennsylvania Press.
Musacchio, A. and Lazzarini, S. G. (2014), *Reinventing State Capitalism: Leviathan in Business, Brazil and Beyond*. Cambridge, MA: Harvard University Press.
Myant, M. (2007), 'The Czech Republic: From "Czech" Capitalism to "European" Capitalism', in D. Lane and M. Myant (eds), *Varieties of Capitalism in Post-Communist Countries*. London: Palgrave Macmillan, 105–23.
Myant, M. and Drahokoupil, J. (2012), 'International Integration, Varieties of Capitalism and Resilience to Crisis in Transition Economies', *Europe-Asia Studies*, 64(1), 1–33.
Naczyk, M. (2022), 'Taking Back Control: Comprador Bankers and Managerial Developmentalism in Poland', *Review of International Political Economy*, 29(5), 1650–74.
Nahm, J. (2022), 'Green Growth Models', in L. Baccaro, M. Blyth, and J. Pontusson (eds), *Diminishing Returns*. New York: Oxford University Press, 443–64.
Naseemullah, A. and Arnold, C. E. (2015), 'The Politics of Developmental State Persistence: Institutional Origins, Industrialization, and Provincial Challenge', *Studies in Comparative International Development*, 50(1), 121–42.
Nattrass, N. (2014), 'A South African Variety of Capitalism?' *New Political Economy*, 19(1), 56–78.
Naughton, B. (2018), *The Chinese Economy: Adaptation and Growth*, Second edn. Cambridge, MA: MIT Press.
Niblock, T. and Malik, M. (2007), *The Political Economy of Saudi Arabia*. Abingdon, Oxon; New York: Routledge.
Noland, M. (2018), 'US Trade Policy in the Trump administration', *Asian Economic Policy Review*, 13(2), 262–78.
Nölke, A. (2018), 'Dependent versus State-Permeated Capitalism: Two Basic Options for Emerging Markets', *International Journal of Management and Economics*, 54(4), 269–82.
Nölke, A. and Claar, S. (2013), 'Varieties of Capitalism in Emerging Economies', *Transformation: Critical Perspectives on Southern Africa*, 81(1), 33–54.
Nölke, A. and Vliegenthart, A. (2009), 'Enlarging the Varieties of Capitalism: The Emergence of Dependent Market Economies in East Central Europe', *World Politics*, 61(4), 670–702.

Nölke, A., Ten Brink, T., Claar, S. and May, C. (2015), 'Domestic Structures, Foreign Economic Policies and Global Economic Order: Implications From the Rise of Large Emerging Economies', *European Journal of International Relations*, 21(3), 538–67.

Nölke, A., Ten Brink, T., Claar, S. and May, C. (2020), *State-Permeated Capitalism in Large Emerging Economies*, 1st edn. New York, NY: Routledge.

Norris, P. and Inglehart, R. (2018), *Cultural Backlash: Trump, Brexit, and the Rise of Authoritarian-Populism*. New York, NY: Cambridge University Press.

North, D. C. and Weingast, B. R. (1989), 'Constitutions and Commitment: The Evolution of Institutions Governing Public Choice in Seventeenth-Century England', *The Journal of Economic History*, 49(4), 803–32.

Oatley, T. and Petrova, B. (2022), 'The Global Deregulation Hypothesis', *Socio-Economic Review*, 20(2), 611–33.

OECD (2018). *OECD International Direct Investment Statistics, 2008-2017*. Paris: OECD Publishing

OECD (2023), *Education at a Glance 2023: OECD Indicators*, Paris: OECD Publishing. Available at: https://doi.org/10.1787/e13bef63-en.

Okimoto, D. I. (1989), *Between MITI and the Market: Japanese Industrial Policy for High Technology*. Stanford: Stanford University Press.

Orenstein, M. A. and Bugarič, B. (2022), 'Work, Family, Fatherland: The Political Economy of Populism in Central and Eastern Europe', *Journal of European Public Policy*, 29(2), 176–95.

Ornston, D. (2013), 'Creative Corporatism: The Politics of High-technology Competition in Nordic Europe', *Comparative Political Studies*, 46(6), 702–29.

Orr, A. M. et al. (2023), 'Not Quite the "Death of the High Street" in UK City Centres: Rising Vacancy Rates and the Shift in Property use Richness and Diversity', *Cities*, 133, 104–24.

Ost, D. (2000), 'Illusory Corporatism in Eastern Europe: Neoliberal Tripartism and Postcommunist Class Identities', *Politics & Society*, 28(4), 503–30.

Owen, G. and Hopkins, M. M. (2016), *Science, the State and the City: Britain's Struggle to Succeed in Biotechnology*. Oxford: Oxford University Press.

Özel, I. (2014). 'Emerging on an Illiberal path: The Turkish Variety of Capitalism', in U. Becker (ed.), *The BRICs and Emerging Economies in Comparative Perspective*. London: Routledge.

Padayachee, V. (2013a), 'Corporate Governance in South Africa: From "Old Boys Club" to "Ubuntu"?' *Transformation: Critical Perspectives on Southern Africa*, 81(1), 260–90.

Padayachee, V. (2013b), 'Introducing Varieties of Capitalism into the South African Debate: Uses and Limits', *Transformation: Critical Perspectives on Southern Africa*, 81(1), 5–32.

Padgett, J. F. and Ansell, C. K. (1993), 'Robust Action and the Rise of the Medici, 1400-1434', *American Journal of Sociology*, 98(6), 1259–319.

Palier, B. and Thelen, K. (2010), 'Institutionalizing Dualism: Complementarities and Change in France and Germany', *Politics & Society*, 38(1), 119–48.

Palma, G. (1978), 'Dependency: A Formal Theory of Underdevelopment or a Methodology for the Analysis of Concrete Situations of Underdevelopment?' *World Development*, 6(7–8), 881–924.

Pan, F., Zhang, F. and Wu, F. (2021), 'State-Led Financialization in China: The Case of the Government-Guided Investment Fund', *The China Quarterly*, 247, 749–72.

Paster, T. (2013), 'Business and welfare state development: Why did employers accept social reforms?', *World Politics*, 65(3), 416–51.

Paterson, M. (2000), 'Car Culture and Global Environmental Politics', *Review of International Studies*, 26(2), 253–70.

Pavlínek, P. (2016), 'Whose Success? The State–Foreign Capital Nexus and the Development of the Automotive Industry in Slovakia', *European Urban and Regional Studies*, 23(4), 571–93.

Pearson, M. M., Rithmire, M. and Tsai, K. S. (2022), 'China's Party-State Capitalism and International Backlash: From Interdependence to Insecurity', *International Security*, 47(2), 135–76.

Perkins, D. (1994), 'Completing China's Move to the Market', *Journal of Economic Perspectives*, 8(2), 23–46.

Perkins, D. H. (2001), 'Industrial and Financial Policy in China and Vietnam: A New Model or a Replay of the East Asian Experience?' in J. E. Stiglitz and S. Yusuf (eds), *Rethinking the East Asia Miracle*. Washington, DC: New York: World Bank; Oxford University Press.

Perkins, D. H. (2013), *East Asian Development: Foundations and Strategies*. Cambridge, MA: Harvard University Press.

Persson, K. G. and Sharp, P. (2015), *An Economic History of Europe: Knowledge, Institutions and Growth, 600 to the Present*, Second edn. Cambridge; New York: Cambridge University Press.

Petry, J. (2020), 'Financialization with Chinese Characteristics? Exchanges, Control and Capital Markets in Authoritarian Capitalism', *Economy and Society*, 49(2), 213–38.

Pettis, M. (2021), *Will China's Common Prosperity Upgrade Dual Circulation?* Washington DC: Carnegie Endowment for International Peace.

Pierson, P. (1996), 'The New Politics of the Welfare State', *World Politics*, 48(2), 143–79.

Pierson, P. (1998), 'Irresistible Forces, Immovable Objects: Post-Industrial Welfare States Confront Permanent Austerity', *Journal of European Public Policy*, 5(4), 539–60.

Pierson, P. (2017), 'American Hybrid: Donald Trump and the Strange Merger of Populism and Plutocracy', *The British Journal of Sociology*, 68(S1), S105–19.

Piore, M. J. and Sabel, C. F. (1984), *The Second Industrial Divide: Possibilities for Prosperity*. New York: Basic Books.

Polanyi, K. (1944), *The Great Transformation: The Political and Economic Origins of Our Time,* Boston, MA: Beacon Press.

Pontusson, J. (2005), *Inequality and Prosperity: Social Europe vs. Liberal America*. Ithaca, NY: Cornell University Press.

Pontusson, J. (2011), 'Once Again a Model', in J. Cronin, G. Ross and J. Shoch (eds), *What's Left of the Left : Democrats and Social Democrats in Challenging Times*. Durham, NC: Duke University Press, 89–115.

Pontusson, J. and Swenson, P. (1996), 'Labor Markets, Production Strategies, and Wage Bargaining Institutions: The Swedish Employer Offensive in Comparative Perspective', *Comparative Political Studies*, 29(2), 223–50.

Popa, M. (2021), 'Political Machines and the Institutional Background of Economic Miracles', *Government and Opposition*, 56(2), 345–64.

Porter, T. (2005), *Globalization and Finance*. Cambridge; Malden, MA: Polity.

Powell, M. and Miller, R. (2016), 'Seventy Years of Privatizing the British National Health Service?' *Social Policy & Administration*, 50(1), 99–118.

Powell, W. W. and Snellman, K. (2004), 'The Knowledge Economy', *Annual Review of Sociology*, 30(1), 199–220.

Power, T. J. (2001), 'Blairism Brazilian Style? Cardoso and the "Third Way" in Brazil', *Political Science Quarterly*, 116(4), 611–36.

Przeworski, A. and Wallerstein, M. (1988), 'Structural Dependence of the State on Capital', *American Political Science Review*, 82(1), 11–29.

Qian, Y. (2000), 'The Process of China's Market Transition (1978-1998): The evolutionary, historical, and comparative perspectives', *Journal of Institutional and Theoretical Economics*, 156(1), 151–71.

Rahman, K. S. and Thelen, K. (2019), 'The Rise of the Platform Business Model and the Transformation of Twenty-first-century Capitalism', *Politics & Society*, 47(2), 177–204.

Rahman, K. S. and Thelen, K. (2021), 'The Role of the Law in the American Political Economy', in J. S. Hacker et al. (eds), *The American Political Economy*. New York: Cambridge University Press, 76–102.

Reinhart, C. M. and Rogoff, K. S. (2011), *This Time is Different: Eight Centuries of Financial Folly*. Princeton: Princeton University Press.

Reisenbichler, A. and Wiedemann, A. (2022), 'Credit-Driven and Consumption-Led Growth Models in the United States and United Kingdom', in L. Baccaro, M. Blyth and J. Pontusson (eds), *Diminishing Returns*. New York: Oxford University Press, 213-C8.N13.

Reiter, J. (2003), 'Changing the Microfoundations of Corporatism: The Impact of Financial Globalisation on Swedish Corporate Ownership', *New Political Economy*, 8(1), 103–25.

Remington, T. F. (2018), 'Bureaucratic Politics and Labour Policy in China', *China: An International Journal*, 16(3), 97–119.
Ringen, S. and Ngok, K. (2017), 'What Kind of Welfare State is Emerging in China?' in I. Yi (ed.), *Towards Universal Health Care in Emerging Economies*. London: Palgrave Macmillan, 213–37.
Rithmire, M. E. (2017), 'Land Institutions and Chinese Political Economy: Institutional Complementarities and Macroeconomic Management', *Politics & Society*, 45(1), 123–153.
Roberts, K. M. (2019), 'Bipolar Disorders: Varieties of Capitalism and Populist Out-Flanking on the Left and Right', *Polity*, 51(4), 641–53.
Rodrik, D. (1997), *Has Globalization Gone Too Far?* Washington, DC: Institute for International Economics.
Rodrik, D. (2016), 'Premature Deindustrialization', *Journal of Economic Growth*, 21(1), 1–33.
Rodrik, D. (2018), 'Is Populism Necessarily Bad Economics?' *AEA Papers and Proceedings*, 108, 196–99.
Rodrik, D., Subramanian, A. and Trebbi, F. (2004), 'Institutions Rule: the Primacy of Institutions Over Geography and Integration in Economic Development', *Journal of Economic Growth*, 9(2), 131–65.
Roe, M. J. (2003), *Political Determinants of Corporate Governance: Political Context, Corporate Impact*. Oxford; New York: Oxford University Press.
Rogers, S. (2020), 'Fidesz, the State-Subsumption of Domestic Business and the Emergence of Prebendalism: Capitalist Development in an "Illiberal" Setting', *Post-Communist Economies*, 32(5), 591–606.
Rogers, S. (2024), *The Political Economy of Hungarian Authoritarian Populism: Capitalists Without the Right Kind of Capital*. Abingdon: Routledge.
Röper, N. (2021), 'Capitalists Against Financialization: The Battle Over German Pension Funds', *Competition & Change*, 25(3–4), 428–52.
Rosenblum, N. L. (2008), *On the Side of the Angels: An Appreciation of Parties and Partisanship*. Princeton: Princeton University Press.
Röth, L., Afonso, A. and Spies, D. C. (2018), 'The Impact of Populist Radical Right Parties on Socio-Economic Policies', *European Political Science Review*, 10(3), 325–50.
Rothstein, B. (2015), 'The Chinese Paradox of High Growth and Low Quality of Government: The Cadre Organization Meets Max Weber', *Governance*, 28(4), 533–48.
Rueda, D. (2007), *Social Democracy Inside Out: Partisanship and Labor Market Policy in Industrialized Democracies*. New York: Oxford University Press.
Rueda, D. and Pontusson, J. (2000), 'Wage inequality and varieties of capitalism', *World Politics*, 52(3), 350–83.
Ruggie, J. G. (1982), 'International Regimes, Transactions, and Change: Embedded Liberalism in the Postwar Economic Order', *International Organization*, 36(2), 379–415.
Runciman, W. G. (1993), 'Has British capitalism Changed Since the First World War?' *The British Journal of Sociology*, 44(1), 53.
Sachs, J. D. and Warner, A. M. (2001), 'The Curse of Natural Resources', *European Economic Review*, 45(4–6), 827–38.
Sachs, J. and Wyplosz, C. (1986), 'The Economic Consequences of President Mitterrand', *Economic Policy*, 1(2), 261–306.
Saez, L. (2014), 'India: From Failed Developmental State Towards Hybrid Market Capitalism', in M. A. Witt and G. Redding (eds), *The Oxford Handbook of Asian Business Systems*. Oxford: Oxford University Press, 55–78.
Saka, A. (2004), 'The Cross-National Diffusion of Work Systems: Translation of Japanese Operations in the UK', *Organization Studies*, 25(2), 209–28.
Sako M. (1997), 'Shunto: The Role of Employer and Union Coordination at the Industry and Inter-Sectoral Levels', in M. Sako and H. Satō (eds), *Japanese Labour and Management in Transition Diversity, Flexibility and Participation*. London: Routledge.

Sako, M. and Kotosaka, M. (2012), 'Continuity and Change in the Japanese Economy: Evidence of Institutional Interactions Between Financial and Labour Markets', in A. Walter and X. Zhang (eds), *East Asian Capitalism*. Oxford University Press, 132–56.
Sallai, D. and Schnyder, G. (2021), 'What is "Authoritarian" about Authoritarian Capitalism? The Dual Erosion of the Private–Public Divide in State-Dominated Business Systems', *Business & Society*, 60(6), 1312–48.
Sally, R. (1998), *Classical Liberalism and International Economic Order: Studies in Theory and Intellectual History*. London: Routledge.
Samuels, R. J. (1987), *The Business of the Japanese State: Energy Markets in Comparative and Historical Perspective*. Ithaca: Cornell University Press (Cornell studies in political economy).
Sancak, M. (2020), 'Partisan Politics of Skills in Middle-Income Countries: Insiders, Outsiders and the Vocational Education System of Turkey', *Competition & Change*, 24(3–4), 291–314.
Sandel, M. J. (2012), *What Money Can't Buy: the Moral Limits of Markets*, 1st edn. New York: Farrar, Straus and Giroux.
Sass, M. (2004), 'FDI in Hungary: The First Mover's Advantage and Disadvantage, *EIB Papers*, 9(2), 62–90.
Schelkle, W. and Bohle, D. (2021), 'European Political Economy of Finance and Financialization', *Review of International Political Economy*, 28(4), 761–74.
Schmidt, V. (2003), 'French Capitalism Transformed, Yet Still a Third Variety of Capitalism', *Economy and Society*, 32(4), 526–54.
Schmidt, V. A. and Thatcher, M., eds. (2013), *Resilient Liberalism in Europe's Political Economy*. Cambridge: Cambridge University Press.
Schmitter, P. C. (1974), 'Still the Century of Corporatism?' *The Review of Politics*, 36(1), 85–131.
Schmitter, P. C. and Lehmbruch, G., eds. (1979), *Trends Toward Corporatist Intermediation*. Beverly Hills: Sage.
Schmitz, C. (1995). *The Growth of Big Business in the United States and Western Europe, 1850-1939*. Cambridge: Cambridge University Press.
Schneider, B. R. (2009), 'Hierarchical Market Economies and Varieties of Capitalism in Latin America', *Journal of Latin American Studies*, 41(3), 553–75.
Schneider, B. R. (2013), *Hierarchical Capitalism in Latin America: Business, Labor, and the Challenges of Equitable Development*. Cambridge: Cambridge University Press
Schneider, B. R. (2015), 'The Developmental State in Brazil: Comparative and Historical Perspectives', *Revista de Economia Política*, 35(1), 114–32.
Schneider, B. R. and Karcher, S. (2010), 'Complementarities and Continuities in the Political Economy of Labour Markets in Latin America', *Socio-Economic Review*, 8(4), 623–651.
Schneider, B. R. and Soskice, D. (2009), 'Inequality in Developed Countries and Latin America: Coordinated, Liberal and Hierarchical Systems', *Economy and Society*, 38(1), 17–52.
Schneider, M. R. and Paunescu, M. (2012), 'Changing Varieties of Capitalism and Revealed Comparative Advantages From 1990 to 2005: A Test of the Hall and Soskice', *Socio-Economic Review*, 10(4), 731–53.
Schnyder, G. (2012), 'Like a Phoenix from the Ashes? Reassessing the Transformation of the Swedish Political Economy since the 1970s', *Journal of European Public Policy*, 19(8), 1126–45.
Schröter, H. G. (2018), 'Germany: An Engine of Modern Development', in A. M. Colpan, and T. Hikino (eds), *Business groups in the West*. Oxford: Oxford University Press, 193–221.
Schwartz, H. M. (2022), 'From Fordism to Franchise: Intellectual Property and Growth Models in the Knowledge Economy', in L. Baccaro, M. Blyth, and J. Pontusson (eds), Diminishing Returns. New York: Oxford University Press, 74–97.
Schwartz, H. M. and Tranøy, B. S. (2019), 'Thinking About Thinking About Comparative Political Economy: From Macro to Micro and Back', *Politics & Society*, 47(1), 23–54.
Seeleib-Kaiser, M. (2016), 'The End of the Conservative German Welfare State Model', *Social Policy & Administration*, 50(2), 219–40.

Sen, S. (2020), 'Financialization, Speculation and Instability', in P. Mader, D. Mertens and N. van der Zwan (eds), *The Routledge international handbook of financialization*. London: Routledge, 448–57.
Shi, Y. (2023), 'Is China Financialised? The Significance of Two Historic Transformations of Chinese Finance', *New Political Economy*, 1–16.
Shiller, R. J. (2016), *Irrational Exuberance: Revised and Expanded Third Edition*. Princeton, NJ: Princeton University Press.
Shleifer, A. (2009), 'The Age of Milton Friedman', *Journal of Economic Literature*, 47(1), 123–35.
Schoenberger, E. (1988), 'From Fordism to Flexible Accumulation: Technology, Competitive Strategies, and International Location', *Environment and Planning D: Society and Space*, 6(3), 245–62.
Shonfield, A. (1969), *Modern Capitalism: The Changing Balance of Public and Private Power*. New York: Oxford University Press.
Sierra, J. (2022), 'The Politics of Growth Model Switching: Why Latin America Tries, and Fails, to Abandon Commodity-Driven Growth', in L. Baccaro, M. Blyth and J. Pontusson (eds), *Diminishing Returns*. New York: Oxford University Press, 167–C6.N14.
Signor, D., Kim, J. and Tebaldi, E. (2019), 'Persistence and Determinants of Income Inequality: The Brazilian Case', *Review of Development Economics*, 23(4), 1748–67.
Sil, R. and Katzenstein, P. J. (2010), 'Analytic Eclecticism in the Study of World Politics: Reconfiguring Problems and Mechanisms Across Research Traditions', *Perspectives on Politics*, 8(2), 411–31.
Silva, E. (1993), 'Capitalist Coalitions, the State, and Neoliberal Economic Restructuring: Chile, 1973–88', *World Politics*, 45(4), 526–59.
Silvia, S. J. (2020), 'The Transnational Activities of German Trade Unions and Works Councils: From Foreign Policy to Active Engagement', *German Politics*, 29(3), 404–21.
Sochulakova, J. and Igazova, M. (2013), 'Foreign Direct Investment in Slovak Regions and Their Impact on Regional Economic Growth', *Economics & Management*, 18(3), 501–8.
Song, J. (2012), 'Economic Distress, Labor Market Reforms, and Dualism in Japan and Korea', *Governance*, 25(3), 415–38.
Song, J. (2014), *Inequality in the Workplace: Labor Market Reform in Japan and Korea*. Ithaca: Cornell University Press.
Song, J. (2020), 'The Political Dynamics of South Korea's Human Capital Development Strategy', *Asian Perspective*, 44(3), 461–86.
Soskice, D. (1999), 'Divergent Production Regimes: Coordinated and Uncoordinated Market Economies in the 1980s and 1990s', in H. Kitschelt et al. (eds), *Continuity and Change in Contemporary Capitalism*. Cambridge: Cambridge University Press, 101–34.
Soskice, D. (2007), 'Macroeconomics and Varieties of Capitalism', in B. Hancké, M. Rhodes and M. Thatcher (eds), *Beyond Varieties of Capitalism*. Oxford: Oxford University Press, 89–121..
Soskice, D. (2021), 'The United States as Radical Innovation Driver: The Politics of Declining Dominance?' in J. S. Hacker, A. Hertel-Fernandez, P. Pierson and K. Thelen (eds), *The American Political Economy*. New York: Cambridge University Press, 323–50.
Soskice, D. (2022), 'Rethinking Varieties of Capitalism and Growth Theory in the ICT Era*', *Review of Keynesian Economics*, 10(2), 222–41.
Stanojević, M. (2014), 'Conditions for a Neoliberal Turn: The Cases of Hungary and Slovenia', *European Journal of Industrial Relations*, 20(2), 97–112.
Stockhammer, E. (2022), 'Post-Keynesian Macroeconomic Foundations for Comparative Political Economy', *Politics & Society*, 50(1), 156–87.
Stockhammer, E. (2023), 'Macroeconomic Ingredients for a Growth Model Analysis for Peripheral Economies: A Post-Keynesian-Structuralist Approach', *New Political Economy*, 28(4), 628–45.
Stoker, G. (2019), 'Can the Governance Paradigm Survive the Rise of Populism?' *Policy & Politics*, 47(1), 3–18.
Stout, N. (2019), *Dispossessed: how predatory bureaucracy foreclosed on the American middle class*. Berkeley: University of California Press.

Streeck, W. (1997a), 'Beneficial Constraints: On the Economic Limits of Rational Voluntarism', in J. R. Hollingsworth and R. Boyer (eds), *Contemporary Capitalism*. Cambridge: Cambridge University Press, 197–219.

Streeck, W. (1997b), 'German Capitalism Does It Exist? Can It Survive?' in C. Crouch and W. Streeck (eds), *Political Economy of Modern Capitalism*. Thousand Oaks, CA: SAGE, 33–54.

Streeck, W. (2009), *Re-forming Capitalism: Institutional Change in the German Political Economy*. Oxford; New York: Oxford University Press.

Streeck, W. (2011), 'Taking Capitalism Seriously: Towards an Institutionalist Approach to Contemporary Political Economy', *Socio-Economic Review*, 9(1), 137–67.

Streeck, W. and Schmitter, P. C. (1985), 'Community, Market, State—and Associations?' *European Sociological Review*, 1(2), 119–38.

Streeck, W. and Yamamura, K., eds. (2001), *The Origins of Non-Liberal Capitalism: Germany and Japan in Comparison*. Ithaca: Cornell University Press

SVT Nyheter. (2018), 'Finskt sjukhus har lockat hundratals svenska cancerpatienter', *SVT Nyheter*, 18 December. Available at: https://www.svt.se/nyheter/lokalt/smaland/cancersjukhuset-lockar-ett-hundratal-patienter-fran-sverige (Accessed: 13 April 2024).

Swedberg, R. (2018), 'How to Use Max Weber's Ideal Type in Sociological Analysis', *Journal of Classical Sociology*, 18(3), 181–96.

Swenson, P. (1991), 'Bringing Capital Back in, or Social Democracy Reconsidered: Employer Power, Cross-Class Alliances, and Centralization of Industrial Relations in Denmark and Sweden', *World Politics*, 43(4), 513–44.

Szanyi, M. (2023), 'Rent-Seeking Business Elites and Populism in Poland and Hungary', in M. Feldmann and G. Morgan (eds), *Business and Populism: The Odd Couple?* Oxford: Oxford University Press, 138–57.

Szarzec, K., Totleben, B. and Piątek, D. (2022), 'How Do Politicians Capture a State? Evidence from State-owned Enterprises', *East European Politics and Societies: and Cultures*, 36(1), 141–72.

Szelenyi, I. (2016), 'Weber's Theory of Domination and Post-Communist Capitalisms', *Theory and Society*, 45(1), 1–24.

Takagi, Y. (2023), 'Technocracy and Populism in the Philippines', in M. Feldmann and G. Morgan (eds), *Business and Populism*. Oxford: Oxford University Press, 202–22.

Takahashi, W. (2012), 'The Japanese Financial Sector's Transition From High Growth to the 'Lost Decades'1', in A. Walter and X. Zhang (eds), *East Asian Capitalism*. Oxford University Press, 201–22.

Tan, Y. and Conran, J. (2022), 'China's Growth Models in Comparative and International Perspectives', in L. Baccaro, M. Blyth and J. Pontusson (eds), *Diminishing Returns*. New York: Oxford University Press, 143-C5.N13.

Tarlea, S. and Freyberg-Inan, A. (2018), 'The Education Skills Trap in a Dependent Market Economy. Romania's case in the 2000s', *Communist and Post-Communist Studies*, 51(1), 49–61.

Taylor, B. and Li, Q. (2007), 'Is the ACFTU a Union and Does it Matter?' *Journal of Industrial Relations*, 49(5), 701–15.

The Economist. (2012), 'The Rise of State Capitalism'. Available at: https://www.economist.com/leaders/2012/01/21/the-rise-of-state-capitalism (Accessed: 26 November 2023).

Thelen, K. (2001), 'Varieties of Labor Politics in the Developed Democracies', in P. A. Hall and D. Soskice (eds), *Varieties of Capitalism*. Oxford: Oxford University Press, 71–103.

Thelen, K. (2004), *How Institutions Evolve: The Political Economy of Skills in Germany, Britain, the United States, and Japan*. Cambridge: Cambridge University Press.

Thelen, K. (2009), 'Institutional Change in Advanced Political Economies', *British Journal of Industrial Relations*, 47(3), 471–98.

Thelen, K. (2014), *Varieties of Liberalization and the New Politics of Social Solidarity*. Cambridge: Cambridge University Press.

Thelen, K. (2018), 'Regulating Uber: The Politics of the Platform Economy in Europe and the United States', *Perspectives on Politics*, 16(4), 938–53.

Thelen, K. (2019a), 'The American Precariat: US Capitalism in Comparative Perspective', *Perspectives on Politics*, 17(1), 5–27.

Thelen, K. (2019b), 'Transitions to the Knowledge Economy in Germany, Sweden, and the Netherlands', *Comparative Politics*, 51(2), 295–315.

Thelen, K. and Kume, I. (2006), 'Coordination as a Political Problem in Coordinated Market Economies', *Governance*, 19(1), 11–42.

Thompson, Mark R. (2016), 'Bloodied Democracy: Duterte and the Death of Liberal Reformism in the Philippines', *Journal of Current Southeast Asian Affairs*, 35(3), 39–68

Thompson, M. R. (2020), 'Explaining Duterte's Rise and Rule: "Penal Populist" Leadership or a Structural Crisis of Oligarchic Democracy in the Philippines?' *Philippine Political Science Journal*, 41(1–2), 5–31.

Thurbon, E., Kim, S.-Y., Tan, H. and Mathews, J. A. (2023), *Developmental Environmentalism: State Ambition and Creative Destruction in East Asia's Green Energy Transition*. New York: Oxford University Press.

Tienhaara, K. (2014), 'Varieties of Green Capitalism: Economy and Environment in the Wake of the Global Financial Crisis', *Environmental Politics*, 23(2), 187–204.

Torche, F. (2005), 'Privatization Reform and Inequality of Educational Opportunity: The Case of Chile', *Sociology of Education*, 78(4), 316–43.

Tormey, S. (2018), 'Populism: Democracy's Pharmakon?' *Policy Studies*, 39(3), 260–73.

Tricker, R. I. (2019), *Corporate Governance: Principles, Policies, and Practices*, Fourth edn. Oxford: Oxford University Press.

US-China Investment Hub (no date), FDI Data. Available at: https://www.us-china-investment.org/fdi-data (Accessed: 3 September 2024).

Vachudová, M. A. (2005), *Europe Undivided: Democracy, Leverage, and Integration after Communism*. Oxford: Oxford University Press.

Valdés, J. G. (1995), *Pinochet's Economists: The Chicago School in Chile*. Cambridge, England; New York: Cambridge University Press.

Vallas, S. and Schor, J. B. (2020), 'What Do Platforms Do? Understanding the Gig Economy', *Annual Review of Sociology*, 46(1), 273–94.

Van Der Zwan, N. (2014), 'Making Sense of Financialization', *Socio-Economic Review*, 12(1), 99–129.

Villalonga, B. and Amit, R. (2009), 'How are U.S. Family Firms Controlled?' *Review of Financial Studies*, 22(8), 3047–91.

Vitols, S. (2001), 'Varieties of Corporate Governance: Comparing Germany and the UK', in P. A. Hall and D. Soskice (eds), *Varieties of Capitalism*. Oxford: Oxford University Press, 337–60.

Vogel, E. F. (1979), *Japan as Number One: Lessons for America*. Cambridge, MA: Harvard University Press.

Vogel, S. K. (1996), *Freer Markets, More Rules: Regulatory Reform in Advanced Industrial Countries*. Ithaca, NY: Cornell University Press.

Vogel, S. K. (2018), *Marketcraft: How Governments Make Markets Work*. Oxford: Oxford University Press.

Wade, R. (2004), *Governing the Market: Economic Theory and the Role of Government in East Asian Industrialization*, 2nd edn. Princeton, NJ: Princeton University Press.

Wade, R. H. (2003), 'What Strategies are Viable for Developing Countries Today? The World Trade Organization and the Shrinking of "Development Space"', *Review of International Political Economy*, 10(4), 621–44.

Waldmeir, P. (1997), *Anatomy of a Miracle: The End of Apartheid and the Birth of the New South Africa*. London: Viking.

Walter, A. (2006), 'From Developmental to Regulatory State? Japan's New Financial Regulatory System', *Pacific Review*, 19(4), 405–28.

Walter, A. (2008), *Governing Finance: East Asia's Adoption of International Standards*. Ithaca: Cornell University Press.
Walter, A. and Zhang, X. (2012a), 'Debating East Asian Capitalism: Issues and Themes', in A. Walter and X. Zhang (eds), *East Asian Capitalism*. Oxford University Press, 3–25.
Walter, A. and Zhang, X., eds. (2012b), *East Asian Capitalism: Diversity, Continuity, and Change*, 1st edn. Oxford: Oxford University Press.
Wang, Y. (2015), 'The Rise of the "Shareholding State": Financialization of Economic Management in China', *Socio-Economic Review*, 13(3), 603–25.
Watson, D. (2019), 'Fordism: A Review Essay', *Labor History*, 60(2), 144–159.
Webster, E. (2013), 'The Promise and the Possibility: South Africa's Contested Industrial Relations Path', *Transformation: Critical Perspectives on Southern Africa*, 81(1), 208–35.
Weir, M. and Skocpol, T. (1983), 'State Structures and Social Keynesianism', *Comparative Sociology*, 24(1), 4–29.
Weiss, L. (2014), *America Inc.? Innovation and Enterprise in the National Security State*. Ithaca: Cornell University Press.
Weitzman, M. L. (1970), 'Soviet Postwar Economic Growth and Capital-Labor Substitution', *The American Economic Review*, 60(4), 676–92.
Whitley, R. (1992), *Business Systems in East Asia: Firms, Markets, and Societies*. London: Sage.
Whitley, R. (2007), *Business Systems and Organizational Capabilities: The Institutional Structuring of Competitive Competences*. Oxford: Oxford University Press.
Wickham-Jones, M. (1996), *Economic Strategy and the Labour Party: Politics and Policy-Making, 1970–83*. Basingstoke: Macmillan.
Wilensky, H. L. (1974), *The Welfare State and Equality: Structural and Ideological Roots of Public Expenditures*. Berkeley: University of California Press.
Williamson, O. E. (1975), *Markets and Hierarchies, Analysis and Antitrust Implications: A Study in the Economics of Internal Organization*. New York: Free Press.
Williamson, O. E. (1985), *The Economic Institutions of Capitalism: Firms, Markets, Relational Contracting*. New York: Free Press.
Williamson, O. E. (2010), 'Transaction Cost Economics: The Natural Progression', *American Economic Review*, 100(3), 673–90.
Witt, M. A. (2006), *Changing Japanese Capitalism: Societal Coordination and Institutional Adjustment*. New York: Cambridge University Press.
Witt, M. A. (2014a), 'Japan: Coordinated Capitalism Between Institutional Change and Structural Inertia', in M. A. Witt and G. Redding (eds), *The Oxford Handbook of Asian Business Systems*. Oxford: Oxford University Press, 100–22.
Witt, M. A. (2014b), 'South Korea: Plutocratic State-Led Capitalism Reconfiguring', in M. A. Witt and G. Redding (eds), *Oxford Handbook of Asian Business Systems*. Oxford: Oxford University Press, 216–37.
Witt, M. A. and Redding, G. (2014), 'China: Authoritarian Capitalism', in M. A. Witt and G. Redding (eds), *The Oxford Handbook of Asian Business Systems*. Oxford: Oxford University Press, 11–32.
Witt, M. A. et al. (2018) 'Mapping the Business Systems of 61 Major Economies: A Taxonomy and Implications for Varieties of Capitalism and Business Systems Research', *Socio-Economic Review*, 16(1), 5–38.
Wolpe, H. (1975), 'The Theory of Internal Colonialism: The South African Case', in I. Oxaal, T. Barnett and D. Booth (eds), *Beyond the Sociology of Development: Economy and Society in Latin America and Africa*. London: Routledge, 229–52.
Wood, S. (2001), 'Business, Government, and Patterns of Labor Market Policy in Britain and the Federal Republic of Germany', in P. A. Hall and D. Soskice (eds), *Varieties of Capitalism*. Oxford: Oxford University Press, 247–74.
Woodruff, D. M. (2004), 'Property Rights in Context: Privatization's Legacy for Corporate Legality in Poland and Russia', *Studies in Comparative International Development*, 38(4), 82–108.

Woywode, M. (2002), 'Global Management Concepts and Local Adaptations: Working Groups in the French and German Car Manufacturing Industry', *Organization Studies*, 23(4), 497–524.

Wren, A., ed. (2013), *The Political Economy of the Service Transition*. Oxford: Oxford University Press.

Wren, A. (2020), 'Strategies for Growth and Employment Creation in a Services-based Economy: Skill Formation, Equality, and the Welfare State', in A. Wren (ed.), *Growth and Welfare in Advanced Capitalist Economies*. Oxford University Press, 255–88.

Wyatt, A. (2023), 'India: Populism, Personalism, and Economic Governance', in M. Feldmann and G. Morgan (eds), *Business and Populism*. Oxford: Oxford University Press, 181–201.

Yamamura, K. and Streeck, W., eds. (2003), *The End of Diversity? Prospects for German and Japanese Capitalism*. Ithaca: Cornell University Press.

Yeung, H. W. (2007), 'Remaking Economic Geography: Insights from East Asia', *Economic Geography*, 83(4), 339–48.

You, J. (2021), 'The Changing Dynamics of State–Business Relations and the Politics of Reform and Capture in South Korea', *Review of International Political Economy*, 28(1), 81–102.

Yusuf, S., Nabeshima, K. and Perkins, D. H. (2006), *Under New Ownership: Privatizing China's Enterprises*. Washington, DC: World Bank.

Zhang, X. and Whitley, R. (2013), 'Changing Macro-Structural Varieties of East Asian Capitalism', *Socio-Economic Review*, 11(2), 301–36.

Zhang, Y. (1997), 'An Intermediary: The Chinese Perception of Trade Unions since the 1980s', *Journal of Contemporary China*, 6(14), 139–52.

Zheng, Y. and Huang, Y. (2018), *Market in State: The Political Economy of Domination in China*. Cambridge: Cambridge University Press.

Zilberfarb, B. -Z. (2005), 'From Socialism to Free Market – The Israeli Economy, 1948–2003', *Israel Affairs*, 11(1), 12–22.

Zuboff, S. (2019), *The Age of Surveillance Capitalism: The Fight for a Human Future at the New Frontier of Power*. London: Profile books.

Zysman, J. (1983), *Governments, Markets, and Growth: Financial Systems and the Politics of Industrial Change*. Ithaca: Cornell University Press.

INDEX

www.ingramcontent.com/pod-product-compliance
Ingram Content Group UK Ltd.
Pitfield, Milton Keynes, MK11 3LW, UK
UKHW051932150926
475560UK00005B/364

9 781350 423091